Andrew Edgar

Old church life in Scotland

Lectures on kirk-session and presbytery records

Andrew Edgar

Old church life in Scotland
Lectures on kirk-session and presbytery records

ISBN/EAN: 9783743342057

Manufactured in Europe, USA, Canada, Australia, Japa

Cover: Foto ©Thomas Meinert / pixelio.de

Manufactured and distributed by brebook publishing software (www.brebook.com)

Andrew Edgar

Old church life in Scotland

OLD CHURCH LIFE IN SCOTLAND:

LECTURES ON KIRK-SESSION AND PRESBYTERY RECORDS.

BY

ANDREW EDGAR,

Minister at Mauchline.

"Shew them the form of the house, and the fashion thereof, and the goings out thereof, and the comings in thereof, and all the forms thereof, and all the ordinances thereof, . . . and all the laws thereof."

EZEKIEL, xliii. 11.

ALEXANDER GARDNER,
PAISLEY; AND 12 PATERNOSTER ROW, LONDON.

1885.

CONTENTS.

                                                              PAGE.

LECTURE I.—*Churches, Manses, and Churchyards in Olden Times,* - - - - - - - 1

    Mauchline Session Records—The Present Church of Mauchline—The Old Church and its Outward Appearance—The Old Church as it was before the Reformation—The Surrounding Monastery—Changes on and in the Church at the Reformation—Few Fixed Seats—Fairs in Churches once—Introduction of Pew System—A Grievance in Connection with the Pew System—The Galleries and Common Loft—The Bell—The Clock—The Windows—Repair of Church Fabrics and Drink to Workmen—Manses of Old Date—Size of Old Manses—Manses Thatched with Straw, and Roughly Finished in many ways—Delivery of Manses by Executors of Former Ministers—Churchyards—Tombstones—Association of Mauchline Churchyard with Burns—Filthy Condition of Churchyards at One Time—Houses on Churchyard Dykes—The Ash Tree in Mauchline Churchyard.

LECTURE II.—*Public Worship in Olden Times,* - - 55

    Readers—The Reader's Preliminary Service—Reading the Word—The Reader's Salary—Precentors—Music and Organs in Church—Amount of Psalm Singing—Mode of Singing—Doxologies—Hymns and Paraphrases—Preachers—Read Prayers and Extempore Prayers—The Bidding Prayers of the Ancient Church—Sermons on Sunday—Week-day Lectures and Sermons—Catechising on Sundays and Week-days—Form of Sermons—The Ordinary—Scottish and free Sermons—Silent Sundays—Disorder in Church—Hats on—Candles in Church—Hours of Divine Service.

LECTURE III.—*Communion Services in Olden Times,* - 117

    Preparatory and Accompanying Services on Week-days—Examination of Congregations—Reconciliations—Purging the Roll—The Preparation Sermon on Saturday—The Fast Day—Object of the Fast —Distribution of Tokens—Monday's Thanksgiving Service—Furnishings for the Sacrament—The Tables—Purchasing of Tokens—Communion Cups—Bread and Wine—Service on Communion Sabbath—Frequency and Infrequency of Celebration—Communion Extended over Several Sabbaths—Communions Early in the Morning—Order of Service—Admission to the Table—Kneeling or Sitting—Assistants at Communion—Communion Crowds—Disorders at Communions—Mauchline Sacrament in Mr. Auld's Day—Number of Communicants and Tables—Month and Day of Communion often Changed.

LECTURE IV.—*Church Discipline in Olden Times,* - 182

Institution of Kirk Sessions—Calderwood's opinion—A Session in Mauchline soon after Reformation—Constitution of Kirk Sessions—The Moderator—Elders—Their Election and Ordination—Subscription of Confession of Faith—Functions of Kirk Sessions—Discipline—Monk's views and Dr. Hill's statement—Complaints against Sessions for over-rigidness—Sessional inquiries: how instituted—All rumours reported—Libellers and consignations—Special districts for elders—Perambulations—Testimonials—Evidence taken—Oath of Purgation—Session's watchfulness over their own Members—Privy censures—Presbyterial visitations.

LECTURE V.—*Church Discipline in Olden Times,* - 234

What scandals were investigated by Kirk Sessions—Insolence to, or slander of any member of Session—Disrespect for the rules or ordinances of the Church—Drunkenness—Brawls and Bickerings—Theft—Murder—Sabbath breaking—Impurity—Witchcraft—Cursing—Heresy—Schism and Secession—Taking the bond.

LECTURE VI.—*Church Discipline in Olden Times,* - 286

Censures—Rebukes—Sometimes in private and sometimes before Congregation—Delinquent sometimes stood in his own seat—Sometimes in the public place of Repentance—Sometimes in usual clothing and sometimes in sackcloth—Repeated compearances for rebuke, called a course of repentance—Cautioners for compearance and for subsequent conduct—Bands for good behaviour—Disuse of cutty stool—Excommunication—Corporal and pecuniary punishment—Session Bailies—Joggs—Fines—Warnings—Deference paid to Kirk Sessions—Cases of Disrespect and Disobedience—Aid of Magistrate needed—Insolence to the Session—State of Parochial morality at different dates—Street fight in Mauchline between a merchant and a lawyer, with the Bailie looking on—Village Rowdyism—Poosie Nansie and her household—Social Progress—Causes to which progress is due—Grounds of hope for the future.

APPENDIX.

		PAGE
A.—*The Exercise, the Presbytery, and the Classical Assembly,*		345
B.—*Fast Days and Days of Atonement,*		348
C.—*Old Oaths of Purgation,*		351
D.—*Presbyterial Visitations of Parishes,*		352
E.—*Rev. Dr. Dalrymple of Ayr,*		355
F.—*Cell, Monastery, or Priory—which? at Mauchline,*		357
G.—*Lecturing on Scripture Lessons,*		360

PREFACE.

THE Lectures published in this volume were in their first draught delivered in Mauchline during the spring of 1884. They formed part of a course of lectures on "Our Parish Church and Parish Records," and the object originally contemplated by them was to furnish the people of Mauchline with such scraps of Parochial History and illustrations of Old Church Life as could be gleaned from the Records of Mauchline Kirk Session.

After I had agreed to publish some of the lectures, it occurred to me that it would be desirable to recast them and widen their scope, so that interest in them might not be limited to people connected with Mauchline Parish. The lectures now published are accordingly altered from what they were when delivered. They are also very much lengthened, and although like a house that has been repaired and added to, they may shew more trace than is desirable of their original design, it is hoped that on the subjects of which they treat they will give a fairly full and correct account of Church Life in Scotland during the seventeenth and eighteenth centuries.

I am aware that the title chosen for this volume is not free from objection, but it was the best title I could think of. There is a great deal of old Church Life that is not described in this volume. The higher forms and aspects of Church Life are little noticed, but that is because the traces and evidences of such life are not to be found in the official records I have had mainly to deal with. It has to be remembered also, that the lectures now published formed only the half of a course, so that the volume viewed as a treatise is incomplete. It was thought that the publication of all the lectures would make too large a book on a subject that is not of very general interest. The topics treated in the lectures not published were, I may here state, the Church's provision for the Poor, the Church's work in providing Education for the people, Marriages, regular and irregular, Baptisms and Burials, and the roll of Mauchline Ministers since the Reformation.

Besides having carefully read over all the extant records of Mauchline Kirk Session from 1669 to the present day of grace, I have had the privilege of examining the Records of the Presbytery of Ayr from 1642 to 1650 and from 1687 to 1796. I have also been favoured with a perusal of the Session Records of Galston from 1626 to (about) 1750, the Session Records of Fenwick from 1645 to 1699, and the Session Records of Rothesay from 1658 to 1662. I have not literally ransacked these Records, but I have appropriated all that on a cursory examination caught my eye as bearing on the several subjects discussed in the lectures. To those who favoured me with an inspection of these valuable documents—my fathers and brethren of the Presbytery of Ayr, the Rev. John Brown of Galston, the Rev. J. K. Hewison of Rothesay, the Rev. John Hall of Fenwick, and Mr. Macnair, Session-clerk, Fenwick—I have publicly to express my thanks and obligations.

It is not necessary to enumerate the printed books that have been consulted and drawn from, in the compilation of the lectures now published, because these books are for the most part indicated by name in the passages where extracts from them are given. It may be stated, however, that as this volume is meant for the general public, and not for such readers only as are well versed in Church history and church law, I have not hesitated, wherever I deemed it advantageous for the purpose of exposition, to make quotations not only from books that might be counted rare, but even from some that are well known and easy of access to people in towns. I have also purposely violated what may be termed one of the canons of literature, by engrossing into the text of the lectures many and sometimes large extracts from session books. This plan of composition, I am well aware, interrupts the flow of writing, and produces dull and heavy reading; but if I should succeed in making my meaning clear and in fully explaining all I attempt to expound, I shall not be dissatisfied with the result.

Nearly half of the volume is taken up with the subject of Church discipline, but in dealing with cases of scandal I have generally withheld the names of persons involved, when I thought it possible that such names could be identified with families still represented in the district of Mauchline. To this rule, however, I have made one notable exception. The public interest in the national poet is so absorbing, and people are so anxious to know the whole truth about his bright and sad career, that I have thought proper to tell nearly all that the Session Records of Mauchline have to say about him and the persons that figure in his poems. And the cause of this insatiate curiosity regarding all places and persons associated with Burns is not far to seek. The poetry of Burns more than that of any British poet, except perhaps Wordsworth, was the outcome of his own life and surroundings. An intimate knowledge of that life and of these surroundings is craved therefore by every one who makes the poems of Burns a study; and although it is not in Session Records that we can expect to meet with what was best and greatest in the poet's life, we still long to hear from these Records the minutest facts they contain about him and his contemporaries.

I have only to add that although I have been at much pains to be accurate, I cannot flatter myself with the expectation that in a book containing so many statements as this does, both on matters of fact and on matters of opinion, no slip nor misjudgment will be found. One point on which, from following with unquestioning faith the statements made in popular works, my remarks are open to criticism and doubt, is the old monastic life at Mauchline. In Appendix F, I have done what I could to set what may be termed the new state of this question impartially before the public.

A. E.

THE MANSE, MAUCHLINE,
2nd May, 1885.

Old Church Life in Scotland.

LECTURE I.

CHURCHES, MANSES, AND CHURCHYARDS.

Mauchline Session. Records—The Present Church of Mauchline—The Old Church and its Outward Appearance — The Old Church as it was before the Reformation—The Surrounding Monastery—Changes on and in the Church at the Reformation—Few Fixed Seats—Fairs in Churches Once—Introduction of Pew System—A Grievance in Connection with the Pew System—The Galleries and Common Loft—The Bell—The Clock—The Windows—Repair of Church Fabrics and Drink to Workmen—Manses of Old Date—Size of Old Manses—Manses Thatched with Straw, and Roughly Finished in Many Ways—Delivery of Manses by Executors of Former Ministers—Churchyards—Tombstones—Association of Mauchline Churchyard with Burns—Filthy Condition of Churchyards at One Time—Houses on Churchyard Dykes—The Ash Tree in Mauchline Churchyard.

THERE is no kind of reading that to the generality of people is more irksome than the old records of church courts. It might be said that if a hundred men were to be apprehended at random on any of the streets of Edinburgh, and told that they must either enter the Queen's service for seven years, or submit to sixty days in the Presbytery House, deciphering the old musty manuscript records of some rural Kirk Session, ninety-seven of the hundred would ask for the shilling and volunteer for Africa. And yet there is interesting information to be culled out of Kirk Session and Presbytery Records that will well repay a deal of trouble. There are both facts of local history to be found and exemplifications of old ecclesiastical life. And it will be admitted that not only is everything bearing on the history of a district interesting to all within its bounds, but that everything illustrative of Church life and Church rule long years ago possesses interest of a general kind to people at large.

Circumstances which need not be here specified have led me to read up the whole of the extant records of our Parish Kirk Session, besides other church records both published and unpublished; and I propose now to submit to the public some of the results of this reading in a series of lectures on old Scottish ecclesiastical life, especially as I have found it illustrated in our own parochial history.

Our Kirk Session Records are neither very voluminous nor very ancient. It is stated in the New Statistical Account of Scotland, published in 1837, that at that date there were ten volumes of our Session Records in the hands of the clerk or minister. Since 1837 another volume has been added to the number, but somehow or other there are now only nine volumes in all instead of eleven. Some of these volumes, too, are very tiny, and scarcely deserve the name of volumes; some are unbound and incomplete; some are scroll books and are headed "Brulie Minutes;"* some are to all intents and purposes duplicates; and some may be described as a miscellany of minutes of different dates arranged or stitched together, without any regard to chronological sequence. The date of the oldest of our minutes is 26th December, 1669, and the records are very far from being continuous after that date. Especially is this the

---

* The word brulie does not occur in any dictionary that I have seen, but I presume it is derived from the French word "brouillon," a scroll or first draught of a document.

case during the forty-four years of Mr. Maitland's ministry. There are no records for example covering the period from 1708 to 1731. And the cause of such a blank in the records of a long peaceful tract of parish history may be gathered from sundry entries in the books of the Presbytery of Ayr.* One Session-Clerk after another made off with a volume of minutes in retaliation for non-payment of salary, or with the view of compelling payment, and the impecunious Session, despite of Presbyterial dehortations, took very languid steps to recover their property.

That there were Kirk Session Records in Mauchline long before 1669 is beyond all doubt. Mauchline is an old parish, and as far back as 1567 there was a complaint given in to the General Assembly, " be the brethren of the kirk of Machlin," against a gentleman for maintaining in his house an excommunicated person who had been " sometyme an elder of the said kirk."

And in saying that no records of the Kirk Session of Mauchline prior to 1669 are now extant, I am virtually saying that the records of what would have been to us the most interesting periods in our parish history are lost. But the records we have, fragmentary though they are, and dating only from the times of the persecution, are interesting nevertheless. They tell tales of parochial and domestic life ; they illustrate old and obsolete laws ; and they reveal antiquated forms of thought that have long since passed away.

With these preliminary remarks I shall now proceed in this lecture to speak of churches, manses, and churchyards, as they were one hundred, two hundred or more than two hundred years ago.

---

* See Appendix. D.

In the article on Mauchline in the New Statistical Account of Scotland it is stated that the present parish church "is reckoned the most elegant church in this part of the country." The expression elegant may or may not be the most appropriate to apply to the church, but that question need not be discussed, for we are not at present concerned with matters of æsthetics. Certainly, however, the church is a goodly and substantial edifice, and one that we have reason to be well satisfied with and proud of, for besides answering the purpose for which it was built, it gives a presence to the village, and forms a notable feature in the surrounding landscape.

But the real import of the phrase "elegant," as applied happily or unhappily to our church in 1837 is that it indicates by comparison the general architectural character or style of churches at that particular date. Now-a-days there are many churches not far off that are a facsimile of ours, or, if the expression may be pardoned, a facsimile with improvements; and there are many other churches in Ayrshire of a different order of architecture that would probably be considered by competent judges much more elegant than ours in their outlines, as well as much more profuse and beautiful in their ornamentation. Indeed an American lady of some distinction, who paid a visit to the village several years ago, has set forth in print that "the kirk is as plain and homely as a house can be made," and that she does "not accede to these barn-like places of worship, while close at hand such lordly dwellings are erected for man's residence." Mrs. Hawthorne's strictures on the church and its internal arrangements, as well as her caricature of the service,*

---

* The minister referred to by Mrs. Hawthorne (the late Rev. James Fairlie) was not only a very worthy man, but a man of eminent attainments in languages and literature.

are it may be admitted a good deal overstrained, and have been the subject of not a little parochial ridicule ; but thus much must be conceded that so common-place in appearance is our church notwithstanding its tower and its gothic windows, that a foreign lady not altogether blind failed to see in it any feature to be admired or commended. Yet in 1829, when newly built, it was the talk and wonder of the country side, and in 1837 it was described in a book which may be called a national work, as the most elegant church in this part of Ayrshire.

What then, it may be asked, were other churches like, fifty years ago? The old church of Mauchline which was pulled down to make way for the building of the present one may be regarded as in many respects a good sample and type of an old parish church. It was not reckoned elegant in 1827, and neither it was, with all the accretions that had gathered round it and all the defacements that had been made on it since the date of its erection many hundred years ago. It was a long narrow low walled building with high steep roof. For many a day previous to its demolition the ground outside the wall was in some places several feet above the level of the floor inside, and at the door on the south wall there was a flight of descending steps that led down into the area of the church. It was buttressed all round too with unsightly stair-cases, one in the centre of each gable and two against the north wall, all leading to separate galleries within. Aiton, in his survey of Ayrshire (1811), says "the churches of Stewarton, Dunlop, Mauchline and Largs are so extremely contemptible that I trust the heritors will soon get them replaced with buildings better suited to divine worship and their own opulence!" But the Church of Mauchline was nevertheless a notable sort of building. It had a pedigree and a history. It was one of the pre-reformation churches in Scotland. It was built in the time of Popery, and it witnessed all the stir of the Reformation. It had been used both for Catholic and Protestant services—both for Presbyterian and Prelatical forms of worship. And so, however dingy or ugly, ill-favoured or antiquated it may have looked in the eyes of people from New York and the cities of yesterday, it had something about it that was venerable and dignified, ancient and honourable. And in its day—the day of its prime, three hundred and fifty years ago—it was considered as goodly and as elegant a structure as the present church was considered to be in 1837. The historian Calderwood, in his account of Wishart's visit to Kingencleuch in 1544, calls the church of Mauchline " a tabernacle that was beautiful to the eye." Its antiquity and honour were thus associated with the tradition at least if not with the visible trace of youthful beauty.

In its latter days the old church was a plain rectangular building—like a barn—and for aught I know such may have been its form always. Many of the most ancient Catholic churches were of that form. More commonly, however, especially in all but the earliest times, Catholic churches were cruciform, and had on their ground plan a representation of the cross. The original rectangle, we might say, had an arm attached to each side about or a little above midway in the church area. These arms were called respectively the north and the south transepts, for the shaft of the cross like the rectangle or basilica always lay east and west. There is no tradition that I ever heard of that the old Mauchline church was cruciform, but the print of the church shews on the south side the trace of a large arch, as if there had been or was contemplated to be a wing at that point.

In the days before the Reformation the old church would of course be divided and furnished according to Catholic notions. Part of the church at the upper or east end would be railed or partitioned off from the part below. Generally this was done by a screen, as it is termed, and as may be seen in many churches and cathedrals in Scotland at the present day. Sometimes, as at Crossraguel, it was by a massive stone wall with a common door in the centre. The east or upper end of the church was called the choir or chancel, and the lower or western end went by the name of the nave. The common herd of worshippers were restricted to the nave, and the choir was the inner sanctuary, where privileged ecclesiastical persons enjoyed the dignity of separation from their fellows at prayers and sacraments.* The choir was always paved—sometimes with plain stones, sometimes with glazed tiles of various hues, and sometimes with tiles of fancy shapes and patterns on which animals and figures were traced in high or low relief. The naves of churches on the contrary were often unpaved, and strewed with rushes for the convenience of worshippers in kneeling. So precise, too, was the order of worship, in at least some places, that the men were ranged on the right hand or south side of the church, and the women on the left hand or north.† At the upper end of the choir, close to the east gable stood the altar,‡ which with the platform on which it was placed, be-

---

* The clergy attached to particular churches were frequently very numerous, very near as many, says an ancient author, as the flock under their care. In the Church of Constantinople there were by imperial determination 60 priests, 100 deacons, 110 readers, and 25 singers.—L'Estrange, *Alliance*, p. 213.

† In the earliest liturgies of the Church of England there was a rubrick which directed that at the close of the preliminary service on days of Communion "so many as shall be partakers of the holy Communion shall tarry still in the Quire or in some convenient place nigh the Quire, the men on one side and the women on the other side."—L'Estrange, p. 198.

‡ "Altars with the Catholics," says L'Estrange, p. 176, "do not observe one regular position, some are placed in the middle of the choir, some at the upper part, endways north and south, and if eye witnesses may be trusted the chief altar

hoved to be by the law of Moses four and a half feet high. Above and behind the altar there were often colossal and splendid specimens of woodwork which formed the architectural glory of the church's interior.*

The old church of Mauchline was attached to a monastery which was affiliated to the Abbey of Melrose and governed by a resident prior. Around the old church, therefore, there must have been monastic buildings, but of these no remains exist now except the old tower or castle. But on two of the sides of the castle there are marks of a roof as if some building of less height had been attached to the castle at these points. In all likelihood, therefore, one line of houses trended north and south from the castle to the church, and another east and west from the castle parallel to the church. And the second of these lines of houses probably extended as far west as the great chestnut tree which stands about forty or fifty yards from the castle, for the foundations of a wall or walls have been traced thus far. Whether these two lines of houses forming with the church a *cul de sac* comprised all the monastic buildings at Mauchline is not known, but if the monastery had been of any considerable size we should have expected that on the south side of the church there would have been either one quadrangle or two quadrangles as at Crossraguel. Be that as it may how-

---

in St. Peter's Church at Rome stands in the middle of the chancel." In Laud's Service Book, 1637, it was ordered that the Communion Table "shall stand at the uppermost part of the chancel or church."

* Spalding says (vol. ii. 216), that in 1642 two of the ministers of Aberdeen "yokit William Charles, wricht, to the doun-taking of the bak of the high altar, standyng upon the eist wall of Bishop Gawin Dumbar's yll alss heiche nar by as the sylving thairof, curiouslie wrocht of fyne wanescot, so that within Scotland there was not a better wrocht peice. . . And in doun-taking of ane of the thrie tymber crouns quhilk they thocht to haue gottin doune haile and unbroken, by their expectation it fell suddanlie upon the kirk's gryt ledder, brak it in thrie peices, and itself all in blaidis, and brak some pavement with the wecht thereof."

ever, there were monastic buildings adjoining the church. These buildings would comprise a chapter house, where the monks met for business; a refectory or dining-room, where they had their meals; a kitchen and pantry, where their food was cooked and stored; cells or dormitories where they slept; perhaps also a library and a schoolroom, and a separate residence for the prior. In front of these buildings, too, there would run piazzas or covered walks which were called cloisters, where the monks arm in arm strolled together and conversed. And seven times a day the monks from their cells would pass into the church to watch and pray according to the precept of the great Master whose words are the golden rules of duty.

And speaking of the monastery I may here say that monasticism is an institution that has been much maligned. The monks are commonly supposed to have been a disorderly community of fast and loose living men who belied profession of religion with scandalous practices. And in support of that opinion the great authority of Luther, who was a monk himself, is cited. "For one day of fasting," says the Reformer, "the monks have three of feasting. Every friar for his supper has two quarts of beer, a quart of wine with spice cakes or bread prepared with spice and salt, the better to relish their drink. And thus, he adds, instead of being pale, and wan, and emaciated, they are stout and robust, and their faces glow like the fiery angels!" But notwithstanding what Luther avers of the monks in the degenerate days that immediately preceded the Reformation monasticism is now acknowledged by most Protestants to have been originally and for many years a noble expression of Christian piety. The monks were then poor and frugal, and their days were divided by rigid rule between prayers and useful labours.

At the Reformation great changes took place not only in

the form of worship within churches, but on the outward appearance of churches and their surroundings. There was a general raid upon monasteries, and as there were then in Mauchline and the neighbourhood not only many staunch but some very violent Reformers we may surmise that the Mauchline cells were dismantled, as well as dispossessed of their tenants. And we may be no less confident that the church itself did not escape rude handling. There was an Act of Privy Council passed for the dismantling of idolatrous houses, and the interpretation put on that act was that churches were to be stripped of all monuments of idolatry and instruments of superstition. Images and altars were to be removed, broken to pieces, and burned. As a matter of course, therefore, the altar which ornamented the east end of Mauchline church would after the passing of this act be taken down, if it had not been previously displaced and destroyed. And as if to make the desecration of the old edifice as complete as possible, the chancel or in other words the holy of holies was, if not just then some time afterwards, secularised by its conversion into a schoolroom. A pulpit with precentor's desk in front was also erected in the church, and either for reasons of conveniency or with the view of uprooting all associations of sanctity with the eastern end of the building, the pulpit was placed against the south wall, and both minister and precentor were directed to set their faces like the seething pot in the prophet's vision towards the north.

In the days when people, still alive, remember its appearance, the old church was crowded with galleries, each of which was approached by a separate staircase. Over the old school room at the east end was the common loft, and at the west end there was a corresponding gallery called the Auchinleck loft. In front of the pulpit against the north wall there were between the east and west lofts two small galleries, separated by a large window, and these were named respectively the Patron's and the Ballochmyle lofts. On the south wall to the east of the pulpit there was another gallery, so diminutive that it looked like a tent bed in a state of elevation. This was the Barskimming gallery. And the probability is, a probability amounting almost to certainty, that each of these galleries was erected after the Reformation, and that the names attached to them indicated at whose cost and for whose convenience they were respectively erected. Down stairs in the area of the church the sitting-room was practically confined to the space between the drops from the east and west lofts. The part under the east loft was partitioned off as has been said for a school-room, and the part under the west loft was unseated, and served as a vestibule to the large north-west door. Down the centre of the church from the vestibule in the west end to the partition in the east end stretched the communion tables with their surrounding seats. From the north and south walls pews extended out to the passages on either side of the space set apart for communion. Under the drop of the west loft and running up to the south wall was the seat known to sinners as the repentance stool, or to speak more correctly the place of public repentance. Its designation, however, was a charitable misnomer, for except the back seats in the galleries it was about the least public place in all the church. I have not heard, but I suppose that a slight elevation above the other seats in front gave to the stool its requisite and much dreaded prominence.

And the old church of Mauchline as thus crowded with galleries and packed with sittings was a fair specimen of country churches about the beginning of this century. But the old church had not always since the Reformation the appearance I have described. It was not till 1775 that fixed tables and seats for communion were erected. Previous to that date the centre of the area was an open space filled on communion days with removable tables and benches. And at a still earlier date there were strictly speaking no sittings at all. Pews are of modern origin. People at one time either stood and knelt by turns during the service, or they brought stools with them to church for their own accommodation.* In 1604 the Kirk Session of Aberdeen ordained that all women of honest reputation who could afford to provide themselves with stools should have stools in kirk to sit upon in time of preaching and prayers. The disposal of these stools was generally entrusted to the beadle, and the gratuities he received for accommodating people with stools formed one of the perquisites by which his pay was made up. In 1662 the mother of the church officer at Fenwick craved the Kirk Session for some of the benefit that

---

* In some ancient churches it was customary for the people to stand during the sermon, and in others for the people to sit. Augustine in one of his sermons says, 'I sit in preaching to you, and you are at the pains of standing to hear me.' In another part of his writings he says "it is better ordered in some foreign churches, where not only the preachers sit while they teach the people, but seats are also provided for the audience lest any wearied with long standing should be hindered from attention, or forced to leave the church." When people, however, had seats for sitting on during the sermon it was customary for them to stand during the reading of the gospel. 'While the holy gospel is being read,' says Chrysostom, 'we do not attend in a careless posture, but standing up with much gravity we so receive the message, yea the greatest potentate on earth stands up also with awful reverence, takes not the liberty to cover his head with his imperial diadem, but in all submissive manner behaves himself in the presence of God who speaks in those sacred gospels." And in the Scottish Service Book (Laud's liturgy) of 1637, it was directed that when the minister should announce the reading of the gospel, "the people all standing up should say 'glory to Thee oh Lord,'" and at the end of the gospel when the presbyter shall say so endeth the gospel, "the people shall answer, 'thanks to Thee oh Lord,' all still reverently standing up."—*Alliance of Divine Offices*, pages 177-8 and 164.

In the Session Records of Aberdeen for 1606 complaint is made of the burgh officers for sitting in public houses and drinking during the time of sermon, and order was given that they "*should stand each before his own bailie in church.*"

her son derived from his lucrative appointment. The Session instructed the officer to allow his mother the fees at baptisms, and "to have what advantage she could make of the church chairs and stools." And these stools were occasionally used for other purposes than letting and sitting upon. As a famous judge, who was a humourist as well, once said in delivering judgment on a question about church sittings, " the area of the church was in former times left void, and people brought their stools with them, which they threw at the minister if they did not like his doctrine."

This account of the interior of old churches enables us to understand how fairs could be held within churches, as from the terms of several old Acts of Parliament they seem to have been. On what were proclaimed as fair days pedlars, with permission of the church wardens, would set up their stalls in the open space of the church, against the walls or wherever they found it convenient, and people would repair to these stalls for all kinds of fancy merchandise, as they would now-a-days go to a bazaar.*

It may seem strange to us that there should have been fairs in churches, or in any of the sacred enclosures around churches. The word fair, however, is derived from *feria*, which originally meant festival, and here is the way in which a modern author,† zealous as any Anglican or Scotch Episcopalian can be for the honour of the ancient Catholic Church, accounts for the origin of fairs. "Monasteries," he says, "were places of such general

---

* In his article on Luther and Erasmus Mr. Froude states that in the great days of the indulgence sales, "The sale rooms were churches, the altars were decorated, the candles lighted, the arms of St. Peter blazoned conspicuously on the roof. Tetzel from the pulpit explained the efficacy of his medicines." In 1571 the General Assembly passed an act inhibiting civil magistrates from holding courts in kirks.

† Rev. Dr. Gordon, author of "Monasticon."

resort that they were often the stage of mercantile as well as sacred transactions. The great concourse of people that generally assembled around religious houses on holy days required refreshment. This suggested the idea of gainful trade to traffickers who repaired thither not only with victuals and drink, but different other articles of merchandise which they disposed of amongst the crowd." The same author in describing the priory of St. Andrews, says that to the west of the prior's house was the cloister, and in it was held the Senzie Fair on the second week of Easter. The stalls of the merchants had thus the advantage of being covered in, and it does not require a great stretch of imagination to suppose that if stalls were once allowed in the cloisters, and the cloisters were found insufficient to accommodate the traders, either charitable or pecuniary considerations would permit still further encroachment on the holy ground.*

The pew system was introduced into the Church of Scotland by degrees. Prior to the Reformation there were at least some desks or seats to be seen in Scottish churches. In 1560, the year of the Reformation, an order was given for the purification of Dunkeld Cathedral. The work was to be thoroughly done. The persons charged with it were "to pass incontinent to the Kyrk and tak doun the haill images thereof, and bring them forth to the kirk zayrd and burn them opinly." They were also "to cast doun the altaris and purge the kyrk of all kynd of monuments of idolatry." But to these instructions there was a postscript added, "fail not bot ze tak guid heid

---

* The constitution or opening of the fair was long after the Reformation a matter of great solemnity. In 1633 the Town Council of Dumbarton ordained that " magistrates, haill burgesses and inhabitants should go out and meet the guiddes coming to the faire, and convoye the samine to stand at this burgh on Wednesday nixt, as they shall be warnit be the officer or be sound of drum."

that neither the *dasks*, windocks nor duris be ony wise hurt or broken." It was long after the Reformation, however, before there were many desks to be seen in Scottish churches, and still longer before churches were filled with pews. From certain entries in old records it would seem that the seats first erected in churches in this country were for the benefit of ladies of rank. In 1603, for instance, the Kirk Session of Stirling refused liberty to the Commissar of the town "to big ane removabill dask for his wyff before that seat pertaining to my Lady Countess of Argyll." The session apparently thought it somewhat presumptuous in the Commissar aspiring to set up a desk for his wife close by the Lady of Maccallum. Four and twenty years later, however, the same Kirk Session were more accommodating to people that had no handles to their names, for in 1627 they gave orders to their treasurer "to build ane seat before Margaret Erskine her seat for the minister his wyff and for all succeeding minister's wyffis efter her." It was not till long after that date that ministers' wives generally were provided with seats in church. In 1700 the minister of Riccarton complained to the Presbytery of Ayr that he had no seat allowed him in the church for the accommodation of his family. And the minister of Mauchline was no better off in that respect, for although it is minuted in the Session Records that on the 23rd Nov. 1698, "the Session appointed the heritors and elders to meet at the kirk by ten of the clock on Wednesday next, the 30th instant, about the business of furnishing a seat in the church to the minister's family," it is stated in the records of Presbytery that Mr. Maitland in 1703 complained that a family seat had not yet been provided for him.*

---

* The minister of Galston had the privilege of a family seat in church in 1650, but he had to erect the seat at his own cost, as the following minute of Session shows, "The same day it was granted to the minister to build a single desk betwix

Down to about the middle of the 17th century there were very few desks or seats in church, and where there were any they were erected generally by individual persons at their own expense and with the sanction of the Kirk Session.* In the session records of Galston we find repeated applications to the Kirk Session between 1626 and 1656, or even later, for liberty to "mak and set up ane desk." In some instances the application is made by an heritor for himself, in another instance by an heritor for his tenants, and in a third case by seven persons for a joint seat. In 1637 a very notable resolution was passed by the Galston session to the effect "that the whole daskes of the kirk be maid of one form, and all of one kind of timber, either of oake or firr." About the time of Cromwell's protectorate seats in churches had become much more numerous than they were twenty years previously, and they were often erected without authority. In the Burgh Records of Glasgow there is an order minuted in 1656 to repair "furmes that they may be kept for the use of old men and young men of quality, and not for every common man as they are now." And in the same year the following minute was entered in the same records. The Council, "tacking to their consideration the great abuse lately begun and crept in by the setting of so many chyris, stools, and other fixit saitis in all the churches within this burghe be all manner of persons promis-

---

the foresaid seatt and the pulpit, provyding it injure not these that sitt beyond nor the standing of the communion tabiles."

* The following minute in the Fenwick Session Records of date February, 1645, gives one a pretty clear notion of what was the interior appearance of a parish church in Scotland about the middle of the seventeenth century. "The Session, considering the prejudice the people sustained by the multiplying of furmes towards the bossome of the church, ordanis from henceforth that no furmes be placed about the cuinzies (that is corners, the church being shaped like the letter T) neither that any persons remove their neighbour's seat without advice of the Session, otherwise to be found censurable."

cuouslie without any warrand," resolve to cause the same to be removed, and to forbid the erection or placing of any seats in churches "but by warrant of magistrates." And very unseemly squabbles about these desks and forms were about that time and fifty years afterwards of frequent occurrence in churches.* One or two such tumults occurred in Mauchline church. In 1677 John Reid of Merkland was summoned before the Session to answer for his conduct on the Saturday before the Communion. The conduct libelled was contention about the occupancy of a church seat. One witness deponed that he saw Merkland "rug at William Ross of Hillhead and two others, and cast away William Ross's bonnet." Another witness deponed that he saw Merkland strike Ross on the back "with his nief and thrust him out at the desk door." And this was not the only row at the communion of 1677. On the same day as Merk-

---

* In the records of the Kirk Session of Dumbarton the following minute occurs, and gives us a good idea of church life and church strife at the period it refers to, 27th Feb. 1620. "In regard . . of the misbehaviour of Johne Robisonne, couper, on the ane part, stryveing to be in ane dask, alledgand to have ryt thairto, and of Umphra Dennie, Walter Boquhanan, couper, to hald him out, the minister being in the pulpit, the session ordainis the said dask to be removit from the part it is, and to set it neirest the kirk door, and none but the por personnis to sit in it quhil it be tryit qho hes ryt to it." In the records of the Presbytery of Ayr there is an account of a wrangle in 1643, in the church of Coylton, between the Laird of Laigland and the gudman of Corbiston about the removal and setting of a seat. It is said that in their contention they waxed so hot that they "offered to strike one another." The same year the laird of Maxwood was summoned before the session of Galston for "doing some abuse and disorder in the kirk," by enlarging his own dask and breaking the dask of his neighbour, and he was found to have done wrong and created scandal thereby. In the Kirk Session Records of Fenwick for 1646 there is mention of people being delated to the session and made to acknowledge their misbehaviour for "removing and braking others seats' in the church." Squabbles about sitting ground seem to have occurred too when congregations met in the fields. In 1647 a man was summoned to appear before the Kirk Session of Fenwick for "his inhuman throwing of Elizabeth White over a brae to the hazard of her life, which was done before the congregation which was necessitat to meit in the fields because of the great confluence of the people of other congregations whose pasture (*sic*) wer from home.'

land was called to account, one John Mitchell was brought before the Session and was "challenged with violently casting Helen Hardie from off the face of a desk upon the communion Sabbath morning." This, it will be observed, was in the saintly days of the persecution, and in a parish that was one of the Covenanters' strongholds.

It might be too general a statement to say that it was out of these squabbles that the orderly pew system originated. It is certain, however, that such squabbles did in some instances at least lead to the introduction of pews in churches. In the year 1658 there was a dispute in Rothesay about "the room of the kirk where Scoulag's desk was," and the dispute we may be sure was characterised by the well known perfervour of the Celtic islanders. Some people of the name of Bannatyne alleged that the said "room" belonged to them, and that their predecessors "had a form there whereupon they sat, and upon a stool before the same." This right they further alleged had been exercised from time immemorial till last Sabbath, when they were desired to rise and make room for some of Scoulag's tenants. The following Monday the Bannatyne stool was broken by Scoulag or one of his agents. "Wherefore the saids claimers desired the Session that the said desk might be removed, and they restored to their own interest, that they might build a desk for themselves" in that part of the church. The consideration of this case opened up the whole question of "sitting room in church." Old records were searched, and the legal bearings of Acts and customs regarding the reparation and maintenance of Church fabrics were considered. "The Provost in name of the town declared that there was a division of the kirk betwixt the burgh and the landward, and that the burgh's part was thirteen cuples nearest the quier," that is nearest the east end. On being asked his authority for that statement, he answered, "that in repairing and roofing of the kirk so much was the burgh's proportion, and that the burgh had given out land for upholding so much of the kirk yearly." It is stated that the Kirk Session on consideration of these premises did, "with consent of the heritors," ratify the said division of the church, and ordain "that the burgh shall have these thirteen cuples which they yearly uphold to build seats in for the townsmen, and that the landward shall have from that down to the west gavill to build seats in" for the remaining parishioners. And the erection of seats was ordered to be proceeded with at once. The landward part of the area was divided among the heritors "according to their interest and free rent," and a wright was employed to erect the seats according to a scheme that will be best, although very ungrammatically, expressed in the words of the minute, "Whensoever the workman is come and builds the first seat, the next in order shall without delay employ him to sett up his also, which if he does not (being advertised twenty-four hours beforehand) it shall be leisum to the next in order after him to employ the workman and to set up the seat in the other's room."

At what particular date seats were first introduced into Mauchline church, and how slowly or rapidly they increased in number it is not easy to determine, because our Session Records go no further back than 1669. From occasional entries in the oldest book of extant minutes of session it would seem that in 1669 the church was well but not fully occupied with seats. The elders had at that date a seat for themselves, for in 1671 there was paid by the Kirk Session a sum of 20s. Scots "for dressing the elders' sait." In the month of August of the same year liberty was granted by the Kirk Session to Robert Miller "to build a seat at the back of Auchmannoch seat." In 1673

William Mershell was allowed in the east loft as much room as would accommodate four persons. In 1693 Robert M'Gavin of Dyke was "appointed to re-edifie his foir-fathers' daske, being next to Merkland's seat." But in 1703 there was no seat for the minister's family, and we may be very sure that when such was the case there would be many other families in the Parish without seats in church. *

It was originally the Kirk Session and not the heritors that granted or refused liberty to people to erect seats in churches. And when pews came to be regarded as a necessary part of a church's equipments we find it minuted in Presbytery and other records that "the heritors, with the minister and session, are to meet themselves and adjust the allocation of the sittings." † Besides granting liberty to individual persons to build seats in churches Kirk Sessions occasionally expended part of the "stock" or funds in their hands for the erection of pews, and then rented or rouped these pews for the accommodation of the public and the benefit of the poor. As recently as 1775 the Kirk Session of Mauchline reported to the Heritors that "there was a decrease in their stock to the extent of £11, 16s. 4d." This decrease, it was explained, was caused by an outlay in erecting seats in the area of the church, but it was added as proof of the wisdom of that outlay that the rents derived from these seats was equal to an interest of 30 per cent. per annum on the sum spent.

---

* In 1710 it was reported to the Presbytery of Ayr that "the kirk of Stair wants a bell, regular seats, and reparation of the roofs and windows." In 1698 the minister of Sorn complained to the Presbytery "that there is not a kirk-yard dyke, nor a pulpit, nor a common loft in the church, nor a schoolmaster in the parish, nor a bridge over the water, nor utensils for the sacraments."

† Case of Riccarton, 1723, in records of Presbytery of Ayr. In 1739 the Court of Session declared that the disposal of the area of a church pertains to the heritors and not to the minister and kirk session.

It need scarcely be said, for all are aware of the fact, that when a parish church is built now-a-days it must be provided with pews to accommodate two thirds of the examinable persons in the parish. The sittings are then allocated by the sheriff of the county among the different heritors, according to their valued rental or their assessed expenses in the building of the church. In the sittings allocated to them the heritors have the privilege of accommodating their tenants in the first instance to the exclusion of all other people. The consequence is that in nearly every parish a large number of parishioners have great difficulty in finding seats in church. They desire to obtain a seat or part of a seat from which they will not be extruded, and it is only by an act of grace and during the donor's pleasure that they can get such a privilege. This state of the law is the most serious grievance that the members of the Church of Scotland have to complain of. The Moderator of the General Assembly 1883, thought the matter of such grave importance that he gave it a prominent part in his closing address. "There is a question," he said, "which will soon press itself on the consideration of the national Church in connection with its home work, viz., how to provide accommodation in our churches for those that desire to wait on our ministrations. The Church would then become more truly the Church of the nation, and the house of God for all. Nay," he went the length of saying, "one is sometimes tempted to go even further, and to wish that our parish churches were replenished with rush bottomed chairs like the naves of cathedrals." And Dr. Rankine has not been the first man to give expression to these views. The well known ecclesiastical lawyer Pardovan,* who wrote in the beginning of

---

* So necessary a part of every minister's library was Pardovan's book considered when it was first published, that Presbyteries enjoined the purchase of it on their members. The following minute occurs in the records of the Presbytery of Ayr,

last century, says, "it would look more impartial like, and resemble more that humility love and sympathy recommended to Christians by the Apostles, and would look liker the subjects of Christ's kingdom which is not of this world, if church members would take their seats in the church without respect of their civil character, as they do at the Lord's table." There is certainly some ground for dissatisfaction with the present law and custom of the church in regard to church sittings. The proposed plan of open pews, however, would probably lead to other evils. It might prevent parents getting their children seated beside themselves. It might lead also to an unseemly scramble for favourite places. Lord Hailes, in the judgment already quoted from, says in regard to the plea, "that the inhabitants of a parish are to have seats at random and indiscriminately, so that he who comes first to the church will have his choice—this might have done very well in former times, when people sat on their own stools, but it will not do in our age." Good order requires a division of church sittings; and there would almost need to be in every country parish some standing committee appointed by the heritors to ascertain what seats are not fully occupied, and to dispose of these from time to time in such a way as will best serve the public interest.

Mention has been made of the galleries that crowded the old Church. The gallery was what might be termed a Protestant institution. One of the chief distinctions between the old Catholic and the new Protestant modes of service, was that

---

1710, January 19th, "Those who have not taken of Pardovan's book are to do it." It would appear too that a few years later a similar injunction was laid on ministers to possess themselves of Wodrow's great work. A minute of Presbytery in 1719 states that "several of the brethren have signed and payed in the money to Mr. Robert Wodrow towards the printing of the history of the sufferings in the Church of Scotland since the year 1660, conform to the Act of Synod, and the deficients have all engadged to do it."

preaching was held of much greater account in the latter than in the former. Long ago it was just occasionally that people were treated to sermon by their Catholic priests, and in some places abroad a sermon is seldom heard of in a church at the present day. There used to be a bell rung at a certain stage of the service when there was to be a sermon.* This was called the sermon bell, because it was rung when there was to be sermon, and it was not rung when there was to be no sermon. And says an old author whom I shall have occasion to quote frequently, " sermons were rare, very rare in these days, in some places but once a quarter and perhaps not then, had not authority strictly enjoined them." People in these olden times went to church to kneel and pray and receive the blessed sacrament from the priest's own hands and it was only on some special occasion (as when some itinerant preacher with the gift of oratory came round to the church on his tour) that there was preaching. But the Reformers in Scotland changed all that. They cried up preaching and cried down priesthood. Every Sabbath they had preaching in church—in fact preaching twice a day on Sunday—and in the course of the week they had a supplementary diet of discourse. It was not an open space therefore for standing or kneeling in that they wanted in church, but as much sitting room as possible for the accommodation of the whole of the parish throughout a long service. They had accordingly to make the most of the room they had in existing churches, and hence galleries.

The galleries in our old church were probably all erected since the Reformation. The only one that could possibly have

---

* " All ringing and knowling of bells in the time of the letany high mass &c., was interdicted by the injunctions of Edward the VI. and Queen Elizabeth, except one bell in convenient time to be rung before the sermon." L'Estrange, Alliance 172.

been erected before that date without interfering with the ritual was the west or Auchinleck gallery. The very name given to that gallery however, let alone other considerations, indicates that it was a post-Reformation structure and was put up at the cost of one particular heritor for the special benefit of himself and his tenantry or dependants. And it was quite common long ago for individual heritors with permission of the Kirk Session to erect galleries in Parish Churches. Very rude structures too these sometimes were. As recently as 1676 an heritor of Galston asked leave from his kirk session to build a loft in that part of the church which had been allowed him by a decreet of the Lord Justice Clerk. The request was granted on two conditions. One of these was that the petitioner should "quat that room of the kirk which he presentlie possesses," and the other was that he should "cover the soles of the loft with deals that it may not be prejudicial to them which are below." The galleries in Mauchline Church were probably erected not very long after the Reformation. There is no reference to the erection of any of them in the extant session records, which go back to 1669, and there are references in our oldest minutes of session to some of the galleries as having been then erected, and so long ago that they were in need of repairs. In 1691 there was a sum of 12s. scots paid to the smith for mending the key and lock of the west loft door, and in 1673 there was liberty granted by plurality of votes in the session to William Marshall, merchant, to have "as much rowme as will contain four persons in the foresyd of the easte lofte beside Alexander Peathin his seat."

One of the galleries I have said was a common loft. And the phrase common loft is one that occurs very frequently in old Session and Presbytery records. Every church was supposed to have its common loft. When there was no common loft in a church complaint was made, and a common loft was ordered to be built. This common loft seems to have been in some cases built by the heritors jointly—in some cases by the Kirk Session with the funds or stock in their trust—and in some cases by private speculators who were allowed by the Kirk Session the privilege of a modified proprietorship, to recoup their outlay and reward them with interest for their public spirit. In Mauchline the common loft had apparently been put up by the heritors, for in 1771 there is reference in a minute of heritors' meeting to the east loft as belonging to them corporately, and as being, with the exception of one seat claimed by Mr. Gibb of Greenhead, let by them for sittings. In Cumnock, however, the common loft had been built by the Kirk Session, as appears from the following sentence in the minute of the Presbyterial visitation of that parish in 1708, "It was complained by Mr. Alexander Drummond that some of the poor's money was employed to build a new common loft in the church, and the Presbytery, judging that this was an alienation of the poor's money, and that the said expense did ly upon the heritors, did recommend it to them to refund the session." In Dunfermline there was a common loft built by a private speculator, and the conditions on which it was built are thus set forth in a minute of Kirk Session, dated 1647,* "Robert Sharp, wright in Pittencrieff, gave in to the minister and elders of the Kirk Session a stent of the haill particular seats and classes within the new loft buildit by him and John Sharp his brother, on the north-east end of the said kirk, for the greater ease and relief to the said Kirk Session." It was then minuted that Mr. Sharp should receive the several stents—or purchase money—from such as should enter and take

---

* See Lee's Lectures, Vol. II. 399.

possession of the seats. " Likewise in case the said seats shall be long in selling the said Robert shall have power to take annual rent therefor, conform to the Act of Parliament, fra those that shall be long in entering thairto. Likeas the said Robert is content herewith and obleiss him no to trouble or crave the Session hereafter for any further payments to him for the said loft and seats therein, and he received the key thereof, providing that those who shall enter to the said seats and rooms shall come to the Session and get their license, and act thereupon fra the Session, acknowledging the poor for the same." The seats in these common lofts were (during last century at least) generally let by roup to the highest bidders. This was not only the best way to recoup outlay and bring in revenue for the benefit of the poor, but it was the only effectual mode of settling claims for sittings between competing applicants. Our records shew that in 1776 (as one example) the seats in the common loft, ten in number, were let by roup for £5, 8s. 10d, one of the front seats realising 22s. 6d, and the other 16s. 6d. And in 1775 the Kirk Session extended the common loft system by seating the central part of the area downstairs, and letting the seats there also with the proviso that on communion days these seats should be used by communicants as table seats.

From pews and galleries I pass on now to the other furnishings and equipments of churches.

A bell is now-a-days considered a necessary part of the equipment of a Parish Church. And from the way in which we read in the very oldest Session Records of the first bell the second bell and the third bell on Sunday we might conclude that every Parish Church in Scotland had always been provided with a bell, and that without a bell congregations could not be convened. And such is the case. The heritors of a landward Parish have always since the burden of providing and upholding churches devolved on them had to procure a bell for the church. There is a curious statement however in a book published in 1715 by a Mr. Morer, who was a minister in London, and had previously served in Scotland as chaplain to a regiment. " Bells, he says, they (the Presbyterians in Scotland) have none or very rare excepting the saint's bell to call the Presbytery or Congregation together."* Whatever we make of that statement however there was a bell attached to the church of Mauchline from the earliest times of which we have any account in our Parish Records. In 1671 there was paid by the session £8. 14s., for "stocking" the bell and in 1673 there was a further sum of £5 paid for dressing the bell and providing iron for it. And long ago there was a stone belfry on the church. There is an entry in the Session Records of payment

---

* The saint's bell as usually defined in dictionaries was just the bell that never was used in the service of the Church of Scotland. Mr. Morer's statement probably means that the Presbyterians use no bell except the great church bell for assembling the congregation, and that they have no such ringing of bells in the middle of service as the Catholics have. Regarding the phrase "the saint's bell" it may be remarked that Dr. Sprott says "our old parish Churches usually bore the names either of New Testament saints, or of the early missionaries who planted the gospel in our land," and that "when these names are forgotten they can sometimes be discovered from the day of the old Parish fair which was usually held on the anniversary of the Parish saint." There must have been more saints in Mauchline once than there are now if there was a separate one commemorated at each of the annual fairs. Can the name of any saint be buried in the word Mauchline? No such origin has ever yet been assigned to the name of our Parish, and so far as I can ascertain none of our fairs has been held on the day of any saint whose name could etymologically form a foundation for the word Mauchline. The Mauchline race has long been held on the last Thursday of April, and in the Book of Days the name of one of the saints associated with the 25th April is *St. Maughold* or *Macallius* of the Isle of Man in the 6th century.—(*Proverbs* 26, verse 19 last clause!!) To speak seriously, however, these were in Ayrshire fairs named after particular saints. The Galston fair is sometimes in the old Session Records (1713 for instance) called St. Peter's fair, and it was held either on St. Peter's day, 29th June, or when Sunday made that impracticable, on the first convenient day afterwards,

to a smith for sundry "pieces of work for the bell house or steeple" and in 1691 there is another entry of 18s. scots expended "at the bringing home of the stones to the steeple." That old steeple however was not so tenacious a piece of mason work as the rest of the church, for in 1775 at a meeting of heritors it was reported that "the whole frame about the bell was loosened and the bell in danger of falling at ringing." In the last days of the old church, there was a wooden belfry on the east gable. It was formed by two parallel upright beams about three feet apart, resting on the staircase and held together by a series of cross bars, while it was bound to the wall by iron brackets. People say that previous to the erection of this wooden monstrosity the bell was suspended from one of the boughs of the ancient ash that stood in the churchyard. This would likely be after 1775 when the frame was so loosened that it was unsafe to ring the bell. Grave elderly persons still flourishing among us like green bay trees, and whom we could scarcely suspect of having ever been guilty of improper pranks, are not ashamed to tell that in their youth it was reckoned one of the highest achievements of village valour to despise parochial authority and set the bell a ringing. Wedding peals were sometimes extemporised in that way and occasionally the villagers were roused from their slumbers by midnight revellers mimicking the monks of old and tolling unholy matins. That was a species of larking which Mr. Auld neither enjoyed nor approved; and in 1773 he represented to the heritors the propriety of so securing the bell rope, that it would not be in the power of every passer by to ring the bell. But it does not seem that this well meant representation had much effect, for in 1778 and close upon the sacrament season if not actually on the very night after the thanksgiving Monday there was a tremendous clanging heard over the town, and then as if the tongue of the bell had been seized by an upper air policeman, there was an instantaneous and dead silence. Next morning when people looked over to the churchyard the mystery was revealed, for there was the bell standing on end, mouth uppermost, like a duck petrified in the act of diving. Such a daring deed of profane mischief was of course not allowed by the kirk session to pass unnoticed. On the Tuesday after the sacrament the session met to distribute the communion charities, and they minuted that they had been "informed of vagrants in the night time causing disturbance by the ringing of the bell and otherwise." An inquisition was therefore set on foot, and the church officer was examined about his knowledge of the affair. And to the credit of the kirk session be it said that the offenders were soon tracked out, and on the following Sunday were brought up for church censure. Not a bad parochial court of justice it will thus be seen was the kirk session in those old rough times and especially when it had for its head and guide such a strong-minded, sagacious man as Daddy Auld.

Besides a bell the old church was graced with a clock, or knock as it is termed in the older records.* The knock house stood in a little gallery called the knock loft, built against the inside of the east gable. A narrow inside stair led to the knock house from the east loft, and people still alive remember this stair and likewise a hole in the gable through which the shaft that bore the handles of the knock protruded. It is evident that the knock was placed in the Church at a very

---

* This it would seem from Mr. Morer's account of Scotland was nothing unusual. While the Scottish churches are generally destitute of all bells except the saint's bell, he says "yet on the steeples besides the hand dial they have an engine to show the change or age of the moon." Whether any such lunar chronometer ever was erected in Mauchline church there is no record that I know of to shew, but there was as I have said a common clock.

early period, long before the date of the first extant minute of Kirk Session. As far back as 1674 there is reference in the Records to the knock. And a very primitive piece of mechanism it had been. The handles were of wood, and it is doubtful if the face was not so also. In 1675, the knock and the knock house were both suffering so much from age, that they stood in need of considerable repairs. Nails to the value of 18s. 6d. Scots were needed for the knock-house, and for work done on the knock-house and repentance stool together, two pounds were expended. There were also at the same time five shillings paid for "nine dales to the Kirk and the palms of the knock." Two years afterwards "the brod of the knock" needed painting, and this cost 10s. The knock was, in fact, both a rickety and a costly piece of furniture—continually in need of oil—and every now and again needing to be replenished with a new cord, a new nut, new rowers, new paces, a new back sprint, or a new something else. But it was regarded as a very useful piece of public property. It was both a civil and an ecclesiastical functionary. It showed the hour both on week days and Sabbaths, and regulated secular as well as spiritual affairs. Part of the cost of maintaining and repairing the clock was accordingly borne by the town. In 1682 the following entry was made in the records, "Given to Patrick Lermont for his dressing of the clock, December, 1680, £4. 0s. 0d., being the equal half of what he got betwixt town and session." This is the latest payment for the knock that I have discovered in the Session Records, but whether the knock was then allowed to run itself permanently down, or whether it continued to be oiled and painted, mended and renewed, from time to time for fifty or a hundred years afterwards, I cannot say. There was no clock face on the east gable of the old church within any living man's memory. But people who remember the old church, remember the bones of an antiquated clock that lay in the old school-room. There is no doubt that that was the old church knock whose "brod" was painted in 1667, more than two hundred years ago. And a vigorous effort was made in the present century to rejuvenate the old clock. When the new church was built in 1829, the old clock was oiled and furbished once more, and placed in the square tower above the present vestry. Many rude repairs, too, were afterwards executed upon it by a village jack at all trades. But it was to no purpose. The clock was done both bodily and mentally. Its old knees knocked against each other, and in damp weather it suffered dreadfully from rheumatism. Its memory was gone too, and it forgot both the hours of the day and the days of the week. Worse than all, it became like an old dotard whom boys make mirth of. The birds of the air mocked at it and made fun of its infirmities. Crows and jackdaws, magpies and blackbirds, sparrows and chaffinches, not to speak of gallant robins and coquettish wrens, perched on its great wooden palms and swung them down to the half hour, and up on the other side to the twenty-five minutes. In fact, the modern idea of a revolving bird cage was doubtless taken from the old Mauchline clock in the year 1830. Public amusement, however, soon got satiated with this monotonous crow and jackdaw performance, and public patience got exhausted with a chronometer, that for giving the time of day could be no more depended on than a weathercock. Once more, therefore, and finally, the old clock was taken down from its post of honour, but not of usefulness, and was superseded by the modern indicator that now regulates the hours of divine service on Sundays, and of labour on week days. But, I am happy to announce to the lovers of local antiquities, that the old knock has not disappeared. Its machinery may still be seen and examined on the landing above the vestry, as also its wooden palms and its copper dial plate, which either is what was called the brod in 1677, or is a more recent substitute for what was originally a wooden face.

The old church was, of course, lighted with windows, and in some parts of the old Records these windows are called glass windows. Now-a-days we should think such an expression redundant. At one period, however, there were windows in Scotland that were not glazed. The traveller Ray, writing in 1661, says, that in Scotland the fronts of the houses were made up with fir boards nailed over each other, with here and there round holes or windows, called shots, for people inside to put out their heads by. In the very best houses, even in palaces, he says, the windows at that date were never glazed all over, but were made up at the foot with wooden shuts to open and admit the air, as well as to let people see out.* There was no unnecessary verbiage, therefore, in calling the windows of the church glass windows. It might mean that the windows so designated were glazed all over, or that it was the upper portion of the windows that was referred to. We can understand also how it should be thought necessary when glass was scarce and costly to provide protection for glass windows. The protection commonly made use of in churches was either a wire trellis, or great

---

* In the Edinburgh Antiquarian Magazine, 1849, there is an extract given from a Kirk Session Record, about a woman who was one Sunday sleeping in the churchyard, and whose head "fell on yee window and broke yee glasse." The writer, who gives this extract, asks, "Are we to infer, that however many windows were in the church only one had been filled with glass." In the Records of the Presbytery of Ayr, there is a statement of the repairs judged necessary to be made on Mauchline Church in 1719, and one of the items in this statement is "for glassing of the whole church 60 foot of glass." Not as much glass as would suffice now-a-days for one window. What disrepairs were put up with at one time may be conjectured from the fact, that in 1701 it was reported to the Presbytery of Ayr, that the Kirk of Dalmellington "is wholly unglassed."

outside wooden shutters which were called storm boards. Among the repairs needed on Maybole church in 1718 there were mentioned to the Presbytery, "glass to the windows of the church that is wanting, and wyer to the laigh windows." At one time there was a wire screen over the windows of Mauchline church, for in the note of repairs on the church submitted to the Presbytery in 1719, there is an entry of "60 foot of glass at 4s. scots per foot, and 64 foot of wyer at the same rate." At an earlier period there were storm boards for covering the windows. In 1676 there was expended, partly in the repair of these storm boards, and partly on lead, a sum of 19s. 4d. And down till near the end of last century there was much need of wire screens or window shutters for the windows of the church, although it would seem that long before that time both the shutters and the wire had been removed.

Till 1789 the school-room was in the east end of the church, and the church windows were consequently exposed to constant danger of breakage from boys. In those grand old times, too, more than a hundred years ago, when there were no policemen to interfere with individual liberty, there was far more mischief likely to arise from juvenile frolics than there is now. It cannot surprise us, therefore, to find that at a meeting of Kirk Session in 1782 it was reported that by reason of boys playing at ball and throwing stones, the glass windows both in the church and school-house had been broken in time past, and were liable every day to be broken in the same manner. It behoved the Kirk Session, accordingly, to take ways and means for protecting the property of which they were custodians, and it is interesting to see how they proceeded in that matter. The records tell us that the Session resolved, with the view of preventing such mischief in future, to warn the inhabitants by tuck of drum that if any person should be found guilty of breaking

c

church or school windows he should be prosecuted for three times the amount of damage done, and that the schoolmaster should be authorised to prosecute either children or parents as he thought proper. One cannot but admire the consummate knowledge of human nature displayed by the Kirk Session in this resolution. The warning by tuck of drum and prosecution for triple damages must have spread dismay over the juvenile community—for it would scarcely occur to boys not old enough to have given over playing at hand ball and throwing stones, that no matter what amount of damages was sued for the court would order payment only of such damage as had been committed. But a loud bark sometimes saves the necessity of a sharp bite, and this seems to have been the kindly principle on which the Kirk Session of Mauchline proceeded in dealing with juvenile offenders.

Now-a-days the maintenance and repair of the church fabric devolves entirely on the heritors of the parish. But at one time it was the Kirk Session and not the heritors that provided the means for defraying the cost of at least tear and wear. The sources from which these payments were usually made were penalties and church door collections, and this application of church door collections, after provision had been duly made for the poor, was, whether legal or not, seldom found fault with.[*] There is a curious minute bearing on this matter in the Session Records of Galston for 1675. The church of Galston had evidently been very ill lit, for in the records of Session there are several entries of permissions being granted to this man and the other to "break out a window above his seat." These small apertures, however, did not suffice to light the body of the church properly, and the Session thought it their duty to provide other windows. And a favour-

---

[*] See Lee's Evidence in Par. Lectures, ii., p. 397.

able opportunity was afforded them in 1675. A general collection had been made that year over the country for the relief of some Christians who had been taken captive by the Turks, but by the time the collection was made the relief was unnecessary. A goodly sum of money thus reverted to the session box, and the Session accordingly in striking out new windows in church resolved that they should "be peyd out of the first end of the Turks' contribution." It was seldom, however, that Kirk Sessions had the luck to fall heir to unclaimed collections, and they had usually to pay their way out of their own proper funds. In 1636 the Session of Galston made an agreement with a slater that he should have four pounds for repairing the Kirk at present, and forty shillings yearly "for halding the said kirk water tight in all tyme coming." In the records of the Mauchline Kirk Session, especially between 1670 and 1690, there are many old and curious entries of payments for church repairs. In some instances the language is antiquated, as "glassing new lozens in the church windows," mending the lock to the "bregan," getting cords for the "paizes," and providing fillet nails, mod nails, and single plainshers. In other cases antiquated customs are disclosed, as for instance, the use of fog in slating. At the present day it is not uncommon in the better class of houses to find a lining of felt inserted between the wood and the slates. Long ago instead of felt it was fog that was used. The slates were rough and coarse, and in order to lie firm and close on the roof they needed a soft bedding. This was supplied by fog. There was some slating done on Mauchline church both in 1677 and in 1686, and on the one occasion there was £1 11s. spent in fog; while on the other there was paid for "seven sackfuls of fog, £2 2s. 0d., Scots." And it was not in Mauchline only that fog was used in this way. In 1626 there was a forfeited consignation given by the Session of Galston to their officer "for powing of fog to the sclaitting of the Kirk." So far as I have noticed, it was always nails that were used for fastening the slates to the roof of Mauchline church. But at one period, not very remote, wooden pins were employed for that purpose in some buildings. At an inspection of repairs on the Manse (or Kirk) of Straiton, in 1725, it was reported to the Presbytery that "both slating and pointing were sufficient, and that having shifted several of the slates the tradesmen found about two inches of cover above the pin." It may seem strange to some of the abstemious people of this age, that a daily allowance of drink was always given to workmen long ago, whether they were employed on churches or on cottages, inside or outside, on *terra firma* or on chimney tops. But such is the case; and we can understand that at a time when both tea and coffee were unknown as beverages, malt liquors may have been more requisite for "the working man" than they are now. In our Session Records there are frequent entries of payments for drink to workmen. In 1677 two slaters were employed on the roof of the church, and for every pound of wages paid them there was an eighth of a pound allowed them for drink. Masons and joiners had each a similar allowance, and charity, which is kind, occasionally gave a small tipple to paupers. In 1674 the Kirk Session devoted the liberal sum of 16s. Scots, for ale to Agnes Hunter on her death-bed.

From the subject of churches I now pass on to the subject of manses, and as this is a subject that does not very much or very directly concern the general community, I shall not enter into it at any great length.

Before the Reformation there were manses in Scotland for the Parochial clergy. In many cases, however, the Catholic incumbents, at or immediately before the Reformation, when they saw what was coming, had the worldly wisdom to give their manses away in feus or long tacks to their relations and friends, and thus on the establishment of the reformed religion, the ministers found themselves excluded from what they considered their rightful residences. In 1563 an Act of Parliament was passed to remedy this state of affairs. In this Act it was declared that whether manses had been set in feu or tack, or had not, the ministers appointed to churches should have the principal manse of the parson or vicar, or as much thereof as should be found sufficient; or else that a suitable "house should be built beside the Kirk" by those having right to the manse in tack or feu. In a subsequent Act of Parliament passed nine years later, it was stated that "na gude execution" had followed on the Act 1563, in respect of its being "in divers pairtes doubtful and uncertain," and on this preamble more precise enactments which need not be specified were made.* Many other Acts of Parliament anent manses followed at later dates.

In the oldest records of our Kirk Session there is little said about the manse here. The earliest reference to the manse that I have noticed in the Session Records is an entry in 1691 of the payment of 14s. scots to a mason, "for repairing the minister's house." The Kirk Session, it will thus be seen, either were burdened or they burdened themselves in 1691 with at least some manse repairs. In the Presbytery Records there is reference in 1646, and that is about as far back as these records go, to the manse at Mauchline.

There have, as everyone knows, been great improvements in the housing of all classes of people within the last three hundred or even the last one hundred years, and this improvement

---

* Dunlop's Parochial Law, 92 and 93.

has been shared by ministers as well as others. Now-a-days the court orders a very high class of house for a manse—a house with at least three public rooms of goodly size and height of ceiling, and at least four bed-rooms, besides kitchen and other appurtenances. The only modern equipments that have not as yet been ordered by the court to be provided in new manses are a hoist and a telephone! But former generations of ministers in Scotland had to content themselves with less roomy and less luxurious upputting. In the records of the Presbytery of Ayr there is a specification of a manse that was proposed to be built at Dalmellington in 1699, and as it was pronounced by the Presbytery to be a complete manse it will serve very fairly to shew us what were the current ideas on manse accommodation at the close of the seventeenth century. The manse is thus described; "threttie-six feet lenth and fourteen foot wide within the walls, threttine foot high of side walls, two fire rooms below and two fire rooms above and cumsciled, with window cases and boards, glasse, partition walls, and all that is necessary to make a compleat manse, with a barn of thrie couple lenth and a stable two couple lenth." And while this was the kind of complete new manse that some fortunate ministers were getting built there were much inferior manses that other ministers not so fortunate had to live in as best they could. In 1705 there was a report given in to the Presbytery of the state of the manse at Symington, and in this report it was said "there is only a hall with a laigh chamber and another high chamber, with a barn and a brew house, by which account the Presbytery judged there is no sufficient manse and office houses."*

---

* The parish of Kirkmichael has been long famed in the county for its model manse. The following is a description of Kirkmichael Manse in 1710, "A dwelling house having a laigh hall, a dry kitchen, a cellar and a chamber in the lowest storrie, as also three fire rooms in the upper storrie, two whereof are ceiled, with a barn, byre,

Early in last century manses were generally thatched with straw.* In the statement of repairs on Coylton manse in 1698, as submitted to the Presbytery, it is said that "to thatch the manse wholly over is needful, which will take of straw sixty threave." And in addition to that quantity of straw there would be required "twenty-six threave more for thatching the laigh house and some divetts thereto." In 1735 the manse of Auchinleck was a thatched house, and in 1746, if not later, the manse of Dundonald was thatched. The practice of slating manses was nevertheless introduced in Ayrshire as far back at least as 1724. In the Presbytery Records of that year it is stated that the heritors of Girvan had "*voluntarily yielded*," which looks very like saying that they had been compelled of their own free will to put a slate roof on the manse of that parish. What is at present called the old manse of Mauchline, which was built, as an inscription over the door states, in 1730, was slated from the first, but the adjoining kitchen and brewhouse, which, according to the common plan of manse and offices would be of one storey, were covered with thatch.

Something has already been said in this lecture about the windows in Scottish houses long ago, and much more need not be added now.† The common size of windows in manses last century was about three feet by two, and in some places, as at New Cumnock in 1707, they were protected by storm boards.

---

stable, and brew house, and a coall fold with a locked door in it, as the office houses thereto belonging."

* Churches also at one time were thatched, as appears from an Act of Secret Council, 1563.

† Aiton, in his survey of Ayrshire (1811) says, "About fifty years ago the farm houses in the county of Ayr were despicable hovels, many of them were built in part and some altogether of turf, or of mud plastered on stakes and basket work. . . . The doors were seldom more than five feet high ; the windows about 18 inches high and a foot wide, into which glass or sometimes only boards, which could be opened and shut at pleasure, were fixed."

In other places, and at a somewhat later date, the clumsy storm boards were superseded by wire trellises. In Kirkoswald manse, in 1720, the whole amount of glass in the windows was a hundred square feet, and for the protection of the glass in the windows of the under storey there were 17½ square feet of wire. The following is what is said in the Presbytery Records about the windows in Dundonald manse in 1725, and it is of special interest, as shewing that at that date windows were not always if even generally glazed from top to bottom.—"Anent the windows *Imp.* to sash them of the upper storey and to make them of the laigh storey good and sufficient half glasse and half boards, will be ane hundred and threttie pounds scots. *Item*, to make the cases and casements of the upper storey, and to fill them with glasse and bands to them, and to make the laigh storey sufficient, ninety-six pounds. . . It will take £200, 12s. scots to make the manse sufficient, providing the heritors agree to the sashing of the middle storey, and it will take £166, 12s. scots, providing the above windows be filled with glasse casements."

It was very roughly that the interiors of manses were finnished a hundred and fifty years ago. The common form of flooring laigh rooms was by pavement. Among the things reported to the Presbytery in 1709 as being "presently wanting" at Dalmellington Manse was "pavement for a laigh room," and in 1744 it was found by the Presbytery on an inspection of Riccarton Manse, that "the west laigh room required to be laid with deals or to be pavemented." And how manse rooms were plastered early in last century, may be surmised from another note of what was presently wanting at Dalmellington manse in 1709, viz., "some lime for *casting* an upper and laigh room." If the upper and laigh rooms were ill-finished, much more so were the garrets. In inspecting a new manse in 1739 the Presbytery of Ayr found that the attics were just one open room—lumber room it might be termed—from one end of the house to the other, and they minuted that "the garret cannot be complete without a partition round the stair case head with a door in it."

It is evident that there had been no such storms hereabouts in the winter of 1732-33, as there were last winter (1883-84), for there could not have been any manse standing the following summer, in the condition in which the manse of St. Quivox was found in the summer of 1733. "The walls of the under storey," it was reported, "are all built with clay and (are weakened) with several bulges, rents and holes; and the foundations of the west gavell (are) undermined, so as a stick of eighteen inches long can be put in through beneath the same." The manse, it was said, was also "very bare of thatch and rigging," and the "office-houses were deplorable." But deplorable as was the state of St. Quivox manse in 1733, it was nothing in comparison with that of Monkton manse in 1737. The Presbyterial power of description was fairly baffled in trying to show how near the verge of dissolution that tottering tenement of clay had come. "The south side wall from corner to corner, about two or three feet from each corner excepted," it was said, "was entirely bulged and flying from the gavills, so that in several parts it hangs nine inches over the plumb at four foot height from the foundation. Of four stone gavills which are in the house only one seems to have been built with lime, the other three with mud, and, upon the whole, we think the house can by no reparation be made sufficient, unless these insufficient walls (to wit . .) be taken wholly down and rebuilt from the foundation, which in all probability would occasion the falling of the other parts."

Pardovan says that ministers are obliged to leave their manses in as good condition as they were found in, but that before ministers can be made liable in that way, the Heritors should move the Presbytery to have the manses in which they are interested declared free. At the settlement of every minister in a parish, therefore, there used to be a regular inspection of the manse by the Presbytery and competent tradesmen, as there is yet, although not now in so thorough a manner, and a formal judgment on the state of the manse was pronounced. There are many reports of such inspections, with the discharges and deliveries that followed thereon, recorded in the Presbytery Books, but the following will suffice to illustrate the practice and procedure that were in common use. In 1708 there was a "committee appointed to meet at Dalmellington anent receiving of the manse from Mr. Aikman's executors. . . . They report it wants eleven feet of glass at five pence a foot to be allowed for it, but the closse that Mr. Aikman causyed on his own charge will counterbalance the said damage of the glass windows. As for the barn, it was never made sufficient for Mr. Aikman, nor did he ever make use of it. As for the manse and the rest of the office houses, they are rather better, excepting the said glasse, than when Mr. Aikman received them. In testimony whereof the said workmen (the Inspectors) gave their oath. . . . Upon all which Alexander Aikman delivered up the keys of the manse and officehouses to the heritors and took instruments in their hands." *

---

* It is stated in the Presbytery Records that at the settlement of Mr. Wyllie in Mauchline in 1646, the new minister and the former minister (Mr. George Young), "did submit what concerned either of them in the matter of the manse of Mauchline, to the determination of the persons (ministers) appointed to induct." The Presbytery Records are a-wanting at the date of the induction of Mr. Veitch, who succeeded Mr. Wyllie, but at the settlement of Mr. Maitland, who succeeded Mr. Veitch, the Heritors reported to the Presbytery that "what was faulty in the manse should be speedily helped." The procedure at Mauchline in 1646, is explained by the tenor of Act of Parliament 1612, which was superseded by other Acts in 1649 and 1663.

I come now to the last division of my subject—the Churchyard. Almost as dear and as interesting to men as the church in which their forefathers worshipped, is the sombre churchyard in which their fathers sleep their long sleep.

Our own churchyard is of great antiquity, but nevertheless there are no tombstones in it with inscriptions bearing an earlier date than 1644. It must be remembered, however, that the erection of tombstones is a comparatively modern custom. Here and there over the country a solitary stone may be found with a date about as old as the Reformation, or an undated stone or cairn of much earlier erection, marking the burial-place of some distinguished chieftain or ecclesiastic whose death was deeply mourned, but it was only people of distinction that in ancient times were honoured with monuments. And although it is quite common at the present day for people to erect tombstones at their pleasure over the graves of their relatives in churchyards, the right of doing so was at one time disallowed, and possibly would, if tried at law, be disallowed still. In the records of the Kirk Session of Stirling it is minuted, in the year 1640, "how certain people without consent of session put in the Kirk yard little stones, one at the head and another at the foot of graves, whereby in process of time they apprehend to have a property," and it is therefore ordained that "all stones not erected by permission of session are to be removed." * In 1634 the lairds of Barr and Galston deemed it necessary to crave liberty from the Kirk Session of Galston to "bigg ane ylle to the bodie of the kirk for their burial places." And liberty was given to each of these magnates to build an aisle at the back of his own desk, on the condition that the "said ylles have pennes joining to the bodie of

---

* Harrie Guthrie was minister of Stirling at that date.

the Kirk with windoes for light glassed and upholden be the saids Lairds." Forty years later the same Kirk Session was supplicated by another heritor to "bound and lay off for him a buriall place and grant him liberty to put up a stone wall about it." And it was only on certain written and stringent conditions that that request was granted.

A few, but not very many interesting, monuments stand in the churchyard of Mauchline. One Covenanter who fought and suffered for Christ's crown has his resting-place marked by a stone. He was a Galston man, and was wounded at a conflict with Captain Inglis' troops at Burn Ann, in the year 1684, and died of his wounds afterwards in Mauchline prison, or what is called in one of the minutes of Session in 1692, the 'keep house." Of worthy Mr. Veitch and his predecessors in the ministry of the Parish, there is no memorial in the churchyard. Messrs. Maitland, Auld, Reid, Tod, and Fairlie, have all appropriate tombstones marking their place of sepulture, but there is nothing to indicate where the ashes of the older line of ministers repose. And henceforth all belonging to the Parish, whether clerical or lay, high or low, rich or poor, famous or infamous, renowned or unrenowned, who wish to be buried in the parish, must choose their graves in the new cemetery that was two years ago laid off in the old moor where the dragoons of Middleton and the yeomen of Clydesdale had their fray in 1684; for an order from the Queen in Council has now closed the churchyard absolutely and without reservation to any favoured party as a place of burial.

Every summer brings to Mauchline visitors from all parts of the world, from Maidenkirk and John o' Groat's, from England and Ireland, from Australia and the great Republic of America. All or nearly all these visitors make a loving and curious inspection of the church-yard. That little enclosure is to them an object of the deepest interest, but it is not because old stern Covenanters are resting there from their warfare, nor because morbid-minded monks, weary of the world, were buried there under the shadows of the old sanctuary, where morning, noon, and night they sang and prayed, and led sad but saintly lives hid with Christ in God. It is because the place has been consecrated by the genius of the national poet of Scotland. Many a time have the feet of Burns trod that hallowed ground. It was in the old church that he worshipped, and I presume it was in the old church that his marriage was "solemnly *confirmed.*" It was in the old church and the present churchyard that those scenes of mingled solemnity and profanation were witnessed, that have been described, perhaps too truly, in his communion satire. It was in the modest mansion adjoining the churchyard, and contiguous to the castle, that Gavin Hamilton, the poet's friend and landlord lived, and where the poet spent many of his gayest and happiest hours. It was about a stone cast beyond, in a green meadow, on the banks of what was then a bright and purling brook, that tradition says the poet first caught sight of the village belle who became his bride, and whose charms he has immortalised in imperishable song. It was in the upper room of a small two-storied red sandstone house, facing the eastern gable of Mr. Hamilton's mansion, that the poet and his wife took up their first abode together. It was in one of the houses that still form the north-eastern boundary of the churchyard, and is separated from Burns' own dwelling

"By a narrow street
Where twa wheelbarrows tremble when they meet,"

that Nanse Tannock had her comfortable and respectable alehouse. It was probably in the large mediæval looking mansion that forms the east side of the cross, that Mary Morrison's window stood, if the Mary Morrison of the song be, as seems disputed, and is doubtful, the Mary Morrison* who lived in Mauchline in the days of Burns. Opposite the church gate, and forming the two lower corners of the Cowgate, were two houses, still more closely associated with the poet's writings. It was in one of these that the Beggars had their high carousals. The other is what a local poetaster and worthy elder of the Kirk has in a somewhat Hibernian style called—

> " The house, *though built anew,*
> Where Burns cam weary frae the plough,
> To hae a crack wi Johnny Dow ;
>   O nights ateen
> And whyles to taste the mountain dew,
>   Wi' bonny Jean."

Immediately to the rear of this house was the one-storied thatched dwelling, with a garret window looking into Dow's hostelry, where the so-called bonnie Jean, in her happy maidenhood, lived with her respected parents.

---

* Mr. Scott Douglas, the latest and best editor of Burns' poems, gives it as his opinion that the person called Mary Morrison was Peggy Alison, and in a letter to me about the inscription on Adjutant Morrison's tombstone in Mauchline churchyard, he says, "This is one of the instances of assumed connection—more or less remote—with Burns, which vanity prompted many weak aspirants to claim, when hero worship of the poet, and hero and heroine hunting in reference to his productions, grew into vogue some 25 or 30 years after his death." In a subsequent letter dated 24th April, 1877, he informed me that he had just been invited to call on the widow of the gentleman who indited the inscription on the Adjutant's tombstone, and to hear the grounds on which it was asserted that the Adjutant's daughter was the heroine of Burns' song. Mr. Douglas expected "more light on Mary Morrison" to arise out of that interview, but I never learned what the result of that interview was. I am informed, however, on authority, that another member of the Adjutant's family who lived to be a grandmother, used to speak of Burns (with aversion, I may add), as one whom she knew personally when he lived at Mauchline, and that she believed her sister Mary was the "lovely Mary Morrison" whom the poet admired. She often spoke of this long lost Mary who died in early youth from the amputation of a foot that had been accidentally injured, as "one of the fairest creatures the sun ever shone upon."

Such a centre of classic ground as the old kirkyard of Mauchline will scarcely be found in all Scotland, for in addition to the immediate surroundings, you look out from the church-tower on Mossgiel and Ballochmyle, the Ayr and the Lugar, the banks of Afton and the braes of Doon.

And in the churchyard lie many that were known and endeared to the poet. Two of his children are buried there, within the railed enclosure belonging to the Armours. Gavin Hamilton sleeps there too, in another railed enclosure on the left hand as you enter the church. A few paces behind Mr. Hamilton's burial-place is the grave of Mary Morrison, and close by the side of her grave is the resting-place of Holy Willie. Elsewhere in the churchyard lie the remains of Posie Nancy, Racer Jess, the bletherin' bodie, Richmond the clerk, and a host of others that were either the companions of the poet or the subjects of his songs.

It is not so much the classic or poetic associations of our own churchyard, however, as the old condition and supervision of churchyards generally, that we are concerned with in this lecture. And although this is not a subject of lofty interest, it is still one that claims from all students of social and parochial history some little measure of consideration.

It might be hazardous to say that distinctive notions on the subject of churchyards are, or have been held by the three great sects of religionists in this country—Papists, Prelatists, and Presbyterians—for neither are all Papists nor all Episcopalians nor all Presbyterians of one mind on that subject, or on almost any other. It is well enough known that in the days of the Papacy churchyards were solemnly consecrated for the burial of believers. But although consecrated, churchyards were sometimes desecrated in the time of the Papacy. They were used as stances for fairs and were made places of merchandise, at least the tenor of some old Acts of Parliament lead us to think so. The Episcopalians may be credited with being the party that in Scotland has held the highest doctrine regarding churchyards. John Row, the Presbyterian historian, expresses his horror and amazement at that doctrine. There is, he says, a singular care had in the book of Canons published by the Bishops in 1636, that the house of God be no ways profaned, nay, nor the churchyard. "Ergo," he concludes, "the bishops would have the place held holy." That seemed monstrous and detestable doctrine to good John Row. But although the Presbyterian Church Courts have never gone the length of calling churchyards holy ground, they have always evinced a laudable desire and have heartily endeavoured, with indifferent success, it may be said, to have churchyards protected against abuse and disfigurement. The Kirk Session of Perth in 1587 ordained that no stables be allowed in the kirkyard of their city after Whitsunday, and that if any stables should be found there the setters of them should pay a penalty of £10 scots. In 1634 the Kirk Session of Galston ordained that "give anie horse or ky beis fund in the Kirkyaird in tymes cuming (the Kirk dyke being at the present sufficientlie bigit and made fenceable), they sall be keipit untill the awners thereof pay 20s. *toties quoties.*" And, as the result of this warning, we find that in 1638 two parishioners of Galston appeared before their Kirk Session and "purged themselffis of the horse being in the kirk yaird ye last Saturday at night." Previous to this latter date, the Kirk Session of Galston had been indicating that they would not allow some other abuses of the churchyard to pass uncensured. They had issued notice that whoever "delves, or breaks the sward of the laigh kirk yaird and common mercat place thereof in tyme coming sall pay £5 toties quoties to the Session with sic punishment as the Session sall injoine."

The mere fact that the schoolhouse in Mauchline was for many a day within the church, and that the churchyard was consequently the village playground, is sufficient to show that at one time the churchyard in this parish was not sanctified as it should have been; and, indeed, enormities much greater than children's games were permitted or committed in the churchyard. In 1708, during Mr. Maitland's ministry, it was represented to the Session as a grievance that beasts were allowed to pasture in the kirkyard, and with the view of putting a stop to that nuisance a committee of Session was appointed to confer with the magistrate. It was reserved to Mr. Auld, however, to make the chief battle in the parish for churchyard purity. He commenced in 1750 by asserting his legal right to the grass of the churchyard, and by consequence his right to exclude every other person from the use of that grass. And in asserting this right he made it clear that it was not for the sake of any pecuniary benefit it could bring himself. It is minuted in the Session Records of 1750, that "the Kirkyard grass, according to use and wont, belonging to the minister, especially as not being sufficiently provided in grass according to law, was rouped and set for the ensuing season at eighteen pence, which the minister gave in compliment to the poor." A large donation satirists will say, but a well considered and manly assertion of personal right as the only means of securing an important public object, is what others who take an impartial view of the case will see and admit. Even this device, however, did not succeed in getting the churchyard made decent. In 1779 the Kirk Session thought it necessary to approach the Heritors with a complaint and petition on the subject. In that complaint it was stated that "by reason of the school kept in the church, by reason of many doors opening upon the church-

c

yard and ready access to it from all quarters, it is altogether a thoroughfare and a place of rendezvous for all sorts of idle and disorderly persons, who break the windows of the church, break the tomb and grave stones, and deface the engravings thereon, and the complainers are sorry to add, that the churchyard is now become a sort of dunghill and common office-house for the whole town, a receptacle of all filthiness, so that one can scarce walk to church with clean feet."

The sentiment that led people to desire burial in the neighbourhood of a church, led them also to cluster their houses as closely under the shadow of the church as possible. In nearly all old towns and villages, therefore, we find houses built on the Kirk yard dyke,* and stringent measures adopted by Kirk Sessions to prevent such houses becoming sources of nuisance. In 1662 the Kirk Session of Fenwick passed a resolution, that "none who have built, or shall build houses hereafter on the Kirk yard dyke, shall have liberty to strike out a door towards the church yard." In 1676 two householders in Galston presented bills to the Kirk Session for leave to strike out doors upon the kirk yard on the north side of their houses. The crave was granted on condition that no prejudice should result therefrom to any burial place. For many years during Mr. Auld's ministry, the question of allowing proprietors of houses adjoining the churchyard in Mauchline to have back doors opening into the churchyard was under discussion. In 1774 a complaint was formally given in to the Heritors against certain feuars for encroaching on the churchyard with "new buildings and

---

* Mauchline was one of those towns in Ayrshire that were said by Aiton in 1811, to be "extremely irregular, the streets narrow, very crooked, ill paved, often dirty, and their general aspect mean." The town, it may be stated for the benefit of people at a distance, is different now.

middensteads." In 1779 the Kirk Session in the complaint already referred to, petitioned the Heritors, as the only means of putting stop to a clamant nuisance, to cause intimation to be "made to every person whose doors open into the churchyard to shut up the same, with certification that if they refuse, the Heritors will proceed to shut up both their doors and windows by building a stone wall just before them, agreeable to the Act of Parliament 15th James VI." At the close of this petition there was a flourishing compliment paid to the Heritors—presumably to engage their good offices the more warmly. "Such honourable regard to the house of God and the burial place of their fathers," it was said, "may well be expected from the Heritors of Mauchline, who in several respects, and particularly in their charity and bounty to the poor, are so honourably distinguished above all their neighbours." There was a legal question, however, involved in the procedure that the Session urged the Heritors to adopt; and in 1788 the Heritors desired the Lord President, who was one of their number, to take the opinion of counsel "how far they have it in their power to shut up the back doors of people who have entries into the churchyard from their houses."

The two things that conduced most in Mr. Auld's day, to the orderly preservation of the churchyard, was the removal of the school in 1789 to its present situation, and the enclosure of the churchyard a few years later with a proper wall. Now that burials have ceased to be allowed in the churchyard and that young trees have been planted among the tombstones for ornamentation, it is to be hoped that in future years the churchyard may become, as it ought to be, a garden of beauty and a fitting centre of classic ground.

The churchyard of Mauchline, we have seen, was in 1779 so

imperfectly enclosed that it was a public thoroughfare, and the Kirk Session demanded that a wall two ells high, should in terms of the Act of Parliament be built round their burial place. And this leads me to say, that long ago there was no want of good and sufficient legislation in matters concerning churches and churchyards, schools and schoolmasters' salaries, maintenance of the poor and punishment of criminals, but the difficulty was to get the laws executed. In most, if not in all parishes, there was an apology for a churchyard dyke, but in very many cases it was only an apology. From the earliest date of which we have record, there was nominally a dyke round the churchyard of Mauchline. Mention is made of that dyke in the Session Records of 1676. It was covered with turf, and the renewal of the turf that year cost the Session 6s. There were other repairs executed on the dyke that year, and these involved the Kirk Session in an outlay of 34s. for sand, and 14s. 4d. for "filling up the Kirk stile with earth and reding (cleaning out) a sink." How dilapidated the dyke had become a hundred years later, may be inferred from a minute drawn up in 1776, which states that "from Dr. Breckenrigg's house to James Smith's yeard, the wall is entirely gone into disrepair, and the churchyard is thereby laid open for cattle to trespass into it." In early records of parishes we read of Kirk stiles, as if there had been, as there doubtless were, several narrow entrances into churchyards. This fact of itself implied imperfect enclosure. In 1783 the Kirk Session of this parish represented to the heritors the propriety of having only one entrance to the churchyard. And although this object was never attained, nor is it desirable, the heritors in 1788 introduced a great improvement on the old-fashioned stiles by recommending to a committee of their number " to get a new great gate made for the approach into the churchyard, to be a bound gate, and to run upon rollers."

It was not unusual long ago, as it still is, to see one or more large trees in a churchyard. They give to the surroundings of the church a befitting look of dignity, antiquity, and solemnity, and in old times they often answered purposes of convenience. Sometimes the church-bell was suspended from one of such trees, and sometimes the joggs were fixed to one of them. In Mauchline there was a magnificent specimen of a churchyard tree. It was an ash of fabulous age and vast proportions. Six feet above the ground it measured fifteen or sixteen feet in girth, and when it fell in 1860, in a gale on the 27th February, its bole yielded more than 200 cubic feet of timber. It was a notable feature both in the churchyard and town of Mauchline, and surprise has often been expressed that no reference to it is found in the Holy Fair or in any other of the poems of Burns.

It will be seen now that since the middle of the seventeenth century, when our forefathers contended to the death for Presbyterian principles, a great and beneficial change has come over the appearance of churches, manses, and churchyards in Scotland. The churches are much larger than they were—more ornate both externally and internally—better lit and better heated—better floored and infinitely better provided with pews, more pleasant in all respects to look at, and more comfortable to sit in. Manses, too, have kept progress with the times, and although churchyards are in many cases far from being what spots so hallowed should be, they are yet more orderly kept than in the proud days of spiritual independence, when cattle strayed into them at will, and slatternly people made them thoroughfares and something worse. These improvements, too, are not matters of trivial importance. They have a civilising influence. People generally feel constrained to live up to the level of their surroundings, and both taste and feeling are silently elevated under the sight of cleanliness, comfort, and beauty. And the apostles of æsthetics who go about preaching the duty of building beautiful churches, and keeping churchyards as trim and tasteful as gentlemen's lawns, are really, whether people see it or not, fellow-workers with those that preach the higher duty of moral and spiritual culture.

NOTE.—Since this lecture was printed I have received an opinion from an eminent authority that there never was, in the popular sense of the term, a monastery at Mauchline. See APPENDIX F.

LECTURE II.

Public Worship in Olden Times.

Readers—The Reader's Preliminary Service—Reading the Word—The Reader's Salary—Precentors—Music and Organs in Church—Amount of Psalm Singing—Mode of Singing—Doxologies—Hymns and Paraphrases—Preachers—Read Prayers and Extempore Prayers—The Bidding Prayers of the Ancient Church—Sermons on Sunday—Week-day Lectures and Sermons—Catechising on Sundays and Week-days—Form of Sermons—The Ordinary—Scottish and free Sermons—Silent Sundays—Disorder in Church—Hats on—Candles in Church—Hours of Divine Service.

A COURSE of lectures on church life would obviously be incomplete without an account of the ordinary service in church on Sundays. One lecture in this course must therefore be devoted to that subject, but I regret to say that it cannot be much illustrated by references to our own parish history as exhibited in either the Kirk Session or the Presbytery records.

Many changes in the form of church service have been witnessed in the Church of Scotland since the Reformation. In the first Book of Discipline, compiled by Knox and others in 1560, it is stated that "to the churches where no ministers can be had presentlie must be appointed the most apt men that distinctly can read the common prayers and the Scriptures to exercise both themselves and the church till they grow to greater perfection." In accordance with this recommendation there were, in parishes where ministers could not be procured to preach and administer the sacraments, a class of men employed in the Church under the name of "readers," whose office was to read the Scriptures and a liturgy of printed prayers, such as is used in the public service of the Church of

England. After the Church became more fully plenished with ministers, readers were still in many places continued. A common arrangement was for one minister to have the pastoral charge of two contiguous parishes with a reader in each to serve as his assistant. For instance, in the Book of Assignations drawn up in 1574, we find the two parishes of Mauchline and Galston united under the pastorate of Mr. Peter Primrois. There was at the same time a reader named Rankyne Davidson stationed at Galston, and although the office of reader at Mauchline is declared to have been vacant that year, it was evidently intended that there should be a reader at Mauchline also, for the "haill vicarage" is mentioned as the stipend assigned to the reader.

In parishes supplied with both a reader and a minister, there were two distinct services in the church on Sundays. There was first of all a preliminary service conducted by the reader. This service consisted of reading the public prayers and portions of Scripture. It usually lasted an hour, and when it ended the minister entered the church and conducted his service of extempore prayer and preaching. The best and most graphic account we have of the primitive form of service in the Reformed Church of Scotland is to be found in a small book published by Cowper, the Bishop of Galloway* (about 1611), and entitled "Seven Days Conference between a Catholic Christian and a Catholic Roman." The two Catholics, the Christian and the Roman, enter a parish church together, and the Roman asks what is this the people are going to do. The Christian says, " They bow themselves before the Lord to make humble confession of their sins and supplications for

---

* It forms *part of one* of the volumes of Cowper's collected works, and it is in that shape, not as a separate publication, that I have seen it.

mercy, which you will hear openly read out by the public reader." After the prayers have been read, the Roman asks what are the people going to do now. "Every one," says the Christian, "is preparing, as you see, his Psalm book, that all of them with one heart and mouth may sing unto the Lord." After the Psalm has been sung, the Roman puts his question again, what comes next—"What doth the reader now—is he making another prayer? No, says the Christian, yonder book which he now opens is the Bible. . . . These are the three exercises which are used in all our Congregations every Sabbath, one hour before the preacher comes in: first prayer, then Psalms, then reading of Holy Scripture, and by these the hearts of the people are prepared the more reverently to hear the word, and you see all is done with great quietness, devotion, and reverence." The third bell then rings and the preacher enters the Church. How shall I behave myself? asks the Roman. Do not trouble yourself about that, replies the Christian, but just do as you see others do, and here is the order of service: " First, he (the preacher) will *conceive* a prayer, at which the people humble themselves, thereafter he reads the text of holy scripture ; this the people hear with reverence ; then he falls to preaching, which some hear with their heads covered,* some otherwise (in that you may do as your health requires). The sermon being ended the preacher concludes all with a thanks-

---

* A sentence pronounced in the General Assembly in 1570 would lead us to suppose that at that date respectable people sat in church with their hats or caps on during the sermon. This sentence runs as follows—" The others that are not excommunicat shall be placeit in the publick place where they may be knawne from the rest of the people, *bare headed the tyme of the sermones*, the minister remembering them in his prayer in the tyme after preaching." Book of Universal Kirk. In 1610 Patrick Simpson of Stirling preached a sermon that was supposed to apply very unpleasantly to Lord Dunbar who was present, whereupon it is said that his lordship "pulled down his hatt in tyme of sermon." Select Biographies, Woodrow Society.

giving, after which there is a psalm sung by the whole congregation, and then the minister blesseth the people in the name of the Lord and so dimits them."

This is Bishop Cowper's account of the Sunday service in a Scotch church about the beginning of the seventeenth century. The reader's service, as he describes it, is what, he says, will be seen "in all our congregations every Sabbath." There has at all times, however, been a little diversity amid the general uniformity of worship in the Church of Scotland, and we find in old records of Kirk Sessions special instructions given to readers to introduce this thing and the other thing into the service. In the year 1578 the Kirk Session of Aberdeen ordained that "howoft the prayers be read on the Sonday in time coming, the reader shall read a portion of the catechism and the bairnis shall answer him." In 1604 the same Kirk Session issued still more specific instructions in regard to both reading and catechising. During his service both on Sunday mornings and on week days, the reader was directed to "repeat at the ending of the prayers the ten commandments as well as the belieff (the creed), that be the oft repeating and hering of them the common people may learn the same perqueir."[*] Then "every Sabbath afternoon between the second and third bell" (that is during the time of the reader's afternoon service), the Session ordained, that "twa scholars of the English school sall stand up before the pulpit, the ane demanding the uther answering with a loud voice in the audience of the people, the short catechism and form of examination of children."

In the year 1580 the General Assembly declared that "the office of a reader is not an ordinary office in the Kirk of God,"

---

[*] Perqueir. French, *par cœur*, by heart.

and the following year it was expressly ordained that readers should not be appointed in any church. It is evident, however, that readers continued to be employed in the Church of Scotland long after that date, both during the episcopacy that subsisted from 1606 to 1637, and during the ascendancy of Presbytery from 1637 to 1645. Indeed the employment of readers is distinctly sanctioned in the acts of the ultra-Presbyterian Assembly of 1638, and in the records of the Presbytery of Ayr from 1642 to 1645, readers are so frequently referred to as to make us think that there was one in every or almost every parish in Ayrshire during that period. At a visitation of the parish of Ochiltree in 1642, "inquisition was made by the Presbytery concerning the reader and schoolmaster, and for his maintenance. The said Mr. John (John Blyth, the minister) declared that William Gilchrist wes thair reader and schoolmaster, and that there wes no exercise of prayer or reading on the week dayes because thair could not ane audience be had in the clauchan, but on the Sabbath day before preaching. And that his maintenance wes onlie thrie score punds money provydit by the laird of Caprington, Patron."* At a visitation of Mauchline the same year it was stated that the "reader and schoolmaster had demitted his places," and that the Session had agreed on a proper person as a successor to him. And what sort of

---

* In 1627 the Kirk Session of Galston allowed a fourth part of all kirk penalties "to the use of the reidar and schuilmaster of this clachan," and in 1633 this allowance was augmented, it is to be hoped on account of the diminution of sin in the parish, from the fourth to the third part of the penalties. In 1639 the Session put an end to this arrangement, which had a look of scandal about it, and was really derogatory to the dignity of the reader's profession, and ordained that "the reidar in the kirk sall have no wages or fie for his service in the kirk with reading of evening and morning prayers, except that quhilk the marriages and baptisms presentlie peyis." The reader, however, felt aggrieved at this curtailment of his income and resigned his office. Shortly after that date there appears regularly in the note of the disbursements of the communion charities at Galston £2 or £3 to the reader.

church service was given by or expected from readers at that date, may be gathered from the fact that the reader at St. Quivox was exhorted by the Presbytery to "concoct prayers although the Brethren did not condemn read prayers in church." The Westminster Assembly * of Divines ignored the office of reader, and when the Westminster Directory for Public Worship was adopted by the Church of Scotland in 1645, it may be said that the service of the reader was ostensibly and almost practically brought to an end in Scotland.

The only offices in the Church that were recognised by the Westminster Assembly were the offices of Pastor, Doctor, Ruling Elder,† and Deacon, and the public reading of the Word was appointed to be done by the Pastors or Doctors. "The Assemblie," says Baillie, writing on the 1st January, 1644, "has past a vote before we (the Commissioners from Scotland) came, that it is part of the *Pastor's* office to read the Scriptures, what help he may have herein by these who are not Pastors is not yet agitat. . . . We are not against the minister's reading and exponing when he does not preach, but if all this work be laid on the minister before he preach we fear it put preaching in a more narrow and discreditable roume than we would wish." The same author says elsewhere in his letters, that the Scots Commissioners at Westminster "would gladly have been at the keeping still of readers," but that after all their study they could find no warrant in Scripture for such an office in the Church. It

---

* The introduction of the Westminster Directory as the rule of public worship within the Presbytery of Ayr is thus referred to in a minute of Presbytery, dated August 1645. The Directory in its principal parts is ordered to be read in all the churches on Sabbath eight-days, and "on the Lord's day thereafter to be uniformlie practised by the whole brethren."

† Instead of ruling elders the Westminster divines said "other church governors," which "reformed churches commonly call elders."

is worth noting, however, that the reader's service was at that time kept distinct from the minister's or preacher's, although both services were conducted by the same person. "Those of best note about London, says Baillie, are now in use in the *desk* (that is, the lectern or precentor's desk) to pray and read in the Sunday morning four chapters, and expone some of them, and cause sing two psalms, and then *go to the pulpit to preach*."* When the General Assembly, in 1645, adopted the Westminster Directory for Public Worship, a very curious regulation was passed for bringing the reader's and the preacher's services into one. It was ordained that the minister and people repair to the kirk half an hour before the time at which the *minister* used to commence *his* service, and that the whole exercise of reading and expounding, together with the ordinary exercise of preaching, be perfected and ended at the time when the service of public worship formerly closed.† In other words, instead of the reader giving one hour's reading of prayers and Scripture, with running commentary on the part of Scripture that was read, and then the minister giving his service of prayer and preaching, the minister was to conduct the whole service, or, as might be said, both services, and to complete them in half-an-hour's less time than used formerly to be occupied by both minister and reader together. Some writers say that when Episcopacy was re-introduced into Scotland, by Charles

---

* In his Dissuasive from the errors of the times, Baillie states that the Independents in his day were in the practice of assigning different parts of the service of worship to different persons. "Sometimes," he says, "they make one to pray, and another to preach, a third to prophesie, and a fourth to dismisse." The order of their service is thus described by one of themselves—"The *pastor* begins with solemn prayer, continuing about a quarter of an houre, the *teacher* then readeth and expoundeth a chapter, then a Psalm is sung, whichever *one of the ruling Elders* dictates, after that the *Pastor* preacheth a sermon and sometimes *ex tempore* exhorts, then the *teacher* concludes with prayer and a blessing." *Diss.*, p. 117, 147.

† Act Assembly, 1645.

II., in 1662, "the reading of Scripture was brought in again."* This must mean that a separate service of reading the Scripture without note or comment was revived as in the days of the former Episcopacy.† Bishop Sage tries to make out that one of the cardinal distinctions between the Episcopal and the Presbyterial form of public worship is, that while in the Episcopal form there is a place assigned to the reading of Scripture, in the Presbyterial there is not. "What a scandal," he says, "would it be to have the Scriptures read in the Presbyterian Churches. . . . ." "The Scriptures," he says again, "must not be touched but by the man of God, who can interpret them, and he must read no more than he is just then to interpret." That these remarks of the Bishop, however, could be applied only to cases where custom had come to supersede law will be evident at once on reference to the Westminster Directory. It is there expressly said that "when the minister who readeth shall judge it necessary to expound any part of what is read, let it not be done until the whole chapter or psalm be ended, and regard is always to be had unto the *time*, that neither preaching nor other ordinances be straitened or rendered tedious." It is, of course, possible, as Bishop Sage alleges was actually the case, that the minister who read the Scriptures in Church always judged it necessary

---

* Chambers' Dom. Annals, 1662.

† In 1657 a petition was presented to the Synod of Aberdeen from the Elders of Kinbettock for a reader to read the Scriptures before sermon. The petition was refused, and orders were given that the Directory for public worship be observed in all points. In 1662, however, on the restoration of Episcopal government in the Church, the same Synod enjoined that there be readers in every congregation. It was directed also that the reader begin his service with a set form of prayer, especially the Lord's Prayer—that he then read some Psalms and some chapters from the Old Testament, and rehearse the creed—afterwards read chapters from the New Testament and rehearse the ten commandments. When there was no reader, the minister was to do this.

to expound what was read, but he was by no means obliged to do so unless by public opinion or prevalent custom.* Indeed, what Sage in 1695 gave out as the doctrine and practice of the Presbyterian Church of Scotland, Baillie in 1645 specified as one of the evil doctrines and practices of the Brownists. "They (the Brownists)," says Baillie, "reject all public reading of the word which is not backed with present exposition." And as his authority for that statement about the Brownists, he quotes the following words from the writings of one of their own apologists:—" Bare reading of the word and single-service saying is an English Popery, and far be it from the Lord's people to hear it, for if they would do so they would offer to the Lord a corrupt thing, and so incur that curse of Malachi. It is certainly very remarkable that a Scotch Episcopalian Bishop should charge the Presbyterian Church of Scotland with doctrines and practices which one of the most eminent expounders of the Church of Scotland's polity imputes, as a grave departure from approved opinion, to the Separatists who were the first to " divert from the high, open and straight way of the Reformed Churches." This is all the more remarkable too that in the Shorter Catechism the reading of the word is expressly mentioned as one of the ordinances. This reading is not private reading at home, but public reading in Church— part, in fact, of what is called the ordinance of the word—

---

* The fact nevertheless remains, that within twenty years or less than twenty years after the Assembly's adoption of the Westminster Directory, the custom referred to by Sage had been introduced. In an Act anent uniformity among ministers passed by the Synod of Galloway (then Episcopal) in 1664, it is said, "that there should be reading of the Scriptures instead of lecturing in the public congregations before ye sermon in ye forenoon." The most extraordinary account, however, of Presbyterian practice, is that of Curate Calder. "For reading the Scriptures in Churches they have abolished that with the rest, and in place thereof he that raises the Psalm reads the sermon that was preached the Sabbath before " ! ! !

and although it is said to be not so important as the preaching of the word, it is nevertheless declared to be by the influence of God's Spirit an effectual means of convincing and converting sinners, and of building them up in holiness and comfort through faith unto salvation.

The adoption of the Westminster Directory in 1645, I have said, virtually put an end to the office of reader in the Church of Scotland.

It has to be stated, however, that readers were nevertheless employed in some parishes long after their office had ceased to be recognised in the constitutions of the church. In the year 1695 the Kirk-Session of Rothesay appointed that "the pulpit be drest and ane readir's seat sett up." In the year 1766 a new church was built at Dalmellington, and the note of cost given in to the Presbytery comprised, among other items, an entry of £12 for the erection of "Minister's seat, Pulpit, Reader's seat, and Baptismal seat." Mr. Morer, in his account of Scotland in 1715, describes the Sunday service in Scottish Churches, as follows:—"First, the precentor about half-an-hour before the preacher comes, reads two or three chapters to the congregation of what part of Scripture he pleases, or as the minister gives him directions. As soon as the preacher gets into the pulpit, the precentor leaves reading, and sets a psalm-singing with the people, till the minister, by some sign, orders him to give over. The Psalm over, the preacher begins confessing sins and begging pardon. . . . Then he goes to sermon, delivered always by heart, and therefore sometimes spoiled by battologies, little impertinences and incoherence." Strange to say the only references to a reader in the Session Records of Mauchline which I have noticed are of comparatively modern date. In the year 1788 there is a minute recording the resolution of the Kirk Session to discontinue the payment of 18s. a year to the reader for reading the Scriptures and Confession of Faith before public worship begins. But the reading was still to be continued as before. The only change in the arrangement was that the Session Clerk was to do the work gratis. At what date the reader's service actually ceased in Mauchline church I am unable to say, and as little can I tell whether it continued without interruption from 1574, when the "haill vicarage" was declared to be the reader's stipend, until 1788, when his salary of 18s. a year was disallowed. It is plain however, that in 1788 the reader's service had been an established, probably a very long established, institution in the parish, and that latterly instead of its being a reading of *prayers* and Scripture, with the singing of a Psalm, it was a reading of Scripture and the *Confession of Faith*, with an "etc.," which may have meant Psalm singing.

The reader was usually also precentor, and it will be a natural transition, therefore, to pass on now to an account of that part of the Sunday service which the precentor conducted. In the Reformed Church of Scotland a very limited space was originally allotted to the service of praise in public worship. "There is perhaps no country in Christendom," says Dr. Cunningham, "in which Psalmody has been so little cultivated as in Scotland. Wherever the Church of Rome reared her altars music grew up under her shadow, and gave a new charm to her sensuous services. But Presbytery gave little countenance to such a handmaid." The use of instruments in the service of praise was repudiated or almost abjured. Organs were not even allowed standing room in church. In 1574 the Kirk Session of Aberdeen gave orders "that the organis with all expedition be removit out of the kirk and made profeit of to the use and support of the puir." On his visit to Scotland in 1617 King James endeavoured to inaugurate a more æsthetic and cultured form of worship in Scotland after the manner of what he had seen in England. Among other innovations he set up an organ in the Chapel Royal at Holyrood. "Upon Satterday the 17th May," says Calderwood, "the English service was begun in the Chapel Royal with singing of quiristers, surplices and playing on organes." And in Calderwood's history there are repeated allusions to the use of the organ in the Chapel Royal. The popular feeling, however, that in 1637 was aroused against the service book was turned against the organ also, and among the outbreaks of 1638 Spalding records that "the glorious organes of the Chapell Royall were maisterfullie brokin doune nor no service * usit thair bot the haill chaplains, choristis, and musicianes dischargeit and the costlie organes altogedder distroyit and unusefull." And in 1644 the General Assembly recorded as one of the "praiseworthy proceedings and blessed events that had caused them great joy, to hear from their Commissioners at Westminster that the great organs of Paul's and Peter's had been taken down" by the Covenanters in England. The old doctrine of the Church of Scotland in regard to Psalmody, is tersely expressed

---

* Considering that it is only within the last twenty years that instrumental music has been introduced into any country churches, it is curious to find Aiton in 1811, who declares himself to be "partial to the Presbyterian Church," lamenting the absence of instruments in the service of praise. "Tasteless must they be," he says, "who have at their command an organ, a harp, and a pipe, and offer in worship the grating and incoherent sounds of people who cannot sing." The feeling of the Covenanters on this subject, or rather of those Presbyterian ministers that afterwards became Covenanters, is expressed by Rutherford in one of his letters to Mrs. Marion M'Naught. The letter is dated 2nd June, 1631, and it begins, "I have received a letter from Edinburgh certainly informing me that the English service, and the organs, and King James' Psalms are to be imposed on our Kirk, and that the bishops are dealing for a General Assembly." Mr. Hill Burton even goes the length of saying that the principles of worship in the various Presbyterian churches the first half of last century, and in the Primitive Reformed Church of Scotland were "the repudiation of liturgical forms, of kneeling at prayer, and of instrumental music."

in the first Book of Discipline. "There be two sorts of Policie," it is said in that book: "The one of these sorts is utterlie necessarie as that the word be preached, the sacraments ministered, and common prayers publicly made. The other sort of Policy is profitable but not necessarie, as that Psalms should be sung and certain places of Scripture read when there is no sermon." And in accordance with this doctrine there is very little singing of psalms prescribed as part of public worship in either Knox's Liturgy or the Westminster Directory. In each of these manuals of worship there are only two psalms appointed or supposed to be sung during the minister's service —one before the sermon and another before the benediction. And in regard to the second of these psalms the directory only says, "let it be sung if with convenience it may be done." It is possible, however, that there was from an early period a third psalm sung in the church by the congregation, although that psalm was not included in the service. Just as in modern churches where instrumental music has been introduced, there is a voluntary played on the organ during the time that the congregation are assembling, so in very ancient times, long before the Reformation, it was customary over a large part of Christendom for the people to "entertain the time with singing of Psalms" till the congregation had gathered. An old Continental author, Durandus by name, who lived more than 600 years ago, states that in his day it was usual for people waiting for the morning services to hasten into the church as soon as they heard the psalm begun. And in this country within quite recent times the epithet of "the gathering psalm" was commonly applied to what we now call the first psalm. Both Knox's Liturgy and the Westminster Directory set down prayer as the first act of public worship ; and Bishop Cowper, in his account of the service of the Scottish Church, mentions prayer as the first part, and the singing of psalms as the second part of the reader's service. The convenience, however, of "entertaining the time" till the congregation gathered must have early presented itself to ministers and Kirk Sessions, and thus a gathering psalm would come to be sung in many churches before the services proper began.*

Pardovan states that "it was the ancient practice of the Church of Scotland, as it is yet of some Reformed Churches abroad, for the minister or precentor to read over as much of the Psalm in metre as was intended to be sung at once, and then the harmony and melody followed without interruption, and people did either learn to read or got most of the Psalms by heart." What is here called the ancient practice of the Church of Scotland in the rendering of praise, is just the practice that is observed at the present day. But soon after 1645 a different practice arose and continued long in the Church of Scotland. Pardovan says that when the new paraphrase of the Psalms was appointed to be sung—that is, when the present metrical version of the Psalms was introduced —it was not at first so easy for the people to follow, and it became customary for each line to be read out by itself, and then sung."† And it is worth noting, that this author, writing

---

* The order of worship followed in our Church before 1661, while the Directory had both civil and ecclesiastical sanction, was as follows :—After an introductory psalm, which was often sung *before* the minister came in, there were 1st, Prayer. 2nd, Reading the Scriptures. 3rd, Praise. 4th, Prayer. 5th, Sermon. 6th, Prayer. 7th, Praise. 8th, Benediction. Sprott, p. 13.

† Mr. A. G. Fuller, in describing the form of worship in his father's (Andrew Fuller's) church at Kettering, less than a hundred years ago, says, "The *machinery* of the Psalmody was something ludicrous. . . . There was invariably a clerk or precentor who would announce the hymn thus—119th Psalm, eighteenth part, long metre ; read several verses, and then, with due regard for the natural obfuscation of the people's intellects, *parcel it out two lines at a time.*" The italics are Mr Fuller's.

in 1709, thought that that new way should be abandoned and the old custom revived. The number of people that can read, he says, is now increased, and if the psalms to be sung each Sunday were intimated the Sunday previous, they might be got by heart by those that can not read. It is doubtful, however, if Pardovan is quite correct in his account of the origin of the practice of giving out the psalm line by line while it is being sung. The present metrical version of the psalms was not introduced into the Church of Scotland till 1650, but the Westminster Directory for public worship was adopted by the General Assembly in 1645, and the Directory recommends that "for the present, where many in the congregation cannot read, it is convenient that the minister, or some other fit person appointed by him and the other ruling officers, do read the psalm, line by line, before the singing thereof." It is more likely, therefore, that it was the recommendation in the Directory rather than the difficulty of following the new version that led first to the practice of giving out the Psalms line by line. It is alleged that the Scots Commissioners at Westminster were much opposed to the insertion of that recommendation in the Directory—it was contrary, they said, to the usage in the Scotch Church, and it was not required by the backward state of education in Scotland—but the English divines were in love with it, and would have it, and as the Scots were anxious for uniformity of worship over the two kingdoms, the General Assembly took no exception to the clause. The practice was accordingly introduced into the Church of Scotland soon after, of giving out the Psalms in instalments of one line at a time, and so popular did the practice become, and so essential a part of revered use and wont, that very great difficulty was found long afterwards in getting it discontinued. Some disorders and abuses doubtless arose out of the practice. It probably in some cases bordered too closely on the ridiculous to be edifying. Pardovan, we have seen, was anxious to have the practice abolished, and for that end he says, "it were to be wished that masters of families would path the way for the more easy introducing of our former practice by reviving and observing the same in their family worship." This suggestion was taken up by the General Assembly, and in 1746 the Assembly recommended to private families that in their religious exercises they should in singing the praises of God go on without the intermission of reading each line. Great resentment arose, however, when attempts were made to abolish the practice in public worship, and it was not till the year 1809 that it was abolished in this parish. In a small scroll minute book of the Kirk Session, stitched up with another scroll book of earlier date, the following entry occurs without any comment or notice of motion or record of discussion about it, "1809, Dec. 10. Began to sing Psalms in the church without reading line by line." *

An old practice in the public worship of the Church of Scotland was to introduce a doxology into the Psalm that was sung. This doxology was just four lines of metre in which praise was ascribed to the three several persons of the Trinity. In the year 1642, however, a great clamour arose in the West of Scotland about this doxology. It was a piece of human ritual people said. It was a commandment of man's that ought not to be accepted as a divine ordinance. Over all Ayrshire there was as much strife about this doxology as there might have

---

* Dr. M'Kelvie, in his annals of the United Presbyterian Church, states that two of the reasons that led people last century to leave the Church of Scotland and join the Seceders were the introduction of the "run-line" and the paraphrases into the worship of the National Church.

been about the most vital article of faith. Baillie, the famous journalist and controversialist, was then minister at Kilwinning, and so serious a matter did he consider the agitation that he made it the subject of a special address to his parishioners, some of whom had apparently been joining in the outcry. "The rejection of the conclusion," that is of the doxology, said Baillie, "is one of the first links in the chain of Brownism. From this beginning seducers have drawn on their followers to scunder at and reject our whole psalms in metre, and then to refuse our prayers. . . As for the putting of that matter—the doxology—in the end of a Psalm, the church which hath power to order the parts of God's worship hath good reason for it, for Christ in that pattern of all prayers and praises teaches us to conclude—for thine is the glory for ever." The General Assembly of 1643 had the question under discussion, and for the sake of peace passed an act, draughted by Henderson, in which all disputation on the subject was ordered to be dropped. At the Westminster Assembly there was no debate about the doxology. "Without scruple Independents and all sang it, so far as I know," said Baillie, "where it was printed at the end of *two or three* Psalms. But in the new translation of the Psalms resolving to keep punctually to the original text without any addition, we and they were content to omit that whereupon we saw both the Popish and Prelatical parties did so much dote as to put it to the end of the *most of their lessons and all their Psalms.*" He adds further that in the letter from the Westminster Divines to the General Assembly there was a desire for the discontinuance of the doxology and of bowing in the pulpit, expressed "in a general courteous clause which we were instructed to make particular." This general courteous clause in the letter of the Divines was as follows, and it might fitly be quoted at the present day to many people for its sterling good sense: "Albeit we have not expressed in the Directory every minute particular which is or might be either laid aside or retained among us, as comely and useful in practice, yet we trust that none will be so tenacious of old customs not expressly forbidden, or so averse from good examples although new, in matters of lesser consequence, as to insist upon their liberty of retaining the one or refusing the other, because not specified in the Directory, but be studious to please others rather than themselves." In 1649 the question of the doxology came up for discussion again in the General Assembly, and it would seem, says Dr. Sprott, that an understanding was come to, that with the view of pleasing the divines of England, the use of the doxology in public worship should be discontinued. Against this concession one man spoke out stoutly. This was Calderwood, the historian, who said that he had always sung the doxology in public worship, that he would sing it to his dying day, and that after his death he would resume it louder than ever in the New Jerusalem. In 1662 when Prelacy was re-established it was enacted by one or more Synods that the use of the doxology should be revived.* And although this enactment was made by the Bishops, it is to be observed that Wodrow, who had great aversion to the Bishops and their doings in general, does not condemn the enactment. The doxology, he says, was a song composed when Arians and other sects denied the deity of Christ, and in 1662 there were many sects who denied that doctrine. It would have been well, he adds, if the Bishops had enacted nothing worse than the singing of a

---

* In the Synod of Galloway's Act, 1664, anent uniformity among ministers, it is stated that "every minister should close his prayer by saying of the Lord's prayer, and should close ye psalm with ye doxologie." Register of the Synod of Galloway from Oct. 1664 to April 1671.

doxology. But the doxology was the symbol of a party, and the mention of it one way or another, in approval or disapproval, excited party feelings. In 1642 the doxology was upheld and used by all the moderate Covenanters—like Henderson and Douglas, Baillie of Kilwinning, and George Young of Mauchline—it was decried and disused by the more vehement Puritans like Nevay of Newmilns, Mowat of Kilmarnock, Hutcheson of Colmonell, and Gabriel Maxwell of Dundonald. In 1649 its disuse was still demanded by the ultra-Puritans, and was conceded and submitted to by those that were zealous for uniformity with England, while it was protested against by the extreme constitutionalists like the historian Calderwood. In 1662 its re-introduction was welcomed or allowed by all of the Prelatical and court party, while its disuse was persevered in by those generally who refused to conform to the new order of things. The re-introduction of the doxology in 1662, it may also be remarked, was in some cases accompanied with a recommendation in regard to postures in worship. In the Synod of Aberdeen it was recommended that in time of public prayers people should observe gestures of reverence by either standing or kneeling, and that in singing the doxology they should stand.* We shall see in a subsequent lecture† how a little disturbance was created and promptly suppressed in Mauchline church at the introduction of the doxology in 1685, but there is nothing said in the records of our Kirk Session about either changes of posture in worship or what postures were at any particular date in use.

The principle on which exception was taken to the singing of doxologies in church should naturally lead people to object

---

* Bishop Sage speaks of the people in Presbyterian churches in Scotland sitting close at prayer.

† Not published in this volume.

to the singing of hymns, and of what in Scotland are commonly at the present day called paraphrases. And in point of fact there has been a great amount of eccentric opinion on the subject of praise propounded and professed in the Protestant Church in all periods of her history. Puritanism has gone to as much excess in the matter of worship as in the matter of Christian life. At the present day there are not a few persons even in the Church of Scotland, and far more among those that are not in the Church of Scotland, who maintain that the only proper subjects for divine praise in public worship are the metrical versions of the old Testament Psalms. But it may very well be contended that the principles on which these people frame their theory of worship should lead them much further than this. The metrical versions of the Psalms are not the Psalms themselves, but the Psalms paraphrased and distorted by human inventions to suit the exigences of rhyme and metre. They are not the verbatim words of inspiration that came from the lips of David and Asaph, or the prophets of the captivity and restoration. They are not even a literal English translation of these words. There have accordingly been strait laced people that have objected to the use in public worship of the metrical version of the Psalms quite as strongly and vehemently as the late Dr. Begg used to object to the use of human hymns. And their argument is just Dr. Begg's argument carried out to its logical conclusions. The first Protestant dissenters and the true fathers of Puritanism in England and Scotland were the Brownists,* and they rejected altogether metrical versions of

---

* So many references have been made in this lecture to the Brownists that some nformation about them and their connection with Scotland may possibly be wished by some readers. The following sentences from Calderwood will perhaps suffice : "Upon Thursday the 9th of Januar (1584) an Englishman called Robert Brown came to Edinburgh out of Flanders. He landed at Dundie, and having gottin support there he came to St. Andrewes, where he purchased a letter of commendatioun

the Psalms as an unauthorised union of divine and human, inspired and uninspired elements. One of their chief apostles says, "what I speak against is not that comfortable and heavenly harmony of singing Psalms, but it is the rhyming and paraphrasing of the Psalms as in your church." And in Scotland during the hot times of the persecution there were a few fanatics that took up these views. Among others there was a crazy man of the name of Gib, the owner and skipper of a coasting vessel in the Forth. He, so to speak, out-covenanted all the covenanters. He not only held that the Episcopal Church established in Scotland at that time was a corrupt and an Anti-christian Church, but that men like Richard Cameron and Donald Cargill came far short of the mark in their contentions for the truth. He founded a sect of his own, therefore, and went over the country preaching and proselytising. Like Messrs. Moody and Sankey at the present day, too, he utilised the softening and sanctifying influences of music in his outdoor services, and indeed so much that he and his followers

---

from Mr. Andrew Melvill to Mr. James Lowsone (minister at Edinburgh). There came in company with him foure or five Englishmen with their wives and families. They held opinioun of separatioun from all kirks where excommunication was not rigorouslie used against open offenders not repenting. They would not admitt witnesses (god-fathers) in baptisime and sindrie other opinions they had. This Brown was their preacher. . . . He and his companie remained at the heid of the Cannongate. . . . Upon Tuesday the 21st, Robert Brown, the ringleader of the Brownists, in conference with some of the Presbyterie alledged that the whole discipline of Scotland was amisse. . . . It was thought good that Mr. James Lowson and Mr. John Davidson sould gather out of his booke and their practice suche opinions as they suspected or perceaved them to erre in and gett them ready against Moonday nixt, to pose him and his followers therupon that therafter the king might be informed. . . . Upon Tuisday the 28th, Robert Brown, with the rest of his complices, were called before the Presbyterie and continued till the morne. He acknowledged and avowed his books and other things. Mr. James Lowson and Mr. John Davidson were appointed to gather the erroneous articles to be presented to the King. But they were interteaned and fostered to molest the kirk,"—that is the king used the Brownists as a means of weakening the power of the church against his own royal prerogative.

were known by the name of the sweet singers. But along with sweet singing he cultivated a most intemperate style of language. He denounced dignities, sneered at statesmen, railed at churches and poured contempt on all ordained ministers. His impeachments of all existing institutions, civil and ecclesiastical, became at length so outrageous that the attention of the government was called to his doings; and for what Wodrow designates "scandals and blasphemies," but what the statesmen of the time would probably have termed seditious and incendiary speeches, he was apprehended and clapt into prison. A more fitting destination for him would have been a lunatic asylum, where laxative medicines, with bodily exercise, were prescribed in copious doses. However, he was lodged in the Tolbooth of Edinburgh, and while lying there, in "the Ironhouse," as he termed it, he emitted a paper that he said was inspired by the Holy Ghost. In this curious document he denounced as sinful every custom that in its origin was either superstitious or heathen, such as the naming of days and months after Pagan deities or Popish saints, the observance of Yule, Hogmanay, and St. Valentine's eve, and what is not the least notable, as indicating a glimmering of sound sense and sober judgment in the midst of his ravings, the prevalent objection to marriage in the month of May. But in his prison-penned paper he said also, "Yesterday being the 26th day of the fifth month (1681), it seemed good to the Holy Ghost and to us to take out of our Bibles the Psalms in metre, for several causes mentioned afterwards, for the Book of the Revelation says if any man should add unto these things God shall add unto him the plagues which are written in this book, and we did burn them in our prison house and sweep away the ashes." In another part of his paper he accused the Church of "usurping supremacy" in saying, by authority of the General Assembly, we allow these Psalms to be sung in churches. This supremacy, he said, I and those enchained with me renounce, and we maintain that nothing but the Scriptures themselves should be within the boards of the Bible. And extreme as these views of Gib were, they were not the most extreme that were put forth in the name of Puritanism. The Brownists allowed the singing of psalms in prose but only as a matter of instruction and comfort, whereby God is glorified, and not as an act of immediate praise. All praise as well as prayer, they contended, must be extempore, and not expressed in any set words, whether found in the Bible or not. The singing of hymns, they said, is an ordinance, and any member of the church exercising his gifts is free to bring a hymn of his own and sing it to the congregation, all the rest being silent and giving audience.* And it was not the Brownists only that held these opinions, but some of the Independents also, about two hundred years ago, were imbued with the same fantastic notions.

It is proper to observe, however, that neither the extreme views of the Gibbites and Brownists, nor the more moderate views expressed by some people at the present day that the psalms in metre should alone be used in the service of public praise, were ever set forth or sanctioned by the Church of Scotland. From the date of the Reformation down to the sitting of the Westminster Assembly, not only were metrical versions of the Psalms, but hymns and doxologies also, generally sung in the public worship of the Church. In all the old Psalters printed and used during that period, there are hymns

---

* One of the Brownists wrote—" The reading out of a book is no part of spiritual worship, but the invention of the man of sin. Books and writings are in the nature of pictures or images, and therefore in the nature of ceremonies, and so by consequent the reading of a book is ceremonial. The Holy Scriptures are not to be retained before the eyes in time of spiritual worship. It is unlawful to have the boo before the eyes in singing of Psalms."—Baillie's Dissuasive, 18, 19.

inserted. The year 1650, however, witnessed a change in that respect. The present version of the Psalms was that year printed for use in public worship,* and no hymns nor paraphrases were appended. But this omission of hymns from the Psalter in 1650 did not indicate that the Church had come to object to the use of hymns in public worship. It may be considered rather, like the discontinuance of the doxology, as a truce with the English Puritans for the sake of uniformity and peace. In the year 1647, when a committee was appointed by the General Assembly to examine and revise Rous' version (or paraphrase, as it was termed) of the Psalms, which is now, and has for more than 230 years been, the version used in the Church of Scotland, Mr. Zachary Boyd was requested

---

* Considered musically, the introduction of the present metrical version of the Psalms, commonly called Rous' version, was a retrograde movement, as the following curious passage in the diary of Lamont of Newton will shew. "A new translation of the Psalms of David in metre, first corrected by the Assemblie of Divines in England, bot afterworde revised by the General Assemblie of this kingdom and their Commissioners, was appointed to be practised in all the kirks of the kingdom, the former discharged. This translation is more neare the original Hebrew than the former, as also the whole Psalms are translated to common tunes, whereas in the former there were many proper tunes (that is, peculiar measures requiring special tunes to suit them). Ther be proper tunes also in this translation, bot with all ther is adjoyned common tunes with them."

In 1631 King James produced a metrical version of the Psalms under his own name, although it is said to have been the work of a well-known poet of that age, Sir Wm. Alexander of Menstrie, and His Majesty would fain have foisted this royal paraphrase on the Church. In alarm at this threatened innovation, reasons against the public use of the king's version were drawn up by some of the clergy, notably Calderwood. One reason was, that people could sing all or most part of the Psalms in the old metaphrase without book ; another was, that a change of version would make the Kirk appear light-headed and unsettled ; and a third was, that the new version contained fantastical words, such as "opposites—exorbitant—gratefully—usher—portend, etc." The real reason of dislike, however, was that the version was "undertaken without direction of the Kirk, or offer made to the Kirk before." —M'Meekan's History of the Scottish Metrical Psalms. Strange to say, although the king's version was much despised by the Church of Scotland, it was largely borrowed from by Rous in the version adopted by the Church of Scotland.—Cunningham's History, ii. 155.

to "be at the paines to translate the other Scriptural songs in meeter, and to report his travels also to the Commission of Assembly." Possibly Mr. Boyd's labours were not found very satisfactory, for his Scripture rhymes have not the melody of Milton's muse ; but whether his labours were satisfactory or not, the deference thought due to the English Presbyterians in 1650, and the rise soon after of engrossing troubles in the kingdom, were sufficient to account for the temporary abandonment of the projected compilation. After the great bubble of uniformity with England in doctrine, worship, and Church government, had burst, and the Church of Scotland was at the Revolution established anew on her old separate national Presbyterian basis, the attention of the General Assembly was again directed to the subject of Scriptural songs, as a supplement to the metrical version of the Psalms. In 1706 a collection of such songs, put into verse by Mr. Patrick Simpson, minister at Renfrew, was recommended to be used in private families, with the view, it may be presumed, of preparing the way for their introduction into public worship ; and in 1708 it was remitted by the General Assembly to its Commission, "maturely to consider the printed version of (these) Scriptural songs, with the remarks of Presbyteries thereupon, and after an examination thereof . . . to conclude and establish that version, and to publish and emit it for the public use of the Church," as was done with the present version of the Psalms in 1649. Mr. Simpson's Scripture songs, however, never established a footing in the public service of the Church.

But in 1742 the attention of the General Assembly was again called to the defective state of the Church Psalter, and a committee was appointed to prepare some Paraphrases of sacred writ, "to be joined with the Psalms of David so as to enlarge the Psalmody." Three years afterwards this committee laid before the Assembly "some pieces of sacred poesy . . composed by private persons," and these pieces of sacred poetry were, with sundry alterations, recommended by the Assembly in 1751, to be published and used in family exercise.* For the next twenty-four years nothing further was done in the matter. But in 1775 the Assembly was overtured by the Synod of Glasgow and Ayr to take such steps as should be judged necessary for introducing the Paraphrases into the Psalter of the Church. In consequence of this overture a committee was appointed to examine and revise the 1751 collection, and to "receive and consider any corrections or additional materials that might be laid before them." The result was that, in 1781, the committee gave in to the Assembly "such a collection of sacred poems as they thought might be submitted to the judgment of the Church," and the Assembly ordered copies of the same to be transmitted "to Presbyteries for their perusal." And while these copies were being examined and criticised in Presbyteries, the Assembly also "in the meantime allowed this collection of sacred poems to be used in public worship in congregations where the minister finds it for edification." This permission, however,

---

* There is an interesting reference to this collection of sacred poems in the Records of the Presbytery of Ayr. The minute is as follows :—" The Presbytery having considered the Scripture Paraphrase transmitted by the late General Assembly to the several Presbyteries of this Church give it as their opinion that the enlarging of our Psalmody is highly necessary, and wish the Assembly would not suffer the design to be dropt. But as Presbyteries have not had leisure in the present confusion (that is, the confusions arising out of Prince Charles' rebellion) to consider them so maturely as they deserve, the Presbytery are of opinion that they should be yet again transmitted, that they should be ranged more methodically, and that several others should be added upon other subjects." The injection of hymns into the Church is more summarily effected now-a-days. The criticism of Presbyteries is avoided, notwithstanding what the Barrier Act says, and what the former practice of the Church has been.

was merely a prudential way of making a virtue of necessity. It was giving a show of authority to what it was known would be done by some people without authority, for in the "advertisement" prefixed to old copies of the 1781 collection, it is stated that the earlier collection of 1751 had been previously "used in several churches." * It is this 1781 collection of paraphrases that is still, after the lapse of more than a hundred years, bound in our Scottish Bibles along with the metrical version of the Psalms of David. This collection, too, is merely a revised and an enlarged edition of the one printed in 1751. The old "advertisement" just spoken of says that "all the translations and paraphrases which had appeared in the former (1751) publication are in substance retained. But they have been revised with care. Many alterations, and, it is hoped, improvements, are made upon them. A considerable number of new paraphrases are added. They are all now arranged according to the order in which the several passages of Scripture lie in the Bible, and a few hymns are subjoined." Strange to say, although these paraphrases have continued to be used in churches ever since their publication in 1781, the interim Act of Assembly that allowed their use "in the meantime" has never been converted into a permanent Act. It is said that the requisite approval of Presbyteries for this purpose was never obtained. But the permission granted in 1781 was never recalled, and it may be held that use and

---

Mr. Hill Burton says he "had great difficulty in obtaining a copy of the original (1751) paraphrases." It may not be out of place therefore to state that this (1751) collection may be seen appended to a large family Bible in a workman's house in Mauchline village. The collection comprises 45 "pieces of poesy" which are termed songs, and are headed Song 1, Song 2, Song 3, &c. In some cases the amendments of 1781 are doubtful improvements on the earlier version. For instance the apparent inconsistency between the 2nd and 3rd verse in the 25th Paraphrase does not appear in the original song.

wont have now given as valid an authority for the singing of the Paraphrases in church as a special Act of Assembly could do. The Paraphrases have, on the strength of their own merits, established a secure place in the psalmody of all the Presbyterian Churches in Scotland. But it was not without contention and controversy, strife and bitterness, that the Paraphrases made their way into use in our public services. People still living remember the hostility with which the use of the Paraphrases was regarded. In the days of Mr. Auld's ministry there were no Paraphrases used in Mauchline church, nor were there any in the days of his amiable and cultured successor Mr. Reid. Nothing but the pure songs of Zion were ever heard then. It was reserved for Mr. Tod to introduce the Paraphrases, and this he did in 1806, two years after his settlement in the parish. There is no notice of this important step in any extant minute of Kirk Session, but allusion is made to it in a small memorandum book of the Session Clerk, in which collections and notes of cases of discipline are entered for transference into the proper journals. The whole entry regarding the Paraphrases in this memorandum book is, " 1806, Feb. 9, began to sing the Paraphrases," and what was the first Paraphrase given out to be sung in Mauchline Church may be conjectured from the fact that the text on that memorable day was " Wherewith shall I come before the Lord and bow myself before the most high God."

From 1806 to 1882 no changes in either the materials of praise or the mode of rendering praise occurred in Mauchline church, but the year 1882 will always be memorable in our parish annals as the year in which the organ and the hymnal were introduced. These events are too recent either to call for or to justify further notice at present, but it may be stated that in order to satisfy the curiosity of subsequent generations a narrative of the movement for purchasing the organ and preparing a place for its reception in the church has been inserted in the Session Records.

Having described the reader's and precentor's service I have now to speak of the service that specially devolved on the minister. It will not be necessary to say much about public prayers, because during the period covered by our extant parish records the service of prayer in the church has undergone no change of form. It is well known that a liturgy was at one time, and for a long time, used in the Church of Scotland. In the year 1564 the General Assembly ordained that every minister, exhorter, and reader should have one of the Psalm books lately printed in Edinburgh, and use the order therein contained in prayers, marriages, and ministration of the sacraments. The order here referred to is what is set down in the book commonly known as Knox's Liturgy; and this Liturgy continued to be used by some ministers and readers down to the year 1637 at least, if not to 1645. Its use was by no means universal, however, during that period. There were both ministers and readers before 1637 that rebelled against set forms of prayer, and laid the prayer book aside. Rutherford, in one of his letters says, " Anent read prayers I could never see precept, promise, or practice for them in God's Word. Our Church never allowed them, but men took them up at their own choice. The Word of God maketh reading and praying two different worships. In reading God speaketh to us, and in praying we speak to God. I had never faith to think well of them. In my weak judgment I think it were well if they were out of the service of God. The saints never used them, and God never commanded them, and a promise to hear any prayers except the pouring out of the soul to God we can never read." And not only were extempore prayers always popular with the general public, but when they were given by a minister of some culture and intellectual power they were not taken amiss even by the professed connoisseurs of devotion. When young and raw readers, however, sparsely gifted and not more than half educated, took on themselves, as they often did, to treat congregations to extempore prayers the guardians of public manners were horrified. It was a shame to all religion, said King Charles, to have the majesty of God so barbarously spoken to, and as a remedy for this deformity, as he termed it, in the public worship of the Church of Scotland, Charles issued a new service book to be used as a liturgy by all preachers and readers.* But neither minister nor people would take the king's liturgy, and extempore prayers became more established in use and favour than ever. The real objection, however, to the king's service book by those that best represented the Church of Scotland in 1637 was not because it prescribed set prayers to be read in public worship. That could have been borne with, and indeed was patiently borne with every Sabbath. But the book was introduced in an offensive manner, and it contained offensive rubrics. It was compiled and introduced into the Church by a royal mandate, and without the Church's examina-

---

* In the preface to Charles' (or Laud's) service book, the following interesting paragraph occurs, "Our first Reformers were of the same minde with us, as appeareth by the ordinance they made that in all the parishes of this realm the common-prayer should be read weekly on Sundaies and other festival dayes with the lessons of the Old and New Testament, conform to the order of the book of common prayer, meaning that of England, for it is known that divers years after we had no other order for common prayer. This is recorded to have been the first head concluded in a frequent council of the Lords and Barons professing Christ Jesus. We keep the words of the history, '*Religion was not then placed in rites and gestures nor men taken with the fancie of extemporary prayers.*' Sure the public worship of God in his church being the most solemn action of us his poor creatures here below, ought to be performed by a liturgie advisedly set and framed, and not according to the sudden and various fancies of men."

tion, revision, or approval. That was an invasion of the Church's rights and liberties, and therefore it was resented by the Church. The book, besides, contained expressions and prescribed ceremonies that were considered to go too far in the direction of Popish doctrine and Popish ritual. It was more High Church than the English prayer book itself. It gave permission to the Presbyter to chant or intone certain portions of the service. Directions were given in it also that at particular parts of the service all the people should stand up and say aloud, "Glory be to Thee, Oh Lord." In the communion service there was a prayer set down that seemed to sanction the doctrine of transubstantiation. Although the Presbyterians in 1637, therefore, could have forborne the use of read prayers in public worship, they would neither submit to have a liturgy thrust upon them *nolentes volentes*, nor would they accept the ritual offered them in the service book. But it must also be said that although extempore prayers were generally cried up in 1637 there were some places where their introduction was not welcomed. "New incum customs," was what Spalding said of them, with a satirical mark of admiration. And even after they had become rooted and grounded in public favour people would still listen respectfully to a liturgy if it was accompanied with ministrations that were otherwise good. It is said of Dr. Gilbert Burnet that during his ministry in Salton from 1665 to 1669 he succeeded by his pastoral care and tenderness, zeal and ability, in completely gaining the affections of all his parishioners, "not excepting the Presbyterians, although he was the only man in Scotland that made use of the prayers in the English Church liturgy."

Although it is, strictly speaking, foreign to the subject of this lecture, which has to do only with the Sabbath service in the Church of Scotland and particularly at Mauchline, at different dates and during different periods, I cannot resist the temptation of giving here a brief account of a very grand old practice that prevailed in England at least, if not in Scotland, in Catholic times. And in doing this I shall just quote from a book called the "Alliance of Divine Offices," which exhibits "all the liturgies of the Church of England since the Reformation, as also the late Scotch Service Book, with all their respective variations, with annotations . . giving a fair prospect into the usages of the ancient Church." The name of the author is Hamon L'Estrange, and the book was printed in 1659, "for Henry Broom at the signe of the Gun in Ivie Lane." "The agenda of religion in our Church before the Reformation were," says the author of this book, "performed, it is well known, in Latin, a language very unedifying to a non-intelligent people. That so many so much interested and concerned in those sacred offices should not be totally excluded as idle spectators, or fit for nothing but now and then to return an Amen to they knew not what, this expedient was devised. The people were exhorted to join in prayers according to certain heads, dictated to them by the minister in the English tongue, observing the method and materials of the then prayers for all states, so that of all the service then used this only could properly be called common prayer, as being the only form wherein the whole congregation did joyn in consort, and therefore the title of it in the Injunctions of Edward 6, Anno 1547 is, 'The form of bidding the common prayers.' Now because it was made by Allocution or speaking to the people, agreeing with what the primitive church called πδοσφώνησιν, it was called bidding of prayers." Nothing could be more proper or more solemn, more impressive or more edifying in public worship than a brief service of this kind reverently conducted.

It is well known that in Protestant churches generally, and in the Church of Scotland in particular, the preaching of the word has always been reckoned the chief part of the service of the sanctuary. The quantity of preaching that ministers had to give and people had to take in olden times was enormous. There were commonly two diets of worship on the Sabbath, and very often what was termed a week day sermon besides. In 1648 an act was passed by the General Assembly reviving former acts which appointed ministers to preach both before and after noon. Pardovan complains that in his day, which was in the beginning of last century, this act had fallen too much into disuetude, and that in many parishes there was only one diet of worship on Sunday.* Till within a comparatively recent date there were in Mauchline two diets of worship on Sabbath, the greater part of the year if not all the year round. In some of the old records there is a note of the service entered, and from these notes we see what the extent of service had been. Opening a volume of records at random I find the following entry under date 28th May, 1732, "Mr. Ferguson, probationer, lectured on Psalm 39 and preached on Psalm 30 and 7. The minister preached afternoon on Psalm 116 and 12." On this occasion the minister had got help in the forenoon, but that was not a common occurrence, and his usual Sabbath-day's work in the pulpit was a lecture and a sermon in the forenoon, and a sermon in the afternoon. In 1736 there is a touching and kindly entry under date 28th March, that "the minister came home this day, and being weary of his journey only preached."

---

* In the records of Galston Kirk Session for 1639 the following minute, which will approve itself to many people for its good sense, will be found, "August 18th. In respect the day is wearing shorter there shall be but forenoon's preaching, with prayers and reading, the time being two afternoon, and this act to be put to continue till March." And so in March 1640 we read of a man's being brought before the Session for profaning the Sabbath "in time of afternoon reading."

Besides two sermons every Sabbath the minister had frequently in olden times to give a third sermon during the week. Pardovan says there was no Act of Assembly enjoining these week day sermons, and he evidently was of opinion that for all the good they did they might have been dispensed with. There was a semi-statutory authority, however, for these sermons. An Act of Assembly passed in 1648 on particular remedies for present corruptions and enormities says that "ministers (should) catechise one day every week wherein also they may baptize and lecture or preach." These catechetical and lecture meetings were a substitute for an older and simpler institution. During the period of Episcopacy prior to 1638 it had been customary to have meetings in churches on the afternoons or evenings of week days, and at these meetings portions of scripture and prayers from the liturgy were read by the minister or reader. The rebellion against set forms and ceremonies which began in 1637 led to these meetings for prayer being changed into meetings for lectures. A somewhat dubious reason for the change is given in the diary of John Nicol,* "In steid of evening and morning prayeris, the ministeris taking to thair consideration that the not reiding and exponing of the Scriptures at the old accustomed tyme of prayer was the occasion of much drinking at that seasoun quhen these prayeris and chaptures wer usuallie red, thairfoir, and to prevent that sin it wes concludit in the beginning of March, 1650, that all the days of the week a lectorie sould be red and exponit in Edinburgh be everie minister thair *per vices*, quhilk accordinglie wes put in practize and so began this holie and hevinlie exercise." That heavenly exercise, however, had been instituted in

---

* An equally *dubious* reason for the change is given by Spalding, "This forme wes brocht in for to mak thair stipend better ! ! "

some places in Scotland before 1650, and although as a rule it was a popular movement it was not universally so. "Upon the 4th May, 1642, Doctor Goold, principal of the College in Aberdeen, began a noveltie," says Spalding, "and to preich upon this weik day within the College kirk. . . His auditoris war few, who had little feist of his doctrein, and at last himself wyreit and shortlie gave over this weiklie sermon moir foolishlie nor it began." The lectures were nevertheless continued by men of more resolute character than Dr. Goold, even although they were denounced as thraldom by the Laodiceans of the northern capital. Three days a week they were held in Aberdeen in 1642 by Andrew Cant and his colleagues, and "the people were compelled to attend these lectures or were cryd out against." During the time of preaching on week days "no merchand nor craftisman's booth durris durst be opnit, that the kirk micht be the better keipit be the masteris and seruandis." And it was neither so far back as 1642, nor so far north as Aberdeen that this rigour was to be seen. In 1661 the minister and Kirk Session of Dumbarton complained to the Town Council that "upon the weiklie days sermon thair ar several merchants and traidsmen within burgh who in time of sermon mak thair merchandise, and wark their wark to the great dishonour of God, contempt of the gospel, and hindrance of thair awin edification," and the Town Council, for preventing of the like in time coming, ordained that every person so transgressing should pay an unlaw of 40s. Even before Goold and Cant introduced the lecture lessons, as they were termed in Aberdeen, there were week day sermons in some places in Ayrshire. The ministry of David Dick or Dickson at Irvine terminated in 1641 by his translation to the chair of Divinity in the University of Glasgow; and Mr. Dickson while at Irvine had week day sermons on Mondays, which were then the market days in that town. "Upon the Sabbath evenings many persons under soul distress used to resort to his house after sermon, when usually he spent an hour or two in answering their cases and directing and comforting those who were cast down, in all which he had an extraordinary talent. In a large hall he had in his house at Irvine there would have been, as I am informed by old Christians, several scores of serious Christians waiting for him when he came from the church. Those with the people round the town who came into the market at Irvine, made the church as throng, if not thronger, on the Mondays as on the Lord's day, by these week day sermons."* In the year 1642 both the old and the new customs were observed at Mauchline. In other words, there were both prayer meetings and lecture meetings. At a presbyterial visitation of the parish that year, Mr. Young said that "he preached twyse on the Sabbath, and every Twysday once, sumtyme by preaching and sumtyme by catechising, and declared the frequent meeting of the people to that effect. And further, he declared that publict prayers wer used and reading of the Scriptures morning and evening, and that familie exercise wes also observed." In 1643 the minister of Coylton was exhorted by the Presbytery of Ayr to preach twice every Sabbath, preach catechetical doctrine once a week, and see if family exercise be constantly practised in the parish. As recently as 1743, Mr. Auld was strictly enjoined by the Presbytery to have week day sermons at Mauchline, as was formerly done on the "mercat days." It was apparently the market day, therefore, that was generally utilised by ministers for their week day sermons, and

---

* Preface by Wodrow to an old book once popular, now little heard of, called Truth's Victory over Error. This book was a translation in English of notes taken n Dickson's Class of Divinity. Its publication had a curious history.

it is easy to understand, therefore, how Mr. Maitland should have complained, as he did, of the number of "mercat days" in Mauchline, making his charge "very gravaminous." *

In the oldest extant records of this parish, those, namely, that refer to the period of Mr. Veitch's ministry, there is little, if any, express mention made of week day sermons, but there are frequent entries of collections on week days, which imply that on such days there were congregational gatherings as in the time of Mr. Young, for either sermon or catechetical examinations. About 1680, during Mr. Veitch's ministry, these week day meetings in church seem to have been held every second Tuesday, that is half as often as they were in Mr. Young's day. Both in Mr. Maitland's and Mr. Auld's days the week day sermon was continued, but not so regularly nor frequently as in earlier times.

While treating of the Reader's duties, we saw that it was customary to have diets of catechising in church on the Sundays, but we see now that there were also diets of catechising held on week days. The Sunday's catechising seems always to have been a catechising of children, the week days catechising was a catechising of all and sundry—young and old, high and low, rich and poor. The catechising of children in church on Sundays was a very ancient custom. In the English Prayer Book there is a rubric appended to the Catechism which states that the curate of every parish shall diligently, upon Sundays and holy days, after the second lesson at evening prayer, openly in the church instruct and examine so many children of his parish sent unto him as he shall think convenient, in some part of the Catechism. "The same rule," says

---

* In 1714 the minister of Coylton reported to the Presbytery at their visitation of his parish that he was in the way of intimating weekly lectures, "but sometimes did not preach because of the paucity of the people that meet."

L'Estrange, " is observed by the Belgick Church, and so did the Palatine divines advise at the Synod of Dort that it should be an afternoon exercise. And I wish," continues that author, "that they of the Presbyterian inclination would more listen to these their friends, and if not for conformity's, yet for Christianity's sake, not suffer preaching so totally to usurp and justle out this most necessary office. The afternoon sermon hath not that countenance of authority in our Church which catechising hath, this being settled by express rule, that only tolerated or entering in by remote implication, and though late custom hath invested it with an honour commensurate with and equal to that of the morning sermon, sure I am, it was of minor reputation in the apostolical and next succeeding ages." Whatever may be said of the Presbyterian Church in England at one period, the Presbyterian Church in Scotland has been more alive to the duty of catechising children on Sunday than Mr. L'Estrange may have been aware of. So recently as the year 1747 the Presbytery of Ayr recommended " that the ancient good custom of repeating the Catechism in church on the Lord's day, before sermon in the forenoon (that is, at the reader's or schoolmaster's service), and betwixt sermons (should be resumed), and that a portion of holy Scripture be read after repeating the Catechism." *

---

* The following account of a Scottish Sunday at Kirkcudbright in 1722 (quoted in Harper's Rambles in Galloway), will be interesting to all to whom it is new. It is by an English traveller who published notes of a journey through Scotland :—"I arrived here on Saturday night. . . . Next day I expected, as in England, a piece of good beef and a pudding to dinner, but my landlord told me that they never dress dinner on a Sunday, so that I must either take up with bread and butter and a fresh egg, or fast till after the evening sermon, when they never fail of a hot supper. Certainly no nation on earth observes the Sabbath with that strictness of devotion and resignation to the will of God. They all pray in their families before they go to church, and between sermons they fast. After sermon every body retires to his own home, and reads some book of devotion till supper, which is generally very good on Sundays, after which they sing psalms till they go to bed." Few people will say that that is not a beautiful picture of grand and quiet Sabbath life.

The week day catechising that at one period formed so important a part of pastoral work in the Church of Scotland, were not restricted to children.* What the object of these catechisings was may be inferred from the tenor of an act of Assembly passed in 1639, which ordained that every minister, besides his pains on the Lord's day, should have weekly catechising of some part of the parish,† and not altogether put off the examination of the people till a little before the communion. Ten years later this act was specially renewed, and a clause was added to it directing "every minister so to order his catechetic questions as thereby the people who do not convene all at one time but by turns unto that exercise, may at every diet have the chief heads of saving knowledge in a short view presented unto them."‡ The carrying out of the Act of 1639 was in some places thought at first rather grievous. At a Presbyterial visitation of the old town kirk of Aberdeen in 1642, it was ordained in terms of the Act of Assembly, says

---

* In 1570 the General Assembly ordained that "ministers and elders of kirks shall universally within this realm take trial and examine all young children within their Parochines that are come to nine years, and that for the first time, thereafter when they are come to twelve years for the second time, the third time to be examined when they are of fourteen years, wherethrough it may be known what they have profited in the school of Christ from time to time."

† The Kirk Session of Galston lost no time in putting that Act into execution. In 1639 they "concludit that there be examination throw the Paroche ane day in ye weik qhuilk is to be keipit on Fryday."

‡ "The chief heads of saving knowledge." Along with the Confession of Faith, Catechisms, &c., there is generally bound up a small treatise called "the sum of saving knowledge." How that treatise should have found its way into what may be termed a collection of the Church's standards in doctrine, worship, and government, is a mystery. The extraordinary estimation in which it was long held is probably the only explanation. It was the joint production of Mr. David Dickson and Mr. James Durham, and, says Wodrow, it was by them "dictated to a reverend minister (who informed me) about the year 1650. It was the deed of these two great men, and though never judicially approved by this Church, deserves to be much more read and considered than I fear it is." Preface to Truth's Victory, signed Eastwood, January 5, 1726. R. W.

Spalding, " that ilk maister and mistres of famelie in toun and cuntrie within this parochin, suld come with there barnes and seruandis to the ministeris catechising. Noysum to the cuntrie people to cum all, cloiss up there durris, and leave none at home to keip thair houssis, thair cornes, cattell, and uther goodis." To meet the convenience of congregations it was customary to have diets of catechising once a year in different parts of the parish, and to gather all the people in each district to some central and suitable place of meeting. In 1658 the Kirk Session of Rothesay ordained that the "landward part of the parish be divided into four quarters for examination, those in each quarter to meet at a special place in the same." Probably there was some such arrangement as this in Mauchline in 1687, and possibly also at such rural diets of catechising there may occasionally have been a sermon and a baptism, for in our Session Records there is an entry dated 22nd December of that year, stating that that day there was collected at Drumfork the sum of 9s. During Mr. Auld's ministry there were frequent diets of catechising held in church, but whether these were for the townspeople only, or for the parishioners generally I have not noticed in the records any statement to shew. In 1750 Mr. Auld complained to the Session "that he and the people that attended catechising in the church were much disturbed by the school being so near, and the schoolmaster being called, promised that for the future he would take care that the school should give no disturbance by noise in time of catechising, and that there should be no ringing of the bell during that time." *

---

* Within the last twenty years an old and respected U.P. minister in Ayrshire was in the habit of convening the people in the different quarters of his diocese to meetings for catechising in the church. The roll of the quarter was at these meetings formally called over, and absentees, of whom there were many, were marked.

It may be supposed that when there was such a quantity of preaching to be delivered week after week there could not have been much work expended on the preparation of sermons. And neither there was. Baillie, in one of his letters written in 1656, laments that the popular election of ministers, which was then in vogue, was spoiling preaching by tempting young men to study *ad captandum* arts of loose extempore oratory, instead of carefully thinking out the subjects on which they wrote and prelected. "Our divinity students (last year) were," he says, "but few, and however they had lessons enough from Mr. John Young and me, yet they minded study bot little, for when they see their weak companions the second or third year after their laureation put in the best place with exceeding poor sufficiencie, it makes the rest the more to neglect all studie, but only to preach in their popular kind of way, which requires little learning." * It was customary for ministers to

---

* *Apropos* of these remarks of Baillie's, it may be mentioned that in the year 1581 the King (James VI.) submitted, among other proposals, to the General Assembly the following suggestions, in favour of which a good deal might be said:—That there be four degrees of stipends for ministers, and that young men new come from schools shall only be promoted to the benefices and stipends in the lowest degree. That the eldest ministers of the greatest learning and judgment be promoted to the highest rank, and for the better eschewing of ambition and avarice so to ascend from one rank to another gradation as they shall be judged and tried worthiest from three years to three years (Calderwood, iii. 521). And not only did he submit that the chief stipends should be reserved for men of the greatest learning in the Church, but in his later years he ordered that the treatment of certain subjects in the pulpit should be allowed to preachers only of a certain standing or rank. No preacher of what title soever under the degree of a Bishop, or Dean at the least, shall presume, he said, to preach in any popular auditory the deep points of Predestination, Election, Reprobation, or of the universality, efficacy, resistibility, or irresistibility of God's grace, but rather leave these themes to be handled by learned men, and that modestly and moderately by use and application, rather than by way of positive doctrine, as being fitter for schools and universities than for simple auditories (Alliance of Divine Offices). To some extent the King's ideas of degrees in the ministry were at one time carried out by the General Assembly. In 1589 the Assembly ordered trial to be made of all ministers in the Church in respect of their

take up a subject or a text, and on that subject or text to preach six or eight Sabbaths consecutively. This was called their ordinary. It is minuted in our records that on the 27th May, 1733, the minister preached on a certain text and finished his discourses on that text. How many discourses he had preached on the said text I have not been able very clearly to make out, but in the course of that same year, 1733, I find that that for nine successive Sabbaths he preached on Isaiah xxix. 9th, "With my soul have I desired thee in the night, yea with my spirit within me will I seek thee early, for when thy judgments are in the earth the inhabitants of the world shall learn righteousness." During the nine weeks that these sermons were being delivered on the Sundays, the week day sermons on three successive Thursdays were on the text, Isaiah lv. 3, "Incline your ear and come to me, hear, and your soul shall live."

I happen to have in my possession several old books of manuscript sermons, utterly worthless as aids for the pulpit, but very valuable from an antiquarian point of view, in showing how sermons were got up and subjects were handled by ministers long ago. One of these volumes is in the handwriting of a man that was famous in his day and district, viz., Mr. Peter Rae, minister first in a parish called Kirkbride, and latterly in Kirkconnel. He is described by Dr. Hew Scott in the Fasti Ecclesiae as having been not only an able preacher and theologian, but a mechanic, mathematician, astronomer and historian. He is best known as the author of a history of the rebellion in 1715. The volume in my possession is written in a hand of

---

gifts and attainments, and sentences pronounced after this trial were to the effect that one minister was "meit to be continued in a better degree," and others were meet to be continued in a good degree, or some reasonable degree, or a low measure, or the lowest measure. A few were absolutely deposed from "the function of the ministry for the present" (M'Crie's Melville, i. 478).

remarkable neatness and elegance. There is not a blot and scarcely an erasure in the whole book. Taking one of the sermons in this book at random as a fair specimen of the sermons in general, I find that it is fully twenty-nine pages in length, that each page consists of six and forty lines, and that each line comprises about sixteen words. The whole sermon is equal in length to six modern discourses that would take each half an hour in delivery. The sermon, however, is made to do for nine discourses, and a marginal date indicates when each part of the sermon was preached. There is no separate beginning and end to each part as if to mark the bounds of a discourse complete in itself, but one part follows another as if the thread of the argument had never been broken, and the preacher had been obliged to stop because time was up. It may be presumed that each discourse would contain a preface recapitulating what had been said the Sunday before, and bringing up the hearers fresh to the new point of departure, and possibly what was written would be altered and amplified, or abbreviated when preached. It will be seen, therefore, that it was not an unusual thing for ministers to make one text serve for nine sermons, as good Mr. Maitland did in Mauchline in 1733.

Another volume of manuscript discourses that I happen to have is a volume written by old Mr. Mungo Lindsay, the minister of Sorn.* It is not written with anything

---

* Historically the most interesting sermon in Mr. Lindsay's book is one preached at Dalgain (Sorn) on the 13th Nov., 1706, "On a fast day relating to a trea ie of union betwixt Scotland and England, laid and lying before the Parliament of Scotland." The text is Daniel xii. 10, "many shall be purified and made white and tried, but the wicked shall do wickedly, and none of the wicked shall understand, but the wise shall understand." Mr. Lindsay speaks of the occasion as a "juncture of dark and critical providences, a darker has scarce been in Scotland since the first Reformation of this land." He argues, however, that all will be over-ruled for good to the godly, and he closes the sermon by an apt quotation of two verses, one of them immediately preceding the text, and the other at the end of the chapter.

like the neatness and elegance of Mr. Rae's book, and there are no marginal references to show when the different parts of each sermon were delivered. But there is no doubt that Mr. Lindsay's sermons were given in instalments like Mr. Rae's, and that like Mr. Rae's and Mr. Maitland's, they sometimes extended over eight or nine Sabbaths. I find for instance that on the 30th April, 1704, Mr. Lindsay commenced a series of sermons on the second part of the 19th Psalm. The passage discoursed on begins at the 7th verse, "The law of the Lord is perfect, converting the soul," and it comprises only eight verses altogether. The discourses, however, on these eight verses occupied a year and seven months, except a few Sundays before and after the communion. One verse alone kept the minister going for two months. The total amount of written matter for this year and a half's stock of instruction is just about equal to the length of ten sermons such as you are in the way of hearing, shewing that what was written long ago was a good deal amplified in delivery, and that perhaps a considerable part of each sermon was occupied with a resumé of what was preached the previous Sabbath. We can understand the point, therefore, of one of the questions that Pardovan says might be put to the elders at Presbyterial visitations of churches, "Does your minister spend too much time in his sermon in repetition of what he said before." This did not mean does the minister

---

"Oh my Lord what shall be the end of these things. And he said, Go thy way, Daniel, for the words are closed up and sealed till the time of the end. . . But go thou thy way till the end be, for thou shalt rest and stand in thy lot at the end of the days." There was much more wisdom in this sermon than in the action taken by some Town Councils at the time, such as that of Dumbarton, who declared the proposed union to be "in their judgment of the most dangerous consequence to all the interests, civil and sacred, of the nation," and instructed their Commissioner, at the Convention of Burghs, to "declare their dislike of and dissent from the said union," as "plainly evacuating all the public oaths this nation lyes under."

dwell too much on any one subject or too frequently revert to particular topics, but it means does the minister each Sabbath before entering into his subject for the day spend too much time in going over what was said the previous Sunday.

This method of adhering to one subject for weeks or months together, was, whatever it might be thought of now, far from being unpopular at one time. One of the questions regularly put at Presbyterial visitations of parishes was, "if the portion of Scripture preached on (that day by the minister) was his *ordinary* text any time before," and the expected and approved answer to this question was "Yes."* In the year 1707 the parishioners of Craigie furnished the Presbytery of Ayr with a criticism of their minister's pulpit services, which is well worthy of preservation as a sample of the state of rural opinion in the West of Scotland at the beginning of last century, " His words in prayer," said the parishioners, " are not connected, and he hath too frequent repetition of God's name in prayer, and he *doth often change his text, and doth not raise many heads*, and doth not prosecute such as he names but scruffs them." Long ago it was customary for meetings of Presbytery to be opened, as meetings of Synod still are, by a sermon. The subject of sermon, too, was not left to the choice of the minister appointed to preach, but was prescribed to him, and these sermons, like old Mr. Mungo Lindsay's of Sorn, were meant to constitute a consecutive and an exhaustive treatment of large subjects. One minister followed up at one Presbytery what another minister had said at the previous Presby-

---

* This style of preaching is expressly recommended in the first book of discipline, chap. xi. 6, " Skipping and divagation from place to place of Scripture, be it in reading or be it in preaching we judge not so profitable to edifie the kirk as the continual following of one text."

tery. For instance, on the 28th October, 1766, the text appointed by the Presbytery of Ayr for the opening sermon at their next meeting was the first verse of the first chapter of the General Epistle of James. Verse after verse of this epistle was then in regular order appointed as the text for the next Presbyterial sermon till the whole epistle had been gone through. The last of this series of discourses was given in the beginning of 1792, more than twenty-five years after the first of the series had been preached! Such a treatise on St. James' Epistle as the legion of sermons preached before the Presbytery of Ayr between 1766 and 1792 was perhaps never given to the world, and along with the lamentation expressed by scholars at the loss of part of Livy's history, the divines of Scotland may fittingly join — disappointment and sorrow that this great Presbyterial commentary, on which the labours of more than a hundred ministers were for twenty-five years expended, has disappeared. In 1792 the Presbytery entered on a similar exposition, verse by verse, of the first Epistle of Peter, but as the most recent volume of Presbytery Records that I have had the privilege of examining comes down only to the year 1796, I am not prepared to say whether or not this exposition of St. Peter's first epistle was ever brought to a close!

It is alleged that some ministers in the Church of Scotland have recently introduced a practice of preaching at large without taking any text from Scripture as the subject of discourse. This practice, too, is regarded by some people as a very startling innovation. Whether a good practice or not, however, it is not a new one in the Christian Church. Baillie says that the Independents in England, during the sitting of the Westminster Assembly, were in the habit of dispensing with Scripture texts when they preached, and ran out on whatever matter they thought most fit and expedient for their hearers.

The same thing was done by the monks of the Catholic Church before the Reformation, and indeed it was also done by St. Paul and our Saviour himself, the great Master and great example, in the first days of Christianity. It may interest some people to be told that in the year 1714 the parishioners of Coylton complained to the Presbytery of Ayr that their minister "read and preached upon an article of the Confession of Faith on the Sabbath afternoon, without reading any text of Scripture before it." The minister did not deny the fact alleged, but explained that he gave an exposition of an article in the Confession of Faith with the Scriptures relative thereto. And the Presbytery apparently did not think that the minister's conduct called for censure, nor even for prohibition in the future, but "considering that this way of preaching is different from what is usual, recommended to the minister to read the Scriptures that relate to the subject he is to be upon, and then the article." Prudent advice, it may be said, to put the horse before the cart.

The sermons of the old Scotch preachers were neither laboured nor polished compositions. They were vigorous off-

---

* All sermons in Scotland long ago were given without paper. This is popularly supposed to have added to the preacher's work in preparation. Such was not necessarily the case. Sermons that are read are usually more carefully prepared than those that are mandated. Still read sermons were thought unsavoury. In the famous Representation and Petition presented to the General Assembly in 1732, which may almost be called the foundation stone of the Secession Church, and in which there is a "correct list" of all the corruptions and enormities in the Church of Scotland at that date the following sentence occurs, "Yea, a young minister appointed to preach before his Majesty's Commissioner to the last General Assembly, had the assurance even on that solemn occasion to add to former innovations, that of reading his sermon openly, though he could not but know it would give great offence both to ministers and people of this church." Some of the old ministers wrote out their sermons in full, but most had notes only. John Livingstone states that at first he wrote out beforehand all he preached, "word for word," Afterwards he preached from notes, and recommended others to do likewise.

hand addresses that went right to the hearts of hearers. Baillie, in the year 1644, when he was sitting in the Westminster Assembly of Divines, spoke of Scotch sermons as a very well understood species of oration. "We had," he says, "from two English preachers, Palmer and Hill, two of the most Scottish and free sermons I ever heard anywhere. They laid well about them, and charged public and parliamentary sins strictly on the backs of the guilty." This was a kind of preaching that was very unpalatable to people in authority, but was immensely agreeable to the public generally. In 1597 an Act of Assembly was passed, at the instigation of the King and his courtiers, forbidding that any man's name should be expressed to his rebuke in public, unless his fault were notorious. But despite this Act of Assembly, Scotch preaching continued long after to be very free and bold. As late as 1650 the Countess of Derby wrote from Kirkcudbright, where she had been staying for a fortnight:—"The sermons which I have heard in this place are horrible, having nothing of devotion in them, nor explaining any point of religion, but being full of sedition, warning people by their names, and treating of everything with such ignorance and without the least respect or reverence, that I am so scandalised I do not think I could live with a quiet conscience among these atheists." That style of preaching, however, as I have said, was popular, and ministers were occasionally requested by their Kirk Sessions to give a genuine Scotch sermon for the special benefit of some particular members of the Congregation. In 1586 the Kirk Session of Perth, lamenting the ruinous state of their church, did with one consent ordain the minister to leave his ordinary text whereof he had been preaching before, and choose for his discourse some portion of Scripture, most able and meet to move the hearts of the people, and especially of the bailies and magistrates, to provide that the church be with all diligence repaired and mended in all honest and decent form." There is no trace in our records of any such application having ever been made to the minister of Mauchline, and if entertainment ever was given to the congregation in Mauchline church by personal allusions of a spicy character the remembrance of it has perished. It might be supposed, from the well known austerity of Mr. Auld, that he would be one of those that laid well about them in preaching. In such of his sermons, however, and I might add such of his rebukes and admonitions as I have seen, there is no trace of any such onslaughts. Mr. Auld was a plain, solid, evangelical preacher, who confined himself to his text and made no remarks that conveyed ridicule or irony. Mr. Veitch was more free in his speech, and more apt to let fly at people that crossed him, and it is not unlikely, indeed it may be considered certain, that his hearers were at times regaled with things that amused and chafed as well as edified them.*

It is commonly supposed that the sermons preached long ago were very lengthy. And no doubt they sometimes were, but I doubt if they were generally so lengthy as is commonly thought. When Latimer was appointed to preach a course of sermons before King Edward the 6th of England, Cranmer wrote to him, "I would ye should so study to comprehend your matters that in any condition you stand no longer in the pulpit than an hour, or an hour and a half at the most, for by

---

* Baillie, in describing the preaching of one of the Protesters in 1654 says that he had "a strange kind of sighing, the like whereof I had never heard as a pythonising out of the bellie of a second person." That strange kind of sighing, however, had been practised as an oratorical device long before 1654, and was objected to by some Protesters as well as by Baillie. John Livingstone, in his advice to preachers, bids them neither use long drawn words nor speak in a singing tone, nor affect a weeping like voice, nor interrupt their discourse with oft sighing.

long expense of time the King and the Queen shall peradventure wax so weary at the beginning (of your course) that they shall have small delight to continue throughout with you to the end." That was what an English prelate wrote more than three hundred years ago. Baillie in his letters gives an account of a Fast-day service that was held in London nearly a hundred years later, during the sitting of the Westminster Assembly. On that occasion extempore prayers of two hours each were succeeded by sermons of one hour each, and the whole service lasted seven or eight hours. In Baillie's days it seems to have been not uncommon for preachers to take an hour to their sermon. Your ministers, said the Brownists, dispute to the hour glass, and they must preach sermons an hour long each. The advice that John Livingstone gave to preachers was, that in their sermons they should not "ordinarily" go beyond the hour, but he evidently meant to say that occasions might arise when that limit might with advantage be overstepped. In his account of the famous sermon he himself preached at Shotts on the Monday after the communion in 1630, he says, "I had about one hour and a half upon the points I had meditated on Ezekiel, xxxvi. v. 15-16, and in the end offering to close with some words of exhortation, I was led on about ane hour's time in ane strain of exhortation and warning with such liberty and melting of hearts as I never had the like in public all my life." Spalding makes an extraordinary statement about the length of sermons in Aberdeenshire on Fast Days—not sacramental Fasts, for there were no such things at the time when Spalding wrote, but fasts on account of public sins or public calamities. The statement looks very like either a cram or a slip, but it is curious and worthy of quotation. "The people," says Spalding, writing in 1642, "for the trespasses of the pastors and estates is thrawin and drawin fra their virtue in hicht of harvest to thir feinzeit fastingis, with four hours doctrin to ilk sermon, quhairby they was sore wyreit and vext, and the gryte God luiking doun upone their hypocriticall humiliations be all appeirans not weill pleisit nor deulie worschippit."* The Westminster Directory does not tie down ministers to any particular time in preaching. It says that ministers should take heed that their preaching be neither straitened nor tedious. And to keep preachers right in this matter it was customary to set up a sand-glass in the church. But it was not an hour-glass, as the Brownists said. It was a half-hour-glass, or at least it was commonly so; and in being of that measure it enabled preachers to gauge their discourses for all occasions. They could give one turn of the glass on a week day, and two or more turns on the Sabbath. John Livingstone tells us that when he went to Stranraer some of the townsfolks wished to come to his house to hear and take part in the family exercise. Instead of taking them into his house he invited them to meet in the church every morning at nine, and he gave them a service there. At this service a few verses of a Psalm were sung, then a short prayer was offered, then a portion of Scripture was read, and on this portion of Scripture he spoke "only as long as ane half hour glass ran, and then closed with prayer." It is easy to understand that on week days it would be considered quite as great a fault for a minister to exceed his glass as not to empty it, and it was probably in reference to week day services that the Presbytery of Aberdeen, in 1603, ordained "thet burials stay nocht the minister to continue his preaching sa that gif he exceid his glasse he sall be censurit in penaltie of gear." There was a limitation, however, of the length of sermons

---

* Wodrow states that on one occasion in 1725 the minister of Kilellan preached without break from eleven to six.

on Sunday also, for one of the faults that the fanatic Gib imputed to the Church was that she limited the Lord's mind by glasses, and instead of allowing her ministers to protract their preaching till they ran their own mental cisterns dry, she made them stop their discourse when the glass was dry. There were not many people that shared Mr. Gib's objections to this limitation of preaching. On the contrary, hearers sometimes wished that the sand would wear out for itself a wider orifice to hasten its progress, and tricks were occasionally resorted to by impatient listeners to make the preacher close his sermon prematurely. At the visitation of Cant's Church in 1642, there was by bad luck a minister in the pulpit who was not very zealous in the cause of the Covenant, and being for the time master of the situation he improved his opportunity by making a merciless onslaught on the new practices which the Covenanters had introduced. Cant was sitting beside the reader who was time-keeper, and did not relish the flavour of the preacher's remarks. With the view of bringing the discourse to a hasty end he " quickly closed the reader's book and laid down the glass before it was run." But the preacher was a quick eyed as well as a quick witted man, and he saw the deception. He accordingly felt himself no longer limited by the glass, but like Mr. Gib free to speak as long as thoughts would breathe and words would burn. And the result was that to Mr. Cant's chagrin he took an extra half hour's grace. There is no record of any such pranks having been played with the sand glass at Mauchline, although from the frequency with which old glasses were replaced by new ones it might be surmised that the church chronometer sometimes met with intentional damage. In 1672 there was a half hour glass bought for 10s., in 1677 another was bought for 11s., and in 1688 a third was purchased for 12s. In the last mentioned year the precaution

Public Worship in Olden Times.

was adopted of procuring for the glass an iron case at a cost of £2 scots.

While preaching long ago was administered in such large and frequent doses there were occasional intervals of relief, unknown to either ministers or people now-a-days, and which would be very much exclaimed against if they did occur. There were now and again what were euphemistically styled silent Sundays—that is Sundays on which there was no preaching in the parish church.

The grandest array of silent Sundays ever witnessed in Mauchline was in 1732. On the 12th March that year the record states, "No sermon, the minister being gone to London on necessary business." For eleven Sundays the minister remained away, and on seven of these Sundays there was no preaching, and what made matters worse, three of these silent Sundays were successive Sabbaths. The same year on the 3rd Dec. the register states, "No sermon, the minister being gone to Edinburgh." His stay at Edinburgh extended over thirteen weeks, and during seven of these there was no sermon. The following summer in the month of July the minister paid another visit to Edinburgh, which lasted six weeks, and the people again were favoured with three silent Sundays. Besides these seventeen silent Sundays there were during the two years 1732 and 1733 at least other five Sabbaths on which there was no sermon at Mauchline, the minister having been either filling by appointment of Presbytery a vacant pulpit, or assisting at a neighbouring sacrament, or attending a meeting of Synod in Glasgow. But we must not draw too harsh an inference from those facts. In 1723 there had been a good many silent Sundays in Mauchline, and the parishioners complained to the Presbytery. But the reply of the minister was that he had been of late under much indisposition of body, and that he had fallen under sundrie difficulties in his affairs, which obliged him to be often abroad contrary to his inclination. It is plain, also, that in 1732 and 1733 he had obtained leave of absence from his parish,* for his place in the pulpit was filled up, except in one instance, every alternate Sabbath by a member of Presbytery. And although it is the case that silent Sundays were of frequent occurrence long ago, they were neither winked at by Presbyteries, nor uncomplained of by parishioners, unless there were known to be good and honest reasons for the silence. In the records of the Presbytery of Ayr there are complaints entered by parishioners against their minister for having no preaching on two successive Sabbaths, or even on one Sabbath, when it was thought preaching could have been provided. During what were considered the more Laodicean times of Episcopacy, too, there were stringent rules laid down and enforced by the Church Courts in reference to the regular supply of ordinances on the Sabbath. In the year 1664 the Synod of Galloway ordained that no minister shall be absent from his charge two Lord's Days together, without leave of the Presbytery. The same Synod, the same year, having been informed that the minister of Kells "is constantly and frequently absent from his charge, sometimes four Sundays and sometimes six together, appointed his Presbytery to take him on trial, and if they found not his excuses weighty and relevant,

---

* The following entries anent Mr. Maitland occur in the records of the Presbytery of Ayr in 1723, besides the report of a visitation of Mauchline parish held the same year, and quoted in appendix D : " The moderator is to write to Mr. Maitland to be present with the Presbytery at the ensuing Synod, that they may enquire into the reason of his long absence of late from his charge, and why he did not provide them with preaching from time to time in that absence, being, they were told, many Sabbaths desolate." The reasons of absence given in by Mr. Maitland were " his civil affairs, and his wyff falling sick at Edinburgh, whom he was obliged to attend." He was then told that when called abroad again he must "take care to have his paroch provided with preaching."

to suspend him from the exercise of his ministry for a competent time, or inflict what other censure his offences should be thought fit to "demerit." Still, as I have said, there were a good many silent Sundays in every parish long ago. With the view of ascertaining what was the usual average of silent Sundays per annum in Mauchline church about the beginning of the present century, I examined the session-clerk's memorandum book for the years 1810, 1811, and 1814, and I found that in each of these years there were five silent Sundays, that is, five Sundays on which the minister required to be absent, or was absent, at neighbouring communions, or for other reasons, and had no substitute in his place.

It is doubtful if in olden times there was as much good order observed in church during divine service as there is now. Certainly there were more cases of flagrant disorder. Civilization, thanks to ministers, schoolmasters, and policemen, has made some progress during the last two hundred years, and the present system of having churches seated all over with rows of fixed pews, gives less occasion for disorder than the old arrangement of an open area inside the church, dotted here and there with a solitary desk.* In some of the old ecclesiastical records we find curious regulations for the preservation of order in church. In the Kirk Session records of Perth we find an instruction minuted that the kirk-officer "have his red staff in the kirk on the Sabbath days, wherewith to waken sleepers and remove greeting bairns." This was after pews with flat book-boards had been introduced for soporific people to lay their weary heads on; but in 1593 complaint was made

---

* The Kirk Session of Aberdeen in 1616 directed that " young bairns not of sic age and disposition that they can take themselves to a seat when they come to the kirk, but vaig through the kirk here and there in time of sermon, should be kept at home."

at Perth of boys in time of preaching running through the church clattering and fighting, and to prevent this disorder application was made to the magistrates that "a seat might be built for the scholars in some commodious part of the kirk where they might hear and learn without troubling either the minister or the auditory." And as another instance of turbulent conduct in the same church, we find it stated in 1621 that one of the merchants was abused by a set of "young professed knaves" casting their bonnets at him. The Kirk Session were alive to their duty on that occasion, however, and made short work with the young delinquents, by having them apprehended and sent to the grammar school to be "scourged with St. Bartholomew's Taws."* The writer of an article in the *Edinburgh Antiquarian Magazine*, 1849, states that in 1813 he witnessed a scene in the parish church of Inverkeillor that for scandalousness might compare with any of the Sunday barbarities of the seventeenth century. Two farm servants, he says, had quarrelled over a knife. In the course of the sermon they suddenly started to their feet, and after swearing at each other exchanged blows, in face of the congregation. A sense of shame came over them at last, and sinking down on their seats they shewed some modesty and sense by burying their heads in their hands.

In the Records of Mauchline Kirk Session there is nothing to be found so lively as the account of these doings in Perthshire and Forfarshire. But there were scenes more lively than lovely in Mauchline church notwithstanding. There were several squabbles about seats we have seen, and in 1693 there was a man faulted for "speaking out in the time of divine worship,

---

*An Act of Parliament in 1551 directed that "bairns who perturb the kirk be leished."

and disturbing the minister in the examination of Kate Montgomerie," whoever or whatever she was. And apparently there had been far more tittle-tattling in church by the better sort of people long ago than was seemly. In 1709 the General Assembly thought it necessary in a special act to "recommend to persons of all ranks that they would forbear bowing and other expressions of civil respect, and entertaining one another with discourses while divine worship is performing and holy ordinances are dispensing." And it may be held as a sign of the times that the Presbytery of Ayr caused this Act to be read from every pulpit within their bounds. Four years previous a general intimation was made from the pulpit of Mauchline that boys and vagabonds would not be allowed to make a disturbance in time of divine service, which implied that disturbances had occurred and had caused annoyance.

It was stated that in Bishop Cowper's days, that is in the first quarter of the seventeenth century, some people sat in church with their hats on, and others had the politeness to take their hats off. There was no ecclesiastical law on the subject, and people were allowed even by the bishops and Episcopal clergy, who had always more regard for forms and ceremonies than their Presbyterian brethren had, to do in that matter as they pleased. This is the more important to be noted, as Bishop Sage makes a statement to the contrary. A very decent and commendable custom, which, he says, obtained in Scotland generally till the latter times of Presbytery, was for people on entering the church to uncover their heads as entering the house of God. But now-a-days, he adds, "tis plain superstition to a Presbyterian not to enter the church with his head covered.[*] Mass John himself doth it as mannerly as the

---

[*] Curate Calder evidently wishes it to be understood that it was common in Presbyterian churches in Scotland for men to have their caps on during the sermon. He

coarsest cobbler in the parish. In he steps, uncovers not till in the pulpit, claps straight on his breach, and within a little falls to work as the spirit moves him. All the congregation must sit close in the time of prayer, and clap on their bonnets in the time of sermon." About the time of the sitting of the Westminster Assembly the question of hats off or hats on in church was made by some people a question of far more importance than that of postures in prayer and praise has been made in churches within the last ten years. Doctrines were supposed to be symbolically expressed by the putting off and putting on of the hat. There was no controversy on the subject in the Church of Scotland, and I imagine that our forefathers in the times of the covenant and after were left free to do as innate breeding prompted them. But the Brownists and the Independents made great ado about their hats. The Brownists in Amsterdam sat during the reading and the preaching of the word with their hats on. Some of the Independents maintained that the right thing was "for the minister in preaching to have his head covered, and the people in time of preaching to sit uncovered." Whatever may have been the date at which men in Scotland began generally to uncover their heads during

---

represents a minister saying to a man that was laughing at his preaching, "do not thou think to gull one of God's ministers that way, lift up your bonnet off your face, think no shame of your shape." In Dr. Scott's Fasti there is an anecdote told of Nathan M'Kie, the minister of Crossmichael from 1739 to 1781, which, if true in all particulars, and that may be doubted, would indicate that in the middle of last century people never sat covered in church except when they suffered from cold. In reading a chapter one day Mr. M'Kie called out, "I see a man aneath that laft wi' his hat on. I'm sure ye're clear o' the sough o' the door. Keep aff yer bannat, Tammas, and if yer bare pow be cauld ye maun jist get a grey worsit wig like mysel." Long ago in Scotland it was reckoned a breach of manners for commoners to stand covered in presence of their social superiors. Brodie in his diary expresses desire "to be humbled under the proud reproof which he gave to John Hasbin for holding on his bonnet irreverently and disrespectfully before his (Brodie's) mother. For what ill did it to her?"

divine worship, it is certain that at a very early period women were forbidden, somewhat contrary, one would think, to the doctrine of St. Paul, to conceal their heads in church. In 1640 the Town Council of Dumbarton took notice in their records of the fact "that the women within this burgh contrair to civilitie cum to the kirk, and in tyme of preiching and prayers keip their playdis about their heids albeit mony tymes dischargit publickly be the minister out of the pulpit." And to put an end to this uncivilized practice, the Town Council ordained that the offence should be punished with fine, and in case of obstinacy with imprisonment. The Kirk Session of Monifieth in 1643 adopted a course that looks more savage, but probably was intended to look so savage as to ensure the certainty of its never having to be carried out. They gave the "bedall 5s. to buy ane pynt of tar to put upon the women that held the plaid above their head in the church." And doubtless it was publicly intimated through the parish that instead of a "red staffe" for sleepers the beadle was henceforth to carry a tarred stick for covered heads!*

Now that we have got gas introduced into the Church at Mauchline to enable us to have occasional evening services in winter, it may interest some of the congregation to hear that in very old times the Kirk Session had a small account to pay every year for candles. In 1670 the following entries occur in the Session book, under date 29th November, "Gevin for a bonet to ye kirk officer 16s., item for ane pound of candles 4s., and for a pair of schoes 24s."† From the way in which these entries

---

* A reason was given by the Kirk Session of Dundonald in 1642 why "no woman be suffered to sit in the time of sommer with plyds upon their heids." The reason was, "it is a cleuck to their sleiping in tyme of sermon."

† Shoes, and I presume a bonnet also, were commonly part of a beadle's allowance. The Session of Galston in 1676 ordained that their officer should "get 2 merks to buy him a pair of shoes according to former use and wont."

are made, one might think that they contain an account of the beadle's outrig, and if so, he must have presented rather a Fijian appearance as he stalked up the church with the Bible under his arm, a candle in his hand, and nothing on his person but a bonnet and a pair of shoes! That interpretation, however, raises historical difficulties, and must be discarded! The expense for candles was probably incurred in connection with some morning or evening service in the church, either on Sundays or week days. Not only is it certain that in old times there were such services in towns, but we have seen that during the ministry of Mr. George Young there were public prayers every morning and evening in Mauchline. It is certain, also, that Kirk Sessions were at expense for candles at these and other services. In 1593 the minister and elders of Perth ordained the Dean of Guild and the deacons of crafts "to cause put ane two penny candle in their pews every Sunday morning in time of the morning exercise, and also the Thesaurer cause furnish ane twelve penny candle to the reader to be lighted immediately after the first bell that all may see to praise God in singing Psalms, which stays for lack of light." In the Burgh Records of Glasgow from 1600 to 1660 there are frequent entries of payments ranging from £4 to £20 for candles to one of the city churches. In one instance the payment is stated to have been made for furnishing candles to the "catechetick doctrine," and in another instance for furnishing candles to what is the same thing under a different name, the "lectour." The allowance to the Mauchline beadle for candle is so small that it may be said it never could have been sufficient to provide light for the church for a whole winter. The common custom, however, at morning and evening services in church, even down to the present century, was for each worshipper to bring his own candle.* The allowance for candle to the beadle would therefore be for his own personal use, or possibly for the reader's desk.

The hours of church service on Sundays, it need scarcely be said, were much earlier long ago than they are now. In 1615 the Kirk Session of Lasswade appointed nine o'clock as the hour on which sermon should begin in the summer months, and half-past nine as the hour of sermon in winter.† These appear to have been the hours at which the church service usually began in Scotland about that date. Speaking of the observance of Good Friday in 1621 Calderwood says that the ministers in Edinburgh "began their sermons about halfe ten, as if it had been a Sabboth day." The following year "the ministers of Edinburgh," he says again, "began their Good Friday sermon at nyne hours as if it had been a Sabboth day." Five and twenty years later, that is in 1646, the common hour of service in church on Sunday I imagine was ten. In the Kirk Session Records of Fenwick for that year there is a minute appointing a delinquent to "stand in the joges from eight till ten, thence to go to ye place of repentance within ye kirk." In 1724 Mr. Maitland was enjoined to convene his congregation at Mauchline by eleven at farthest, which shows that an earlier hour than

---

* On the pulpit of the Fenwick meeting-house there were in 1830 two brass brackets, each holding three candles. The old beadle "every now and then during evening service docked the candles with snuffers." The members of the congregation brought their own candles with them (Account of Jubilee of Rev. Mr. Orr). In the ancient church, candle-light prayers and candle-light hymns were common expressions. And one of the bidding prayers of the Catholic Church was, "Also ye shall pray for all those that have honoured the church with light-lamp, vestment or bell, or with any other ornaments by which the service of Almighty God is the better maintained and kept " (Alliance of Divine Offices, p. 98, 181). For a curious case of endowment of candle, see Dumbarton Burgh Records, 1627.

† The reader's service commenced an hour earlier, namely, at 8 o'clock. In 1603 the Presbytery of Aberdeen ordered that every Sunday at seven in the morning there be teaching of the Catechism in church by the minister to servants and others.

eleven for public worship was not uncommon at the beginning of last century.

Sometimes lamentation is heard at the present day about the extent to which public ordinances are neglected. There are many people, it is alleged, that seldom or never enter the house of God on the Sabbath, and when there are two diets of worship there are very few even of regular church goers that attend both diets.* Many devices are said to have been tried to remedy or abate these evils. Those resorted to by the Covenanters in Aberdeen in 1642 were perhaps as ingenious as any that have ever been adopted. "Our minister," says Spalding, "teaches powerfullie and plainlie the word to the gryte comfort of his auditores. He takes strait count of those who cumis not to the communion nor keipis not the kirk, callis out the absentis out of pulpit, quhilk drew in sic a fair auditorie that the seatis of the kirk was not abill to hald thame, for remeid quhairof he causit big up ane loft athwart the body of the kirk and enterit the wrichtis thairto in November." That was what Mr. Strathauchin did. Mr. Cant did not go quite so far, but being annoyed that his afternoon diets, especially on Fast days, were sparsely attended, he naively dismissed his forenoon audience without a benediction, and reserved his blessing for those that returned to the second sermon. Perhaps he was right.

---

* In 1603 there were complaints given in to the Presbytery of Aberdeen that many people were in the habit of leaving the church in the middle of sermon, or during the prayer after sermon. The Presbytery, in consideration of this scandal, ordained that officers should be appointed to stand at the church door, "quha sall hald in and bring back sic as removis befoir blessing be endit, except they be seik and may not indure sa lang." In the town of Aberdeen absentees from church were ordered both in 1578 and 1603 to be fined 3s. 4d. each. As late as 1646 people were made to confess a fault in Galston Session, when they were delated and found to have been absent from a diet of worship. In 1634 the Galston people for either absence from the examination or not keeping the kirk had both to " mak their repentance and pay 10s."

LECTURE III.

Communion Services in Olden Times.

Preparatory and Accompanying Services on Week Days—Examination of Congregations—Reconciliations—Purging the Roll—The Preparation Sermon on Saturday—The Fast Day—Object of the Fast—Distribution of Tokens—Monday's Thanksgiving Service—Furnishings for the Sacrament—The Tables—Purchasing of Tokens—Communion Cups—Bread and Wine—Service on Communion Sabbath—Frequency and Infrequency of Celebration— Communion Extended over Several Sabbaths—Communions Early in the Morning—Order of Service—Admission to the Table—Kneeling or Sitting—Assistants at Communion—Communion Crowds—Disorders at Communions—The Mauchline Sacrament in Mr. Auld's Day—Number of Communicants and Tables—Month and Day of Communion often Changed.

HAVING shewn how the ordinary services of the Sabbath were conducted in the Church of Scotland long ago, I have now to give an account of the communion services. Notwithstanding the great notoriety that the Mauchline communion has acquired, I am sorry to say that the references to the communion in our existing Parish Records are so few and brief that, as in last lecture, I shall be obliged to draw my illustrations mostly from the Records of other Parishes.

The first matters to be considered in connection with communion celebrations are the old law and the ancient practice of the Church of Scotland regarding preparatory and accompanying services on week days.

The Directory for public worship, framed by the Westminster Divines, and in 1645 adopted by the Church of Scotland, states that when the Sacrament of the Lord's Supper cannot with convenience be frequently administered in a parish, there should be some services in the way of preparation for that solemnity. Public notice of the administration should be given the Sabbath before, and either then or some day of the intervening week something concerning the ordinance and its proper observance should be taught from the pulpit. This direction was in accordance with the old customs of the Church of Scotland, but it was not passed at Westminster without considerable opposition. "The unhappy Independents," says Baillie, "would mangle the sacrament of the supper. No catechising nor preparation before, no sacramental doctrine or chapters in the day of celebration, yet all this and much more with God's help we have carried over their bellies to our practice."* In another of his works, the same author, in describing the uncouth customs of the Independents, brings out indirectly what was the practice of the Church of Scotland *per contra*. "They, the Independents," he says, "have no preparation of their flock before, they are so happy as to have all their members prepared always sufficiently for the Lord's Table from their first entrance into their Church to their dying day, for all this time there is no catechising among them, this exercise is below their condition and altogether needless in any of their congregations. They will have no sermon in the week before, nor so much as any warning of the communion. They use not so much as a little application of the doctrine in the sermon before it to that occasion."

The book from which this last quoted passage is taken was published in 1645, and the passage quoted may therefore be held as shewing that at that date it was the settled practice in the Church of Scotland to have both an examination of the congregation and a week day preparation sermon before the communion. The Westminster Directory says nothing about

---

* *Letters*, Vol. II., 91.

this examination, and in regard to the preparation sermon it says that that sermon may be given either the Sunday before the communion or on some day of the week immediately preceding the communion Sabbath. When the Westminster Directory was adopted by the Church of Scotland in 1645, a number of resolutions on points left open or untouched in the Directory were also framed and agreed to by the General Assembly. One was that congregations be still tried and examined before the communion according to the bygone practice of the Kirk, and another was that there be one sermon of preparation delivered in the ordinary place of public worship upon the day immediately preceding the communion. The preparatory work for the communion, enjoined by Act of Assembly in 1645 (conform as we shall see to old use and wont), was thus, in the first place, an examination of the whole congregation, old and young, proposing to communicate for either the first or the fiftieth time; and, in the second place, one sermon on the Saturday before the administration.

The trial or examination of congregations before the communion is expressly stated in the Act of Assembly, 1645, to be an old custom in the Church. As far back as 1566 it was a thing of use and wont. A minute in the Records of the Canongate for that year states that the Kirk ordained examination to begin before the communion, and appointed the minister publicly to warn and exhort all communicants "to cum and keep their aun quarter with thair households for guid example unto the waiker." Other kirk records, of dates nearly as old, speak of the examination as an understood and an invariable preliminary to the ministration of the Lord's Supper. A minute in the records of the kirk-session of Perth, for the year 1595, relates that "for as meikle as sundry within this congregation are found ignorant of the principles and grounds of religion, notwithstanding that there is a yearly trial and examination before the celebration of the Supper of the Lord, therefore the minister and elders appoint in time coming, on some days of the week, a particular trial and examination of particular persons within families, that all may be instructed and catechised."*

This examination was a special examination in view of participating in the sacrament, and was quite distinct from the weekly catechising all the year round, except in seed time and harvest, referred to in last lecture. This fact is brought out very clearly in a complaint that the parishioners of Craigie made against their minister at a Presbyterial visitation of the Parish in 1644. "There was no catechising," they said, "but once in the year by examination before the communion." And how essential before communion this examination was regarded, is shewn in a petition to the Presbytery of Ayr, by the Kirk-Session of Cumnock, in the year 1642. The parish was then vacant, but the Kirk-Session petitioned the Presbytery to allow the sacrament to be administered "because the people were all examined by John Somervail," a probationer at Cumnock. The practice, however, of insisting on an examination as an essential preliminary to admission to the Lord's Table led, in the course of time, to some evils. Its non-performance was made by ministers an excuse for putting off the communion. An overture was accordingly moved in

---

* "Anent the examination before the communion, the General Assembly of 1590, 'thought meet for the common profit of the whole people that an uniform order be kept in examination, and that a short form of examination be set down by their brethren, Messrs. John Craig, Robert Pont, Thomas Buchanan, and Andrew Melville, to be presented to the next Assemblie.'"

At one time people went at a very early age to the Lord's Table. John Livingstone states that he communicated at Stirling when he was at school there, and he left school in 1617, when he was only fourteen years old.

the Presbytery of Ayr, in the year 1710, that the fact of a minister's "not having examined all of the paroch every year is not a sufficient argument" for not having the sacrament celebrated, because "those who have been examined and admitted before, may be admitted of new upon the former evidence of their knowledge, and those of whom the minister is doubtful, or who are known to be ignorant, may thus be more easily overtaken." But it was specially mentioned as a proviso in that overture, that this course "should hold only in case of palpable inability to examine all the communicants, lest otherwise it furnish encouragement to negligence."*

It may be assumed that this sacramental examination would be gone about much more strictly and faithfully by some ministers than by others. It is not unlikely that by some easy-going men it would be altogether neglected. Not the least valued privilege which the city of Aberdeen enjoyed before the days of the covenant, was immunity from this annual and oppressive inquisition. The Aberdonians took it much amiss, therefore, when Mr. Andro Cant deprived them of that comfortable privilege. The town council entered on their records a vehement protest against what they considered Mr. Cant's innovations, especially "that none should be admitted to the communion except such only, as in ane pharisaical way, offered themselves to be tried by him and those whom he

---

* It is probably to such examinations that the following minute of the kirk-session of Dumbarton refers. The date of the minute is 28th May, 1620 :—"The quhilk day the sessione ordained that everie persoune being warned to come to the examination, if they refuse to cum ane of the two days quhilk sall be appointed to them sall pay everie ane 4s. Leikwayes that if any persoune so cumes to be examined be fund ignorant of the prayer, belief, or commands, in that case they sall pay for everie ane of thes quhairof they sall be ignorant 12s., except that within the space of sax weiks theraftir they lerne them." This resolution was passed, not in the rigorous days of the covenant, but in the pleasant days of Episcopacy.

called his Elders." And the whole community in Aberdeen had cause to feel sore at Mr. Cant's procedure, for it led to the casting of a very great slur on their reputation. No communion, says Spalding, in 1642, was given by Cant for two years' space to the town of Aberdeen, till first " they wer weill catechist, because he alledgit they war ignorant."* In our own Parish Records we find traces of these sacramental examinations at dates comparatively recent. In the year 1735, during Mr. Maitland's ministry, it was intimated from the pulpit, on the 16th August, that the sacrament would be celebrated that day fortnight. Diets of examination were also appointed as they had been the two previous Sabbaths. On the following Sunday, being the Sabbath before the sacrament, the minister further "intimated Monday for examination of absents, and Tuesday to converse with such as never communicated in this place, and have now a design."

Either at these examinations, or at special meetings called in Church on some week day shortly before the communion, the labours of the Kirk Session were directed to the removal of offences in the congregation and the reconciliation of people at variance. And this was not a practice peculiar to the Church of Scotland. It is expressly laid down in the book of Common Prayer for the Church of England, that the Curate shall not suffer those betwixt whom he perceiveth malice and hatred to reign to be partakers of the Lord's Table until he know them to be reconciled. For the removal of evelists and offences before the communion, it was at one time common in Scotland to convene publicly and specially the "haill brethren and

---

* Mr. Cant's zeal for purity was not accompanied with much compassion for frailty. He not only debarred the profane and the grossly ignorant from presumptuous approach to the Lord's Table, but he prohibited all that were "ordinarie sleepers in tyme of sermon if they were strong and healthy persons."

honest neighbours within each congregation;" and ministers as well as people were considered unfit and unauthorised to take part in communion services if they were at variance with any one and had not made overtures of peace.* So recently as the year 1716, complaint was made to the Presbytery of Ayr, by Lady Coilsfield, that her parish minister, the minister of Tarbolton, went to the Lord's Table at St. Evox, in July last, without seeking to have her husband, the laird of Coilsfield, reconciled to him. It turned out, however, that the minister was free from blame in that matter, for the "very night in which Coilsfield did him injury, he shewed inclination to have all differences done away, and his overtures were declined." The procedure that took place in the reconciliation of persons at variance is shewn to us in an old minute of the Kirk Session of Galston. The date of the minute is 1634, and the subject of the minute is an accusation brought by a woman against a man for defaming her character. The man pled guilty to the woman's charge, but averred that he was under the influence of drink when he spoke the words libelled, and that "he kend nothing to hir bot honesty." In token of contrition he then humbled himself before the Session —that is, went down on his knees—and the woman, in token of her satisfaction with that abasement, "tuke him up be the hand."

---

* Pardovan says, "When notour scandalous breaches and differences do happen in that case the parties should be obliged to a formal agreement by conversing in presence of those whose work it is to compose such differences, but even then they can be obliged to continue in no more friendship than a common converse imports." A hundred years before Pardovan's time there were people 'who abstained from the communion under colour of deadly feuds and other light causes,' but the Assembly (1600) gave orders that every person of age should communicate once a year at least, under pain of being delated to the King's Majesty as a contravener of a penal act. Both in Episcopal times (1633) and in Presbyterial times (1647) we find in the Galston Records cases of people delated and rebuked for 'byding at home on the communion Sabbath and neglecting the communion.'"

These public meetings for examination and reconciliation came in the course of time to be altogether abandoned. Meetings of Kirk Session, however, were held before the communion, to go over the "examine roll,"* deal with delinquents, and determine who should be admitted or refused admission to the Lord's Table. About the beginning of last century, the Kirk Session of Galston met for this purpose on a week day, "at nine of the clock in the forenoon," and after spending "a good time of the day"—several hours it is stated in one or two instances—in prayer, they proceeded to business. In 1752 a very questionable practice was introduced in Mauchline by Mr. Auld, as appears from the following minute of date 2nd August :—" The Session being constitute, and having the celebration of the sacrament in view, the examination roll was read over in order to know who in the Parish were unfit to receive tokens, at which time also the Session took a list of the scandalous persons, and in consequence of an intimation from the pulpit, about three months before, that all scandalous persons who should not apply to the Session to get their scandals issued in a regular way, should have their names read publicly before the congregation. This, accordingly, was appointed to be done." What authority beyond their own sweet wills Mr. Auld and his Kirk Session had for this procedure I cannot tell. More than once the General Assembly had directed that the names of people under particular scandals should be publicly

---

* It may be presumed that the examine roll was generally very carefully and conscientiously made up by the minister. But there were cases in which this work was alleged to have been slopped. In 1714 it was complained by the people of Coylton, that their minister was in the way of making up his examine roll, by taking the "names of those who, after intimation, come to attend catechising, from the beddal who informs him who are present." And it was further objected that his roll was incomplete, for if people did not come forward at the hour advertised, he declined to catechise them, though they came within "an hour or half-an-hour after."

read out from the pulpit before the communion. In 1705, for instance, it was ordained that the names of all persons under the censure of lesser excommunication should be so announced. And in 1649, when extreme measures were thought necessary to stem the tide of grievous and common sins in the land at that "present time," it was propounded among other things that persons grossly ignorant be debarred from the communion, and that when persons were so debarred for the third time, their names should be expressed. It will be seen, however, that what Mr. Auld did in 1752 was quite different from what the Assembly ordained or propounded in 1705 and 1648. And whatever may have been the precedent that Mr. Auld had for his procedure in 1752, experience taught him long before his death the expediency, if not necessity, of discontinuing all invidious disclosures from the pulpit.*

The Saturday's preparation sermon, enjoined by the General Assembly in 1645, was also, I have said, an ancient institution in the Church of Scotland. Bishop Sage says otherwise. The Saturday's preachings, he says, were never heard of till they were recommended by the Committee of the Innovating Assembly, which introduced so many novelties, in 1645. That these preachings were never enjoined by special enactment before 1645 may be true, but they were certainly in general use long before that date. They were known too all over the Church by the name of the Preparation Sermon. For instance, in the year 1643, the six sessions of Edinburgh instructed a committee

---

* John Livingstone states in his autobiography, that when he was in Ireland, about 1630, it was customary there for delinquents to confess their scandals before the congregation at the Saturday's sermon before the communion, and then they were absolved and admitted to the sacrament. Such delinquents as did not do so had their "names, scandals, and impenitence," declared to the congregation, and were publicly debarred from the Lord's Table. This proclamation, says Livingstone, inspired such a wholesome terror, that very few contumacious people were found.

of their number to urge on the town council the expediency of appointing a collection for the poor, "upon the Saturday immediately preceding the celebration of the communion, while the people is convening to the sermon of preparation, and that according to the *custom universally practised through the whole kingdom.*" As far back as 1567 there is mention, in published records, of the Saturday service as a customary preliminary to the communion. On the 11th January of that year, the Session of Canongate appointed the minister to intimate from the pulpit that the communion would be celebrated on the 19th of that month, and that "the exhortation would be given on the Saturday afternoon afoir." And in the records of our own parish we have notice of a Saturday's service preparatory to the Lord's Supper as far back as 1680, and I may say constantly ever afterwards when the sacrament was administered. But just as the Westminster Directory leaves the precise day for the preparation sermon unfixed, so did ministers and kirk sessions before the passing of the act 1645 consider themselves not exactly restricted and tied down to the Saturday for the service. Spalding, in his journal for 1641, incidentally mentions, that on "Frydday, 4th June, our minister preached ane preparation sermon befoir the giving of the Communion the nixt Sabboth."*

The Saturday's sermon of preparation, however, came in course of time to be completely overshadowed by the solemnities of another preparatory service. This was the sacramental fast. Such fasts, we all know, are nowhere prescribed in Scripture, and they were never observed by the Apostles and

---

* In 1634 the communion was celebrated at Galston, on Sunday, the 27th April, and on Sunday, the 4th May. On the Saturday preceding each of these days there was service in Church and a collection made for the poor. On the one Saturday the collection amounted to 16s., and on the other to 21s., whereas, on the Sabbath before the communion, it was only 14s., and on the Sunday after the communion 10s.

first Christians. They never were enjoined either by any Act of the General Assembly of the Church of Scotland. They are simply a custom or the special appointments of particular Kirk Sessions. It is admitted that they were at least not common in Scotland till after 1651, but it is contended by some people that there are on record one or two instances of sacramental fasts previously. In the appendix to Principal Lee's lectures, it is stated that "there appears" to have been a fast ordinarily observed at St. Andrews[*] in connection with the communion as far back as 1574, and that the good custom was still kept up in 1598. I have looked over the Session Records of Galston from 1626, and I have not noticed, or at least not noted, any instance there of a week day sacramental fast till long after 1651. There was at one time a Sunday fast before the communion, in Galston. In 1626 the communion was held on the 30th July, and Sabbath the 23rd July was called "the day of Fast." In the records for 1645, I find the expression,[†] "Sunday, the 1st of June, being the fast

---

[*] In support of this opinion, Principal Lee quotes from a reply of the minister of St. Andrews, to a charge of neglecting an Act of Assembly appointing a special fast in 1574. The words founded on are, the fast "wes observit and concludit with ye ministration of ye Supper of the Lord, according to the order observit hidderto in our kirk." But what is the meaning of these words? Is it that a fast was always observed in connection with and in preparation for the Lord's Supper, or is it the converse, that the Lord's Supper was always celebrated in connection with and as a completion of the observance of a solemn fast? That the latter view is not without historical support, may be inferred from the following words of Calderwood, vol. ii., page 324, Anno, 1566 :—"It was appointed a publick fast sould be holden the two last Sabboth dayes of Julie, in respect of the dangers imminent wherewith the kirk is like to be assaulted, and *that the Lord's Supper be ministered upon the same day if it can be done convenientlie.*" Fasts sometimes lasted a whole week, with two diets of worship daily.

[†] The Sunday fast before communion seems to have been not uncommon at that date. In the Records of the Presbytery of Ayr for 1642, we find the following appointments minuted for the vacant Parish of Cumnock,—Messrs. A. and B. "to celebrate the sacrament respectively on Sunday come twenty days and Sunday come a month," also, "Mr. Summervail to celebrat the *publict* fast thair upon Sunday

before the Communion," and a similar expression occurs in the records of the previous year. In 1642 the sacrament was administered at Galston, on the 18th and 25th September. Each day of communion was preceded by a Saturday's and followed by a Monday's service, and the Wednesday before the first day of communion is described as "being ane fasting day." I cannot but think, however, that if that fasting day had any connection at all with the communion, its appointment must have been due to some very exceptional circumstances.* Neither in 1641 nor in 1643 was there any such week day preparatory fast at Galston. In 1640 there were two Sabbaths of communion, each preceded by a Saturday service, but neither of them preceded by a Wednesday's fast nor followed by a Monday's thanksgiving. On the Monday after the sacrament in 1673, a minute was made regarding the collection which was gathered "upon *Sabbath* was eight days being the *Fast* day and upon Saturday, Sabbath, and this day." It is quite certain, therefore, that week day sacramental fasts† were not common till after 1651, and they were in some

---

come a fyfteen dayes." Possibly this was not a Sacramental Fast, but it looks like one in the light of other minutes.

* Somtimes a fast appointed for one purpose was made to serve for another. In the Records of Galston Session for 1726, there is a minute which states that the Kirk Session desired that "the national fast which falleth the Thursday following, be observed as a day of preparation before the sacrament."

† So far from Parochial fasts before communion being universal even after 1651, we find religious men providing for their own necessities by holding private fasts. Brodie of Brodie, in 1652, made the 3rd May, which was a Monday, a day of humiliation for four specified reasons, the second of which was that the Lord would fit him for participation at the Lord's Table at the coming communion. John Livingstone, in 1634, made the Saturday before communion a day of private fasting, prayer, and sacramental preparation, and it may be mentioned here that the custom of holding private fasts for reasons personal, had not altogether died out a hundred years ago. In 1794, Andrew Fuller, the celebrated English baptist, took to himself, at the age of forty, a second wife, and shortly before his marriage he thus wrote in his diary,—" I devoted this day to fasting and prayer on account of my expected marriage, to entreat the blessing of God upon me and her who may be connected with me."

Communion Services in Olden Times.

cases not introduced till 1700. It was the Protesters of 1651 that made the sacramental fast what is vulgarly called an institution. And from their point of view, Fast Days were a necessary preparation for communion. The whole Kingdom was in a state of variance,—neighbour against neighbour and brother against brother,—and not only so, but the King and his Government, and all who complied with their proceedings, were guilty of treason against high heaven in repealing the Act of Classes and allowing malignants to hold office in the army and the state. Communion services had consequently to be suspended altogether for a while, and when they came to be administered, they had to be preceded by a special humiliation which was most fittingly expressed in fasting. "The Protesters," says Bishop Burnet, "gave the sacrament with a new and an unusual solemnity. On the Wednesday before the communion they held a fast with prayer and sermons for about eight or ten hours together. On the Saturday they had two or three preparation sermons, and on the Lord's day they had so very many, that the action continued above twelve hours in some places, and all ended with three or four sermons on Monday for thanksgiving. A great many ministers were brought together from several parts, and high pretenders would have gone forty or fifty miles to a noted communion." It might be expected, as a matter of course, that if Protesters introduced Sacramental Fasts, Resolutioners would set their faces against Fasts, and such was the case. Both in pamphlets and sermons the Resolutioners inveighed loudly against the new custom as a violation of the order established in the Church, and as causing prejudice against faithful ministers who would not adopt the new ways. These new ways, however, were popular; and more and more ministers, year after year, went in with them, till by-and-by the holding of

I

Sacramental Fasts, although neither enjoined in Scripture nor instituted by Act of Assembly, came to be an universal practice over Scotland. And for a long while these Fasts, if not Fasts in the literal sense of the term, were at least days of genuine humiliation and devotion. Wodrow, writing about communions in his neighbourhood, in 1729, says, "there is something like a spirit of wrestling and prayer on our Fast Days." And no Christian will deny that, so long as that was the case Fast Days did good ; but when they came to be spent not in humiliation, but in gaiety—not in prayer, but in the pursuit of worldly pleasure—not in sobriety, but with a good deal of public drunkenness—not in the house of God, but as far from it as possible—not with any view to communion with Christ, but in railway excursions and sometimes on racecourses, where sport was provided for the occasion—they were a public scandal to the Church, and a means of demoralising far more than of spiritualising men's minds.*

What, then, it may be asked, was the special purpose of the Fast Day's service as distinguished from the Saturday's preparation sermon? Long ago, it was very common, in appointing Fast Days, whether National, Synodical, Presbyterial, or Parochial, to specify their causes and occasion. When a National Fast was appointed, some national sins or

---

* Zeal for fasting amounted to a mania about the time of the Westminster Assembly, and for many years after. The divines at Westminster kept a monthly Fast. This was for a special reason. They were engaged in a great work which concerned the Church of Christ and the glory of God. The Protesters are said by Baillie to have instituted monthly Fasts in Scotland, and these lingered in some places till near the end of the seventeenth century. Curate Calder, who wrote after the coronation of William the III., speaks familiarly of them and says, " once in the monthly Fast Day I heard Mr. Kirkton discourse." In the Session Records of Fenwick, I find that in 1693 "John Stiel was delated for driving kine to Strathaven mercat upon the monthly Fast Day in Julie instant, and was appointed to be summoned to the next Session."

national calamities were specified as the causes of the Fast, and when Parochial Fasts were appointed, some Parochial sins or Parochial calamities were mentioned as the reason for the appointment. In the Records of this Parish, for instance, I find that in 1703 the Kirk Session appointed a day of humiliation "for the outbreakings of sin and wickedness in the Parish." And so when Sacramental Fasts were first instituted, it was not unusual to indicate the reason of their appointment. In the Records of the Kirk Session of Dunfermline there is a minute dated July, 1656, in which it is said that "it is thought fit that there be a day of fast before the communion for the sins of the people in this Paroche." This minute shews that Sacramental Fasts were originally appointed as Kirk Sessions thought fit, and that the object of these Fasts was humiliation on account of the prevalence of sin in the Parish. Pardovan says that some people think it not very proper that stranger ministers should conduct the Fast Day services, for "the design of that day being a Congregational Fast, on which the sins of that Parish are to be mourned before the Lord, no other minister can have such particular knowledge thereof as he who labours and travels among them." And at one time it was not uncommon for the minister of the Parish to officiate part of the day at least on his own Parish Fast. In the Records of this Parish it is minuted that on the Sacramental Fast in 1732 the minister preached in the forenoon and Mr. Lindsay of Sorn in the afternoon, while in 1734 the minister preached in the afternoon and a stranger in the forenoon.*

At what date it will now be asked were Sacramental Fasts

---

* Judging from the heading of a sermon in a manuscript volume of Mr. Lindsay's in my possession, I think it must have been common in Sorn as well as in Mauchline about 1730, for the Parish minister to preach one of the sermons on his Sacramental Fast Day.

introduced into this Parish? Bishop Sage, writing in 1695 about "the practice of our present Presbyterians" in regard to the ministration of the Lord's Supper, says, that "in many places, particularly in the west, a Fast is kept on some day of the week before the sacrament is celebrated." It would seem, therefore, that before the end of the seventeenth century, Sacramental Fasts had become common, but not universal, in Scotland, and that they were most common in the west. I was very hopeful of finding information about early Sacramental Fasts in the Session Records of Fenwick, but I was disappointed. Fenwick was a famous covenanting Parish, and its minister, William Guthrie, was a noted Protester. The old records of Fenwick, however, say little about the ministration of the sacrament. The earliest notice of a Sacramental Fast that I happen to have observed in them, occurs in the records of the year 1693. That year there was a day formally and specially appointed by the Session "to be observed as a day of fasting and humiliation by the congregation before the communion." A similar appointment was minuted in 1694. In the Records of Galston Session there is mention of a man's being in 1697 delated and publicly rebuked "for the scandal of breaking the Fast Day (which was keeped before the communion) by leading coals." Both the offence libelled and the clause bracketed in this minute, indicate that the Sacramental Fast was then a new institution in Galston Parish.

In the extant records of Mauchline Parish, there are entries shewing clearly that a communion was held here in 1673, and there are entries of early date which make it appear probable that the communion in 1673 was not the first that Mr. Veitch had after his return to the Parish in 1669. But it is not till 1680 that we find any entry to shew what extra days of preaching there were at the communion time. That year there was a

Fast on the Sunday preceding the communion, and from what has been said about the Fast Sunday at Galston, we may suppose this Fast to have been in preparation for the sacrament. All that is said about this Fast, however, is contained in two entries of collections. The first of these entries is "Collected, October 10 and 11, being the Fast Sabbath and the Monday thereafter, £13 12s. 0d.," and the other entry is "Collected, 16, 17, 18 days of October being the Saturday before the Communion, the Communion Sabbath and the Monday thereafter, £50." The next year in which we have an account of preaching days at the communion of Mauchline is 1691, and that year also there was no week day Sacramental Fast. Nor is there anything said about the previous Sunday's having been a Fast Sabbath; but, whether it was or was not, it was at least a day of unusual interest, on which there was a more than common congregation in the Church, for the collection amounted to £4 9s. 2d., whereas on ordinary Sabbaths it reached little more than half that sum. It might be an open question whether the records shew that in 1702 there was or was not a week day Sacramental Fast in Mauchline, but in the records for 1705 the following explicit statement occurs:— "August 9th, being Wednesday, the Fast before the communion, there was collected £3 1s. 10d." And it may be assumed, in absence of proof to the contrary, that from 1705 to 1882 there was always a week day Fast before and in connection with the summer communion here. But the fact that for many years prior to 1882 there was no Sacramental Fast before the winter communion, shews that Fasts were never reckoned essential preliminaries to the celebration of the Lord's Supper. And that Fasts were for long considered not so closely connected with the communion as the Saturday's and Monday's service is proved by the fact, that for many, many years, the collections on the Saturday, Sunday, and Monday, were slumped together as one, and were sometimes specially stated to be "for the poor," that is, for immediate distribution among the poor, while the collection on the Fast Day was entered by itself, and nothing was said about its destination. In later times, 1750 for example, the form of entry was changed, and the phrase used was "collected on *Fast and* following days," shewing that the Fast Day's collection was then considered part and parcel of the charities of the communion season.

One of the ends commonly served at present by Sacramental Fasts or preparation services on the Saturday before the communion is the distribution to intending communicants of tokens for admission to the Lord's Table. In very ancient times, however, it was not the practice of Kirk Sessions to distribute tokens in Church on either the Fast Day or the preparation Saturday. In 1574 the Session of Edinburgh ordained that the "haill communicants cum in proper person upon Friday next, at twa hours efternoon, and ressave their tickets in ye places of examination." But to come nearer home and nearer the present day, the Session of Galston, in 1673, "laid down a way how to distribute the tickets to those that are to communicate," and that way was, to give to the Elder of each quarter, a certified list of all the communicants within his district, and as many tickets as there were names upon his list. In Fenwick, the Kirk Session, in 1698, met a week before the Fast Day "for the judicial distribution of the tokens," and the following year it was minuted that the Session " divided themselves into committees in order to the admission of persons to the Lord's Table." There is nothing in our own records to shew what was the practice in this Parish with regard to the distribution of tokens two hundred years ago. But it is stated that on the Fast Day in 1732, the minister "*intimated how* the people were to be served in tokens for the communion," and that in 1735 the Session met after sermon on the Fast Day, and "the Elders received tokens to distribute to their respective quarters."

It is not necessary to say much about the Monday's service of thanksgiving after the communion. This service, like the Fast Day service, had neither Scriptural nor statutory origin. It was simply a custom of spontaneous generation. If it did not exactly originate in 1630, it at least was popularised then by the signal blessing that was seen to attend the preaching of John Livingstone, at Shotts, on the memorable Monday after the communion there in June of that year. By 1644 it must have become a common communion custom in Scotland, for Baillie, in one of his Westminster letters, expresses astonishment at the Independents having not only no preparation sermon before, but no thanksgiving sermon after, their communions. In this Parish there was a Monday service after the communion in 1680, which is the first year in which we have any account or enumeration in the Session Records of the different preaching days in connection with the celebration of the sacrament.

The word thanksgiving, which was the name given to the Monday's service, almost implied that the Monday was a more joyous day than the other preaching days. It was a day on which the bow was unstrung and the long pent up spirits were relaxed. It was a day to eat the fat and drink the sweet, and send portions unto them for whom nothing was prepared. But so apt is festivity to degenerate into jollity, and the natural reaction from intense emotion and restraint to pass into hilarious excitement, that the communion Mondays soon came to be a byeword and a matter of slight reproach to the Church. As far back as the year 1697, the Presbytery of Ayr were exercised on the subject, and a committee of their number was "appointed to think on some overture anent the inconvenience and offence of great preparations and multitudes dining on the Monday after communion." The outcome of this appointment was a resolution by the Presbytery to forbid ministers "to invite any to dinner on the foresaid day, but such as have been assisting at their communion." And that this prohibition was not to be considered a mere farce, threat, or *fulmen brutum*, the Presbytery ordered the clerk to transmit a double of it to each minister within the bounds. Far be it from me, however, to insinuate that the Monday's sociality always or usually verged on either excess or levity. On the contrary, gatherings more pure and pleasant than these Monday meetings at the social board generally were, could scarcely be either wished or conceived.

What may be termed the furnishings and material preparations for the communion in olden times, are the next things we have to consider. Some of these furnishings and preparations seem rather odd now. At the present day, communicants, when receiving the elements, either sit in their ordinary pews, the book-boards in front being covered for the occasion with clean white linen, or they sit in special pews linked together (as in Mauchline Church, between the two passages) so as to resemble a long table. At the Westminster Assembly the Independents kept the divines in discussion "long three weeks upon one point alone, the communicating at a table." They were content, says Baillie, that the elements should be received by the communicants sitting, instead of kneeling as the Episcopal ritualists in Scotland at one time insisted on, but they did not see the necessity for communicants rising out of their pews and going to a table. They did not raise the question either whether communicants should sit at the table with their hats off or on, although some of them held that the covering of the head was significant of their table honour, and of their sitting there as children not as worshippers. They considerately waived that crotchet, and directed all their efforts to overthrow the table system. And the result of their debate was that some vague and general expressions were devised, which could meet the views and suit the purpose of all parties, but which, said Baillie, would "by benigne exposition infer our (Scottish) practices." The general expressions thus referred to by Baillie are to be found in the following clause, in the Directory for Public Worship:—"the table being before decently covered, and so conveniently placed, that the communicants may orderly sit *about it* or *at it.*" By a benign exposition this clause might be taken to mean that all the communicants were to sit round or about the table in the sense of sitting *at* it; but by a benign construction it might also mean that the communicants were to sit in their pews around the table, in the sense of being *about* it on the same floor. The General Assembly perceived the ambiguity, and in approving the Directory for Public Worship, they made a special declaration that the clause in the section on the Lord's Supper "which mentioneth the communicants sitting about the table or at it, be not interpreted as if in the judgment of this Kirk it were indifferent or free for any of the communicants not to come to and receive at the table."* So much importance being thus attached to the seating of communicants at a table, it was generally in the olden times a literal table, and

---

* And as recently as 1827 the General Assembly pronounced a deliverance declaring that it is the law, and has been the immemorial practice of the Church of Scotland, to dispense the Sacrament of the Lord's Supper to the people seated at or around a communion table or tables, and enjoining Presbyteries to use their best endeavours when Churches are rebuilt or reseated to have a suitable table or tables provided for the solemn service of the Lord's Supper.

frequently it was a table specially made for the occasion, that was used at the sacraments. Sometimes too the table was fenced in a literal sense, not by words of warning and threatening from the minister, but as was the case in Edinburgh in 1562, by a wooden paling, or as it is termed, "ane travess for holding furth of ye non-communicants."

In Mauchline, the erection of the tables for the communion was for many years a matter of regular contract. In May, 1673, two of the elders were appointed "to meet with George Wilson, carpenter, and search what will be found necessar for mounting and making readie tables and formes for the communion, that it may be done betwixt and July 10th." And among the items of expenditure by the Kirk Session in December of that year was a sum of £6 (Scots) "for eight dales to be the communion tables." Twenty years later, in 1693, there was again given to George Wilson, for setting up the communion tables, £4, besides a sum of 8s. to the "wright for morning drinks." In 1674 two trees were purchased at a cost of £2 14s., to mend the tables, and Wilson was paid £5 8s. for work. As late as 1753 there is an entry in the Session Books of £2 14s. 10d. for setting up tables. And long ago there was expense incurred also, as there still is, in dressing the tables. In 1681 there was given to Bailie Hunter, who seems to have been either a draper or a merchant, £6 for table cloths at three communions." In 1691 there happens to be minuted a very full and detailed account of communion expenses. The fitting up of the tables cost £3 ; the furnishing of the table cloths with knittings cost £2 3s. 0d. ; and there was given to a man for helping at the tables, whatever that may mean, £2.*

---

* The Records of Galston contain a similar tale of expenses, such as for "setting the table buirds and mending the bridge ;" "for nails to fix the communion tables, 13s. 4d., and for timber to be standers to the tables, 5s. 8d. ;" "27 elnes linning cloth

Another source of expense to Kirk Sessions in connection with communions in olden times was the purchase of tokens. These tokens, although generally called tickets in old writings, were made of lead. But although they might have lasted for ever, they somehow did not. They were either worn out of shape or they were lost, and new ones had to be provided from time to time. In 1672, the Session of Mauchline, paid to the smith, a sum of 40s., for casting communion tickets. A slight economy, however, was effected under this head in 1768, by the presentation to the Session of a set of cams or moulds, from a good Samaritan named Muir, who lived at Gadgirth. The famous Water-of-Ayr stone, of which so much has recently been heard in the courts of law, had thus, we see, been used and prized for some works of art—even ecclesiastical art—a hundred and twenty years ago. And the Kirk Session had, at least, an opportunity of trying the capabilities of Mr. Muir's cams, for in 1779 it was found that there were only 1026 tokens to the fore, and that 300 more were needed.*

Communion cups were also, like tokens, sources of occasional and indeed of very considerable expense to Kirk Sessions. This expense, as well as the expense of providing communion tables and table cloths, has ever since 1617 fallen, by Act of

---

to cover the table buirds, and to be keipit for that use, at 10s. 4d. the elne, £3 19s. ;" "new furmes and renewing table buirds, £9 17s. 4d. ;" and paid "to the bedall for the sope to wash the baptisme cloth this last year, 6s." In 1676 the Galston Kirk Session found it necessary to invest in a full equipment of communion linen, and the account of the "table cloathes" shews what appearance the communion service must have presented. "One (cloth) the lenth of the Church betwixt the two north doors, another of equal lenth, divided in two, for the south side, item, a short one for the midd table. Two napkins and linen to be a codware to keip them in."

* At the first communion of the Seceders, at Ceres, in Fifeshire, which was held in August, 1743, and at which it is said there were 2000 communicants, the tokens distributed "were circular pieces of leather, about the size of a shilling, with a hole perforated in the centre."—M'Kelvie.

Parliament, on the heritors. But just as Kirk Sessions had, long ago, notwithstanding the Act of Parliament, to provide tables and table cloths for the communion, so had they to provide communion cups. In 1691 there was paid by the Session of Mauchline, £3 12s., for dressing the cups, and in 1777 the Session minuted that they were "determined to get new communion cups, as the old ones can serve no longer." The Session seem to have been determined also not to pay for the new cups, for although beautiful silver cups were got that year, it was not at the Kirk Session's expense, nor at the Congregation's expense, but at the cost of the Heritors. Lovers of antiquities will be pleased to hear that these cups are still in use, and that they look as fresh and bright as on the day they were made.*

One of the questions asked by Presbyteries long ago at the visitation of Parishes was, what utensils have been provided for the administration of the sacraments? In the year 1698, Mr. Maitland reported that in Mauchline there were neither any mortifications for the poor nor any utensils for the celebration of the sacraments. Five years later, however, Mr. Maitland informed the Presbytery that there had been mortified for the poor, 100 merks Scots, by the Laird of Glenlee, and six pounds Scots by Mr. Hodge. Also that there were provided for sacramental use, two silver cups, but no other utensils. In 1719 matters had still further improved in the Parish, and not only were there "two silver cups for the sacrament, but there were also a peuther plate for carrying the bread and a basin for

---

* A not uncommon form of gift to a parish by an heritor or an heritor's lady was Church plate. Lady Anne Whiteford, for instance, gave to the Session of Mauchline, in 1788, a beautiful baptismal basin, and in 1730 the Kirk Session of Galston received " Four silver cups, dedicated by the late Lady Polwarth, for the use of the Parish."

baptism." And Mauchline was no worse off in respect of sacramental utensils than other Parishes in the district. In 1706 there were many Parishes reported to be wholly unprovided with such articles. In 1709 there were at St. Quivox "no communion cups nor other utensils for the sacraments except a basin to hold water." The only sacramental possessions in other Parishes that same year were table cloths. In 1723 the whole stock of sacramental utensils at Auchinleck were "a siller queff, ane stoup, table cloaths, and two cloaths used when children are baptized."

The question may well be raised, how came it that after the re-establishment of Presbytery in Scotland, at the Revolution, there was such a scarcity of sacramental utensils in so many Parishes? Did the outed Episcopal ministers make off with all the Church belongings they could lay hands on? It is just possible, and the ministers may have thought that in so doing they were preventing old benefactions from being misappropriated. After the establishment of Episcopacy in 1661, the Bishops complained that the outed Presbyterian ministers had stowed away their decreets of locality.* Thirty years later, when tables were turned, Episcopalians may have taken their revenge, and made off with what they could seize, on any feasible pretence. Certain it is, that a great many ecclesiastical records, pertaining to the second period of Episcopacy, have disappeared. In the Records of the Presbytery of Ayr there is a blank from 1650 to 1687. It is but a few years since the Record of the Synod of Galloway from 1664 to 1671 was accidentally discovered; and that communion cups have been lost to Parishes by ministers in much the same way as Church Records have been lost by the Clerks of Church courts, is at least com-

* See Register of Synod of Galloway from 1664 to 1671, page 10.

monly believed, if not positively ascertained. In the Session Records of Irongray there is a curious entry anent the loss of communion cups. In 1697 the elders of that Parish were directed to make enquiry about the loss of the utensils of the Church,—cups, table cloths, and other things,—and a week later they reported that nothing could be heard of the missing articles except "that they were carried away by Mr. John Welsh, his plenishing."* It is quite possible that a similar fate befell many parochial possessions at transition and troublous times. But it is pleasant to have to say that there are instances of Episcopal ministers endowing Parishes with communion plate. Among the Parishes reported in 1696 to have had no utensils for the sacrament, was the large and wealthy Parish of Maybole. Forty years later, at a visitation of that Parish, the minister and elders informed the Presbytery that they had "got two silver cups for the sacrament of the supper, from Mr. Alexander ————, their late Episcopal minister, which he hes mortified to the Paroch for the said use."

The plenishing of the communion table with bread and wine is an expense that at the present day falls on the minister, but it is an expense for which a fixed allowance is appointed, by the Court of Teinds, to be paid to the minister by the heritors. In some Parishes, but Mauchline is not one of these, when the sacrament is administered oftener than once a year, there is an extra grant for communion expenses, made to the minister, by the Kirk Session. But in the old Parishes it is only in the case of *extra* communions that Kirk Sessions make any payments for communion elements. And this present practice is of old standing. An Act of Parliament, passed in 1572, imposed

---

* Harper's Rambles in Galloway. This John Welsh, grandson of the great John Welsh of Ayr, was not an Episcopalian but a Presbyterian.

on the parsons of all parish kirks* the burden of furnishing bread and wine to the Communion as often as it should be administered.† The General Assembly of 1638 made an addendum to this Act, and declared that where allowance was made for furnishing communion elements only once a year the charges should rather be defrayed out of the day's collection than that the congregation should want a more frequent celebration.‡ It might be supposed, therefore, that subsequent to the year 1572, when the above cited act of Parliament was passed, there would not be found in Kirk Session Records any entries of expense for communion elements, unless the communion had been celebrated oftener than once a year. Nor are there in Session Records many entries of expense on that score. But there are some. In the Galston Records for 1642 there is an entry of £11 18s. od., "to mak out the elements by and attour the 40 merks qlk Cessnock, Barr, and Gastoun peys." And it is proper to explain that the Act 1572 is apt to be misunderstood by lay readers. The parsons on whom was laid the burden of providing the communion elements were not the stipendiary parish ministers, who received only a stipend out of the parish teinds, but the few ministers who at that date were parsons in the strict sense of the term, and had for their livings the whole benefice of the parish. In parishes where there were no parsons, but only stipendiary ministers, the burden of providing the communion elements was held by some authorities to devolve on the titular of the

---

* Pardovan, 281.

† In 1572 the General Assembly "concluded that the persone (parson) should find bread and wine to the communion, unless the vicarage exceed the sum of forty pounds, and in that case the vicarage to furnish the same in time coming."—Book of Universal Kirk.

‡ The communion collections and their distribution fall to be considered in the Lecture on Provision for the Poor.

teinds; and I refer to this matter chiefly because this construction of the Act possibly affords the explanation of a curious entry in our own Session Records. In 1680 there is an entry "given to Thomas Stewart, servitor to my Lord Loudoun for carrying the elements, 13s. 8d." The carrying of the elements probably meant the carriage of the elements to Mauchline, for in 1674 and 1691 there are similar entries in the following words, "for bringing the wine to the communion, 12s.," and "for bringing home of the bread and wine, £1 2s. 0d." Lord Loudoun, it is well known, was the patron of the parish and the titular of the teinds, and if the construction just mentioned of the Act, 1572, was held by Lord Loudoun to be the proper construction, we can understand his providing the elements and the Session's being at the expense of conveying them to Mauchline.* In the Galston records we find similar entries of outlay for the "wyne fetching."†

---

* Since this paragraph went to press, I have chanced to light on the following note in Chalmers' Caledonia:—"Acta Parl., iv. 323. Lord Loudoun and his heirs were obliged to pay to the Crown 100 merks Scots yearly, and to pay to the ministers serving the cure at the Church of Mauchlin, 40 bolls of oatmeal and 300 merks Scots yearly, and to furnish bread and wine for the celebration of the communion."

† The following extracts from the Records of the Presbytery of Ayr are interesting, as shewing how communion elements were provided or failed to be provided long ago:—

1642—"It was regreated by the said Mr. Johne (the minister at Kirkoswald), that some of the Parochiners refused to pay their part for the furnishing of the elements to the communion, according to the direction of the platt thereanent, through the which neglect and omission the communion wes not celebrated twyse in the year, as the minister affirms he would willingly do, if the said neglect were helped."

1644—The town of Ayr furnished the communion elements for the Church.

1697—"At Symington the minister reported that he had not wherewith to defray communion elements."

1702—The minister of Kirkoswald reported that he has "a decreet of ocality containing allowance for communion elements for which he gets nothing, the Heritors alleging they are out of use of payment. No utensils for sacraments.'

The peace of some congregations has recently been broken by a controversy regarding the particular kind of wine that should be used at the communion. It may perhaps not be generally known that the wine commonly used now is not the same kind of wine as was used very long ago in Scotland. The wine now in use is port wine, the wine used long ago was claret, and the quantity of it consumed at a sacrament was enormous. It was at the cost of the city that the communion elements for the churches of Edinburgh were in the sixteenth century provided, and in the Dean of Guild's accounts for 1590 the following entries occur, " 1st communion ane puncheon of claret wine, £36 10s., 9 gallons mair, £16 16 ; 2nd communion 1 puncheon of claret wine, cost £35, 6½ gallons mair, £14 6s." And these quantities were not beyond common. In 1578 there were used at one communion in Edinburgh 26 gallons of wine which cost £41 12s. 0d. ; in 1575 at what is called the second table, "ane puncheon of wyne, £27 10s., mair bocht fra Gilbert Thornetoune's wyfe, 11 quarts and ane pynt, £5 15s. ; in 1574 ane puncheon of wyne, £30 ; and in 1573 ane puncheon of wyne, £18, and sax quarts mair, 32s."* Coming down to the times of the Covenant we find that in 1641 there was paid by the town of Glasgow to Robert Campbell and others for "wyne to the communion," the sum of £84 10s. 8d., while in 1656 there was purchased by the same liberal corporation for the same good purpose a hogshead of wine at the cost of £160. It is quite plain that in these old Reformation and second Reformation days communicants had partaken at the Lord's table in a different way from what they now do. For one thing the wine used was lighter, and more of it might be rationally and innocuously taken by each person. It is not unreasonable to think, also,

---

* Lee's Lectures, Appendix.

that the laity, after having with no small effort secured for themselves the privilege of communicating in both kinds, with wine as well as bread, might, by way of protesting against the popish practice of refusing the cup to the people, have made a point of shewing that they appreciated the privilege by returning the "queff" either empty or visibly lightened of its contents.*

The question what kind of wine should be used at the sacrament was copiously debated by ecclesiastical writers long before the present wise generation of disputants came into being. Pardovan in his collections refers to the question, and says, "Any kind of wine may be used in the Lord's supper, yet wine of a red colour seemeth most suitable." † And, what will be

---

* I have had the privilege of examining a selection of old papers belonging to the Kirk Session of St. Cuthbert's, Edinburgh, with manuscript notes thereon by George Lorimer, Esq., and I find that the following account for wines, etc., was given in to that Session in 1687, by the beadle, who was by trade a publican. The bill is not large as compared with those quoted above, but the congregation is estimated, by Mr. Lorimer, to have been not more than two or three hundred. It will be seen from this bill that in old times, when the services were very protracted, a considerable amount of liquor was at least provided for, if not consumed by, the several sets of Church officials, viz. :—the minister and his assistants, the precentor and his helps, the elders and deacons, the officers and the attendants. The wine was light wine, either Claret or Burgundy :—

To the Kirk, 9 pynts wyne and 2 pynts ale,	- -	£8	6	0
,, Mr. Hepburn (Minister), 4 pynts wyne,	- -	3	12	0
,, John Wishart (Precentor), 2 pynts wyne,	- -	1	16	0
,, Elders and Deacons, 4 pynts wyne, -	- -	3	12	0
,, William Byers (Beadle), 2 pynts wyne,	- -	0	18	0
,, The Officers, 3 pynts wyne, - -	- -	2	14	0
,, The Baxter, 1 chopin wyne, 2 pynts ale,	- -	0	13	0
,, Ane pynt of ale to the man yt drew ye wyne,	-	0	2	0

A Scotch pint was equal to three bottles, and a chopin half that quantity. The sums quoted both in this note and in the text above are of Scots money.

† The fact of the wine being a symbol of the *blood* shed for sinners is perhaps why Pardovan thinks that red wine is more suitable than white wine for the sacrament of the supper. Some strange conceits, however, on the subject of red and white wine have been enunciated by religious writers of what may be termed the allegorical school. In a book printed at Paris in 1575, under the title of *Quadragesimale*

grateful to the ears of total abstainers, he adds, "in case a society of Christians should want [not be able to procure] the fruits of the vine of all sorts, I cannot think but it might be supplied by some composure as like unto it as could be made."

In the first liturgy of Edward the VI., there was a rubric which directed the Priest on pouring the wine into the chalice or some fair convenient cup, prepared for that use, to add thereto "a little pure and clean water." This was a very ancient custom in the Christian Church, and it was, says a learned author, "in opposition to two contrary sects, first the Arminians, who held that it was only lawful to use wine alone without water; secondly, against the Hydroparastatae, who officiated with water unmixt with wine. The reason of this mixture was partly in imitation of our Saviour's act in the first institution of the Eucharist, agreeable to the custom of that hot climate, which constantly used to allay the heat of the wine with water, and partly because that when our Saviour's side was pierced with the lance there issued out both water and blood." The same custom was at one time attempted to be introduced into the Church of Scotland, and in some places the attempt met with success. In Aberdeenshire it continued to be more or less general for a hundred and fifty years. But in Ayrshire popular feeling was against it. The Covenanters denounced it, and it was regarded consequently with all the

---

Spirituale, or Lent's Allegory, it is said, "there are two kinds of wine, white and red, the white signifieth the hope which is in Christ Jesus, and the red the love which he hath shewed us in purchasing of the foresaid glory. . . . The white teacheth us the way to heaven, for it giveth good courage to a man, legs of wine and bodlines of joy. The red sharpeneth the wit and understanding, and helps the memory to remember that the precious blood of Christ gushed out of his side for our salvation. This wine is chief of choice among all liquors, *electus ex millibus*." Stephen's World of Wonders, London, 1607. Wodrow states that in his day the wine used at communions in Holland was white wine, and that in Norway and Denmark it was not wine at all that was used but malt liquors.

aversion that anything supposed to be associated with Episcopal ritual encountered in the west. Common people, who knew nothing of the philosophy of Christian symbols, exclaimed against the mixture as an intake, an imposture, and a shameless adulteration, and they attributed its introduction to clerical parsimony. So dangerous is it for ministers to attempt to do anything, however reasonable in itself, if the reason of it is not apparent to the most benighted of his flock.

It may not be generally known that there has been almost as much diversity of opinion and custom in regard to the bread used at communions as in regard to the wine. The Roman Catholic monks, as might be expected, were very particular about the preparation of bread for the communion. The corn, if possible, was to be selected grain by grain, and, before it was ground, the mill was to be so purified that the flour for the host would not be polluted with any fretts. The table on which the flour was baked was to be without spot, and the servant that held the irons for baking was to have his hands covered with rochets. During the process of baking there was to be dead silence in the room, and the baking was to be done over a clean fire, made of very dry wood, prepared on purpose many days before. After the bread was baked, it was put by the monks themselves, with ceremonies and prayers, into a mould marked with sacred characters; and before consecration, it was cut in the form of a cross, by a special knife, and was mystically divided into nine parts with different designations.* It was deemed heresy to make the host of fermented bread; and I may add that many of the Reformers, like the Catholics, have thought that the bread should be unleavened. In some parts of Scotland, short bread was till quite recently chosen as the most appropriate bread

---

* Gordon's Monasticon, p. 21.

for the Christian passover. During the first year of my own ministry in Galloway, I was one day accosted by the beadle, and told that he and his friends were hoping I would give them short bread at the sacrament. We used to have it till three years ago, he said, and we thought it very shabby in the minister to change the old custom and give us plain bread. My answer was that altogether apart from the question of expense, I considered plain bread the most suitable for the occasion, and that, in this view, I was backed by the great ecclesiastical authority, Pardovan, who says, that "ordinary bread is to be used, and it is most decent that it should be leavened wheat bread." I cannot make out whether shortbread was ever used or not at the communion in Mauchline. I have heard old people say that in their fathers' or grandfathers' days it was used in some Parishes in Ayrshire, and the expression in our records two hundred years ago, "bringing home the bread," rather indicates that it was not ordinary bread that was used, but bread that had to be brought from a distance.* At the present day, as may be seen from the last published volume of the Queen's Journal, the communion bread in some parts of Aberdeenshire is cut into small cubes like dice. These are put on large plates, and on the top of them are two or three longer pieces of bread for the ministers to break before distribution. The plates are then passed down the tables, and each communicant helps himself to one of the small cubes. If this mode of preparing the communion bread

---

* This is not an absolutely certain inference. Two hundred years ago there may possibly have been no baker in Mauchline. As recently as 1725 "there was only one baker in Dumfries, and he made bawbee-baps of coarse flour, chiefly bran, which he occasionally carried in creels to the fairs of Urr and Kirkpatrick." Letter from Maxwell of Munches to Herries of Spottes, quoted in Stat. Account of Scotland, Kirkcudbrightshire, page 207. The man to whom the West Kirk Session of Edinburgh made payment for communion bread in 1688 designated himself " Clark to the comon Beackhows."

in the north is of very ancient origin, we may understand the astonishment of Spalding in 1643, at what he called the new in come customs, introduced then by Cant, although these are customs that in this part of the country we have been familiar with from our earliest years. "The communion breid, he says (was not), baikin nor distribute as wes wont, bot efter ane new fashion of breid, for it wes baikin in ane round loaf, lyke ane trynsheour, syne cuttit out in long schieves, hanging be ane tak. And first the minister takis ane schieve efter the blessing, and brakis ane piece, and gives to him who is narrest, and he gives the schieve to his nichbour, who takis ane piece, and syne gives it to his nichbour, whill it be spent, and syne ane elder gives in ane uther schieve whair the first schieve left, and so furth. The lyk breid and scruice wes nevir sein in Abirdene, befoir the cuming of Mr. Andro Cant to be thair minister."

I had occasion to indicate how the cost of the elements at communions in the Church of Scotland is defrayed. In the old Catholic Church, expenses of that kind were generally met by voluntary beneficence, stimulated by public praise and the hope of future reward. One of the old bidding prayers was,— "Ye shall pray for the good man and woman that this day giveth bread to make the holy loaf, and for all those that first began it, and them that longest continue." Whether the communion bread was supposed by its consecration to have some spiritualising influence impressed on it, or was merely endeared and made sacred to people by its use in the great mystery or symbol of redemption, it is certain that even in Scotland, and at no remote day, some communicants were in the habit of carrying fragments from the table, to shew or give to their friends at home. According to the learned author I have so often quoted, this was a very ancient practice in the Christian

Church. At first, he says, the analects and remains of the supper were *sent* to absent friends "as pledges and tokens of love and agreement in the unity of the same faith." The custom came at length to be abused, and was interdicted by the Council of Laodicea, which ordained that the consecrated bread be sent no more abroad to other Parishes at Easter, under the notion and in resemblance of the "blessed loaves." "As for the order of our Church" (the Church of England), adds our author, "it is very circumspect, for by saying the curate shall have it to his own use, care thereby is taken to prevent the superstitious reservation of the sacrament as the Papists practised."*

Having thus described the material preparations for the communion in olden times, I now pass on to describe the Church service on the communion Sabbath.

The Church of Scotland has always recommended frequent celebrations of the Lord's Supper, although the practice of the Church would scarcely lead one to think so. In the first Book of Discipline, 1560, it is stated that "four times in the year, we think sufficient to the administration of the Lord's Table, which we desire to be distincted that the superstition of times (Easter, Christmas, &c.) may be avoided." To wean the people from the observance of old popish holidays, Knox and his friends recommended that the communion days in the Church of Scotland should be the first Sundays of March, June, September, and December. The Westminster Directory,

---

* I am informed that in some districts of Scotland it was customary for the minister and his assistants to consume what was left of the consecrated bread. This was done to prevent the distribution of the fragments becoming a source of superstition. In 1703 a man was delated to the Kirk Session of Galston "for his scandalous and offensive carriage at the Lord's Table the preceding year, in putting up part of the bread in his pocket." He was cited to appear before the Session, and the charge having been found proven, he was publicly rebuked in Church.

and the Acts of Assembly subsequent to the second Reformation of 1638, only recommend that celebrations of the communion should be frequent, without specifying how frequent. There could, however, in the opinion of the most approved exponents of the Church's polity, be such a thing as over frequent as well as too infrequent celebration of the sacrament. Says Baillie, "Those who have seen the manner of celebration used by the Independents, professe it to be a very dead and comfortlesse way. It is not as in New England, once in the month, but as at Amsterdam, once every Lord's day, which makes the action much less solemn than in any other of the Reformed Churches, and in this too much like the daily masses of the Church of Rome."

Till within a very recent date there has been great irregularity, in respect of time and frequency, in the administration of the Lord's Supper by ministers in the Church of Scotland. As far back as 1565 that irregularity had become noticeable. At the General Assembly, held in the month of June of that year, there were ministers, says Calderwood, complained of and ordered to be tried and censured for "not ministering the communion for six years bypast." It was after the great disruption in 1651, however, that this irregularity became most scandalous. It is stated in some histories that the Protesters, in their zeal for the promotion of godliness, "ordained that the Sacrament of the Supper should be dispensed every month."*

---

* See Cunningham's Church History of Scotland, vol. ii., p. 171. Possibly the source of this error is a sentence in a letter of Baillie's, dated 19th July, 1654. This sentence is sometimes given as follows,—"From their meetings in Edinburgh they were instructed to have monthly fasts and communions." In Dr. Laing's edition of Baillie's letters, however, vol. iii., p. 245, the sentence is somewhat different, and if a comma be inserted after the word *fasts*, the meaning is very much altered,—" From their meeting in Edinburgh they were instructed to have monethly fasts, and communions as they could have them."

That must be a mistake. In all or most of the towns where the chief Protesters exercised their ministry, the sacrament remained unadministered for years. The chief of the Protesters was James Guthrie of Stirling, and in the Session Records of Stirling the following minute occurs, under date, 5th Nov. 1657 :—" The Congregation have been without the enjoyment of that healing ordinance (the Lord's Supper) for the space of nine years."* It was then appointed that the communion should be celebrated on the two Sabbaths, 15th and 22nd of the current month, and that the 12th of the month " be set apart for public solemn fasting and humiliation." In Edinburgh and St. Andrews, and I cannot tell how many other places, the communion was in like manner uncelebrated for years, notwithstanding the entreaties of congregations. Both Protesters and Resolutioners had a difficulty in regard to celebration. The whole community was at variance. Was there to be a communion without reconciliation? There were charges and counter charges of sin heard everywhere—charges of spiritual defection and counter charges of ecclesiastical contumacy—charges of denying Christ and counter charges of rebellion against the Church of Christ—and who was to judge in these matters or settle who should be received and who should not be received at the Lord's table? At a meeting of the six sessions of Edinburgh in April, 1652, it was concluded that the communion " cannot conveniently be celebrate, as is now thought, till there be a lawfull judicatorie of the kirk to determine anent the present course of defection carried on amongst us anent the Covenant, and what censure it deserves."† After

---

* This extract given me by Rev. Mr. Smith, North Parish, Stirling.

† In August of that year the General Assembly passed an act, ordaining ministers and Kirk Sessions "to debar from the Lord's table all such persons as are found not to walk suitably to the gospel, and being convinced and admonished thereof do not reform." Even this enactment, however, did not satisfy the Protesters.

the deplorable schism in 1651 about a bagatelle, a question of politics and statecraft, it might have been said of the Church in the words of the prophet, "the ways of Zion do mourn, because none come to the solemn feasts, all her gates are desolate, her priests sigh, her virgins are afflicted and she is in bitterness." Not only, however, in the troublous times of the 17th century, but during the still times of the 18th century, there were many instances of a communion not being held in a parish for five, ten, or even more years. One of the grounds on which the General Assembly in 1705 deposed the minister of Urr was that he neither had "dispensed the sacrament of the Lord's supper to others nor partaken thereof himself for more than sixteen years." And this minister was not a man that was unconcerned and uninterested in things spiritual. He was, or affected to be, an extreme Puritan, and "asserted that communicating with persons scandalous made people guilty of communicating unworthily."

I am not prepared to say with what degree of regularity or irregularity the communion was celebrated in Mauchline before 1695, when Mr. Maitland became minister, nor indeed for a good many years after, but judging from such entries as I have seen, both in our own Kirk Session Records and in the Records of the Presbytery of Ayr, I am more than doubtful if the sacrament was administered every year in this parish for a considerable part of the seventeenth century if not also of the eighteenth.*

From the second Reformation in 1638 till the Disruption in 1651, it seems to have been the common practice with

---

* All the years in which I have noted that a communion was held in Mauchline prior to the settlement of Mr. Maitland are 1673, 1674, 1677 (probably), 1679, 1680, 1681, 1691; and 1693. At the visitation of the Parish in 1723, during Mr. Maitland's ministry, it was stated that there had been no communion for three years.

ministers in Ayrshire to have two communions a year. We have seen that in 1642 the minister of Kirkoswald "regraited" that the communion had not been celebrated twice a year in his Parish, and expressed his anxiety that it should be. In 1643 the minister of Coylton was admonished by the Presbytery to give his people the opportunity of communicating twice a year. Judging from the following expression, which occurs in a minute of Presbytery, "the reasons that hindered the brethren to celebrate the Lord's Supper in their paroches this last season," it would seem that in 1710 it was neither expected nor required that communions should be held in a Parish more than once a year. And for a long while, from that date down, it was the practice of the Presbytery of Ayr to ask each minister in the bounds if he had had a communion in his Parish that season, and if not, what was the reason for the omission. In 1749, however, the Presbytery recommended that "every Parish should have the Lord's Supper celebrated twice in the year, and that there should be, besides a Fast Day observed as usual, one sermon on the Saturday, dropping the Monday's meeting altogether." The following year the Presbytery again declared their opinion that the more frequent celebration of the sacrament is highly desirable. They were constrained to admit, however, that this was "in a great measure impracticable without abridging the number of sermons that have been long in use on these occasions, and that there was difficulty in bringing about a reformation in this matter owing to the prejudices of the people, who seem to look upon such numbers of sermons as in some degree essential to the celebration of that sacred institution." All that the Presbytery could therefore do was to recommend that every minister in his public sermons, catechisings and visitations of families, should endeavour to remove from people's minds mistaken notions on this point, and that till the effect of this labour became, by the blessing of God, visible, enquiries should be made at every minister "once at least in two meetings of the Presbytery" what had been his diligence in this particular business.

Scarcely a year passed, from 1710 to 1750, in which there were not more or fewer ministers who reported to the Presbytery of Ayr that they had been hindered from having the communion celebrated "this last season." * The reasons why they were hindered from that necessary work were also stated, and sometimes the reasons given were sustained and sometimes not. When the reasons were not sustained an admonition followed, which was recorded, like the Second Book of Discipline, *in rei memoriam perpetuam.* Some of the reasons might be called laughable, and others lamentable. In 1711 one minister gave as his reason for having no communion "that the kirk being like to fall through the shutting out of both the side walls he could not venture to have a considerable meeting of people in it." This excuse was not sustained, and the minister was told that rather than have no communion he should have it in the churchyard. In 1716 one minister assigned as his reason for having no communion that some of his congregation were so scrupulous as to take exception to the brethren he had asked to assist him, on the ground that "these brethren had taken the oath of abjuration." † This excuse was sustained

---

* In 1716 it was reported to the Presbytery that the sacrament had been administered at Tarbolton only three times during the last eight years. An explanation, however, was given, which the Presbytery accepted as a sufficient excuse. The minister of Cumnock had no sacrament for many years on account of an unhappy state of feeling in the parish about an Act of Parliament. In 1717 the moderator was appointed to write to the minister of Coylton that the Presbytery were dissatisfied that the sacrament had not been celebrated in his parish for several years.

† In an Act passed by the General Assembly in 1715 it is said, "The General Assembly, considering that the distinguishing course taken by ministers in the choice of their assistants at the celebration of the holy sacrament of the Lord's Supper,

because it showed that the minister had at least endeavoured to have a communion. The same year another minister stated that the communion in his parish was hindered because of "disorders occasioned by some irregular ministers that came into his bounds." In other words, the parish had become so demoralised by these itinerant preachers and so much bad feeling between neighbours had been created, that it was inexpedient to convene the congregation to a banquet of love in their present state of mind. These reasons, however, for postponing communions are neither so paltry nor so amusing as one that the great Samuel Rutherford gravely relates in one of his letters. "To my grief," he says, "our communion at Anwoth is delayed till Sabbath come eight days, for the laird and lady hath earnestly desired me to delay it, because the laird is sick and he fears he be not able to travel because he hath lately taken physic. The Lord bless that work. Commend it to God as you love me, for I love not Satan's thorns cast in the Lord's way. Commend the laird to your God."

In olden times it was very common to have the communion celebrated on several successive Sabbaths. And this was done not only in large towns but in country parishes. In the records of the Presbytery of Ayr we find that during a vacancy in Cumnock in 1642 the parishioners petitioned to have the sacrament administered to them, "whereupon the Presbytery did voyce and nominate Mr. William Scott to celebrate the communion at Cumnock upon Sunday come twenty days, and Mr. James Nesmyth on Sunday come a

---

wh'ch ought to be the bond of unity and love among Christians, does exceedingly contribute to the confirming of people in their unjust prejudice against ministers, and in their divisive practices, do therefore earnestly obtest all the ministers of this church carefully to guard against this, as they would not be found to lay a stumbling block before the people."

month." In the Session Records of Galston, too, we find it was for many years the usual practice to have two successive Sundays set apart for the communion in that parish. In his history of the sufferings of the Church, Wodrow states that Mr. Thomas Wyllie of Kirkcudbright, and formerly of Mauchline, had, on the 8th June, 1662, his *first* day of distribution of the sacrament, because he had so many communicants and such numbers joined with him that they could not all communicate in one day. We might infer from this statement of Wodrow's that no person was allowed to communicate on two successive Sabbaths in the same church. But there was no such restriction of spiritual privileges. Spalding says that in 1642 the communion was given in Old Aberdeen for the first time on the 17th April, for the second time on the 24th April, and for the third time on the 8th May, and that on each of these occasions Dr. Forbes of Corss communicated, although he had never, as was required, subscribed the Covenant "and still stood out." The practice of having communions extending over successive Sabbaths had been either entirely or generally given up in the Church of Scotland before the date at which the extant records of Mauchline parish begin, and in these records there is therefore no trace of the old custom.

At a very early period there used to be a morning service at the communion. This service commenced at five or sometimes at four or even at three o'clock, and doubtless it originated in the old Popish notion that the sacrament should be taken fasting, not after a Fast Day, but fasting,* and that nothing common should be eaten for so many hours afterwards. These matutine communions involved an expenditure on lights. In

---

* "For the honour of that great sacrament the body of Christ should have the precedence of entering in at our mouths before ordinary meat." Augustine Epist., quoted in Alliance of Div. Off. 152.

Edinburgh, for instance, in 1563, there was expended on two dozen torches for the communion, a sum of £3, and on candles for "baith the days," 18d. or more probably 18s. And in those days there were in large cities simple and effectual arrangements for raising money for all legitimate Church purposes. The Kirk Session of Canongate, for instance, just passed a resolution and framed a minute appointing the magistrates to supply torches for the communion, and the magistrates had the goodness to do as they were directed by their spiritual rulers. In 1565 that Session required "everilk bailyie, everilk diocone of craft with uther faythful men that thai and everilk ane of them have ane torch agane the morning service (of the communion), the quhilk they promisit to do." In 1613, however, the Session of Canongate, in appointing the days of communion, specially minuted and caused to be intimated that the communion was to be "without morning service." This resolution probably indicates the date at which morning services at communions came to be generally given up in the Church of Scotland.

There is no doctrine so self-evident or demonstrable, that some people will not stoutly maintain the truth of its contrary; and so, while morning communions, after the manner of the Catholics, were common in the Church of Scotland for fifty years after the Reformation, there were other denominations of Christians that took the opposite course of having their communion services at night. This was one of the discordant practices of the Independents about the time of the sitting of the Westminster Assembly. The Lord's Supper, says Baillie, they desire to celebrate at night, after all other ordinances are ended. And, indeed, it may well be a matter of wonder that these views have not been more strongly and more widely held than they have been, for it was certainly in the evening that the original supper, which is the recognised pattern of the sacramental banquet, was partaken of by our Lord and His twelve Apostles.

Except during the periods when Episcopacy was established in Scotland, the form and order of the Sabbath service on communion days have from the earliest times been very much the same as they are now. Public worship began as on ordinary Sabbaths, with prayer and praise, reading and preaching of the word. The sermon preached on that occasion was called the action sermon or the sermon at the action, in distinction from the sermon of preparation preached on the Saturday or other preaching week day. As far back as 1574, the manner of the holy communion and the order thereof at Edinburgh are indicated as follows in a minute of Kirk Session:—"Ye bell to begin to ryng upon Sonday at four hours in ye morning, ye sermon to begin at five hours, and ye ministration to begin at sex and sua to continue. Item, the bell of new agane to begin to ryng at aucht hours, ye sermond to begin at nyne and sua to continue."*

Previous to the distribution of the elements there are three ministerial acts performed in the communion service. One is called the exhortation or fencing of the tables, another is the reading of the words of institution, and the third is the blessing of the bread and wine, or prayer of consecration. The order and manner of performing these acts have varied slightly at different times, and probably vary slightly yet in different parts of the country, or with different ministers. In the book which Charles attempted to thrust on the Church in 1637, the order of service before communion was, first, exhortation,

---

* In 1765 public worship in Edinburgh on the communion Sunday began at ten.

then confession, and thirdly, absolution. After which it was directed that the "minister kneeling down at God's boord" shall say a collect of humble access to the holy communion, and "then the Presbyter standing up shall say the prayer of consecration."

It is commonly supposed that the Presbyterian ritual always forbade kneeling at the Lord's Table. This is not exactly the case. The Presbyterians set their faces against communicants receiving the elements kneeling, but Presbyterian ministers sometimes knelt in prayer at the table. Spalding writes, that in 1643, after Episcopal ritual had been fairly suppressed, the minister at Old Aberdeen, on the day of communion, "when the first table was full of people, said ane prayer upon his knies, the people at the table pairt sitting, pairt kneeling. There-efter, and efter sum schort exhortation, he gave the communion to the people all sitting at that table." Both minister and part of the people therefore knelt in prayer at the table, but the people all received the elements sitting. Apparently Mr. Cant did not allow the people to kneel even at prayer, for in the same year, 1643, Spalding writes that the communion was given in New Aberdeen, "not efter the old fashion kneilling, bot sitting, nor the people suffered to pray when Mr. Andro Cant prayed, as thair custom wes befoir, bot all to be silent and dum." The tendency in the Scottish Church has been rather to magnify exhortation and to depreciate the importance of devotion in Church services, and consequently the fencing of the tables came, in the course of time, to be regarded as one of the chief parts of the communion service. In the hands of not a few zealous but indiscreet ministers this act degenerated into something very like a profane farce. The different sins that disqualify people from partaking worthily of the Lord's Supper were elaborately detailed,

L

and among these were specified by name the various forms of minced oaths and senseless interjections used in common parlance.

It may be remarked here in connection with the fencing of the tables, and the debarring of unworthy persons from the communion, that one of the subjects most vehemently and lengthily discussed in the Westminster Assembly was the principle on which admission to the Lord's table should be regulated. In different churches different standards of requirement have been set up. The historical principle of the Church of Scotland has been that three things are required of those that seek access to communion privileges, first, "that they have a good measure of knowledge, and profess to believe the truth; secondly, that in their life and conversation they be without scandal, and thirdly, that they be submissive to the discipline of the Church.".* To these three qualifications some Churches have added a fourth, and have required that all applicants for communion privileges publicly declare "such clear and certain signs of their regeneration" as will satisfy the minister and the elders, and sometimes the majority of the congregation, that they are true Christians born of God and sanctified by the holy spirit.† What the English Parliament however, wished the Westminster Assembly to do was to enumerate all the sins and shortcomings that justify the exclusion of a man from the Lord's table, and to make this list of scandalous offences in the hands of a magistrate the hard and fast rule of admission and rejection. The Assembly complied so far with this request as to draw out a long list of offences that would justly exclude a man from the enjoyment of communion

---

* Baillie's Dissuasive, p. 22

† The Protesters held similar views. See their declaration in Peterkin's Records, p. 645, Section 6.

privileges. But there were two things that the Assembly would not do. They would never say that their list was complete, and they would never allow that the title of a man's admissability to the Lord's table was to be judged by the civil magistrate in accordance with the tenor of this list of offences.* The Parliamentarians said to the Divines—give us your advice as to what sins should exclude from the communion, and we will ratify your advice so far as it meets with our approval, and then leave it to the local magistrate to decide on communion claims as on any other matter of civil law. One member of Parliament, in advocating this erastian scheme, took on himself to say, "the civil magistrate is a church officer in every Christian commonwealth. In Scotland, the nobility and gentry live commonly in the country, and so the clergy are moderated as by a scattered parliament." The divines, however, would not yield to the erastian demands of the statesmen, but maintained that the right to judge of the fitness of persons to come to the sacrament belongs to the officers of the Church.† "To these officers," they said, "the keys of the kingdom of heaven are committed, by virtue whereof they have power to shut that kingdom against the impenitent both by the word and cen-

---

* The catalogue of deadly sins drawn up by the Westminster Assembly was very lengthy, and it included "drinking of healths." And apropos of this it may be here stated that in 1646 a list of enormities and corruptions observed to be in the ministry with the remedies thereof, was drawn up in the General Assembly of the Church of Scotland. Among the enormities specified in this list were "dissoluteness in hair and shaking about the knees, tippling and bearing company in untimous drinking in taverns and alehouses." And among the remedies propounded were that "care be had of godly conferences in Presbyteries even in time of their refreshment, and that ministers in all sorts of company labour to be fruitful, as the salt of the earth seasoning them they meet with, not only forbearing to drink healths (Satan's snare leading to excess) but reproving it in others."

† "The Zurichers did by their *civil* law seclude from the sacrament vitious or scandalous persons, and did compel these to communicate who neglected it." Brodie's Diary, p. 94. This was true erastianism.

sures, and to open it unto penitent sinners by the ministry of the gospel and by absolution from censures as occasion shall require." In the end the divines carried their point, and the admission and exclusion of people to and from the communion have been ever since allowed to lie with Kirk Sessions, subject to the directions of the superior courts of the Church. And the terms of admission to the Lord's Table have not been always the same in the Church of Scotland. Three years after the adoption of the Westminster Directory, the General Assembly enacted that all persons must subscribe the Covenant before their first admission to the communion. Hence the argument of the Protesters, that defection from the Covenant excludes from the sacrament. It is stated in the Records of the Presbytery of Ayr, that in November, 1648, the attention of ministers was called to an Act of the Commission of the Kirk, which must have been even more stringent than the Act of Assembly of that year. This Act of Commission was entituled an "Act anent those who suld be debarred from renewing of the Covenant and from the Lord's Supper." And the act seems to have been promptly and lovingly put into execution in Ayrshire, for, at a meeting of Presbytery soon after, the brethren reported the names of those whom they had so debarred. Of course in the year of the engagement at Mauchline Moor, it could not be supposed that there would be in this Parish any outcasts from the covenant. Neither were there, and in this respect Mauchline was honourably distinguished from some other Parishes in Ayrshire. In the Revolution settlement of the Church, the covenants, it is well known, were ignored, and subscription of the covenant was never, after 1690, made in the Church of Scotland a condition of Christian communion.*

---

* The Presbytery of Ayr, in 1648, ordered all subscriptions of the covenant, by

Except during the times of Episcopacy, when a more imposing and ornate ritual was observed, it was always the custom in the Scottish Church for communicants to receive the sacrament at the table, and in a sitting posture. At the Westminster Assembly there was no discussion about posture. Both Presbyterians and Independents held that the bread and wine should be received by the communicants sitting. The discussion between the two parties at Westminster was whether it was necessary or not for communicants to rise out of their seats and take their places at a table. But in earlier times there was a great controversy in Scotland about kneeling at the communion. In 1633 King Charles gave orders that in the Chapel Royal at Holyrood, which was in a manner his own private chapel, all that received the blessed sacrament should receive it kneeling. The King gave warrant also that the Lords of Privy Council, the Lords of Session, the Members of the College of Justice, and others, " be commanded to receive the holy communion * once every year, at the least, in that our Chapel Royal, and kneeling for example sake to the kingdom." What was ordered by the King to be done *for example sake in the Chapel Royal*, was of course done in many other places,† and in some places so much against the

---

malignants, to be *deleted*. Among other subscriptions deleted by the Presbytery was that of Lord Montgomerie. The Commission of Assembly, however, to whom the case was referred, advised his subscription to be received anew.

* Baillie, i., 423.

† In 1619 also the kneeling posture was enjoined, but to no purpose. "Those that kneeled, says Calderwood, were of the poorer sort, and kneeled more for aw nor for devotion, or were members of the Secret Council or of the College of Justice. Cold and graceless were the communions, and few were the communicants," Vol. VII., 359. John Livingstone states that when he was at Glasgow College in 1619 or 1620, Law, the Bishop of Glasgow, urged all the people at the communion to fall down and kneel. "Some did so, but we (Livingstone and another student) sat still. Law came to us and commanded us to kneel or depart. Somewhat I spoke to him that there was no warrant for kneeling. He caused some of the people about us to rise, that we might remove, which we did."

mind of the people, that the communions were deserted.* In
other places the innovation was approved. Spalding states
that when the communion was celebrated at Aberdeen by
Mr. Cant in 1642 the elements were received by the communicants "sitting at the table bot not kneilling as wes usit befoir,
whereat sindrie people murmurit and grudgit but could not
mend it." At the time when the communion was received
by the people kneeling the elements were delivered by the
minister personally to each communicant. This had a priestly
look which some of the self-assertive Presbyterians of Scotland
did not like. In 1620, therefore, the citizens of Edinburgh, on
the morning of the communion, desired that communicants
might be suffered to distribute the elements among themselves.
That, said the ministers, is what we are not at liberty to allow.
Then followed a scene which for irreverent humour and sacerdo-
tal bewilderment could not easily be matched out of Scotland.
The minister "gave the thesaurer a shaive of bread, and the
thesaurer made it to serve other five that were next him. The
minister, perceiving his own error, would have given each of
the five the element of bread again, but they answered they
were already served!" The objection to ministerial distribution,
however, was not shared by every one in Scotland, and after
people got accustomed to it some thought it the more excel-

---

* Some people, says the author of the *Alliance of Divine Offices*, think that
kneeling is too good for the sacrament. " Miserable infatuation. Good God, how
well mayst thou say to these misled souls as Augustine to him that entertained him
meanly,—' I did not think you and I had been so familiar. Blessed Jesus, wert
thou so gracious to us wretches as to leave and bequeath us this mystery of our
eternal redemption, and great charter of all thy benefits, and shall we dare to
receive it in any other than the lowest and humblest posture. . . . . .
The danger of reverting to Popish idolatry is altogether vain, but the danger of
apostatising from Christ is very great, and no way sooner occasioned than by a
sitting posture, it being observed by the Popish church that the men who lapsed
there into the Arian heresie were all such as addicted themselves to that posture at
the communion,'" page 219.

lent way. In 1641 Spalding was horrified when, after seeing the minister give the bread to one or two on each side, he saw " the bassein and breid lifted by ane elder, and ilk man tak his sacrament with his own hand. Not done as wes befoir," exclaimed the simple citizen, " for the minister gave ilk person communicating the blessed sacrament out of his own hand, and to ilk person the coup."

One of the graceless practices of the Independents, complained of by Baillie in 1644, was the "carrying of the elements to all in their seats athort the church." This was a practice that the Independents inherited from the Brownists. These were in the way of sending the elements from the pulpit by the hand of the deacon to all the congregation sitting up and down the church in their usual respective places. But Baillie's horror at the uncouth practice was mild compared with that of more ritualistic men. To him it seemed inorderly, to them it was worse. It was unchurchly, and contrary to the sacred usages of antiquity. "Certain it is," says our old author (of the *Alliance of Divine Offices*), "that the priest in primitive times did not run ambling with the elements up and down from man to man, but that the communicants came to him." The Service Book which Charles the First attempted to thrust on the Church in 1637, directed that the communion should be received kneeling. The words of the rubric on this point are,—" The Bishop, if he be present, or else the Presbyter that celebrateth, shall first* receive the communion in both kinds himself, and next deliver it to other Bishops, Presbyters, and Deacons (if any be there

---

* The old approved custom among Presbyterians, as well as Episcopalians, was for the minister to take and eat of the bread himself before distributing it to others, and to drink of the cup also before he handed it to the person next him, A minister in the south-east of Scotland tells me that the old custom is still the common practice in his district. It is certainly founded on good Scriptural authority, " He took the cup *when he had supped,* saying," &c.

present), that they may help him that celebrateth, and after to the people in due order, all humbly kneeling." In 1638, when the people of Scotland had risen up in a body, and by public voice had put down the Erastian Episcopacy of Charles and Laud, we find it gratefully and pathetically minuted by the Kirk Session of St. Andrews, that "the holie communion was celebrate with great solemnity *in the old fashion, sitting.* My old Lady Marquess of Hamilton, my Lord Lindsay, and sundrie uthers Barons, ladyies, and gentlemen, strangers, being present thereat."*

A question has been raised whether the present or rather the late practice of having a host of neighbouring ministers to assist at communions is of ancient standing. The minutes of the Kirk Session of Canongate shew that in 1566 the communion was administered according to the order, namely, once at four in the morning, and a second time at nine, that eleven hundred persons or thereby communicated, and that both of the services were given by the minister himself. In later times, when tables multiplied, it continued common, some people say, for ministers to celebrate the communion without assistance.

In support of this statement the instance has been adduced of old Carstairs, the father of the Principal, doing the whole work of a communion Sabbath himself, and addressing as many as fifteen tables. That, however, was a very special occasion, and was no illustration of common practice. The story is told by Wodrow, and is to the effect that Carstairs, with some other preachers, was engaged to assist at the sacrament at Calder. The minister of Calder took unwell on the Sunday morning, and Carstairs was requested to take the minister's place and give the action sermon. This Carstairs did, and he likewise addressed

---

* Lee, i., p. 400.

the first table; and with so much power and unction did he speak, that the other preachers were overawed and could not be induced to undertake their parts in the service. The consequence was, that Carstairs had to serve all the tables; " I know not, says Wodrow, whether ten, twelve, or sixteen," but the effort was *at the time reckoned prodigious*, and it was long before Carstairs recovered from the fatigue. It is certain that on the famous Monday after the communion at Mauchline in 1648, there were seven ministers at the political gathering * which Middleton dispersed. It may be presumed that these or most of these ministers were at Mauchline ostensibly for the purpose of assisting in the communion service, more especially as some hundreds of men all the way from Clydesdale had come to communicate before rising in rebellion. Not only, therefore, were there crowds of people at communions as early as 1648 and many years earlier, but there were sometimes also great bevies of ministers taking part in the services. On the other hand the tenor of several appointments by the Presbytery of Ayr in 1642 rather indicates that, while communions were then extended over several days, little or no ministerial help was usually required on the sacrament Sunday.

The addresses at the table were by Act of Assembly, 1645, directed to be brief, but it is difficult to say what *brief* was understood to be. In the newspaper account of an old centenarian, who died at Brechin last year, it is stated that in her youth (about the year 1800), sacramental services in small country Parishes like Dreghorn lasted from ten in the morning till five in the afternoon, and that there were a dozen or more tables served. According to that statement, the filling and serving of each table would occupy about twenty-five minutes, and as

---

* Baillie, III., p. 48 and 53.

tables were small, the addresses before and after communion would average in length about eight or ten minutes.* The words of the Act, 1645, anent the addressing of tables (and that Act has not been superseded by any more recent enactment), are, that "there be no reading in the time of communicating, but the minister making a short exhortation at every table, there be silence thereafter during the time of the communicants' receiving, except only when the minister expresseth some few short sentences suitable to the present condition of the communicants." Bishop Sage complains of this act as a grievous innovation, both in respect of its prohibition of reading during the time of communicating, and in respect of its institution of table addresses. "In the time of celebration," he says, "the Reformers had no exhortation at all, neither extempore nor premeditated. But the First Book of Discipline appointed thus —"during the action we think it necessary that some comfortable places of Scripture be read. . . This," he adds, "continued the custom of the whole Church for more than eighty years after the Reformation, without any attempt to innovate till the often mentioned Assembly, 1645."†

The records of this parish contain no entries that either serve to illustrate or are explained by any of the old laws and customs I have described, regarding the mode of administering

---

* Many of the table addresses of both the seventeenth and eighteenth century that are in print, are brief, in the modern sense of the term, some of them indeed very brief. Many of these addresses too, such as those of John Welsh of Irongray, are printed as if the address before and after serving the elements were one unbroken discourse. The words of distribution appear in the middle of the address. In the volumes of sermons published by Mr. Dun of Auchinleck, in 1790, there are one or two samples of table addresses printed in this form, and after the words of distribution, the following instructive note is added to shew the common custom of ministers at that date :—"Here a pause for a considerable time that communicants may devote themselves to God, etc. . . . Many ministers choose to speak on, but don't they rather disturb than assist?"

† Sage's Fundamental Charter, 365.

the communion. The older records of the parish generally say little more about the communion than that it was administered on such and such a day. What amount of assistance the minister had is rarely if ever mentioned. But in a little memorandum book of a session clerk, which happens still to be in existence, there are several entries that show with what amount of oratorical parade the sacrament was administered in the beginning of the present century, and we may safely say during the greater part of last century.* In the year 1801 the sacramental fast was held on Thursday the 6th August, and on that day Mr. M'Clatchie (then a probationer, and afterwards minister of St. Giles, Edinburgh), preached forenoon and afternoon. On Saturday there were two preparation sermons preached, one in the forenoon by Mr. Moody of Riccarton, and one in the afternoon by Mr. Lawrie of Loudoun. On Sabbath, the day of communion, Mr. Reid, the minister of the parish, preached the action sermon and served the first table. The second table was addressed by Mr. Smith of Galston, the third by Mr. Lawrie, the fourth by Mr. Gordon of Sorn, the fifth by Mr. Ritchie of Tarbolton, the sixth by Mr. Moody and the seventh by Mr. Smith, who preached the thanksgiving sermon in the evening. And all the while that these table services were going on sermons were being thundered from a tent in the churchyard to such as were not communicating. On the Monday the preaching was resumed, and sermons were preached in the forenoon and afternoon by Messrs. Ritchie and Gordon respectively. It will be seen that including the parish minister there were six ministers occupied in the communion service on Sabbath, and that besides a table address (and in the case of

---

* Burns, in his account of the Holy Fair, refers to five different sermons preached in the tent by five different ministers, and seems to say that these were not all.

some, a sermon in the tent), each had a sermon to deliver in the church on one or other of the preaching days. Whether in the time of Mr. Auld there was or was not a still greater number of ministers taking part in the communion service I am unable to say, but it is certain that in Mr. Auld's time there were more than twice as many tables as there were in 1801.

The General Assembly never encouraged but rather discouraged the gathering of crowds from neighbouring Parishes at communions, and the employment of a host of ministers to assist in communion services. Bishop Sage would have it considered a part of Presbyterian polity, that great crowds be collected at communions, and he would have that polity considered a grave scandal on the Presbyterian Church. A great parade, he says, the Presbyterians must have at their communions. "Though there are but some scores, or at most but some hundreds to communicate, yet the communion is not solemn enough, there's a cloud upon the minister's reputation, something or other is wrong, if there are not some thousands of spectators." And he adds, "who knows not that hundreds, generally strangers to one another, who have no sense of, no concern for, no care about serious religion may meet on such occasions for novelty, for curiosity, for intrigues not to be named, for a thousand such sinister ends." These remarkable words were written by a bishop of the Scotch Episcopal Church ninety years before the famous satire of Burns was composed, and yet they bear the same testimony as Burns did to the abuses of communions. But before blaming the Church, as the Bishop does, for encouraging communion crowds, we must enquire a little into the facts of the case. The time when communion crowds began was during the establishment of Episcopacy, before 1638. The communion was then given in many places in a ritualistic way which the people disliked, and the malcontents made a practice of going at communion seasons to other Parishes where the ordinance was administered in a plain manner which was more to their mind. The Episcopalians, therefore, by their high-handed procedure, were the persons mainly responsible for the introduction of communion crowds. They forced people to have inter-communion out of their own Parishes.* What began under Episcopacy in 1619 was, it may be admitted, carried much farther under Presbytery in 1651, when the great split took place in the Church, and Protesters would have no intercourse with Resolutioners.† The Protesters gathered from far and near to their own communions, as if these solemnities were meant for demonstration. And so also in the times of the persecution, birds of a feather flocked together. The true blues mustered in full force at hillside communions. There was a spiritual exhilaration too, if not a spiritual benefit of more lasting kind derived from these great confluences. They accordingly became popular, and tended as time went on to increase. But the Church came to see very early that there were great evils as well as some, or perhaps much, good in the system, and she did what she could to repress these evils and introduce a more excellent way. She can hardly be said, therefore, to have been responsible, however much so some of her ministers may have been, for the state of matters that Sage denounced and Burns ridiculed. In 1701, a little after the time when Sage wrote, the General Assembly passed an Act recommending Presbyteries to take care that the number of ministers serving at communions

---

* In 1634 a Royal Proclamation was issued forbidding this practice. Chambers' Domestic Annals.

† In Galston Records it is minuted that in 1673 "several hunders of tickets ar distribute among strangers with sufficient testimonials from several places."

"be restricted, so that neighbouring churches be not thereby cast desolate on the Lord's day." In 1724 the Assembly further enjoined Presbyteries and Kirk Sessions "to endeavour to reform disorders that sometimes take place at the celebration of the Lord's Supper"; and for this end the Assembly ordered "Presbyteries to take care that on the Lord's Day, upon which the sacrament is to be administered in any Congregation, the neighbouring Congregations be supplied with sermon;" and likewise ordered "ministers on the preparation day to give public warning that such as are guilty of disorder shall be censured according to the degree of the offence." Wodrow, who was minister at Eastwood, near Glasgow, writes in regard to his own communions about 1729 or 1730,—"We have many irregularities in the celebration of that holy ordinance that cannot yet be rectified, at least, not soon, especially here. I lie in the neighbourhood of the city of Glasgow, and we have confluences and multitudes. Perhaps I may have about 300 of my own charge who are allowed to partake, and yet we will have a thousand, sometimes eleven or twelve hundred at our tables. I am obliged to preach in the fields a Sabbath or more sometimes, before our sacrament, and a Sabbath after it. We must bear what we cannot help, and amidst our irregularities we want not a mixture of good tokens." This was the way in which good and godly ministers, so far back as 1729, lamented the confluences that took place at communions. As the communions in Mauchline Parish a hundred years ago have unfortunately acquired an immortal notoriety, and will for ever, by the readers of Scottish literature, be associated with grave scandals,[*] either real or fictitious, some

---

[*] In a note to one of his printed sermons (1790), Mr. Dun of Auchinleck complains of the way in which the solemnities of the great communions in Scotland were caricatured and misrepresented by hostile critics. The following is what he

people will naturally be curious to know whether any disorders at these communions are noticed in the Session Records, and whether any censures for such disorders were ever inflicted. I am happy to say that there are not many such cases on record in the Session books, but I would suppose that if cases of drunkenness and other sins occurred at the communion the parties guilty of such misconduct would generally not be parishioners, but strangers, who had come, as Bishop Sage says, for novelty, curiosity, and intrigues. There are, however, one or two cases of communion scandal recorded in the Session minutes. In 1774, a villager was reported to have been seen the worse of drink on the night of the Monday after the communion, and in his drunkenness to have committed outrages that alarmed sundry respectable families. In 1775 three men minuted as "belonging to —— parish," which implies that it was not Mauchline parish, were reported to the Session as having been guilty of a riot on the night of the Monday of the sacrament. In 1780 a case came before the Session, of which it is needless to say more than that it is minuted "the confession answered to the Monday of the sacrament," the date at which the guilt was alleged to have been contracted. In the same year it is recorded that the Session were informed that a certain parish-

---

says about Burns,—"A late author, indeed, who has abused his God and his King, has ridiculed the communion in the Parish where he lived, under the sarcasm of a holy fair. He pretends to be only a ploughman, though he mixes Latin with his mixture of English and Scottish, and is not like 'thresher Dick who kept at flail.'" Mr. Dun did not stick to his own flail either, for immediately under this note—in a volume of sermons be it remembered—he enters the lists against Burns in the field of poetry, and prints a squib of his own under the title of "The Deil's address to his verra freen, Robin Burns." The Rev. Hamilton Paul, who also, like Mr. Dun, was a Parish minister, calls the Holy Fair a delightful satire, and says that it contains "not a single sneer at the solemnity itself."

ioner, whose name is given, was seen the worse of drink on the Monday of the sacrament, in both of the years 1779 and 1780, notwithstanding that he had been a communicant in both years. These are all the cases of disorder and scandal at communion times that I have found in the Parish records, and although it is to be lamented that there should have been two or three persons in one year that so far forgot themselves at a season of special solemnity, as to merit censure, it may yet be said, what are these among so many as the crowd comprised. It must be admitted, however, that there were scenes at these great communions that although unrecorded in Session Records were a scandal to religion. An old parishioner, who still lives amongst us, tells me that he remembers having seen at the Craigie sacrament a band of Kilmarnock "lads"* passing from the public house through the churchyard when the solemnities were proceeding, and pitching with drunken jeers the remains of their luncheon at the preacher in the tent. Many similar or even worse stories about these old communions could doubtless also be gathered from equally good authority. And yet there was a wonderful solemnity and refreshing from the Lord about these vast gatherings. People that came to them with a desire to be benefited seldom went away disappointed. They were worked up to a higher state of feeling than usual, and that elevation of spirit was a substantial boon to them. But the system was too open to gross abuse for any one to lament its discontinuance.

Notwithstanding all that the Church in her General Assemblies said, crowds did repair to communions from other parishes. Even Acts of Assembly, if they did not give an implied sanc-

---

* "Batch o' Wabster lads blackguarding frae Kilmarnock."—Holy Fair.

tion to such promiscuous gatherings, at least made provision for their spiritual entertainment. In the Act 1645, so often referred to, it is said that "when the parochiners are so numerous that their parish kirk* cannot contain them the brother who assists the minister of the paroch may be ready if need be to give a word of exhortation in some convenient place, appointed for that purpose, to those of the paroch who that day are not to communicate, which must not be begun until the sermon delivered in the kirk be concluded." It was assumed in this act that at communions the minister would have a brother assisting him. It might have been presumed, therefore, that a neighbouring congregation would be left without a service at home. It was anticipated that there might be more people present than the church could hold, and arrangements were made for giving an out-door service to such as could not find accommodation inside the church. Besides a church, therefore, every parish required a tent. This tent was not like the so-called gospel tent which some zealous brethren are in the way of pitching in benighted districts now-a-days. It was not a tabernacle of canvas for sheltering the worshippers, but a moveable pulpit made of wood for the preacher to stand in. From an early period there was such a tent in Mauchline. How early the records do not indicate, but it was so early that in 1770 the tent had fallen to pieces with age, and its "remains," so says the minute of Session, were ordered to be rouped as soon as convenient. Whether a new tent was procured in 1770 is not said, but if one was procured then, it must have been like the

---

* This was not uncommon, for churches were as a rule very small, and the number of communicants bore a large proportion to the entire population. It is stated in the records of the Presbytery of Ayr that in 1642 the number of communicants in the parish of Ochiltree was 1200, that the number in Cumnock was 1600, and that "the kirk cannot contain the half of the communicants."

Publican's Psalm-book, "ill bund," for in 1786 the Session again agreed that another tent should be got ready against the following summer.

Some idea of the size of the crowds that came to the communions at Mauchline may be gathered from the number of persons that are said to have sat down at the table at different dates. We have no account of the numbers that communicated at any one time during the ministry of either Mr. Veitch or Mr. Maitland, but from the year 1750 downwards, the number communicating at each sacrament is pretty regularly given. And that we may see what proportion the number communicating bore to the population of the Parish, I may state here that the earliest census on which much reliance can be placed, was taken in the year 1791. In that year the population of Mauchline was 1800. In the year 1755, a census that, more strictly speaking, was only an estimate of the population of the country, was drawn up by the Rev. Dr Webster of Edinburgh. According to Dr. Webster, the population of Mauchline in 1755 was only 1169. This number may confidently be put down as an under statement, but we have no known data for correcting it. Now in 1750 the number of persons that communicated at Mauchline sacrament was 578, and ten years later it was about the same. In 1771 the number rose to 850, in 1773 to 1000, in 1779 to 1100, in 1780 to 1300, and in the years 1786 and 1788 the number was the highest on record, 1400.* Mr. Auld died in 1791, and the first notice we have of the number of communicants at a sacrament after his death was in 1793, and in that year the number had dwindled to 700, while in the following year it dwindled still further to 600. In

---

* The Holy Fair was written in 1786.

1805 the number went down to 500, and at that figure it continued a good many years, but in 1819 it declined to 400. By that date customs had changed, and the better way had come in, or was coming in, of people contenting themselves with their own parochial ministrations.

It may be asked how many tables did there use to be at the communions in Mauchline. It happens to be recorded that in 1752 there were "nine tables, wanting five or six persons at the last." In the year 1777, it is stated more expressly in the minutes, that there were "twelve tables and a few, amounting to about 1000." According to this statement, each table would hold about 80 persons. Suppose then that 80 was the number of communicants that each table held in 1788, when there were 1400 communicants, there must that year have been 18 table services. And I may mention that one of the old stories I have heard of the Mauchline communions is that on one occasion a boy, whom I remember as an old man, was present at the sacrament, and heard the beadle call to the preacher in the tent to "fire away, for the 17th table was filling, and there was no end to the work." Bishop Burnet says that in the days of the Protesters, communion services sometimes lasted twelve hours. It is difficult to see how the services at the Mauchline communions, in the latter days of Mr. Auld's ministry, could have been concluded in less than nine hours, and if table addresses were as prolix then as they were fifty years later, it may have taken an hour or two longer to get over the work. Wodrow states that at communions in his day it was sometimes late in the evening when the service ended.

I have just to add that the date of the communion—the month, and week of the month, in which the communion was celebrated—in this parish, has been frequently changed. It rests with Kirk Sessions to appoint the ministration of the sacrament at whatever date they think convenient In 1674 the communion was held on the 12th July, in 1691 on the 9th August, in 1680 on the 17th October, in 1706 on the second Sabbath of June, in 1751 on the 20th October, in 1786 on the 13th August. For a long time the communion continued to be held on the second Sunday of August, but in 1812 it was changed to the third Sabbath of June, and a few years later to the fourth Sabbath of June.

In the year 1711 the General Assembly "considering that in some places the sacrament of the Lord's Supper is administered only in the summer season, wherethrough people are deprived of the benefit of that holy ordinance during the rest of the year, did therefore recommend to Presbyteries to do what they could to get it so ordered that the Lord's Supper might be administered in their bounds through the several months of the year." Two years previously there had been discussed in the Presbytery of Ayr an overture to the same effect, with a recommendation that parishes having "clachans or touns at or near their church should have the communion in the winter season." In 1724 a scheme was drawn up by the Presbytery, appointing the sacrament to be administered at Ayr and Mauchline in January; at Monkton, Dalrymple, and Stair in April; at Dailly, Auchinleck, Coylton, and Craigie, in May; at Barr, Dalmellington, Riccarton, Ochiltree and Tarbolton, in June; at Galston, Straiton, New Cumnock and Muirkirk in July; at Kirkmichael, Dalgain, Dundonald and Kirkoswald, in August; at Maybole and Symington, in October; and at Cumnock, Girvan and St. Evox, in November. In 1727 all the members of Presbytery reported that they had celebrated the sacrament at or about the time appointed, except Mr. Reid, of St. Evox, "who told he was desirous, but that his Session would not concur with him because they judged it very inconvenient to the people." The Records of Presbytery state that Mr. Reid was excused, and his Session were to be dealt with to comply with the Presbytery's appointment. But it is evident that the Presbytery's scheme was not adhered to for any length of time. Parochial convenience had more sway than Presbyterial orders. The first notice of a sacrament in Mauchline that I have observed in our Session Records subsequent to 1724 is in the register of 1735, and the sacrament that latter year was administered in October, as it was also at Tarbolton, whereas the Mauchline communion should have been held in January, and the Tarbolton communion in June.

LECTURE IV.

CHURCH DISCIPLINE IN OLDEN TIMES.

Institution of Kirk-Sessions—Calderwood's opinion—A Session in Mauchline soon after Reformation—Constitution of Kirk-Sessions—The Moderator—Elders—Their Election and Ordination—Subscription of Confession of Faith—Functions of Kirk Sessions—Discipline—Monk's views and Dr. Hill's statement—Complaints against Sessions for over-rigidness—Sessional inquiries: how instituted—All rumours reported—Libellers and consignations—Special districts for elders—Perambulations—Testimonials—Evidence taken—Oath of Purgation—Session's watchfulness over their own Members—Privy censures—Presbyterial visitations.

BEFORE proceeding to describe the way in which Kirk Sessions in former times exercised their functions, it will be proper to state a few particulars regarding their institution and constitution.

The question, when were Kirk Sessions instituted as courts in the Church of Scotland, is one that has received different answers from different writers. It is quite certain that from the date of the Reformation there were in most parishes what might be termed ecclesiastical boards, which consisted of the minister and a number of elders, and that these ecclesiastical boards were to all practical intents and purposes Kirk Sessions, and were so designated. In the very year of the Reformation, John Knox and others drew up a form of ecclesiastical policy for Parliament to establish; and in this form of policy, which is commonly called the First Book of Discipline, elders are referred to as office-bearers in the Church, and it is said that their office is "to assist the ministers in all publicke affairs of the Kirk." Then in 1592, when the Presbyterian government was established in the Church by Act of Parliament, Kirk

Sessions were invested by the civil power with certain privileges and authorities. The words of the Act are, " Anent particulare kirkis. Gif they be lauchfully rewlit be sufficiente ministeris and sessioun, they haif power and jurisdiction in their awin congregation in materis ecclesiasticall." And that this really meant that Kirk Sessions were to be regarded as separate Church courts, is made evident by the tenor of the Act 1690, for settling Presbyterian Church government anew, after it had been twice over subverted by Prelacy. In this Act of 1690 the government of the Church, as ratified and established in the former Act of 1592, is expressly declared to be "by Kirk Sessions, Presbyteries, Provincial Synods, and General Assemblies."

But a strange incident occurred at the Westminster Assembly in the end of 1643, or the beginning of 1644. The Scots Commissioners at that Assembly drew up a paper wherein they "asserted a congregationall eldership for governing the private affairs of the congregation." Such an eldership they evidently supposed, and never imagined that any one could doubt the fact, was part of the established order in the Church of Scotland. They maintained also that it was founded on Scripture. But when Calderwood the historian, who was reckoned a great authority on questions in ecclesiastical law, although a cranky man, and singular in many of his opinions, heard of this Act of the Commissioners, he wrote them a letter, in which he sharply censured their conduct. " Our books of discipline," he said, "admit of no Presbyterie or Eldership but one ;" and an acknowledgment of Congregational Eldership, he added, will be a great step towards Independency or Congregationalism, as opposed to Presbyterianism.* Baillie, who records this in-

---

* It is very strange that Calderwood, in his own history, should speak of the *Session* or consistorie of the Kirk of Edinburgh. And this he does in quoting the

cident, states that Henderson felt the force of Calderwood's criticism, and that all the Commissioners at Westminster were in a peck of troubles about it. On the ground of this letter of Calderwood's, some subsequent historians maintain that it is uncertain whether Kirk Sessions in the Church of Scotland were originally distinct and constituted courts, or only committees of Presbyteries.

Calderwood's opinion is very strange in many ways. It is at variance with the terms of the Act of Parliament 1592, and it was at variance with the commonly received opinion in the Church at the date of his writing. But it is particularly strange in this respect, that only three years before he wrote his letter the Parliament of Scotland had passed an Act ratifying all the conclusions of the famous Assembly of 1639—granting, in short, to the Covenanters of that period every thing they desired—and in that Act it was expressly provided that not only should General Assemblies be kept yearly, but " also that Kirk Sessions . . . be constitute and observed according to the order of this kirke." This was an Act passed with the view of satisfying the Covenanters in every point, and yet Calderwood would fain have made the Covenanters quarrel with it.

The probable explanation of Calderwood's argument is this. Just as the Covenanters of 1638 maintained that the Book of Canons and Service Book thrust on the Church by the King and his Council were not lawfully imposed, because they were imposed without the consent, approval, or antecedent judgment of the Church, so in the Acts of Parliament

---

terms of an appointment made by the General Assembly in 1562.—Vol. II., 207. In 1573 John Row was complained of to the Assembly for solemnising a band of matrimony irregularly, and he replied that "he did nothing but (without) the command of the *Session of his Kirk* and my Lord Ruthven, a special elder of the said kirk." Book of Universal Kirk, 134.

establishing Presbytery, nothing was to be held as part of the Church's constitution, if it had not been previously declared so by the Church herself. The measure of the Church's liberty might be defined by Act of Parliament, and people might, in matters indifferent, comply with ordinances they did not wholly approve; but the constitution of the Church was to be ascertained from the acts and declarations of her own Assemblies, and from these alone. Calderwood, therefore, I suppose, argued, that if you want to find out the Church's doctrine in regard to questions of discipline and government, you must look neither at the terms of Acts of Parliament which she submits to as the best she can get, nor at her custom and practice based on laws she had no hand in making, but at the words of her own authorised documents. And in the book of policy known as the Second Book of Discipline, which was not only drawn up, as Knox's book was, by a few individuals, but was passed by the General Assembly, there are, as Calderwood states, only four recognised courts in the Church; and although the fundamental court is so vaguely defined that it looks nearly as like a Kirk Session as a Presbytery, it was, nevertheless, in respect of its functions, a Presbytery and not a Kirk Session. But as was said before, Kirk Sessions were, notwithstanding Calderwood's opinion, popularly considered from the earliest times, and were in 1592 declared by Act of Parliament to be courts of the Church.*

But something more may be gathered from Calderwood's letter. That letter shows unmistakeably that the Covenanters,

---

* The Second Book of Discipline seems to say that the office-bearers of a *single* kirk or congregation *may* be constituted a particular eldership or separate presbytery, but that, as a rule, there should be several kirks included in a Presbytery. The Act of Parliament 1592, on the other hand, seems to give congregational jurisdiction to particular kirks *within* Presbyteries, when these kirks are lawfully ruled by ministers and Sessions. Regarding erection of Presbyteries see Appendix A,

from 1638 to 1651, were not very anxious about the extension of popular rights and privileges in the Church. They were zealous against Erastianism and Episcopacy,—they impugned the authority in the Church of Kings and Parliaments, Bishops and Lay Patrons,—but it was not with the view of setting the Church on a popular basis. They wanted all ecclesiastical power conferred not on the Church members, but on the Church officers. They were furious in their invectives against Popery, but their ecclesiastical polity was to a large extent founded upon the Popish system. With them Presbyter was Priest writ large, and Calderwood feared that enormous evils—all the evils of Congregationalism—would result from the institution of Kirk Sessions as Parochial Courts of the Church. The Westminster Assembly did not concur in Calderwood's views. The conclusion to which it came was that "for officers in a single congregation, there ought to be one at the least both to labour in the word and doctrine and to rule; it is requisite also that there should be others to join in the government: and that these officers are to meet together at convenient and set times for the well ordering of the affairs of the congregation, each according to his office."

The Records of the General Assembly shew that from a date close to the Reformation there were Elders as well as a Minister at Mauchline. In 1567 "the minister and ane part of the elders of the Kirk of Machlin" gave in a complaint to the General Assembly. This complaint, which is interesting as an illustration of the state of ecclesiastical law at the time, set forth that whereas "the brethren of the Kirk of Machlin had be the just law of God pronounced the sentence of excommunication against John Spottswood of Foulde (or Fowler), sometyme an elder of the said Kirk, for the horrible crime of adultery committed be him. Notheless Sir William Hamilton of Sanquhair, Knight, now ane elder of the said Kirk, plainly maintaineth the said John in his house, to the great sclander and offence of God his law." The outcome of this complaint was that the Assembly "ordained ane letter to be sent to the said Sir William," requiring him in the name of the eternal God, and as he looked to reign with Jesus Christ for ever, to remove from his society that wicked person, John Spottiswoode, otherwise the censures of the kirk would be used "alsweel against the maintainer as the committer of manifest crymes."

With these remarks on the institution of Kirk Sessions in the Church of Scotland, I pass on now to speak of the constitution of Kirk Sessions long ago. At present Kirk Sessions are composed of a minister and a quorum of ruling elders.

There must be a minister present at all meetings of Kirk Sessions. This minister (if there be only one present) acts as moderator, and both opens and closes the meeting with prayer. If at any alleged meeting of Kirk Session the minister, or an authorised ministerial substitute, did not preside, the alleged meeting would be declared no meeting, and all its acts would be pronounced null and void. It would seem, however, that this rule about a minister's sitting as moderator in all meetings of Kirk Session, was not in the first period of the Church of Scotland's history universally observed. Wodrow states with surprise that on looking over the Session Records of Ayr he found that in Mr. Welsh's time, when the minister was absent, an elder, and particularly one called MacKerrell, was designated moderator.* In reality there was not cause for very great

---

* There was nothing unprecedented in this matter which so surprised Wodrow. The like occurred at later periods, On the 8th March, 1658, the Kirk Session

surprise at this circumstance. Although, as the Act of Assembly 1638 implies, it was the ancient and well understood practice in the Church for ministers to moderate their Sessions, yet all that is said on the subject in the Westminster Form of Church Government, approved by the General Assembly in 1645, is that " it is most expedient that in these meetings (of Kirk Session) one whose office is to labour in the word and doctrine do moderate in their proceedings." It is not said to be requisite, but only expedient, that a minister should preside at meetings of Kirk Session. In the year 1600 a schoolmaster was elected moderator, and sat as moderator of the Presbytery of Glasgow ; and it is well known that George Buchanan, the famous scholar, who was neither a pastor nor doctor, once sat as moderator in the General Assembly.* In the Records of Mauchline Kirk Session there is no minute to show that any meeting of Session was ever formally constituted with prayer by an elder ; but there are several minutes of Session so worded as to lead one to think that the elders occasionally met as a Session in the minister's absence, and transacted pieces of business that did not involve a judicial deliverance.

The Kirk Session is made up chiefly of " such as are com-

---

of Aberdeen minuted that " in respect of Mr. Andro Cant, Moderator, his long sickness and infirmity, they did appoint George Meldrum, one of their number, Moderator, till it should please God to enable the said Mr. Andro to moderate himself." And this George Meldrum was not the person of that name who was at that time a regent in the University, and shortly afterwards one of the Ministers of Aberdeen ; for on the Session's election of this regent Meldrum, in December, 1658, to be one of the city ministers, "George Meldrum, one of their number (was appointed) to acquaint the said Mr. George with the said call, etc."

* Originally there was no Moderator in even the General Assembly. The first appointment of Moderator in the Assembly was in 1563, and the minute of Assembly on the subject was as follows,—" It was proposed be the haill Assemblie that ane Moderator should be appointed for avoiding confusion in reasoning, but that every brother should speak in his own roome."

monly callit elders."* But the word elder needs to be explained. In the Church of Scotland elders and presbyters mean the same thing.† Elder is just the English word for presbyter, and presbyter is the Greek word for elder. A Presbyterian Church accordingly means a Church that is governed exclusively by presbyters or elders, and in which there is no prelacy or prelation or precedence of one presbyter over another of the same kind. All the courts of the Church might with perfect propriety be called either Presbyteries or Elderships. The General Assembly might be called the general or "haill" Presbytery of the Church, the Synods might be called Provincial Presbyteries. Presbyteries

---

* This phrase is of very old standing. It occurs in a list of articles read and allowed by the Assembly as meet to be proponed in the year 1582. A phrase very like it occurs also in the Westminster Form of Church Government.

† It is only fair to say that while this statement undoubtedly represents what was the doctrine of the Church of Scotland regarding elders and presbyters at one period, it is declared by some eminent authorities to be not the Church's doctrine now. Principal Campbell says, "We reject the theory that the lay rulers of the Church are in the proper sense presbyters or elders." He adds that in the Westminster Assembly a proposition was brought forward that "there be other *presbyters* who especially apply themselves to ruling, etc.," but that the Grand Committee excluded the word presbyters, and even the word elders, and said, "*some others besides* ministers." He says further that when the question about naming church governors came up for decision in the Assembly, "whether to call them ruling elders or no," it was at last determined to adopt the phrase "such as in the Reformed Churches are commonly called elders." This proposition did not satisfy Gillespie, the chief exponent of the views of the Church of Scotland, who moved, but without success, that the Assembly itself call them ruling elders. It is plain that Gillespie's motion indicated the views that prevailed north of the Tweed, and the adoption of the Westminster generalities does not imply repudiation of the old historical doctrine of the Church. Dr. Sprott says, "The Westminster Assembly definitely rejected what is called the presbyter theory of the office, and regarded them (the elders) merely as laymen representing the laity in the government of the Church." There is not a word in the Westminster Form of Church government about the elders "*representing* the laity," or about their election by the laity as representatives. Their mode of appointment, their ordination, and their usual designation, support the presbyter, and militate against the representative theory.

used to be called sometimes the particular Elderships, and sometimes the classical Assemblies,* and Kirk Sessions might be called the Parochial Presbyteries: because, as has been said, each of these Courts is composed exclusively of Presbyters, or, what is the same thing, of Elders.† But there are two kinds of Elders in the Church of Scotland. There are those that not only exercise authority and take part in government, but labour in word and doctrine. These are the Ministers or Pastors, and the Doctors of Divinity. The other class of Elders have no license to preach, or administer sacraments or solemnise marriages. Their office is simply to rule, and for that reason they are called ruling Elders. There is a common notion, however, that the ruling Elder is some specially important personage in the Kirk Session,—some one that in virtue of higher rank, special office, or commanding influence, is exalted over the other Elders. This is not the case. All Elders are ruling Elders. Ministers, too, are ruling Elders, but they are something more. They are Elders that both rule and preach. And yet although these facts are as plain as the Shorter Catechism to every person that has given the least attention to the constitution of the Church, they have

---

* See Appendix A.

† In the General Assembly the proportion of ministers to elders is as three to two or thereabouts. In Synods and Presbyteries the number of elders is nominally the same, or nearly the same as the number of ministers. But it was otherwise once. In 1582 the General Assembly declared that "the number of such as are associat to the Elderschip (Presbytery), for discipline and correction of manners, that are not Pastors nor Doctors, who travelleth not in the word, be not in equal number with uthers but fewer—the proportion as the necessity of the Elderschip craves." The same Assembly declared also that the attendance of ruling Elders at Presbyteries was not to be very imperative. "Concerning such elders as verses not in the word," the Assembly said, "thair resort to the Presbytrie shall be no farther straitit but as the weightinesse and occasion, upon intimation and advertisement made be the Pastors and Doctors, shall require, at quhilk time they shall give their godly concurrence."

not always been understood by Church officials. In the records of this Parish the Elder appointed to represent the Session in the Presbytery and Synod is more than once designated the ruling elder. On the 21st Sept., 1691, for instance, it is minuted that "Kingincleugh is chosen by the Session to be ruling elder for half ane year ensuing," and on the 10th July, 1692, it is minuted that "the vote of the session this day appoints Ballochmyle to be ruling elder until the next Synod." And the use of this peculiar phraseology was not confined to the Kirk Session of Mauchline. In the Session Records of Rothesay it is stated that in 1658 one of the members of Session was "chosen ruling elder for the next Presbytery." Occasionally, too, one person was chosen by the Session of Rothesay to be ruling elder for the Presbytery, and a different person to be ruling elder for the Synod.*

At one period ruling elders were elected annually, and held their office for only one year. In the First Book of Discipline, compiled by Knox and others, it is said that the election of elders and deacons ought to be made every year "lest of long continuance of such officers men presume upon the liberty of the Kirk." But it is added that "it hurteth not that one be received in office more years than one, so that he be appointed yearly thereto by common and free election." In the Second Book of Discipline which was agreed to by the General Assembly in 1578, very much under the guidance of Andrew Melville, "the eldership is declared to be a spiritual function as is the ministerie, and Eldars anis lawfully callit to

---

* At one time it was the practice at Galston for the Kirk Session to nominate two or three of their number to keep the Presbytery by turns. In 1639 no fewer than five members of the Galston Session were so appointed commissioners, as they are termed in their minute of appointment, to the Presbytery. Lockhart of Barr for the first two turns, Cessnock for other two turns, and so on.

the office and having gifts of God meit to exercise the same may not leive it again." Since that date elders have, as a rule, held their office for life, or till deposition or resignation. But that rule has not been uniformly observed in Kirk Sessions. In 1653 it was minuted by the Kirk Session of Fenwick that "the whole elders and deacons do resolve and voluntarily condescend to lay down their charges, and to submit *per vices* to be determined by the voices of the remanent eldership whether presently to take up the exercise of their office or to surcease from it." The elders then retired separately from the room, and a vote regarding their continuance in office was taken in their absence. Some were voted to continue, and others were politely informed that they might "surcease, and be eased of that burden for a while, according to their own desire."

In old times the form of ordination of elders was very simple. In 1689 four elders were ordained in Mauchline Church, and the following is the minute of their ordination:— "Being all four present before the Session, and being spoken to by the Minister in presence of the Session, they did all of them accept of the said office, whereupon the Minister took their oaths for their faithfulness in the said office of being elders and deacons in the said Parish, and so did admit and ordain them thereto." It is in like manner minuted in the Galston records for 1639, that certain persons whose names are given, were "admittit and received elders before the Congregation, and sworne to be faithful and upright in their calling." Sometimes, however, in these old days, the ordination service was conducted with considerable pomp and show of solemnity. In the printed records of the Kirk Session of Stirling, it will be found that in 1628,—that is, in a time of Episcopacy—the officer was directed to warn the Elders against Sunday next to sit in the merchants loft, and there to hold up their hands before the congregation, in sign and token of fidelity in the office of the eldership for one year to come. The special engagement entered into by elders at their ordination two hundred years ago, it will thus be seen, was faithfulness in the exercise of their office, and possibly a return to that simplicity would be hailed by many good men at the present day as a movement in the right direction.*

In the year 1690 it was ordained by the General Assembly that "all elders received into communion with us in Church government, be obliged to subscribe their approbation of the Confession of Faith . . . and that this be recommended to the diligence of the several Presbyteries." In 1700 this Act of Assembly was re-enacted with two important additions: first, that both ministers and ruling elders put their signatures likewise to what is commonly known now as the Formula; and secondly, that they do so before next General Assembly. The Presbytery of Ayr were at great pains in 1701 to get the Confession of Faith signed by ministers and schoolmasters, but it was long after that date before much zeal was shewn in urging the subscription on Elders. In 1726 the Presbytery reported some progress in the matter, but the whole progress amounted to this :—that

---

* In 1582 the General Assembly approved the order used at Edinburgh as "ane general order of admissione to the office of Elders." Universal Kirk, p. 250, article 10. This order or form is said to have "consisted of a short address, a prayer to be read, ending with the Lord's Prayer and the rehearsal of the Belief." Spalding writes, in 1644, that "upon Sonday the 11th Aug. oure elderis wes chosin in the Kirk of Sanct Maucher befoir the pulpit. Bot Mr. William Strathauchin, Minister, be himself and by (without) thair knowledge, had drawin up certain articles in wreit quhilk he causit everie Elder to stand up and swear with his hand halden up, . . whiche the Elders and deaconis wondred at, neuer seeing the like befoir. Yit they war, man be man, sworne to the samen, suppose against thair willes, and that the minister and thay both knew thay war unhabill to keip the forsaid aith. Yit suche wes the pryd of oure minister to thrall menis consciences efter his fantasie."

the Kirk Sessions of Straiton and Ayr had signed the Confession, and most of the brethren had elicited from their Sessions a declaration of willingness to sign. It was nevertheless reported to the Presbytery in 1733 that there were still a good many Kirk Sessions that had not signed the Confession, and that this omission did not arise from inattention, but from scruples, is made plain by what occurs in the minutes of Presbytery the following year. It is there stated that the brethren who had not yet prevailed on their Sessions to sign the Confession of Faith, "reported that they are using diligence to gett it done, and that members of Session are perusing it in order to sign it with judgment." It may be mentioned, however, that at that date there was a great commotion over the whole kingdom about the subscription of creeds. There were numbers of people that on principle objected to sign any confession of faith, whether they concurred in its doctrines or not. Wodrow in his letters refers repeatedly, and with much distress, to this movement for "opposing Confessions and exalting reason under pretence of search after truth." In one letter he says there are great divisions in England and Ireland on the subject, but he adds, with obvious gratefulness and satisfaction, that subscription "being required by our reverend Parliament, keeps us (in Scotland) free from these flames." And what Wodrow says about the state of public feeling over the country in 1725, and for years after, will probably explain how it happened that the Church Courts in Scotland were at that time so urgent in requiring from all office-bearers in the Church a subscription of the Formula, while at the same time so many Kirk Sessions were slow and reluctant to subscribe.

The functions of Kirk Sessions were at one time much

more numerous than they are now. In the words of the First Book of Discipline, it fell to Kirk Sessions to take cognisance of all the public affairs of the Kirk within the bounds of their Parishes. They not only administered discipline,—rebuked and censured, kept the keys of the church, admitted into membership and expelled from membership,— but they took charge of the poor, looked after education, and superintended arrangements for burial. In short they were, in a very wide sense of the words, the local authority in their respective Parishes.

In this lecture, and in the next two lectures, I shall confine myself to the subject of Church discipline.

As we all know, there have during different periods been different forms of government in the Church of Scotland. Episcopacy and Presbytery have each been established twice over at least. The discipline of Episcopacy is understood to have differed considerably from that of Presbytery, but even under Presbytery itself discipline has undergone much change.

A very memorable statement was once made by the celebrated General Monk in reference to Church government and Church discipline. This was in the spring of 1660, when people were much concerned lest an attempt should be made to set up Episcopacy again in Scotland. General Monk, who was at the head of affairs in the kingdom, was sounded on the subject, and he wrote to his questioners that he considered Presbytery the best expedient for healing the bleeding divisions of these poor nations, "so it be moderate and tender." And the Presbyterianism that has for long existed in Scotland has been "moderate and tender" both in profession and in practice. The accepted theory of Presbyterian discipline is nowhere better stated than in Dr.

Hill's view of the constitution of the Church of Scotland, which was published about the beginning of the present century. "In that temperate exercise of discipline which the general practice of the Church of Scotland recognises as congenial to her constitution, care is taken," says Dr. Hill, "to avoid every appearance of intermeddling officiously with those matters that fall under the cognisance of the civil magistrate: no solicitude is ever discovered to engage in the investigation of secret wickedness: counsel, private admonition, and reproof, are employed in their proper season, and the *public* censures of the Church are reserved for those scandalous sins which bring reproach upon religion, which give offence to the Christian society, and which cannot be overlooked without the danger of hardening the sinner, of emboldening others to follow his example, and of disturbing and grieving the minds of many worthy Christians."*

---

* The following contrast between Episcopal and Presbyterial discipline will be found in Baillie's Dissuasive, 1645, and may perhaps surprise some people who have been taught to consider Presbytery as tyranny, and Episcopacy as loving kindness. "Episcopal courts were never fitted for the reclaiming of minds,—their prisons, their fines, their pillories, their nose-slittings, their ear-cuttings, their cheek-burnings, did but hold down the flame to break out in season with the greater rage. But the Reformed Presbytery doth proceed in a spiritual method, evidently fitted for the gaining of hearts: they go on with the offending party with all respect and at so much leisure as can be wished, appointing first the fittest Pastors and Elders in the bounds to confer and instruct him in private: if this diligence do not prevaile then they convent him before the consistory of his congregation: there by admonitions, instructions, reproofs, and all the means appointed in the gospel, they deal with him in all gentleness, from weeks to months, from months often times to years, before they come near to any censure, and if so it fall out that his insuperable obstinacy force them to draw out the terrrible sword, their proceeding here also is so exceeding leasurly and full of sensible grief and love to the party, of fear and religion towards God, that it is a singular rarity among them to see any heart so hard as not to be mollified and yeeld before that stroke be given. Excommunications are so strange in all the Reformed Churches, that in a whole Province a man in all his life will scarce be witness to one, and among them who are cut off by that dreadful sword, very few do fall in the State's hand to be troubled with any civil inconvenience," pages 7, 8. The Acts of Assembly, especially one in 1643, anent using civil execution against excommunicate persons, shew that the Church

But while this statement expresses the doctrine on Church discipline that has been held by the Church of Scotland for many, many years, the discipline administered in the Church of Scotland in ancient times was not what most people would consider either tender or moderate. It is proper to remark, however, that people's notions of tenderness are constantly changing, and that in every age there have been men who have maintained that the discipline of the Church in their own day was tender enough. Robert Douglas, one of the Scots Worthies, and one of the worthiest of them all, could not brook the insinuation of Monk that the discipline of the Church of of Scotland had ever been over-rigid, and yet in Douglas's time censures of the severest character were frequently witnessed. And not only was the discipline of the Church at one period what would be counted over-rigid by us in the latter part of the nineteenth century, but it was complained of for being so by people who lived in the time of its rigour. Both Episcopalians and Latitudinarians have uttered loud and fierce denunciations of its severity. One Episcopalian author says, " Every parish had a tyrant who made the greatest lord in the district stoop to his authority. The kirk was the place where he kept his court, the pulpit his throne or tribunal from which he issued his terrible decrees, and twelve or fourteen sour, ignorant enthusiasts, under the name of elders, composed his council. If any, of what quality soever, had the assurance to disobey his orders, the dreadful sentence of excommunication

---

was less mild than Baillie represents her to have been. In the Assembly of 1638 Henderson the Moderator said, "Anent our cariadge toward excommunicat persones I thinke civill affairs may be done with them,—a naturall duetie done to them, but civill dueties verie sparinglie." The theory of the Presbyterians, however, was that spiritual courts should inflict nothing but spiritual censures, and that Magistrates only should inflict fines and imprisonment.

was immediately thundered out against him, his goods and chattels were confiscated and seized,* and he himself being looked upon as actually in the possession of the Devil, and irretrievably doomed to eternal perdition, all that convened with him were in no better esteem." That, of course, is the language of a partisan, and must be largely discounted, but still it shows that Presbyterian church discipline was complained of for over-rigidity. A recently deceased historian, who, in an unfinished work, has left behind him a wonderful monument of his learning and philosophic genius, but who, unfortunately, wrote under the strong bias of irreligious prejudice, and with a bitterness and rancour which strangely belied his professions of ultra-liberalism, says, that "when the Scotch Kirk was at the height of its power, we may search history in vain for any institution which can compete with it, except the Spanish Inquisition." And it may be added that in the letters of Burns the same word inquisition is rightly or wrongly applied to the Kirk Session of Mauchline Parish only a hundred years ago.

It lies beyond the scope of this lecture either to assail or defend old institutions. My object is simply to tell what was done in old times, so that we may see what the character of these times was. It will not be out of place, however, to remark that, as a rule, institutions represent the spirit of the age in which they flourish, and as times change institutions change also. And there is no doubt of the fact that both two hundred

---

* At one time excommunication inferred civil penalties, but by an Act of Parliament passed soon after the Revolution, "no civil penalty such as escheat of movables or caption doth now follow on the sentence, so that the liberty and estate of Church members are not endangered by it, nor do they depend upon churchmen." See Pardovan. One of Wyclif's demands was that imprisonment for excommunication should cease (Green). And Baillie says that even when excommunication inferred civil penalties, very few excommunicated persons fell into the State's hands to be troubled with civil inconveniences,

years ago and one hundred years ago, the manners of people were much ruder than they are now. Certain virtues may have been more conspicuous than they are now, but there was also a much greater amount of coarseness prevalent. More rigid methods of discipline accordingly were needed to deal with the iniquities that abounded. Gentle admonition touches only gentle minds, and where there is a hard hide there needs to be a sharp censure. It must be remembered, too, that in olden times far less was done than is now, by the civil authorities, to restrain and prevent disorder. The Church, among other good offices, was expected to save the nation police rates. She had not only to shew men what is good, but she had to keep down the unruly, and to bring the thoughts of people's hearts into subjection to the laws of Christian duty. And whatever the Church may be or may do, whether she is tender or rigid, whether she punishes or passes over transgressions, she will always have enemies and detractors to speak evil of her procedure. When her discipline was strict she was called intolerant and tyrannical, now that her discipline is milder she is said to have lost her power and influence, and is blamed for leaving the masses to perish in brutality and atheism. There is no form of action on the part of the Church that will stop the mouths of gainsayers. All that the Church in her discipline can do is to seek men's good in the way that experience shews to be most practicable.

I have used the word inquisition in reference to Kirk Sessions, or at least I have quoted that word as having been applied to Kirk Sessions by both an historian and a poet. Strictly speaking, inquisition means enquiry and investigation, and no one will deny that Kirk Sessions long ago were, and perhaps they still are, courts of enquiry. They enquired into all migrations into and out of the parish—into the ecclesiastical profession of all parishioners—and into all famas affecting the moral or religious character of the people under their jurisdiction. And what in this lecture I mean to set forth is the mode of inquisition that was adopted long ago by Kirk Sessions in general, and by Mauchline Kirk Session in particular. In next lecture I shall indicate the different kinds of offences that were taken notice of by Kirk Sessions, and in a subsequent lecture describe the censures and penalties that Kirk Sessions inflicted.

How, then, we have to ask, did the Kirk Session conduct its inquiries or inquisitions long ago? It is quite clear that enquiries may be made either in a way that is oppressive and objectionable, or in a way that is inoppressive and unobjectionable. The extortion of confessions by thumb-screws and boots is an oppressive inquisition. But the Kirk Sessions of Scotland never made inquisition after that fashion. It must be admitted, however, that Kirk Sessions long ago were very inquisitorial and very zealous in their efforts to elucidate the mysteries of iniquity. Dr. Hill, as we have seen, says that "no solicitude is ever discovered by Kirk Sessions to engage in the investigation of secret wickedness." That for many a day has been the case, but it was not so always. One of the most marked distinctions between the procedure of Kirk Sessions in modern days and their procedure a hundred years ago or more, is that alleged cases of scandal are not taken up now unless there is a decided *fama clamosa* and some palpable facts to proceed on. But in olden times if either a minister or an elder happened to hear a word of calumny regarding a parishioner, the minister or elder, as the case might be, thought it his bounden duty to report to the Session what he had heard, and the Session thought it their duty to ascertain without delay whether the report was true or false, and then to deal as circumstances required. In the printed records of the Kirk Session of Aberdeen we find the elders, in 1568, sworn to secrecy regarding all that passed in the Session, and to faithfulness in delating all that they heard affecting the Christian character of people within their bounds. As shewing what the practice of Kirk Sessions was, I may mention that I have seen old minutes of Session (Galston, for instance, 1692) which commenced by stating that "enquiry being made if there were any public scandals known to any of the elders, it was reported" that some one had been seen under the influence of drink, or had been heard using profane words. Very strange enquiries, too, were at times ordered to be made by Kirk Sessions. It is minuted, for instance, in the Session Records of Mauchline that on the 15th August, 1697, "Alexander Baxter, an elder, was appointed to enquire if the woman that lived with Bryce Allan was his wife or not, as also anent Andrew Rob, whether he was a thief or not, as was reported." It need not surprise any one to be told that Mr. Baxter himself was made very soon afterwards to suffer from calumny. A man sent to enquire into scandals about other people is almost certain, especially if he shews any zeal in his inquisition, to hear something said to his own discredit. Despite the greatest prudence in his walk and conversation, there will be something or other discovered which will be made the foundation for an unwarranted story. And so it happened with Mr. Baxter. In less than a twelvemonth after he had been sent to inquire into Andrew Rob's alleged theftous habits, a report reached the Session that Alexander Baxter, one of their number, "had resett some stolen goods which Allan M'Crae, a notorious thief, had brought to his house." It turned out on investigation that Mr. Baxter was perfectly innocent of the charge. Stolen goods were found in his house, and these goods had been left there by

M'Crae, but of these facts Mr. Baxter was as ignorant as an unborn child. A daughter of Mr. Baxter's confessed that, in her simplicity, she had allowed a vagrant to leave his goods in her father's house, but declared she was not aware that the goods had been stolen. For her simplicity and incaution, however, she had to bear the brunt of a Sessional rebuke in her father's presence. Endless are the cases in which it is minuted in old records that this person and the other person was reported to have been guilty of some sin or another—cursing, swearing, drunkenness, and such like—and in every instance the report was thoroughly investigated. No rumour was disregarded, and no offence was deemed too frivolous to be enquired into.* In 1771 an unlucky lad in Mauchline gave a sixpence instead of a token to the elder that was lifting tokens at one of the communion tables. The lad was a communicant admitted to the table on that occasion for the first time. The tokens were in size as like sixpences as possible, and the act of the lad was evidently a mistake for which none could be more sorry than himself in respect that it threatened to involve him in the loss of sixpence. The matter could not be overlooked, however. It was formally reported to the Session, and the lad was duly cited to compear before his betters and answer for his conduct. His innocence of any intention to profane the sacramental ordinance was made clear by his sorrow for the mistake he had made, and he was dismissed, but, like Mr. Baxter's daughter, with a

---

* Even the sin of penning or singing poetical squibs was duly cognosced, as the following curious entry in the Session Records of Ayr will shew:—" In case ony persoun or persouns at ony time sall find, heir or see ony ryme or cokalane, that they sall reveil the same first to ane eldar privatlie, and to na uther, and in case they faille therein in reveiling of the same to any uther, that person sall be esteemed to be the authour of the said ryme, and sall be punished therefor conforme to the Acts of the Kirk and ye laws of ye realme."

Sessional rebuke for his carelessness, and with an admonition to be more observant in future. So much punctiliousness is what we would now-a-days account over rigidity. But whatever may be our opinion of the wisdom or expediency of such ecclesiastical fuss, we must do the worthy men that held office in the Church long ago, the justice to say that in acting as they did, they only did what they believed they were bound in Christian duty to do, and that their aim and object were to put away all evil and reproach from the Church, and to educate the people in strict and high notions of Christian life. Their chief function was well described in a minute of the Galston Kirk Session, in 1647, which stated that "the Session did consider they had need of some more elders for watching over the manners of the Congregation."

And it was not only sins of commission but sins of omission that kirk sessions took cognisance of. In the Records of Galston it is stated that in December, 1639, "the minister presentit ane book and red it in the sessioune quhilk is to be put in practice conforme to the Act of the General Assembly, intituled Familie Exercise, that everie familie sould have morning and evening prayers, publict and private reading, psalms and uther exercises of God's worship, as in the said buke is conteinit. And to this end, for the better ordering heirof, and that this service be not neglectit in families, it is thought meit that ilk elder within the paroche, in his pairtis nixt about him, have ane speciall care and charge hereof, and see what religion, what prayer, what reiding, and what uther exercise of God's service they use in their house." Indeed, so recently as 1700, the Synod of Glasgow and Ayr passed an Act, which was appointed to be read in all kirk sessions within the bounds, requiring among other things " that elders make conscience of visiting families within their districts, exhorting heads of families to set up the worship of God in their houses, reproving those who neglect it, and *delating* them upon their continuing neglect, etc." Kirk Sessions were even at pains, in some instances, probably in many, to promote Christian fellowship in their parish by means of district meetings for prayer and conference. In the year 1700, the Synod of Glasgow and Ayr recommended and enjoined such action, and in at least some parishes, of which Galston might be named as one, the Session, on this injunction, " did divide themselves into district societies, to meet the first Wednesday of each month, and spend the day in prayer and Christian fellowship."

But to return to the subject of delations, it occasionally happened that stories of misconduct turned out, on investigation, to be gross exaggerations of very paltry matters, and as injury was done to people by the circulation of such stories, the Session sometimes thought it necessary to undo such injuries by public intimation of the result of their enquiries. In 1702, for instance, a report reached the Kirk Session of Mauchline, that there had been some gathering in a house at the Pathhead of Ballochmyle. A formidable committee of Session was thereupon appointed to investigate the scandal, and this committee reported that " the people who mett only took a civil drink, and did no harm so as to raise such a talk." The minister was then desired by the Session " to intimate ye nixt Sabbath to ye people from ye pulpit," that the meeting at Pathhead had not been so bad as was supposed, and to "give a caveat to all to cause others bewar in time to come of the like sin." The intimation, it will be admitted, was a proper act of justice to the people at Pathhead, but as no sin had been committed on the occasion libelled, it may be said that the caveat was uncalled for. The Kirk Session seem to have thought, however, that a good admonition can never be applied untimeously, and that although people have not been in a fault they may possibly be on the way to one.

Very often parishioners brought charges against one another before the Kirk Session. These charges, whatever they were, always received attention. If one woman complained of being cursed or bewitched or defamed by another, the Session always gave an open ear to the complaint. But there was one salutary regulation that the Kirk Session adhered to in such cases. Every accuser had to table so much money as a pledge that the accusation would be proved, and the money so pledged was forfeited to the Session for pious uses in the event of its being found that the charge was either false or not proven. This pledge was called a consignation,* and the common amount of it was 40s. Scots. The following minute in our Parish Records, 1682, will give a good and clear specimen of the Session's mode of procedure in such cases:—" Bessie Edwards' supplication being renewed, and the particulars specifiet, it's admitted relevant, and she is appointed to consign £2 0s. 0d., and if she prove not the particulars laid to the delinquent's charge, she is to forfeit the £2 0s. 0d., and the names of the witnesses are to be given in to the Clerk against the next Session." The complaint of Miss Edwards was that she had been reviled by a neighbour with some railing speeches. In this case the consignation was not forfeited. The delinquent,

---

* The word consignation was more frequently applied to another pledge which will be fully treated of in the lecture on marriages. But it was a general term equivalent to pledge, and used in reference to many things. For instance, in the Galston Records for 1633. there is an entry, "Margaret Smyth gave in ane bill upon Janet Richmond, and consignit her bill silver in ye minister's hands;" and in another entry it is said that A. B. having given in a bill upon C. D., "his *consignation* was maid, and the witnesses were ordained to be summoned."

as she is termed, confessed her fault, and was admonished "to carry more suitably in time coming." In many cases the consignation was forfeited, and lifted by the Session. For instance, in our Records, 1670, it is minuted that Janet M'Connell, having previously given in "ane bill of complaint against John Marshall, clerk, for calling her a witch, and with it having consigned fourteen shilling, nothing being proven by the witnesses, the Session declared her consignation forfaltit." In 1671 it was minuted that "Margaret Fisher, wyffe to W. Ronald in Holhous having gevin in a complaint of sclander against W. Anderson and Margaret —— his spous in Killoch, and upon their denyall, the sclander not being proven, the Session decernes the said Margaret to have forfaultit her consignation, 40s." The Records of Galston Session tell of a man that in 1643 gave in a bill against another man "for slandering his name anent ye selling of some silk buttons, which he alleadgit he had stolen or resett, . . . some long tailed buttons of silk which was upon the Laird of Cessnoch's clook the tyme that it was stolen." The slandered man, however, saw reason not to press his complaint any further in the face of facts, and allowed his consignation to be forfeited.

At the present day it is quite customary, both in country and town parishes, to assign special districts to the charge of special members of Kirk Session. This arrangement is not supposed to be, nor is it really, made for any purpose of espionage, but with the view of securing that the wants of the sick and the poor shall be duly attended to. But the arrangement was at one period enjoined for purposes of discipline. In the year 1648 it was enacted by the General Assembly "that every elder have a certain bounds assigned to him that he may visit the same every month at least, and report to the Session what scandals and abuses are therein, or what persons have entered without testimonials."* And it was doubtless in consideration of the great amount of work that this Act of Assembly entailed on elders, that Kirk Sessions long ago comprised so many members. In the Records of Mauchline Parish for 1684, there is given in one minute "a list of the elders the minister afterwards chused." This list comprises fifteen names, and although it is not quite clear from anything that subsequently appears in the register whether all the fifteen persons named were actually ordained and admitted elders, there were, at any rate, nine of them present at the first meeting of Session held after the list was drawn up. On the back of a small minute or rather scroll minute book, there is written out "the order that the elders are to collect for the poor and their names;" and in this order or memorandum, dated 1707, there are fifteen persons named and described as elders. Some of the biographers of Burns, among others Dr. Chambers, have stated that in the later years of Mr. Auld's ministry there were only three elders in this parish, and that they were men of discreditable character. This statement is simply untrue, and on what worthless authority it could have been made I cannot conceive. It is very difficult to make out from the Session Records how many elders there have been in the parish at different dates. The roll of elders is seldom entered in the Records, and the sederunts, or names of elders present at particular meetings of Session, are seldom given. In the time of Mr. Auld the Kirk Session was probably not so large as it was at the dates 1684

---

* The following entries in the Fenwick Records illustrate the old customs in regard to this matter, 1646—" The Session nominates these persons following for elders, viz., for the lands of Rowallan (six names), for the lands of Polkellie (three names), for Fenwick (one name), for Craufordland (three names) for the lands of Raith (two names), for Hartshaw muir John Paton in Meadow head." These sixteen were all ordained elders. In 1653 the same Session made formal appointment of their " several quarters to the elders for special oversight."

and 1707, but that it never was reduced to three members is absolutely certain. In the year 1785, which was one of the four years in which Burns lived in the parish, the names of at least six elders may be clearly made out from two minutes of Kirk Session, which are both in print. The only period in Mr. Auld's ministry in which I could have thought it possible that the Kirk Session had dwindled down to a mere quorum, or little more, was at the time of his death. I find, however, from the Records of the Presbytery of Ayr, that at Mr. Reid's induction, in 1792, the Kirk Session comprised seven elders.

Less than might have been expected is said in our Session Records about the allocation of the elders to special districts in this parish; but the fact of such an allocation is indicated more than once. In 1707, the year in which we have seen that there were fifteen elders in the parish, there is a minute which states that a woman who had been summoned to appear before the Session did not appear. The finding of the Session thereupon was, that the elder of the "quarter" to which the woman belonged be instructed to inform her that if she will not compear before the Session she must go to the Presbytery." On the Sacramental Fast in 1734 it was minuted that "tokens were given out to the elders to serve in the several quarters of the parish." There is no doubt, therefore, that long ago every elder in Mauchline Parish had his district assigned to him, and that by this means the whole affairs of the parish were brought very directly and very closely under the surveillance of the Kirk Session.*

---

* Kirkton, the Church historian, boasts of the perfection of discipline in the Church of Scotland in 1650 in these words—" No scandalous person could live, no scandal could be concealed in all Scotland, so strict a correspondence there was betwixt ministers and congregations." I may add that the Records of the Presbytery of Ayr show that it was common between 1640 and 1650 for Presbyteries to send

Sundry perambulations, too, used to be appointed by Kirk Sessions with the view of checking and correcting disorders. In Mauchline one or two elders were generally directed to attend the race and the fairs, and to report if anything censurable came under their notice. In January, 1702, for instance, three elders were told off "to goe through the faire and take notice of what immoralities they hear or see." Four years before that date it is recorded that two elders were in like manner instructed to take notice of any abuse that might occur at the race, and it is satisfactory to know that the elders reported in due course that they had gone to the race, and "heard nothing scandalous at it." And there was nothing exceptional in this procedure of the Mauchline Kirk Session. The same line of action was adopted at Galston, and with even greater zeal. In the beginning of last century and down to the end of at least the first quarter of that century, elders were appointed in Galston to visit all the alehouses in the village between nine and ten at night during the fair, and disperse those that were found drinking. And this was an old custom in Galston; for as far back as 1640 I find it minuted that two of the elders were "ordained to go throw the clachan at ten at night and advertyse the minister, that the hour may be neir keiped." On the margin of an old minute in the Records of Galston these ecclesiastical scouts are called the "civillisers."

It was chiefly, however, for the detection of Sabbath desecration, that Sessional perambulations were appointed. There was nothing that gave the Church of Scotland more trouble in old times than the enforcement of Sabbath observance. Acts of Assembly, Acts of Presbytery, and Acts of Kirk Sessions

---

one of their members as a correspondent to neighbouring Presbyteries. There was constant correspondence of this kind between the Presbyteries of Ayr and Irvine.

were made ever so often for the repression of some form or another of Sabbath profanation. And the reason why the Church had so much difficulty in the matter was that the people, both under Popery before the Reformation and under Episcopacy after the Reformation, had been allowed and had been accustomed to great liberty on the Sabbath. Not only was corn-stacking at the end of a late harvest done without compunction as a reasonable work of necessity, but both corn milling and salmon fishing were carried on without any necessity whatever. King James himself, the first Protestant King of Scotland, one of whose titles was Defender of the Faith, was so zealous for Sunday liberty that he published a work called the Book of Sports, in which he specified a number of amusements and field exercises that he thought might be lawfully and innocently enjoyed on the Sabbath. When the Church awoke to a sense of the sanctity of the Sabbath, and to the binding duty of a holy resting all that day, even from such worldly employments and recreations as are lawful on other days, she found that she had a very arduous work to do in putting down Sabbath desecration. Both the importance of the work and the obstacles that lay in the execution of the work made her all the more zealous and stringent, therefore, in carrying out an inquisitorial and rigid discipline. Solemn denunciations of the sin of Sabbath breaking and solemn warnings of the consequences that would attend that sin were time after time issued from pulpits, and elders were deputed to scour the streets and enter the premises of publicans, to see if any in the parish were not remembering to keep the Sabbath holy to the Lord. In this parish such warnings and perambulations were of frequent occurrence. In 1672, at a meeting of Session in Mauchline, on the 26th March, " intimation was appointed to be made the next

Sabbath day that people vaig not abroad on the Sabbath, and that they tak care that their children vaig not." On the 22nd February, 1676, it was further appointed "that the two elders who collect on the Sabbath shall goe through the town and search who are in the houses the tyme of sermon." And what resulted from these perambulations may be surmised from an entry that occurs fourteen years later in the Records. On the 7th September, 1690, two of the elders "delated George Miller in Mauchline and his (wife) to the Session, for their selling aill and drinking it in their house with incomers, which they did find with them in the tyme of the forenoon sermon."

In 1699 a very important recommendation was minuted by the Presbytery of Ayr, that "each Session apply to and concur with the civil magistrate and principal leading men of the Paroch, that *censors* be appointed in each paroch to go about, visit, and delate delinquents for cursing, swearing, drunkenness, &c.: and where there is a town or clachan in the paroch that the censors go through the town or clachan and delate such as shall be found in taverns or ale houses in tyme of divine service; as also on week days, especially on mercat or fair days, they go through the said town or clachan to notice and delate delinquents for the foresaid crimes; and likewise that the said censors or visitors go through the town or clachan and delate delinquents that are in ale houses at unseasonable tymes of the night." In other words, the Presbytery of Ayr in 1699 wished a rural police established, and it was doubtless because such a system of police supervision was not established that elders continued long afterwards to do police duty, and that this police duty was reckoned an important part of elders' work. As late as 1718 a complaint was made to the Presbytery of Ayr by the parishioners of Maybole that there was no delation in the Session "of immoralities on the streets and in taverns at untimely hours, in drinking, swearing, and the like . . . tho instances thereof have been seen in private persons, and elders too, to the offence of some."

Another and a very effective means employed long ago for making kirk sessions fully cognisant of all the antecedents of their parishioners was the requirement of a testimonial from every person that came to live or even stay for a few months in the parish. This testimonial shewed whether the incomer was married or single, and whether he was under scandal or free from scandal.* An Act of Assembly passed in 1648 made it imperative that "all persons who flit from one paroche to another, have sufficient testimonials," and this requirement was declared "to be extended to all gentlemen and persons of quality, and all their followers who come to reside with their families at Edinburgh or elsewhere." Ministers were over and above enjoined to advertise the minister to whose bounds their parishioners flitted, whether or not the emigrants left under scandal; and for a long period this law was carried out with great strictness. The receiving and the granting of testimonials were regarded as formal sessional acts, and were duly recorded. In our own Session Records for 1672 there is a whole page filled with an account of testimonials granted and testimonials received. By this means it was made almost impossible for scandals to be covered. A sinner might flee from Barr to Banff, and settle down in a district where nothing was known of his family or his history, but if he brought no sufficient testimonials with him, he became in the

---

* The oldest entries about testimonials that I have seen in Session Records simply certify to the bearer's "civil carriage" for so many years or from birth. At later times they very often, if not always, stated what was the bearer's condition, married or single. In 1716 a man confessed to the Presbytery of Ayr "that he was guilty in forging a testimonial, adding Mr. M'Viccar, Minister at West Kirk in Edinburgh, his name to it, to bear that he was an unmarried person."

eye of the Church a scandalous person. And if it should be found out where he had fled, a letter from the minister he left, let the minister and Kirk Session of the Parish to which he had gone know all about his sins and delinquencies.

Our records tell that in 1671 a woman in this parish was " ordainit to be publicly declared a scandalous woman, and not to be owned for a parishioner till she produce a sufficient testimonial." In 1694 there was intimation made from the pulpit that none would be entertained within the parish unless they produced testificates. And following up this resolution, the Session, in April 1705, directed the church-officer to go to the Haugh and "tell Jean Kennedy and her mother to remove from this parish at the 1st May, because they can produce no testificates :" and to understand that in the event of their failing to remove by the time stated "the Session would apply to the civil magistrate." The Haugh seems to have been about that time infested with uncertificated visitors. In 1703 "Jean Wat, and the wife in the Haugh and her daughter, that lives in the house belonging to the holm, which William White possesses, was discharged from staying there because she could produce no testificat." And people were obliged to remove for that cause at the Session's order. In 1697 "George Petersone being called and compearing was interrogate if he had as yet gotten a testimonial as he was appointed. He answered he neither had got one nor expected to get one." He was then told that if he did not produce a certificate before Whitsunday the Session would apply to the magistrate. Whitsunday came, but George's testimonial was not produced, and the minister was therefore desired by the Session "to speak to the Sheriff Depute to take notice of Petersone so as to compel him to go out of the parish." And Mr. Petersone had to remove pretty quick, although it is difficult to see where he could go and fare much better. It was the 18th of July when the minister was instructed to speak to the Sheriff, and on the 27th July the minister reported to the Session that Petersone was off. As recently as 1777 there is notice in our records of a man that had come to this parish and had not brought with him any testimonials. He was not summarily ejected, as he might have been a hundred years earlier, but he was laid under censure, and although the faults for which he was censured were legion, it was minuted that one of these was "his bringing no testimonials of his christian character to this place, and the bad report of him from other parishes where he had resided." Instances beyond number might be cited in which kirk sessions and presbyteries enforced this law anent testimonials. In 1648 the magistrates of Ayr were politely requested by the Presbytery ". to be careful that no person whatever, coming to dwell and make residence in that town, be receaved therein by any without testimonial from the minister of the Paroch from whence they came." In 1707 the Presbytery were informed that there was a family living at Cumnock which refused to give testimonials to the Session. The Presbytery thereupon ordered their Clerk to "write to the magistrate of the place, to oblige them to obtane ane, or that he remove them from thence." The Kirk Session of Fenwick, in 1691, forbade all landlords in the parish to let their lands or houses to any persons that had no certificates from their former place of residence, and when a landlord in 1692 declined at the Session's order to put away his cottar, the Session "resolved to commit the said (landlord) to the civil magistrate." In 1700 the elders of Galston were ordered to report every three months what persons had come into the parish, so that enquiry might be made if they had testimonials. And very chary were the Session of Galston in granting testimonials. All were refused that benefit who neglected the catechising.*

It often happened that when charges were brought against a man in the Kirk Session the person so charged denied his guilt. From the days of St. Peter downward, and perhaps in the days before St. Peter, it seems to have been natural for people to deny even with the vehemence of an oath whatever has been laid to their charge, till the accusation has been established by indubitable testimony. Whether this tendency has shown itself more strongly in Kirk Sessions than in other courts only those historically acquainted with the proceedings in different courts can tell, but there is nothing that to the reader of Kirk Session Records gives a lower notion of parochial morality than the effrontery with which people conscious of guilt have protested their innocence. When accusations were received by a Kirk Session, therefore, and guilt was denied by the persons accused, it became necessary, in many cases at least, for the Kirk Session to take evidence. This disagreeable duty is often evaded now-a-days, and with much advantage by the Kirk Session's delaying procedure till the question has been decided in the civil court; but in olden times Kirk Sessions were more self-reliant, and they entered upon and went through probations without scruple or misgiving. They cited witnesses, and witnesses were obliged under pain of censure to come forward after citation and give evidence. All evidence was required to be taken in a fair and an open way. The witnesses were examined in presence of the accused party,

---

* It was not unusual at one time to call people before the Session "for harbouring a scandalous person" in their house, or to order people to remove from their house this and that scandalous person. In 1628 a woman appeared before the Session of Galston and "obleist her under the paine of £10 that she suld keip her house clein of all vagabonds and strangers in resetting thame without advyce of the Sessione."

and the defender was at liberty to desire the moderator to put such cross questions as might invalidate the proof. It was expressly provided, however, that "no accused person is to interrupt the witnesses or speak during the time of deposition." From the earliest times, too, witnesses were put on oath by Kirk Sessions. In the Mauchline records we find that in 1671 a woman was convicted of scolding and cursing " partly on her own confession and partly by sworn evidence." Opening a more recent volume of the same records at random I find that in 1780 it was common for witnesses to be "solemnly sworn, purged of malice and partial counsel," and then interrogated. Occasionally it is minuted that both parties agree to accept a witness's "solemn declaration, instead of his oath for the present," and on such occasions the oath was dispensed with. In the "brulie minutes" for 1780 there is a curious sentence deleted, "Compeared Hugh Widrow, smith, and refuses to give his oath unless paid for his oath. The Session having considered the refusal look upon." Here the minute ends abruptly. The Session had evidently shewn their intention of regarding this refusal to be sworn as a greater offence than the pawky blacksmith was aware of, and on second thoughts Mr. Widrow agreed to take the oath without reward or fee. Whether there was an intentional touch of sarcastic humour in Mr. Widrow's refusal to take an oath, unless paid for it, my ignorance of his cerebral structure prevents me saying; but the Session must have had their own thoughts at his extreme punctiliousness, for they had not long previously been calling him to book for being too free in the use of oaths, both to the dishonour of God and the terror of nervous neighbours.

As might be expected, cases have often occurred in which the evidence submitted to a Kirk Session did not clearly point to one conclusion or another. In these cases the accused did not as in criminal courts get the benefit of the doubt. The law of the Church was, and still is, that procedure must be sisted till Providence sheds further light on the case, or the oath of purgation must, with the sanction of the Presbytery, be administered to the accused. Long ago, processes before Kirk Sessions were occasionally sisted for ten, twenty, thirty, or forty years, the accused remaining all the while under scandal, and without the benefit of church privileges. In 1757, a man made application to the Kirk Session of Mauchline for a testimonial of good behaviour. The man had been under scandal for thirty-eight years, and he had often offered and still offered to clear himself by the oath of purgation. The Session, however, had never thought proper to allow him to take the oath. As a last chance the man respectfully demanded either to be allowed to clear himself by oath or to be assoilzied without oath. The Session doubtless felt that whatever was the strict rule of law there was justice in this requisition, and so the man was allowed to take the oath and relieve himself of his long sorrow and long reproach. In the letters of Burns there is reference made to a man's being under the inquisition in Mauchline in 1786. Thirty-two years later, that is, in 1818, the same man appeared before the Kirk Session and requested absolution from the scandal that Burns refers to, and which at the time of investigation was left not proven. And the Kirk Session, in 1818, under the guidance of Mr. Tod, gave a deliverance that, whether in accordance with evidence or not, was at least in respect of sentiment and feeling worthy of a Christian court. " The Session," so ran the deliverance after a narrative of circumstances, " considering this whole affair, are of opinion that James Bryan hath suffered greatly by being kept so many years from enjoying church privileges, and that his affair is long ago prescribed."*

Kirk Sessions have been known to put all the people of a parish on oath in regard to their guilt or knowledge of misdeeds. It is minuted, for instance, in the Galston Records that on the 11th October, 1635, "all the inhabitants of the Galstone being summondit against this day compeircit and purgeit themselves be their aith that nane of them tak, nor knew who tak, ane daill from ye kirk."

The form of process states that the oath of purgation is never to be administered without the sanction of the Presbytery. It is not to be administered, either, unless the presumptions of guilt are so great that nothing but the oath will remove suspicions of guilt, and unless, also, it is thought probable that the oath will remove suspicion and put an end to scandal The reasons for such extreme caution are obvious. Perjury is a very grievous sin, and there is temptation to commit perjury whenever people are allowed to swear for their own benefit. Hence the caution that was ordered to be used in the administration of an oath of purgation. The form of process was enacted by the General Assembly in 1707, but how much the spirit of its provisions appeared in the proceedings of Kirk Sessions at an earlier date may be gathered from the following cases. In 1696 a Mauchline man accused of a sin which inferred civil consequences was loud in his denial of guilt, and pressed to be permitted to clear himself by the

---

* The following minute, however, will shew how exacting Kirk Sessions once were, and how cruel at times were even their tender mercies:—"Mauchline, 1736, January 11. The Session agreed to absolve Agnes —— after a Sessional rebuke, she having stood twice publicly about nine or ten years ago, and think it would not be edifying that she appear publicly, she now being old and infirm, and it a *scandalum sopitum*" (that is, a scandal gone to sleep or fallen into oblivion).

oath of purgation. The minutes state, however, that "the Kirk Session, too much fearing he was guilty, did not admit him to swear." Again, in 1698 a man, described as a merchant in Kilmarnock, having his good fame and worldly credit traduced by a Mauchline belle, came to the Session under the pressure of injured feelings to declare his innocence. He offered, like a merchant and a gentleman, to give the oath of exculpation, but the Session considered, to use the words of their minute, "that it was not safe to be rash in taking his oath, and appointed both him and his accuser to be cited to the next meeting" for further examination. And the wisdom of the Session's caution in this instance was vindicated, for at the next meeting of Session the man being asked if he adhered to his denial of guilt, "paused a little, and being urged to give an answer" confessed to the guilt. In 1704 one James Millar appeared before the pulpit in Mauchline church after sermon and declared himself content to take the oath of purgation, which was read to him by the minister. The minister, however, was "in such a consternation he would not administer the oath till the next Lord's day." It is not made clear whether when next Lord's day came Miller failed to come forward or that the minister's consternation was not removed, but it is stated that the administration of the oath was postponed till the Sabbath following. On that second Sabbath Miller was allowed to take the oath, but with what solemnity on his part, and with what consternation on the part of the minister, may be imagined from the fact recorded, that the man had to go down on his bended knees before the congregation. In our records prior to 1707 several instances occur of people being positively refused the privilege of clearing themselves by oath. Sometimes a copy of the oath was given to a man that he might consider whether it would be safe and proper for him to swear according to its tenor.* In the Mauchline records of 1787 there is engrossed a copy of a curious protest and appeal by a man against a sentence of the Session appointing his accuser, a woman, to establish her charge by oath. In this singular document the appellant takes on himself to lay down to the Session the ecclesiastical law on the subject. "That law," he says, "requires men charged as he was to swear before the congregation after carrying a copy of the oath for twelve or more months, and surely," he adds, "no less occasion is necessary to be used before taking a woman's oath, many of whom would require great pains and diligence used to make them to understand the very nature of an oath." It is scarcely necessary to say that there never was such a law in the Church as was stated by this consequential man.

It is only in cases where there are strong presumptions of guilt that the form of process, 1707, allows the oath of purgation to be administered. In early times, however, Kirk Sessions were not always particular on this point, and oaths of exculpation were occasionally allowed, if not even required, when nothing but innocence should have been presumed. In 1680 a woman in Mauchline was slandered by a man, and the Session allowed her the privilege of clearing herself by oath before the congregation. Such a privilege as that came very far short of women's rights. It is monstrous to think that any person should need or be expected to disprove an unsupported accusation against him. The burden of proof clearly falls in justice on the accuser, and the civil law very properly allows

---

* There are several cases on record in the books of the Presbytery of Ayr in which persons offering to take the oath of purgation got a double or copy of it to consider. How dreadful the old oath, prior to 1707, was, will be seen at Appendix C.

people injured by false accusation the right of not only proving innocence but recovering compensation for damages.

While Kirk Sessions were so zealous and strict in looking after the morals of parishioners it ought to be mentioned that they were no less zealous and rigid in dealing with the members of their own courts. No *fama* supposed to have the slightest foundation was allowed to pass uninvestigated: and every accusation brought to the Session against an elder was thoroughly sifted, in the same way as an accusation against any other person would have been. And there are cases in the Parish Records in which accusations or reports against elders were received by the Session of Mauchline. On the 29th May, 1698, it was minuted that "there being a flagrant rumour that J. R., one of the members of Session, should be guilty of theft, the Session took notice thereof, and caused summon several men who were presumed to have some knowledge of that affair, . . . and appointed the minister going to the Presbyterie that week to consult them about it." The case was called at next meeting of Session, and witnesses were examined "severally." One witness deponed that some corn found in the elder's house "by the searchers was very like to his (the witness's) in colour, quantity, and smell." Another declared "that he was very clear to depone upon oath, that some materials belonging to a plough, such as a team, tugs, and heme, found by the searchers in the elder's house were his." A third deponed that he and others had "tracked a horse's footsteps from the barn where the corn was stolen to the elder's house," and that when the house was searched "a lamb's skin was found in the bedstrae which was very like the skin of a lamb that another man wanted." The elder's statement in defence is not recorded, and the absence of that statement makes the Session's deliverance difficult for one to understand. If it were the case that either the elder had been guilty of theft or that the witnesses had been guilty of perjury, then undoubtedly one or other of the parties was amenable to church censure. But apparently such had not been the case. It seems as if the Session thought that the facts deponed to may have been true or been believed by the witnesses to have been true, and yet that the facts did not infer theft, for the deliverance of the Session was that "the thing was rather civil than ecclesiastick, and that the elder should be informed to pursue these persons who, as he said, had slandered him, before the civil magistrate." It is proper to remark that this case occurred during the incumbency of Mr. Maitland, who, whatever were his merits as a man and a preacher, was rather a feeble minister of justice. It was he that was in such a state of consternation in 1704 about giving the oath of purgation. And whether in the days of his stronger-nerved and more legal-minded successor, Mr. Auld, such a negative deliverance on a charge of theft against an elder would have been pronounced, is very doubtful. The Session would probably have found ways and means of making either the innocence or guilt of the elder more clear, not only to themselves, but to all future ministers and elders that should happen to see the record of the case. In 1708 a very painful incident occurred in the parish, which is brought out sufficiently clearly in the following minute of the Presbytery of Ayr, which I shall give verbatim, —"Compeired Robert Miller of Willoxhill, and gave in a petition wherein he desired the Presbytery would relax him from the sentence of minor excommunication and suspension from the office of an elder, which they passed against him upon his striking of a woman upon her refusal of a poynd, and the woman having dyed in a few days thereafter, her friends alledged the said stroak was the means of her death, as is recorded formerly. Withal, he produced an absolvitor under the Sheriff Principal's hand, who had made all search therein, and found nothing to evidence the said aledgiance, and the minister of Mauchline, in whose bounds he lived, told their Session found nothing to make the said aledgiance evident to them : and the Presbytery having considered the said petition, and the Session of Machlyne's account thereanent, did and hereby do absolve the said Robert Miller from the said sentence of minor excommunication, and they refer it to the prudence of the Session of Machlyne whether to invite him to officiat again as an elder or not."

What the Kirk Session did in this matter I cannot discover. The only distinct reference to the case that I have found in the Session Records is the following :—" May 2nd, 1708, Willockshill offeired ane petition to the Session in order to take away aspersion laid upon his name, as supposed to be accessory to the death of Janet Hudd, spouse to John Aird in Barloyse, and it's resolved therein to be carried to the Presbytery for an absolvitor, seeing they first passed a sentence upon him."

During the ministry of Mr. Auld there were at least four, but so far as known to me only four instances of an elder being brought up for censure in the Session for an act that inferred scandal. One of these instances was the case of the schoolmaster for an irregular marriage he had contracted, and which will be noticed in its proper place under the head of marriages. Another of the four instances occurred in 1747. It was the case of an elder, who was also Kirk Treasurer, and who was accused first of giving away, or allowing to be taken away, " part of his household plenishings," which he had assigned to the Session as payment in part of what he owed the Session ; and secondly, of absenting himself from public ordinances ever since the Session had taken steps to recover from him what he owed. Both charges were admitted by the elder, who had been unfortunate in business, and, to keep the wolf from his door, had used the poor's funds, doubtless hoping that some day he would be able to repay all he had taken,—

> "And look the whole world in the face,
> For he owed not any man."

But these expectations were never realised. Deeper and deeper the poor man floundered in debt, and all hope of extricating himself died away. And his appropriation of the kirk money was an offence which could not be condoned or overlooked. Poor and heart-broken though he was, therefore, he was ruthlessly and of necessity deposed from his eldership.

The third of the four instances referred to, occurred in 1774. In this case the elder and two of his sons were accused of having beaten a man in the Haugh with sticks and tongs and pint stoups, to the effusion of blood, and of having accompanied their blows with profane swearing. It transpired in evidence, that on the night of the February fair the elder had endeavoured to persuade an angry and presumably a half-drunk man to leave a house where a quarrel was being made up, and that on the man's refusing to go away peaceably, the elder, with the assistance of others, had turned him out. In the process of ejection some blows had been struck, but by whom was not clearly proved. It was deponed also that the elder, in the excitement of such an unusual scene, had given vent to some comminative words that are not expected to escape the well-guarded lips of ecclesiastical persons. After a full and patient hearing of the case, the Session found the elder, along with others, guilty of fighting. And although wars on a great scale, where thousands of men are mowed down like thistles, are often called righteous contentions and noble exhibitions of public spirit, a small scuffle between unarmed citizens, resulting in nothing worse than a black eye or a nasal hemorrhage, is always pronounced a very wicked and unchristian act. For the sin therefore of doing what in itself was proper, but was improper in being done by means of tongs and pint stoups, the elder was sentenced to be rebuked and to be admonished to behave better in time coming. But he thought himself a maligned and much injured man, and would not submit to the indignity of a rebuke. He was accordingly continued under scandal, and allowed time to reflect on his conduct. Two months later he came back to the Session and acknowledged that "he was not absolutely certain of his being guilty or not guilty, but if he was guilty in any respect he professed his sorrow for it, and likewise with respect to an expression just now uttered, viz.: Dear, keep me, he owns that it was rash and sinful."

This confession looks very like an artifice on the part of the accused to withdraw attention from the greater charge by a frank admission of the lesser. If such a ruse, however, was intended by him, it did not succeed. The order was renewed that he be rebuked and admonished. And although he was, on submission to this sentence, at once absolved from scandal, and "admitted to the privileges of a Christian," he was suspended from the exercise of his office as an elder, until the Session should have sufficient evidence of his being qualified by his after behaviour."

The last of the four instances I have noted of an elder being brought before Mauchline Session by delation or *fama clamosa* for a scandalous offence was that of William Fisher —Holy Willie, as he is called—for an instance of drunkenness in 1790. Of that case there is no record in the extant minutes of

Kirk Session. But the reason of this omission can be clearly made out from what is stated in the Session Records two or three years later and from what appears in the Presbytery Records between 1790 and 1792. In 1790 the Session Clerk had been suspended from his office for some alleged fault, and that was at least the *fifth* charge of one kind or another which had been brought against him in the Church Courts. During the time that the legality of this dismissal was being contested at law, the proceedings of the Kirk Session were scrolled by an *ad interim* clerk whose papers have not been recovered. It is not unlikely that that *ad interim* clerk was Mr. Auld himself, for on a former similar occasion he so acted. Be that as it may, however, there is a blank in the Session Records from August, 1790, till September, 1792, and it was during this period that Fisher's frailty was brought to light The rebuke given to Fisher I discovered in a small manuscript volume in Mr. Auld's handwriting, which contains the admonitions, or the greater part of the admonitions, delivered to delinquents by Mr. Auld during the last twenty-five or thirty years of his ministry.* It contains, for instance, the public rebuke given to Burns and Jean Armour in 1786, and a rebuke that in 1782 was given to Janet Gibson, who figures in Burns' poems under the soubriquet of Racer Jess. And I may remark that while in Mr. Auld's manuscript book Fisher's offence is called "an instance of drunkenness," the admonition rather insinuates that by 1790 Willie had come to be too free in his habits. He was bidden shun bad company, avoid taverns as much as possible, and abhor the character of a tippler. He was reminded also that drunkenness is a bewitch-

---

* This interesting manuscript volume is in the possession of the Rev. John Ritchie of Langside, Glasgow.

ing sin, and he was exhorted therefore to seek wisdom from heaven to guide him, and grace to enable him to walk steadfastly in sobriety and holiness all his days. It is well enough known, however, that charges of a worse kind than drunkenness—charges of dishonesty and of pilfering the alms of the poor—have been made by Burns and Burns's biographers against Fisher, but of these alleged misdeeds there is no trace so far as I have seen, in any part of the Kirk Session records. And these records were carefully kept and have come down to us apparently entire from the date of Fisher's ordination as an elder till the Session's quarrel with their Clerk in 1790. Of course it is well enough known that cock and bull stories about elders appropriating the poor's funds have always formed part of rural gossip. The records of this parish tell of a man that was called to account by the Session in 1735, for saying that some of the elders drank the poor's money. That is just a sample of the idle fables that senseless or ill-conditioned people would make themselves and others believe. And William Fisher was the kind of man that people were apt to raise stories about. He was what was termed a great professor, not exactly in the sense of being a pretender, but in the sense of making his convictions known and his light shine in full blaze before men. He is spoken of by old people, whose parents knew him intimately, as a man of wonderful gifts in prayer, and we may suppose that both at sick-beds and at funerals his gifts would be conspicuously displayed. He was a zealous disciplinarian too, and was frequently sent by the Session on delicate missions of enquiry into *famas* affecting members of the congregation. As Antony said of Lepidus, he was—

> "A slight unmeritable man
> Meet to be sent on errands."

To a certain class of people he must accordingly have been

obnoxious, and all latitudinarians would naturally enjoy the pleasure of finding some little rent in his garments. Stories to his discredit would be eagerly received, not examined very carefully, industriously circulated, and adorned with exaggerations. Myths would eventually assume the form of historical facts.* But whatever were his merits or demerits, it is to my mind simply incredible that any serious allegation of his tampering with the funds of the poor could ever have reached the ears of the Session without leading to a searching investigation. The rights and welfare of the poor were subjects on which Mr. Auld and his Session were zealous to excess. It was zeal for the good of the poor that first led Mr. Auld to quarrel with Mr. Gavin Hamilton, and it was probably owing to the way in which Mr. Auld displayed his zeal that Mr. Hamilton became remiss in his attendance on religious ordinances. And the noise that Mr Auld and the Session made for whole nine years about Mr. Hamilton's declinature to account for his incomplete return of poor's rates during the short time he collected the assessment, proves that if the Session had been cognisant of any *fama*, to which the slightest credit was attached, of an elder's appropriating parish or poor's funds, that *fama* would have induced a searching enquiry.† And there is no notice, as I have said, of any

---

In Cunningham's life of Burns it is alleged that the satire of the poet "made holy Willie think of suicide." It is not to be wondered at, especially if Willie was innocent of what Burns laid to his charge. It is indeed not impossible that the annoyance suffered by Fisher from the circulation of baseless slanders against him may have fostered his tippling habits.

† There was no charge of dishonesty brought against Mr. Hamilton. He was simply complained of for declining to do one of two things—either pay to the Session the total amount of assessment laid on the heritors for support of the poor, or shew what heritors had failed to pay their assessment. It was very common last century for heritors to decline payment of poor's rates. In 1737 the heritors of Galston gave orders that those who had not paid their stent for the year 1735-6 should be

such *fama* regarding William Fisher in any part of the Session Records. The only person called to account by the Session of Mauchline for tampering with the poor's funds during or near to the time of Burns's connection with the parish was the kirk-officer, and his misbehaviour was not of a very flagrant kind. He was appointed by the Session to distribute the pensions to the paupers, and he deducted, out of each payment he made, a half-penny as recompense for his trouble. And for doing so he was very sharply reprimanded by the Session.

The Kirk Session of Mauchline were, if possible, more strict with their own members than with the rest of the community. Not only did they take up all *famas* and reports against elders, but every year, especially during Mr. Auld's ministry, they held two special meetings for prayers and privy censures, or, as it might be better expressed, for private censures of their own members.* The appointment of these meetings as a standing part of Sessional procedure in this parish, was minuted in December, 1752. Such meetings may have been held long before that date, but a formal resolution to hold them was then minuted and carefully adhered to. As far back as 1705 the Presbytery of Ayr instructed all ministers within the bounds to meet for prayer with their elders; and in

---

"poynded and distrinzied." About the same date (1737) some of the heritors of the West Kirk Parish, Edinburgh, refused to pay rates on the ground of their being not legally exigible. In 1740 the Kirk Session of that parish instituted a prosecution of these heritors for payment, but the court decided in the heritors' favour.

* Such meetings for privy censures date almost from the Reformation. See Records of Kirk Session of Aberdeen, 1568. There were also meetings of Presbytery for privy censures, and how these meetings were conducted the following minute from the records of the Presbytery of Ayr, of date 1723, will shew :—" After Messrs. ——— had prayed by courses, and had given answers to the usual questions, they were removed two by two, and nothing being found but what was suitable, they were called in and encouraged to go on in their work." At other times things unsuitable were found, and admonition was given.

1723 the following appointment was entered in the Presbytery records:—"In order to comply with the act of last Synod as to Sessions' observing a day for prayer and privy censures, the ministers of Air are to draw up a formula of questions to be put to members of Session." In 1752 the Presbytery once more appointed "that ministers and Sessions meet frequently for prayer, and be put on privy censures." This last quoted appointment explains the occasion of the minute of December, 1752, in our parish records, that I have referred to. Our Session minutes do not indicate the form of procedure gone through at these meetings for censure, but the law of the Church directed that the elders one after another should be removed, and when one was absent the others told tales about him, and declared if they had seen or heard of anything in his behaviour requiring rebuke.

It may be said that, as a rule, nothing worthy of censure was found against the elders, nor against the session-clerk, nor church-officer either; for the obvious reason that scandals about men in honourable positions are of rare occurrence. The common entry in the minutes was, "the elders were taken on privy censures and were approven of, likewise their session-clerk and officer were approven of." But there was occasionally an exception to this rule. In 1755 two of the elders of Mauchline were censured, one for entertaining a company in his house to a late hour, and the other for being in that company. It is certain, therefore, that no elder in Mauchline Parish, especially in Mr. Auld's days, could have been known by the Session to have committed any impropriety or breach of decorum without being taken to task for it, and having his misconduct placed on permanent record.

In addition to all these modes of inquisition for the discovery and correction of faults and misconduct, there was another still more formidable than any. This was the visitation of the Parish by the Presbytery. There is no notice of any such visitation of Mauchline Parish in our extant session records, but it would be erroneous to conclude from this fact that no such visitation ever took place. The records of the Presbytery of Ayr contain accounts of many such visitations at Mauchline, and in some instances the visitations were not very pleasant, especially in the days of Mr. Maitland's incumbency. The official reports of some of these visitations I shall give separately, but here I may state what was the general form of procedure adopted on all such occasions.* First of all the minister, after having given auricular proof of his pulpit gifts, by preaching a sermon from "his *ordinary* text," was removed, and the elders were questioned about his ministerial diligence and manner of life. The questions that might be asked about him were, according to Pardovan, almost infinite in both number and variety. Among those that now-a-days would be thought most *outré* were the following :—" Is he a haunter of ale-houses? Is he a swearer of small minced oaths, such as, before God it is so? I protest before God, or Lord what is that? Saw ye him ever drink healths? Is Saturday only his book-day or is he constantly at his calling? Doth he preach plainly, or is he hard to be understood for his scholastic terms, matter, or manner of preaching? What time of day doth he ordinarily begin sermon on the Sabbath, and when doth he dismiss the people? Doth he ever censure people for idleness, breach of promise, or backbiting? Doth he restrain abuses at penny weddings? Doth he carry any way partially so that he may become popular?" After the elders had been questioned regarding the minister, the elders were themselves

---

* Appendix D.

removed, and heads of families were interrogated concerning the life and conduct of the several members of Session. The precentor and beadle were in like manner put under inquisition, and the full circle of inquiry was subsequently completed by removing heads of families and questioning minister and elders if they had any thing to say about the congregation generally, or about any individual members of it in particular. A great many other matters were inquired into,—such as the state of the church, manse, churchyard, church Bible, communion cups, the session registers, the number and names of books in the minister's library, and the provision made for the poor. Some of these inquiries were doubtless very proper and very useful, but the visitations were in many respects calculated to do a thousand times more evil than good. They encouraged a spirit of criticism, gave opportunity for the venting of calumnies, created bad feeling in the Parish, and in general produced all the mischievous effects that usually accompany or flow from vexatious interference. One cannot wonder that ministers winced a good deal under such inquisitorial visitations, and that they were tempted at times to reply somewhat tartly to remarks on their sermons, by alleging, as the minister of Maybole did in 1718, that "some tastes are more perverse and peevish than delicate." As an illustration of the tattling criticism that Presbyterial visitations evoked, the following account of what took place at the Kirk of Holyrood House, in June, 1583, may be adduced :—" John Brand, minister, being removed, it was asked if any person had aught to lay to his charge in respect of doctrine, office, life, or conversation. *Inter alia*, some persons accused him of negligence in seeking to reconcile people at variance. The said John being recalled, answered that with sundry trifling exceptions, the very contrary of that was the truth. And to justify his conduct in these exceptional cases, he added that as touching wives flyting, he found that by frequent reconciliation and removal of all fear of punishment, they were the more encouraged in their sin!" Previous to the Secession of 1843, when party feeling ran very high in the Church, the visitation of Parishes was resumed in some Presbyteries, and it is alleged was both carried on in a partisan spirit, and was made to serve party purposes.

In a previous lecture I indicated some of the complaints that were given in to the Presbytery of Ayr at Parochial visitations, and I may in subsequent lectures have occasion to indicate others. As the subject of this lecture is Church discipline, I may here state that objection was often taken by Parishioners to the way in which discipline was exercised. And, strange to say, it was to the laxity rather than the rigidity of discipline that objection was usually raised. In 1644 the Parishioners of Craigie complained "that discipline was not particularly exercised, nor order taken with sundrie persons who absented themselves on the Lord's day from the public worship, but wer spending the day in sleiping and drinking or in going to uther kirks. Also that no order wes taken with beggars and tinkers fighting and drinking about the Kirk of Riccarton (then in Craigie Parish), not only on the week days, but also on the Sabbath."

It will thus be seen what a strict and rigid system of supervision the Church in olden times exercised in every Parish. "The only complaint of profane people," said old Kirkton, "was that the government was too strict, and that they had not liberty enough to sin." It need not surprise us that remonstrances from the profane were occasionally heard.

LECTURE V.

CHURCH DISCIPLINE IN OLDEN TIMES.

What scandals were investigated by Kirk Sessions—Insolence to, or slander of any member of Session—Disrespect for the rules or ordinances of the Church—Drunkenness—Broils and bickerings—Theft—Murder—Sabbath breaking—Impurity—Witchcraft—Cursing—Heresy—Schism and Secession—Taking the bond.

IN last Lecture we considered the mode of inquisition adopted by Kirk-Sessions long ago in dealing with scandals. We saw that, for the purpose of Sessional supervision, each parish was divided into a number of districts, and that each district was assigned to the care of a particular elder, who was required to report to the Session what scandals and misorders existed within the bounds of his charge. People coming to a parish were required to bring with them testimonials, and on leaving a parish they were required, if they wished to have the benefit of Church privileges and to escape the inconvenience of Church censures, to take testimonials with them. When scandals were reported to Kirk Sessions, the parties delated were summoned to appear before the Session ; and when guilt was denied, witnesses were examined on oath. In certain cases, where proof of guilt was not established, but presumptions of guilt were not removed, persons accused were, with the sanction of the Presbytery, allowed to take an oath of exculpation, either before the Session in private or before the whole congregation, as was thought best, and then they were assoilzied and treated as innocent.

In the present lecture we have to consider the different forms of scandal that Kirk Sessions condescended or thought it their duty to take cognisance of.

It is plain that if I were to draw materials from all available sources this lecture might be expanded to the dimensions of a cyclopaedia. I propose, therefore, to confine myself in this lecture very much to what is contained in our own parish records, and by this means I shall more truly and faithfully shew what Church rule actually was in an average Ayrshire parish long ago. I shall however refer occasionally both to the laws of the Church and to the records of other Sessions than our own, so as to shew to what extent the discipline in Mauchline conformed to general usage.

The practice of Kirk Sessions at the present day is to take up no cases of scandal but such as are forced on their attention and are of such gravity that they cannot be overlooked without bringing reproach on the Church. Kirk Sessions now-a-days consider that it is not for edification that they should be officiously zealous in the exercise of their judicial authority, and that the reformation of manners in a parish is more likely to be promoted by pulpit counsel and social education than by the pains of infamy and censure. But Kirk Sessions long ago took a different view of their duty. To overlook a fault was in their opinion to connive at sin, and had a tendency to harden the sinner in his iniquity. All offences, therefore, of word and deed—such as cursing and swearing—defamation and false-hood—uncleanness and drunkenness—fighting and stealing—Sabbath breaking and venting of heresy—were taken instant notice of by Kirk Sessions, and when proved were visited with quick and sharp censure. The scandals mentioned in our records—scanty as these records are compared with the records of larger and more wicked parishes—as having come under the notice and reproof of Mauchline Kirk Session, are so many and miscellaneous, that it is no easy task to bring them all under review, and many of them are so paltry that there is risk of their recapitulation proving very tedious.

To shew, however, what was the kind of discipline exercised long ago by Kirk Sessions, I must, though it be at the risk of proving tedious, enumerate all the different sorts of charges, frivolous as well as serious, that Kirk Sessions were in the way of receiving and investigating.

Kirk Sessions, in the first place, were very careful to maintain their own dignity and good name. Any word or action that could be construed as an intentional insult to the Session, as a shew of contempt for their authority, or as a slander on any of their members, was promptly resented. And in this matter all kirk sessions were much alike, whether north of the Tay or south of the Tay, and whether urban or rural. In 1645 a man, whose name, Malcolm Fleming, betokened international pedigree, was by the General Kirk Session of Edinburgh fined in 40 merks for some act of incaution or unrestraint, which is vaguely and dubiously described as a "misbehaviour that escaped him in presence of the Session"! No liberties, it will thus be seen, were allowed to be taken in the Session's presence. In last lecture it was stated that on one occasion a man was called to account by the Kirk Session of Mauchline, for alleging that some of the elders drank the poor's money. The slander, for of course it was a slander, was simply the hasty utterance of a passionate man who wished to avenge himself on some members of the Kirk Session for the zeal they had shown in inquiring into some parts of his own conduct which could not bear investigation. And there are on record several other instances of similar speeches, made under similar circumstances, against one or more of the elders of this parish, or all of them together. These speeches, although foolish and unworthy of notice, were all declared scandals by the Session, and the utterers of them were brought to book. In 1674 and 1675, one Adam Reid was twice over summoned to the Session and rebuked for "cursing and railing on ye elders." In 1707 another case of similar misconduct was reported to the Session. The culprit, in this instance, was a woman whose quarrels with a neighbour had been the subject of ecclesiastical inquisition. She had been found in the wrong and she thereupon accused the Session of injustice, and went the further length of calling one of the members a Judas Iscariot. The last occasion on which, so far as I have observed, the Session of Mauchline took notice of any outside speeches made against themselves was in 1735, during the ministry of Mr. Maitland. And it was one of those speeches which so far overshoot the mark that they might be laughed at and let alone. The railer had been provoked by the Session's refusing him a token of admission to the Lord's Table, and he gave vent to his wrath by calling the whole Session—"ane and a'—a pack o' villains." Such ebullitions of bucolic temper, it will now be admitted on all hands, were scarcely worthy of serious consideration, and when kirk sessions condescended to take notice of such petty faults, we may be sure that in their high ecclesiastical state they did not eat the bread of idleness.

Prior to the date at which our Session Records begin, there were people in Mauchline Parish faulted by the Church for their disrespect, both to the Kirk Session and minister. The records of the Presbytery of Ayr shew that in December, 1646, George Campbell of Brigend, in Mauchline, compeared before the Presbytery and " wes gravely challenged for his wicked miscarriage against Mr. Thomas Wyllie, his minister, and against the Session of Mauchline and magistrat there. The Presbytery appointed a letter to be written to the

Commission of the Kirk for joyning in supplication with the parochinars, that order may be taken with the said George." A few months later, "Robert (George?) Campbell, in Mauchline, compeared in sackcloth for abusing his minister, Mr. Thomas Wyllie, both in speech and carriage, and was ordained to satisfie in sackcloth in the Kirks of Machlin, Gaston, Tarbolton, Uchiltrie, and Cumnock, and thereafter to compeir before the Presbytery."* But in respect of slandering their spiritual rulers, Mauchline people were no worse than their neighbours. In Fenwick records there is notice of a man's being delated to the Session of that Parish in 1646 for "calling one of the elders a mansworn slaverie loon."

It is not to be supposed, however, that the carefulness shewn by kirk sessions to maintain and vindicate their own good name was caused either entirely or chiefly by jealousy of their personal honour and dignity. They considered that reflections on themselves were reflections on the service in which they were engaged, and that contempt for the officers of the Church would lead to, if it did not spring from, contempt for religion. We find, accordingly, that kirk sessions were particularly strict in seeing that no slight, or appearance of slight, should be shewn towards any religious ordinance. Twice over at least there are notices of men's being summoned before the Session, in Mauchline, for returning small pieces of coin instead of tokens to the elders at the communion table. On one occasion a farmer gave a farthing instead of a token, and on another occasion a young lad gave a sixpence instead of a token. Both of these acts could have been done by mistake, and the wonder is that some such mistakes did not occur at every sacra-

---

* Such penitential tours were not uncommon in the seventeenth century, and the discipline they constituted was called "circular satisfaction."

ment. The tokens were small round pieces of lead: some were about as thin as a sixpence, and others were about the thickness of a farthing. But it was just within the bounds of possibility that the substitution of a coin for a token was a device for obtaining, or helping some one to obtain, an unauthorised privilege. Indeed, it was not unusual for persons under scandal to force, or fraudulently find, their way to the Lord's table. In the year 1775, at a meeting of the Kirk Session after the communion at Mauchline, it was reported that a woman under scandal had been seen at the communion table, and that she had a token. Her name was on the list of those to whom tokens were to be refused, and yet she had obtained what it was minuted she was not to get. There was another person whom the Session were surprised to see at the sacrament that year, and it was resolved that he should be asked to tell the Session how and where he had procured his token. And incidents like these occurred in other parishes. As far back as 1647, when the Covenanted Church was in the height of her pride and purity, a man was called before the Session of Galston for "giving a ticket to a strange unknown woman, to whom the minister refused a ticket for manifold reasons"; and the said woman was also called before the Session "for taking a ticket from ——, and coming to the Lord's table." At a still earlier date than that, namely, in 1634, a man was taken to task by the Kirk Session of Galston for "breech of the act set down anent these qho keipit not their tickets but gave them to uthers," and having pled guilty he was ordained "to mak his repentance and peye 10s." *

---

* The Kirk Session of Galston in 1628 "statut and ordained that quhatsumever persone quha hes the credit of the keiping quhat the kirk orders upon the communion daye, that brings in or admittis any persones quha ar reflectabill to this kirk or disobedient to the same in any wayes, without the consent of the haill Sessioune, sall pay £10 to the use of the kirk."

When a man presented a coin, therefore, instead of a token, it was deemed necessary for the Session to take notice of the matter formally and officially, so that all the congregation might know that the Lord's table was not to be approached without a Sessional pass. Wodrow mentions in one of his books a strange, and for the moment a very painful scene, which occurred at his own communion at Eastwood, in the year 1711. Two or three English soldiers presented themselves at that communion, and one of these came forward without a token. He happened to be seated near the upper end of the table, within whispering reach of Wodrow himself. He was seen by Wodrow to have no token, and he was desired by Wodrow to come out to the churchyard for a moment's private conference. He was then asked outside why he had presumed to seat himself at the Lord's table without a token of admission. "In my native country," said the man, "there is no such custom as you refer to, and if I have given offence it was not of intention, but in ignorance of Scottish ways." Wodrow then examined him at the church-door regarding his knowledge of the gospel and his faith in Christ, and being well satisfied with his answers gave him a token and told him he might go forward to the next table. The position that Kirk Sessions took up was this, —All our discipline, in its main provisions, at least, is of divine authority, and we ourselves are solemnly ordained to rule for Christ in Christ's Church, and we dare not therefore let either our discipline or our ordination suffer contempt at the hands of any profane or ignorant person.

Among the sins named by St. Paul as excluding people from the kingdom of God, drunkenness is mentioned. It may be presumed, therefore, that drunkenness would be one of the scandals that Kirk Sessions would visit with censure, and so it was. The Church of Scotland never went the length of

Jonathan the son of Rechab in forbidding the use of either wine or ale or alcohol, and she never made total abstinence from intoxicating liquors a pre-requisite for Church membership. Her principle has always been that men should never in zeal for any cause that seems good in their own eyes, go beyond what Scripture has commanded or prohibited, never exclude whom God has not ordered to be excluded, nor curse whom God has not cursed.* But she denounced all untimeous and excessive drinking, and forbade publicans to supply drink at unseasonable hours. In the year 1675, there was a publican named Campbell brought before the Kirk Session of Mauchline; and the minutes state that, "being convict, by his own confession and the deposition of one witness, of selling ale until the four hours in the Sabbath morning, he was appointed to be rebuked publicly," that is, in the presence of the congregation, the following Sabbath. And in 1702 "the Session," I quote *verbatim* from the records, "appointed the minister to give a public rebuke to all the brewers in the toun for selling drink beyond the ordinary time of the night." What was counted the ordinary time of night in 1702 was probably ten o'clock. At least it is stated in the Records of the Burgh of Aberdeen that in 1601 the magistrates issued an order that no ale nor wine should be sold after that hour, and in Calder's squib we read of a man's being called before the Kirk Session "for drinking after the ten hour bell." †

---

* The Galston Records of 1640 describe the two kinds of censurable drinking as "excessive and exorbitant drinking in the day tyme," and "extraordinarie drinking after ten hours at even."

† It may be stated that there was an old Act of Parliament which ordained that "na man sall be found in taverns after *nine* hours at night and the bell, under the pain of prison, and gif the aldermen or baillies puttes them not to prison they shall pay 50 shillings."—Regiam Majestatem, Part 2nd, p. 58. In 1646 the Kirk Session of Fenwick ordained that "if any be found drinking in any change-house

But it was not merely the sellers of ale that the Kirk Session came down upon. It was stated in last lecture that in 1755 two elders were rebuked in the Session for drinking after elders' hours. Neither of these elders was alleged to have been the worse of drink, but they were said to have created scandal by the length of time they sat at their potations. And while untimeous drinking was censured, much more was excessive drinking. Our records contain many entries of rebukes for drunkenness, especially when aggravated by swearing or violent conduct. One extract will suffice to shew what was the practice of the Kirk Session when a case of drunkenness was reported. And to prevent its being supposed that the instance adduced was in any way exceptional or antiquated, I shall quote from a minute of comparatively recent date. In 1772 " James Craig (I purposely change the name) being charged with the sin of drunkenness, was called and compeared, and acknowledged his guilt and his sorrow for it, Declared also his resolution to behave well in time coming."

---

within the parish after nine hours at night, they shall acknowledge the same publicly before the congregation and pay ane merk, as also ye seller of the drink to give satisfaction in like manner." The Kirk Session of Galston in 1634 caused proclamation that wherever "hostlers within the parochine sells drink or keips people drinkand in their house after ten hours at even ather upon ye Sabbath night or oulk night, they sall underly the censure and acts of the kirk in penaltie and repentance." In 1720 the Galston Session appointed "that the bell be rung at 6 in the morning and at 9 at night, ye drum to go at 5 in the morning and at 10 at night." An old ballad says,—

"There were four drunken maidens
Together did convene,
From twelve o'clock in a May morning
Till ten rang out at e'en,
Till ten rang out at e'en,
And then they gie'd it ower."

Elders' hours is a phrase that has long been in use to designate ten o'clock at night, and the most probable way of accounting for the phrase is that ten o'clock was the hour at which people were sent home by the elders from the ale-house.

As a rule, people accused of drunkenness were very civil to the Kirk Session, and like Mr. Craig were ready to profess any amount of sorrow for their sins, and to promise good behaviour for the future. There were exceptions to that rule, however, as there are to most rules. One whose conduct formed very marked exception to that rule, was Agnes Ronald, better known to the readers of Burns's poems as Poosie Nansie. Agnes had the privilege of receiving many admonitions from the Kirk Session, but to no purpose. In 1773 it was reported to the Session "that Agnes Ronald, wife of George Gibson, is habitually drunk, troublesome to her neighbours, and frequently disturbs the sober passengers." Agnes was summoned, therefore, to appear before the Session and give an account of herself. And she was not reluctant to make appearance. She did not need to be bidden twice, and when she came to the Session she was quite at her ease, and had her mind made up what to say. The minute states, "compeared Agnes Ronald, and declares before the Session that she is resolved to continue in her disorderly way." And as if that were not plain enough speaking, she more pointedly "declared her resolution to continue in the sin of drunkenness." Such a declaration would have flabbergasted many a Kirk Session. Poor Mr. Maitland would have been thrown into "consternation" for months if such a speech had been made to him. But Mr. Auld was of sterner stuff, and his equanimity was not disturbed by Mrs. Gibson's vapouring. He did not even condescend to reply to her insolence, but got it minuted that "the Session, considering the foresaid foolish resolution and expression, do immediately exclude her from the privileges of the Church until she shall profess her repentance." When, if ever, she was induced to profess repentance, I have not noted; but I have observed that for years and years her name appeared regularly on the list of those to whom tokens of admission to the Lord's table were to be refused.

Occasions sometimes occurred on which stronger measures than those I have indicated were adopted by Kirk Sessions in their laudable desire to reclaim drunkards from their evil habits. In 1646, a man at Galston was found the worse of drink after having promised to abstain from the use of intoxicating liquors. He was thus guilty of a breach of promise, as well as of an act of intemperance, and he was accordingly made "to sit down on his knees before the Session and confess his fault." The Kirk Session of Fenwick had to deal with a similar case the following year, and with the delinquent's own consent they entered on their register, that if found guilty of drunkenness again he would be made to stand in the joggs at the kirk door, and afterwards in the public place of repentance within the kirk, and pay for penalty the sum of 40s., with duplicate every time that the offence should be repeated. Sometimes, however, Sessions were so baffled in their dealings with these habituals that they had to invoke Presbyterial wisdom for advice and Presbyterial authority for correction. In 1710 it was minuted by the Presbytery of Ayr that an inebriate whose name was mentioned had been "frequently guilty of drunkenness since the time he promised to the Presbytery to amend his life," but that Lord Cathcart and others had "taken some course to oblige the said David to live more soberly." And very strict inquisition was made by Presbyteries into all sins of jollity. In 1693 a probationer within the bounds got a surprise one morning in being taken to task by his reverend fathers for "drinking and learning others to drink healths." Singular words of wisdom, too, were occasionally emitted by the culprits who were brought in their sober senses before the Presbytery to answer for outbreaks of insobriety. A philologist from Cumnock made a statement in 1697 that might have immortalised a German. He comprehended the wide significance of the word intemperance—as applicable to words of haste and deeds of violence, as well as to states of intoxication—and on hearing his charge read over therefore he confessed himself guilty of "intemperance, and particularly of drunkenness."

Besides drunkenness, all the other common kinds of immorality, such as swearing and fighting and purloining, were taken strict cognisance of by Kirk Sessions. Many of the cases of cursing and beating reported in the earlier pages of our Parochial records were of such a domestic nature that it might have been better if they had been overlooked. A quiet word in season by the elder of the district when he went his monthly rounds might have done more good than a citation to the Kirk Session. But these old broils and bickerings, although they ought perhaps to be buried in oblivion, had occasionally a humorous aspect, and great is the temptation to unearth one or two of the least unmentionable of them. In 1682 Jean Campbell and John Campbell, it does not matter of where, were summoned to answer to a charge of scolding and railing. Both parties, *mentibus consciis recti*, innocent as doves, presented themselves before Mr. Veitch and his covenanting elders. Jean smiled at the charge when it was intimated to her, and explained that she had only "reproved John for lowsing a beast and letting it goe amang the corn." John, on the other hand, assured the Session that all the extent of his delinquency was calling Jean "an ill-favoured blade," for putting on him the blame of a cow's misdeeds. At the present day we are sometimes shocked to read in the newspapers of cruel and cowardly cases of wife-beating, but two hundred years ago some married women were more than able to take care of themselves, and be-pommeled husbands had to creep for shelter under the wing of ecclesiastical protection.* In 1672, Jean Edwards appeared before the Kirk Session, and, "partly by her own confession (for she gloried in her shame), and partly by witnesses that were sworn, was convict of frequent scolding, cursing, swearing, and fighting with her husband, Hew Smith, and beating of him." For these unwomanly practices, Jean was ordered "to be publicly rebuked and suspended from the sacrament of the Lord's supper." And the merry wives of Mauchline were not content with rattling tattoos on the backs of patient husbands, but they now and again had bouts with each other. As recently as 1773 information was lodged with the Session that a woman in the village had attacked her mother-in-law, and "had wounded her in the head by a stroke with the iron tongs." And tongs were not the most lethal weapons that the Amazons of Mauchline flourished in the days when our great-grandfathers were under petticoat government. In 1777 a report came to the ears of the Session that "Kitran Angus had threatened to stick Robert Gibb with a grape." Kitran was instantly called to account, but when the charge against her was announced she jauntily told the Session that she had not meanly taken any

---

* Mr. Burton in his History of Scotland quotes an interesting account of the people of Scotland sent to Ferdinand and Isabella by Don Pedro de Ayala in 1498, in which the following sentences occur:—"The women are courteous in the extreme. I mention this because they are really honest, *though very bold*. They are absolute mistresses of their houses, and even of their husbands, in all things concerning the administration of their property, income as well as expenditure." In the records of the Kirk Session of Ayr for 1605, in John Welsh's time, there is a minute regarding a delinquent, who is described as "ane verie vitious woman, . . . quha in face of Session threatened her guidman."—Select Biographies, Wodrow Society. Galston wives too were delated (1694) for "unchristian behaviour towards their husbands and children," and even (1647) "wronging their goodfathers by casting peas at their faces."

undue advantage of her antagonist, for "if she had a grape he had a flail." It is devoutly to be hoped that Kitran and Robert came to be thankful to the mercy of an over-ruling Providence that they were both spared to compear before the Kirk Session, and that nothing worse befell them than a well-merited rebuke. The weapons of their warfare were fearful, but the story of that warfare has its moral. Passion in its fury overleaps the mark. Had Kitran been content to brandish a broom, and Robert to use a whip, each might have left on the other's person enduring marks of degradation. But their vaulting ambition, in its scorn of things familiar, moved them to lay hold of weapons, destructive and deadly enough in all conscience, but too unwieldy for dexterous handling.

The cases of theft that came before the Kirk Session of Mauchline, I am happy to say, comprise a very light calendar. Neither in number nor enormity were they much of a reproach to the parish. The notice that was taken of them, however, shows how rigorous was the Church discipline. In 1757 a woman was delated for stealing coals out of the minister's close—in 1773 a man was delated for abstracting a hive of bees from the cooper's garden—in 1774 a woman confessed that at last fair she had lifted a jug from a pewterer's stall, but only, she said, for the inspection of a friend who wished to purchase a jug—and in 1777 there was entered on the list of those to be excluded from the Lord's supper the name of Jean Mitchell, "for stealing a hen as alleged."* These are, if not all, at least the principal cases of theft that, so far as I have noted, were

---

* In 1773 the Kirk Session declared themselves unanimously of opinion that "George Gibson keeps a very irregular house, and that his wife and daughter (Poosie Nansie and Racer Jess) are guilty of resetting stolen goods, knowing the same to be stolen."

ever reported to the Kirk Session of Mauchline. And there is a sorrowful story to tell about Jean Mitchell, the last-mentioned of the Mauchline thieves. Although guilt had never been brought home to her, and she was only "alleged" to have stolen a hen, yet for five years her name was placed on the black list of those that were to be debarred from communion, with the same words each year appended to her name, "for stealing a hen as alleged." And what is more sad to state, the scandal was never removed during her lifetime, for in the records of the year 1782 there is a stroke drawn through her name and her alleged offence, and on the margin of the book is written the word that can never be recalled or deleted, "*dead*." The impression left on my mind from reading old Session Records, is that the people of Ayrshire long ago were wonderfully free from sins of covetousness. The charges of theft that came before Kirk Sessions were far fewer and more paltry than I expected to find, and there was often great sensitiveness exhibited under accusations of dishonesty. In 1633 there was an honest man, for I cannot doubt that, both in the ancient and the modern sense of the word, he was honest, that could get no sleep to his eyes nor slumber to his eyelids, because a prating and malicious neighbour had said of him, "Thow wes followit out of Loudoune with stolne yairn." Would that more people now-a-days were distressed with such reproaches!

It will not surprise any one to be told that in our extant Session Records there is no case of murder, because if such a thing as murder had happened in the parish we might have expected that "hanging of the author should have prevented all further censures." There was, however, a case of murder in this parish, which was taken up by the Church courts, and apparently by them alone.* The murder was committed in 1642, which was nearly thirty years before the date of our oldest extant minute of Kirk Session. There is no reference to the murder, therefore, in our Session Records; but in the records of the Presbytery of Ayr there is a full account of the ecclesiastical procedure that was taken against the murderer. In the month of June, 1642, the Presbytery ordained "Mr. George Young, minister at Mauchline, to summond from pulpit Mungo Campbell, sone to Hew Campbell in Netherplace, to compeir before the Presbyterie to be holden in Ayr, the 20th July next to come, to answer before them for the cruel and unnaturall murthering and killing, in the town of Machling, of John Campbell in Mossgavill, as wes gravely related by the said Mr. George." This pulpit citation was disregarded by Mr. Mungo, more probably from fear than from disrespect, and we may presume it had to be renewed oftener than once. At length, on the 12th April, 1643, it was minuted in the Presbytery book that Mungo Campbell, being called and not compearing, "Alexander Peden, his brother-in-law, presented a supplication in his name, subscribed with his hands, wherein was declared the willingness of the said Mungo to give obedience and satisfaction to the Presbyterie, if possiblie he might compeir befoir them without hazard of his life. The quhilk supplication being read and considered, the Presbyterie fand themselves satisfied with the samen, and therefore appointed Mr. George Young and William Campbell of Hollhouse to speak the partic offendit, and to deal with them, to give assurance not to persew the said Mungo till he gave signes of his public repentance as he

---

* In 1648 the General Assembly enacted that for the sin of murder people should make public profession of repentance fifty-two Sabbaths, in case the magistrate do not his duty in punishing the crime capitally.

suld be enjoyned." If Mungo was troubled by a sense of sin at all, he was at least not shamed by it into good conduct, for the next account we have of him in the Presbytery records states that to his former transgression he had added recent iniquity. In November, 1645, "report was made," so runs the minute of Presbytery, " that Mungo Campbell in Machlin, who this long tyme hes lyen under the scandall of murther, not yet satisfied, hes fallen in ye sinne" that always implies a partner in guilt. " The Presbytery, considering the hynousnes of the said scandalls, thought meit that they shuld be represented to the nixt ensuing Synod at Hamilton, thaire to be advysed upon, for course taking with him thereanent." Synodical authority, combined perhaps with a sense of the inconvenience of long continued isolation from society, induced Mungo at last to make peace with the Church, and it is to be hoped to seek peace also with his Maker. In September, 1646, therefore, he appeared before the Presbytery " in the habite of sackcloth, and in all humility confessed the unnatural murther and killing of John Campbell, his cousin-german. As also he confessed his frequent falls in . . . (sins of affection) sensyne. The Presbyterie, considering thereof, ordained the said Mungo to compeir in the habite of sackclothe in the Kirk of Machlin in the place of public repentance two Lord's dayes till the Presbytery advyse at thair nixt meeting what further order shall be enjoyned to him." After this he was directed to make a tour of some half-dozen neighbouring kirks in sackcloth, on successive Sabbaths, and ultimately, in December, 1646, he was referred to the Session of Machlin, and his minister, Mr. Thomas Wyllie, to be received by them "betwix and the next Presbyterie, he giving sufficient signs of repentance." Some may perhaps think that Mungo was let off lightly for such a crime as murder, but it depends altogether on the constitution of a man's mind whether he would consider public execution, or public humiliation in sackcloth for three months, the greater ordeal.

Of what may be termed common offences, the one that, next to impurity, figures most prominently in our Session Records, and I may say in all Kirk Session Records, is Sabbath breaking. In last lecture it was explained how Kirk Sessions came to be so stringent in maintaining the sanctity of the Sabbath. I have now to shew how rigorous and vigorous the Kirk Session of this parish was in putting down every form of Sabbath desecration. In the Appendix to Principal Lee's Lectures on the History of the Church of Scotland, there is an interesting abstract of the cases of Sabbath breaking that came before the Kirk Session of St. Cuthbert's, Edinburgh, from 1587 to 1699. This abstract shows what a great variety of both works and games were, during the period in question, engaged in on Sundays, and complained of in Kirk Sessions as breaches of the Sabbath.* Among the works so enumerated

---

* Among the forms of Sabbath desecration for which people were delated to the Kirk Session of Fenwick, I have noted the following in the records of that parish.

    1645—Making butter and cheese upon the Sabbath.
    ,,   Going to Mearns market to be fee'd on the communionSabbath.
    ,,   Cursing within the kirk on the Sabbath before the minister came in.
    ,,   Mawing and sheiring of grasses.
    ,,   Weiving on the Fasting Thursday (this was counted the same as Sabbath desecration).
    ,,   Staying from the kirk on the Sabbath day, and keeping a drunken beggar in her house in tyme of sermon.
    ,,   Drying of clothes on the Sabbath.
    1646—Bearing of burdens on Sabbath and travelling.
    1647—Driving a cow towards Kilmarnock fair on the Sabbath.
    ,,   Selling milk on ane Satturday night after ten o'clock.
    1658—Going to Newmilns on the Fast Day, and receiving some money there, and paying a pctt.
    ,,   Cleaning a byre and making cheese on Sunday.
    1699—Going to Rutherglen fair with a horss and cow a little after the setting of the sun on Sabbath.

were the shearing of corn and the stacking of corn—the baking of bread and the selling of milk—the pulling of peas and the staking of peas—the carrying of parcels—and the subscription of bonds. Among the pastimes detailed were dancing and football, bowls and pennystones, fishing trout and catching laverocks. There is not such a large and varied table of Sabbath sins to be found in the records of this parish, but there are still a few not unnotable instances of what was held to be Sabbath profanation. Between 1670 and 1680 there were several cases of people's being charged before the Session with playing at the " pennystone " on the Lord's day, but so far as I have noticed there is no other game that the parishioners of Mauchline have, ever since 1669, been alleged to have played on the Sabbath. In 1675 two men of the name of Campbell were "delated for travelling to Glasgow on the Sabbath day, and for bringing a cow from Eaglesham on the Sabbath," and for these offences they were subjected to a public rebuke. The same year five persons were delated in the Session for bringing home herrings on Sunday. In 1703 a woman confessed to the Session that she " was almost washing yearn on the Sabbath," but she wished to exculpate herself of such a dreadful approximation to sin by alleging a mistake in her reckoning of

---

In the records of the Kirk Session of Ayr for 1604 and 1605, we read of people's being delated to the Session for "playing at ye carts on Sabbath," and for "playing at the coppiehoall in the kirk door on Saboth."

Long ago there was a good deal of Sabbath profanation in Galston, and some queer instances of it might be cited. For example, in 1705, a man was delated for causing a dog to catch a sheep, and calling witnesses to prove that the sheep was his. The Session, it may be said, however, did their best for a *hundred years* by rebukes and penalties to restrain the evil. In 1648 they appointed two elders to "visit the town and gatesyd on the Sabbath night about seven hours, and see that none be in toune except the inhabitants thereof." They prohibited on the Sabbath all journeying, all blocking or niffering, and all drinking, "passing an hour after both sermons."

the days of the week. There are mistakes, however, and mistakes—mistakes that are innocent and mistakes that are culpable—mistakes that are excusable and mistakes that are inexcusable—and the Kirk Session held it inexcusable that any person in this parish should not know Sunday from Saturday. Strange to say, a similar mistake was made by a married couple in Mauchline Parish so recently as 1777. One John Hunter and his wife went to the harvest rig and cut corn till they were checked by a neighbour that was better versed in the calendar. In 1780 a strange complaint and an equally strange counter-complaint were sent in to the Kirk Session. The complaint was by a man who alleged that a woman whom he named had paid him a visit in men's clothes, and told him several falsehoods. The counter-complaint of the woman was that her accuser had been guilty of sundry "immoralities, particularly of profaning the Sabbath by employing a barber on that day." For this particular offence the barber was of course as much to blame as the man whose beard had been trimmed, and indeed rather more so, for he had previously been brought to book for the same offence, and had been made to sign a bond, which still stands in the Session records, that he would never again exercise his craft on the Sabbath. But what signifies a bond to a man without a conscience? The barber had been too long accustomed to do evil to take kindly to well-doing. Both the restraints and the services of the Sabbath were irksome to him. In 1781 he was reported to have become "negligent in his attendance on ordinances," and the minister was instructed to speak to him on the subject. In 1784 his negligence was again commented on, and he was named in the Session along with a gentleman widely known from his connection with Burns, as requiring to be admonished of his sin, and warned to beware of a presumptuous approach to the Lord's table.

The zeal of Mr. Auld in enforcing Sabbath observance has, as we all know, become historical, and that zeal has been attributed to "pique and ill-nature." It will be seen, however, from what has been said, that Mr. Auld's conduct in reference to Sabbath observance was all of a piece throughout the whole course of his ministry. His zeal for the Sabbath did not begin in the days of Burns, and it was not confined to his dealings with any one particular person. It was also, whether we may think it expedient or not, in strict conformity to both the written law of the Church and the immemorial action of the Kirk Session in the parish as far back as our records extend. And it was nothing unusual a hundred years ago. The same strict discipline as he exercised was exercised in many other parishes, both in the neighbourhood and at a distance. In the Parish of Lumphanan a man in 1785 was taken to task by the Kirk Session for going to see his mother on a Sabbath day, and carrying a stone of meal to her. He refused to admit that that conduct was any breach of the Sabbath, and for his obstinacy in maintaining that view, he was, the present minister writes to me, solemnly excommunicated. The Sabbatarianism of Mr. Auld and the Kirk Session of Mauchline, between 1784 and 1788, was just part of the religious spirit of the age, and if that Sabbatarianism seems to us rigid and oppressive, illiberal and inexpedient, it must be allowed to have at least the virtue of logical consistency. There was also something grand and dignified in the conduct of these old Sabbatarians. They had none of the frivolity of our modern pleasure-seekers, who seem to think that duty consists in denying ourselves nothing that is pleasant and enjoyable. They surrendered freely and unreservedly a whole day in seven to their Maker, and it may be questioned if in that act they did not display a statelier and purer pattern of Christian life than those people who boast of their enlarged views and their wide humanitarian sympathies.

It might be expected that I should here enter at large into the successive dealings that the Kirk Session of Mauchline in the days of Burns had with Mr. Gavin Hamilton in regard to alleged Sabbath breaking. These dealings have been much commented on by some of the poet's biographers. It would occupy too much space, however, in this lecture, to detail the tedious controversies that arose out of the action which the Kirk Session thought it their duty to take in this matter. I may here state summarily that the charges brought against Mr. Hamilton, not all at once, but on different occasions specially libelled, were—irregular attendance on divine ordinances, setting out on a Sabbath day on a journey to Carrick, habitual if not total neglect of family worship in his own house, and giving orders for a dish of new potatoes to be dug on a Sunday forenoon. Whatever may be said or thought of the particular circumstances under which these charges were made, and of the spirit and temper in which they were made, there can be little doubt that all the offences specified were matters that, both by law and custom, fell under the Kirk Session's cognisance.* In 1733 the Presbytery of Ayr passed and

---

* On the one hand the Kirk Session maintained that they were merely executing the laws of the Church—which is true—and on the other hand Mr. Hamilton and his friends alleged that pique and ill-nature were at the bottom of their zeal —and quite possibly their zeal may have been associated with baser feelings. Where is there absolute purity? Burns has stated the question concisely from Mr. Hamilton's point of view.

> " An honest man may like a glass,
> An honest man may like a lass ;
> But mean revenge and malice fause
> He'll still disdain ;
> And then cry zeal for gospel laws,
> Like some we ken."

minuted a special resolution that "each minister shall deal privately with such of their people as neglect to worship God in their families, and that prophane the Lord's day by absenting themselves from ordinances, or that travels on it by journeying"; and that "an account of their success be enquired in next privy censures." In 1755 the Presbytery again, "considering the too frequent profanation of the Lord's day by unnecessary travelling and absenting from public worship, resolved to have the proper remedies of this growing evil." *

By far the most notable case of Sabbath desecration that ever came before the Kirk Session of Mauchline was one that occurred six-and-thirty years before Mr. Auld's settlement in the parish. It was mentioned in this lecture that one of the forms of Sabbath desecration taken notice of by the Kirk Session of St. Cuthbert's, Edinburgh, was the subscription of bonds. In 1649 several persons were, for writing out, subscribing, and being witnesses to a bond on the Lord's day, severally rebuked and fined by that Session twenty shillings each. In Mauchline there was a similar case in 1706. The bailie of the burgh (whose name was John Baird), the clerk of the burgh, the

---

* Brodie of Brodie wrote in his diary in 1653:—"Lord, for a blessing. And put it in their hearts to do for the Lord and to set family duty on foot again in this parish in every yeoman's house and other man's, and in Forres, and to debar from sacrament these that worship not God in their family." In 1604 the Kirk Session of Aberdeen ordered family worship to be made twice a day in every house. The General Assembly passed an Act of similar tenor (not identical) in 1694, and again in 1711 and 1819.

The Synod of Galloway in 1671 (during Episcopacy), "taking to their serious consideration the great profanation of the Lord's day by people assuming to themselves a liberty needlessly to travel, yea, to begin their journeys on the Lord's day, . . . publicly testify against the samen, and warn their people to abstain therefrom, with certification that such as shall be found guilty shall be censured for the same."

In 1731 two people were brought before the Presbytery of Ayr for gathering nuts on a Sunday.

treasurer of the burgh, and the officer of the burgh—all the civil dignitaries and officials in the town—the administrators of the law and the custodians of the public peace—were that year cited to appear before the Session "for attesting a man to be a soldier with the young laird of Kerse, the last Lord's day, betwixt six and seven o'clock in the morning." All the parties honourably obeyed the citation, and frankly acknowledged the act with which they were charged. But this acknowledgment brought the Session of a sudden to their wits' end. They were not quite prepared for such a *denouement*. They were at a loss what to do. They did not know what censure to inflict. If they had been brought before Cæsar and been condemned by Cæsar to the stocks, they could have lifted up their testimony and declared their joy at being thought worthy to suffer. But they were placed in a far more embarrassing position than that. Cæsar was brought before them, and Cæsar had pled guilty to their impeachment, and the question was what to do with Cæsar. In one of his letters Baillie writes:—" I know of no people that have so much need of a Presbytery as the people of London." The Kirk Session of Mauchline, in their dealings with Cæsar, felt the same necessity—the necessity of a Presbytery to guide them in their difficulties and strengthen them in their weakness. They minuted, therefore, that "the manner of rebuke is to be delayed till the next Presbytery—till the Session get the mind of the Presbytery." As a rule, Presbyteries indicate their wisdom by judicious reserve, and remit cases to Kirk Sessions to be dealt with according to the laws of the Church—leaving Sessions where they were, when Sessions don't happen to know the laws of the Church—but in this case the Presbytery of Ayr was more communicative, and gave express injunction that the Sabbath breakers should be rebuked publicly in face of the congregation. Only people that have sat in chairs of state can imagine the astonishment of the

Mauchline bailie when he got notice of this finding. "My conscience!" he exclaimed, "are the magistrates and officers of this burgh to be marched off some Sabbath morning from the Council Chambers to the repentance stool, and to be set down there alongside of half-a-dozen limmers, as if we had been all in the same transgression? This would not only make municipal dignity ridiculous, but would subvert all civil authority in the parish." A consultation of the burgh officers was held, therefore, and the Presbytery were supplicated to relax their sentence. But when Presbyteries have a duty to perform, they despise threats and entreaties alike. They take their stand on Scripture and conscience, and refuse to resile. And so the Presbytery told the Mauchline supplicants that in matters of discipline there could be no respect of persons, and that the sins of magistrates were not less but more hurtful to the public than the sins of common people. The Presbytery, therefore, so runs the entry in our Session Records, adhered to their former appointment, "that ye fornamed persons be rebuked publicly the nixt Lord's day." When next Lord's day came the parish dignitaries did not appear in the place of rebuke, and "the appointment of the Session and Presbyterie" was continued till the following Sabbath. During the intervening week the dignitaries made another effort to get the rigour of the Presbytery's sentence modified. They sent in to the Session on the Thursday a humble petition, entreating to be rebuked in private, and to have the rebuke signified to the congregation next Lord's day, by the minister's "calling on their names, and them owning that they were in fault." The upshot was, that on Sunday "the fore named persons were called on before the whole congregation, and confessed they were faulty, and sorrie for the same, and promised a more circumspect life." The Session, it will thus be seen, carried their point, and enhanced their victory with moderation, by treating the subject Cæsar with all the respect and courtesy due to his rank and title.

It need scarcely be said, for it is a matter of public notoriety, that a very large part of the contents of Kirk Session Records is taken up with cases of impurity. But on this subject I do not mean to say much. There is one entry, however, in the scroll minutes of the Mauchline Session for 1788, so very extraordinary, that, partly because it is extraordinary, and partly because it has been seen by literary men interested in the writings and history of Burns, and may therefore any day come to the light without proper explanations, I can scarcely pass it over. In Mr. Auld's time it was customary for the Session to hold a special meeting every year, before the administration of the Lord's supper. The purpose of this meeting was to go over the "examine roll," and to make out a list of persons under scandal. This list, in 1788, was what most people would think very large, and there had been a considerable talk in the neighbourhood about the prevalence of impurity in the parish. The Session-Clerk, however, was a man of peculiar notions. He did not like to hear of the parish getting an evil name, and he thought that prattling people were making too much ado about the moral and spiritual condition of the congregation. At the foot of the list of "persons under scandal since last sacrament," he entered, therefore, a private postscript of his own, which, if it were not outrageously absurd, might be thought very improper. "N.B.," says the clerk, "notwithstanding the great noise, there are only twenty fornicators in this parish since last sacrament!" At this ridiculous entry in a church register where sin was meant to be called sin, Americans and Frenchmen have laughed till the foundations of their midriff threatened to give way, and stolid Scotch divines, who were too much scandalised to laugh, have lifted up their spectacles in blank wonderment, and looked and stared. In point of fact, however, the list of persons under scandal, in 1788, was unusually large, and so far from its being lightly thought of by Mr. Auld and the Kirk Session, it lay very heavy on their minds. The annotation was the Session-clerk's own, and it was not copied into the extended minute. The Session-clerk, too, was not, although Dr. Chambers erroneously says he was, a member of the Kirk Session. On the contrary, he was a man loaded with reports, and it was just all he could do to keep himself in his office of Session-clerk. And what the Kirk Session thought about the "noise" that was in the district, is made very plain by a warning or admonition against the sin of uncleanness, which they drew up at that date, and ordered to be read from the pulpit, and to be engrossed in the records as a testimony in all time coming to their zeal for the cause of pure religion. In this admonition, which is still extant in the minute book, the Kirk Session specially acknowledge and deeply lament the prevalence of the sin in question, both over the country at large, and in this parish particularly—they declare the sin to be one that brings "many woes and sorrows on men and women both now and for ever,"—they "warn, obtest, and beseech, in the name of God, every person, man and woman," to maintain the honour and purity of their Christian profession by avoiding every approach to that scandalous iniquity ; and then they conclude with a statement of sundry resolutions they had passed, with the view of making people feel more seriously than they had yet done the social and pecuniary consequences of transgression in that line.*

---

* To prevent even the appearance or suspicion of evil, the Kirk Session of Fenwick in 1653 caused intimation to be made from the pulpit, that "no young woman shall live alone without fitting and beseeming company." Finding "that none excepted against this resolution when it was intimated the Session afterwards ordained "the same to be in full strength and effect as it is enacted." In 1654 several women were suspended from the sacrament, as the phrase is, for living alone.

In the records of the General Assembly we find a good many acts anent witches and charmers, and we know that at one period the Church shewed extraordinary zeal in the detection and punishment of such evil doers. It may be asked, therefore, if there is no case of witchcraft to be found in the Kirk Session Records of this parish. Dr. Chambers, in his Domestic Annals of Scotland, states that, on the 8th May, 1671, Marion M'Call, spouse to Adam Reid, in Mauchline, was tried before the Justiciary Court in Ayr for "drinking the good heath of the Devil,"* and being found guilty of that profanity, was ordered to be taken to the Market Cross of Edinburgh "to be scourgit be the hangman from thence to Netherbow, thereafter to be brought back to the Cross and have her tongue bored and her cheek burned, and not to return to Ayrshire on pain of death." The barbarity of this sentence is horrible. It may be admitted to have been a very unladylike and blasphemous toast, that Mrs. Reid, sitting over her cups proposed, but a much milder punishment might have sufficed for all the harm she did. In the eye of the law, however, Mrs. Reid's offence was witchcraft. It was, to quote as nearly as possible from a book on the old criminal law of Scotland, an act of treason against God, in preferring to the Almighty his rebel and enemy, and in thinking the Devil worthier than God of being served and reverenced. It may be asked then, if there is any reference to this case of witchcraft in our Session Records? The trial at Ayr took place in May 1671, and our Records date back to December, 1669. Strange to say, there is no reference in our Records to this case of

---

Forty years later, in 1694, information was made to the Session and minuted that a man in the parish "transgresseth an act of the Session publicly intimated, by living in a house with a young lass his alone, contrary to order." Entries of a similar kind may be found in the Galston records.

* It is to be feared that this profane toast was not uncommon among irreligious

witchcraft.* We have seen that in 1674 and 1675 there was an Adam Reid censured on two separate occasions for cursing and railing on the elders. If this man be the Adam Reid that had Marion M'Call for wife, as the name would lead us to infer, we can say with certainty that the witch's husband was both a profane man and an habitual drunkard, for both his profanity and his drunkenness are expressly referred to in the Session Records.

But although in our Records there is no notice of Marion M'Call's toasting the health of the enemy, there is a case of scolding, cursing, and fighting, in 1673, which looks very like a sequel to the case tried in Ayr. The names of the parties in this scolding match were Reid, and one of them is said to have been a daughter of Marion M'Call's. Some of them are called "witchgets," and some are accused of handling articles that were bewitched. The whole story is of the earth earthy, but the following points will suffice to shew the gist of the case. The two principals on the one side were Elizabeth (or Isobell) Boswell and her daughter, Marion Reid; and the adversaries on the other side were John Reid and Janet Reid. The ball was opened by Marion Reid, who accused Janet of having "drunk five mutchkins of wine." Marion admitted to the Session that she had used the words complained of, and said further that her authority for the statement was Janet Reid's own mother, Marion M'Call. Janet Reid had not the self-restraint to listen unmoved to Marion's impeachment, but retaliated with the retort courteous, that she at least never "drew any man's ale, and that she never took a fey apron off the dyke." This was the skirmish between the light weights in the

---

and ill-conditioned people. As recently as 1710 an ex-schoolmaster of Galston was accused in the Session *inter alia* of "having moved the drinking of the Devil's health."

* The Presbytery records at this date are awanting.

combat, but the real tug of war had to come. Marion Reid and Janet Reid were but in their maidenhood. The one was under the wing of her mother, and the other had her brother beside her. Neither of the guardians could stand to see injustice or injury done to one of near kin. The old lady and the gentleman accordingly went at it with a will. Isobell Boswell, the mother of Marion Reid, fell on John, the brother of Janet Reid, and both cursed and beat him, and in particular called him by the elegant epithet of "witchget." John's patience seems so far to have been commendable that he never raised a hand against his assailant, the "guidwife of Drumfork," as she is designated ; but he was accused of calling her witch and something worse. There had been a nice distinction, however, in John's speech which the old lady, as she thumped on his back, had not observed. John did not call her a witch or any thing worse,—but only that she lied like a witch or something worse,—an important distinction, showing that John was cautious in his use of terms and aimed at accuracy in his defamation. Enough was elicited by the confessions of the parties to warrant public censure all round, but Kirk Sessions in those days were not content with scratching the surface of scandals. They probed to the very core. Witnesses accordingly were summoned and evidence was led. All the witnesses deponed that there was a lively interchange of compliments between the parties, and that it was difficult to say which had the advantage. One witness summed up the whole case and the philosophy of it by saying that she thought both the guidwife of Drumfork and John Reid were drunk,—which it is very likely they were,— and that the one cried up "witchget," and the other cried down "liar like a witch." The story is not one to be dwelt on for edification, but it nevertheless conveys instruction of a kind. We are sometimes told to look back to the days of the

Covenant and the persecutions as being days specially distinguished for all that is pure and lovely and of good report. It is quite plain, however, that in the days of the Covenant, as well as in the days before the flood, men not only prayed and held up holy hands, nothing doubting, and contended to death for principles they held as dear as life, but some ate and drank, cursed and swore, did not marry and get married as they should have done, and both fought with and defamed each other like Turks and Trojans.

Although there is no famous case of witchcraft in our Session Records, there are several cases of people complaining that they were called witches, said to be connected with witches, or accused of actions that were thought to infer witchcraft. In the year 1707 two women named Jean Reid and Jean Gibson came to words. It was alleged that in this altercation one of the damsels called the other witch and witch-bitten. The Session got wind of the scandal and summoned both parties to compear on a charge of slander. Jean Gibson gladly responded to the summons, and complained of Jean Reid for saying that " her (Gibson's) parents went both to the hollow pit, and that corbies conveyed them thither." Jean Reid, at a subsequent meeting of Session, stoutly denied the charge as stated by her accuser, but confessed that she had once on provocation said to Jean Gibson, " There were not corbies on my grandfather's lum-head, as there were on your father's when he died." This statement, however, was considered by the Session to bear the construction put on it by Miss Gibson, for it was part of the current superstition in those days that Satan occasionally assumed the form of a corby, and consequently when corbies were seen fluttering about the lum-head at the time of a death in the house an obvious inference was suggested. But while defamation is never justifiable, there are many evil thoughts that people would keep to themselves if they were not provoked to express them. And so Jean Reid argued that what she had said about the corbies was excusable, because it was said by way of retort. She had been bidden by Jean Gibson "go home and see her luky climb the walls." The whole case between the two Jeans was simply an affair of temper and dialectic talent, and would not have occupied a modern Kirk Session two minutes. But it actually occupied the Mauchline Kirk Session, in 1707, several months. Witnesses were called and put upon oath. Evidence was heard, and the more evidence that was led made confusion all the more confounded. It was on the 8th June that the two women were first cited to attend the Session. On the 4th August "Ballochmyle was appointed to attend the next Presbytery and . . . . . . was directed . . . to consult the Presbytery anent the affair." On the 31st August a committee of Session was instructed to confer with the parties and bring them to some reconciliation. On the 7th September the committee reported that the parties were irreconcilable, and the Session ordered the witnesses to be cited and examined anew. It was not till the 28th December that the case was brought to an end, and it ended in both parties being sessionally rebuked for so much of the slander that each was proved to have uttered.*

---

* Apropos of this superstition about the corbies, the following sentence from the close of Thackeray's lecture on the first of the four Georges may be quoted :— " It is said George promised one of his left-handed widows to come to her after death, if leave were granted to him to revisit the glimpses of the moon, and soon after his demise a great raven actually flying or hopping in at the Duchess of Kendall's window at Twickenham, she chose to imagine the King's spirit inhabited these plumes and took special care of her sable visitor. Affecting metempsychosis—funereal royal bird ! How pathetic is the idea of the Duchess weeping over it ! When this chaste addition to our English aristocracy died, all her jewels, her plate, her plunder, went over to her relations in Hanover. I wonder whether her heirs took the bird, and whether it is still flapping its wings over Herrenhausen !"

There is an old saying, that it never rains, but it pours. And it certainly very often happens that when one scandal breaks out in a district two or three others of similar character follow soon afterwards. Old philosophers and divines would have accounted for this circumstance by saying, that when Satan comes in force to any particular locality, he puts two or three people on the same track of mischief. Perhaps the modern scientific farmer would say in his lecture at the Corn Exchange that all sin and all cattle disease are the results of special atmospheric conditions, and that all persons and animals within the sphere of the vitiated atmosphere are under influences, that if favoured by suitable subjective congenital receptivities, will result in violent disorganisations! Laying aside, however, these philosophic explications as being too profound for ordinary understandings, it is a curious fact that while Jean Reid and Jean Gibson were raking up their ancestral traditions, and associating each other with the father of falsehood, there were other cases of reputed witchcraft jumbling the judgment of the Mauchline Kirk Session. A young damsel complained to the Session that her feelings were injured by the slander of a great lout who averred that on a certain Sabbath evening she had frightened him. How the sprightly little lass should have felt aggrieved by an accusation which seemed to reflect more on her accuser's courage than on her modesty requires to be explained. We must get at the facts of the case, therefore, and the best way of doing so will be to give the man's own statement, verbatim, when he was called before the Kirk Session. He declared, so runs the minute, that "he came to the Kirk on a Sabbath, and going through the Muir home he heard a person say to another, 'hold afore.' He looked again and saw a person at his foot, and he judged it to be Bessy Pethin. He asked her where she was going this time of night. After which he came to

Barheipe land foot, he heard the sound of a fair, and then he heard a dog after a sheep. He says he knew or he thought it to be her by her voice and garment." What it may be asked could be the meaning or wherein could lie the slander of such a rigmarole of nonsense? A sentence from the Table Talk of Luther will probably enable us to answer these questions. "The Devil," says Luther, "is so crafty a spirit that he can ape and deceive our senses. He can cause one to think he sees something which he sees not, that he hears thunder or a trumpet which he hears not." The man meant, therefore, to say that enchantment and sorcery had been used upon him, and that Miss Bessy Pethin, who had perhaps jilted him or rebuffed his advances, was the agent of the fiend in that diabolic business. Hence Bessy's distress about the damage that might be done to her good name, both in the world generally and in the matrimonial market particularly. And hence her righteous determination not to be squashed by the calumnies of a despised or rejected suitor. She made a Session case of the story, therefore, and the case, as presented to the Session, seemed a very hard nut to crack. There was, of course, such a thing in the world as sorcery,—no man who believed in spiritual existence could deny that fact,—and although sorceresses were usually old and haggard beldames, they were not necessarily so. Lucifer had transformed himself into an angel of light, and there consequently was nothing in Bessy's youth or beauty to make it impossible that she could have been the agent of the evil one. Witnesses were called, therefore, and evidence formally taken. The case was then referred to the Presbytery, and the Presbytery shewed what a grand divine institution a Presbytery is. It evinced no hesitation or dubiety in coming to a deliverance, and it spoke with no uncertain sound. It at once declared the man guilty of fabricating lies, and ordered him to be rebuked publicly.*

Superstition dies hard, and as recently as the year 1779 there was a complaint lodged in the † Kirk Session of Mauchline, by a merchant, against the wife of another merchant, for using maledictions that were regarded as savouring of witchcraft. No one now-a-days would think that a malediction has any power whatever. How, as Balaam said, can man curse where God hath not cursed. But in old times there was in Scotland a wide-spread fear of maledictions. The old Papist dreaded the curse of the Priest.‡ The Protestant Congregation, for many a day, not less truly dreaded the excommunication of the Church as the shutting of the kingdom of heaven against men. People even quailed under the imprecations of enraged and half-drunken beggars. To lie under a curse seemed a sore evil. And in criminal indictments for witchcraft, such averments as these were found,—" By your cursings and imprecations ye wrang and hurt man and beast, quhilk evil is brought to pass by the power and working of (Satan) your maister." The Mauchline merchant, therefore, was much

---

* The Presbytery of Ayr seems always to have had, on good grounds of course, plenty of self-reliance and a high opinion of its own superior wisdom. In 1699 the Presbytery instructed its Commissioners to the Assembly "to propose that some be appointed to supervise the press at the printing of the Acts of Assembly, because of ill grammar which is to be found in them and also some unnecessary letters are added."

† In the judicial testimony drawn up by the Seceders in 1742, one of the steps of defection and apostacy complained of, was the repeal of the penal statutes against witchcraft, "contrary to the express letter of the law of God—'thou shalt not suffer a witch to live.'"

‡ Protestant presbyters as well as Popish priests often pronounced from the pulpit solemn curses which were thought to be prophetical. In 1605, John Welsh, the Presbyterian, thundered out a curse on Spotswood, who was one of the King's chief agents for the inbringing of Episcopacy into the Church. "I denounce," he said, "the wrath of an everlasting God against him, which assuredly shall fall unless it be prevented."

aggrieved that the wife of his brother-in-trade had not only defamed him, but had said "that he would not thrive, and that all his cattle would die, with other predictions and expressions too tedious to mention." So far as the imprecations went, it turned out on evidence that the accused had expressed a wish that "George Merkland's cow might die as the other two had done which he had lost," and that her reason for expressing such an evil wish against a neighbour was the bad treatment she had got from Mr. Merkland and his family. The Session found that nothing had been proved to establish any serious charge, and the complaint was accordingly dismissed. The accused thereupon turned accuser, and lodged a libel "against Agnes Shaw, spouse to George Merkland, and against Jean Merkland, their daughter, for having said that she had killed two of their cows, and should be bled above the eyes," which was the commonly supposed way of making a witch powerless, and of undoing the evil she had done. The Session would fain have shelved the case, but the libeller forced them to go on. The evidence broke down, however,—especially Poosie Nansie's, who was one of the witnesses, but swore the wrong way, —and the libeller had to desert her cause.* The whole story,

---

* How closely allied to witchcraft the practice of physick was supposed to be, may be judged from the following extracts from the Records of Rothesay Kirk Session :—1660. "The Session finding that there is a report throw the countrie that Jeane Campbell, wife to Robert M'Conachie, gangs with the faryes, appoints the elders to tak tryell thereof, and how the scandall raise, and to mak report to the next Session." It was found that there was no ground for the scandal, and this was intimated from the pulpit. The woman had had an illness and vomited her food, and she got a "salve to rub on her breast, which was good for comforting the heart against scunners." 1661. "Considering that the said Janet goes under the name of a witch or a deceiver by undertaking to heal desperate diseases by herbs and such like, the Session did discharge the said Janet, in time coming to use the giving of any physick or herbs to any body under the certification that she shall be esteemed a witch if she so do." A good deal of what was called witchcraft long ago would be called quack-doctoring now. In 1640 a well-meaning woman was accused by the Session of Galston of charming and using such

as I have outlined it, was a miserable, paltry scandal, unworthy of repetition, but for the interest given to it by its association with Jean Merkland. This was the Mauchline belle whom Burns pronounced divine. We cannot but think it must have been true what the poet's brother said of these belles. They were invested with fictitious attributes. But no discredit to the poet for that. Well would it be for the world if there were more men in it to invest the earth with happy and purifying illusions—"the consecration and the poet's dream." The subject too has practical bearings. For assuredly if the genius of the poet has exalted and consecrated so much that was commonplace, and made the world look brighter and more joyous than it was, much might be done even by ourselves to augment the stock of happiness, if we would only turn away our own eyes and the eyes of others from what is least lovely in people's ways and manners, and bring into light what in their conduct and aims is best and purest and most praiseworthy. It is unquestionable that we all look through coloured glass, and well would it be if the glass we looked through were bright and roseate rather than blurred and muddy—in a word, that we were idealists and optimists rather than caricaturists and pessimists.

The remarks that have just been made on the subject of maledictions will serve to explain several matters regarding cursing. The words cursing and swearing are usually coupled

---

like devices "with sik bairnes and beasts and douges." In 1746 a "doctrix" was consulted in Galston about the recovery of a sick child. The "doctrix" attributed the child's illness to a neighbour who "had a bad eye, and could not help it." This neighbour was ordered to say, "God bless the child," and to surrender some of her hair to be used for a charm, which she did. In 1724 a Galston man was rebuked "for his scandalous and offensive behaviour in going to consult a supposed wizard in order to the discovery of goods stolen from him." The man justified his action, and "refused all conviction." His rebuke was therefore intimated to the congregation, and he was publicly pronounced a scandalous person.

together, and the acts of cursing and swearing very commonly go together. But the two things are still distinct. To swear is to take an oath or vow, and to swear profanely is to take a vow in a profane manner.* To curse is to invoke evil. And long ago cursing was sometimes regarded as a form of profanity, and sometimes as a form of sorcery or what approached to sorcery. For instance, there is an Act of the General Assembly of date 1699, intituled an act against profaneness, and in this act cursing as well as swearing is mentioned. There is little doubt that this is the common view taken of cursing. But cursing was sometimes looked upon as a more serious thing—an appointment of some one to divine wrath or misfortune.† And in our own Session Records we find one or two cases of cursing in this sense of the term. In the year 1677, one Agnes Reid was delated to the Session of Mauchline for flyting and scolding. Whether Agnes belonged to the witch family of Reids there is nothing in the records to indicate, but it is a curious fact that a considerable number of the people that in Mauchline were long ago censured or delated for cursing and imprecating were of the name of Reid. Letting that pass, however, the misconduct of Agnes was inquired into by the Session. One witness, "John Adam, being sworn, deponed that he heard Agnes say that she should sit down on her bare

---

* In old Session Records there is a distinction drawn between "sweiring and mansweiring." The former meant profanity and the latter perjury.

† Cursing in that case is rather a form of witchcraft than of profanity. Pardovan, the Church lawyer, in discussing the question—What acts are relevant to infer witchcraft? says that "when threatenings are specified, bearing a promise to do a particular ill, and when charms are used to obtain its execution, and when it is known that the threatener had a preceding enmity against the person threatened," the acts libelled would seem to be relevant. But to this observation he appends a remark of his own which the common sense of modern times will heartily approve. "It is safer to punish threatenings with some milder punishment than death, as *crimen in suo genere* (that is, as a special offence, called by the proper name of threatening) and not as witchcraft."

knees every morning and give them God's curse that takes ye maling over yer heads." Janet Richmond deponed that she heard Agnes Reid "curse John Fisher and his wife and say God hunt them to death." This was a sample of cursing, not in the sense of profane levity, but in the sense of earnest, malicious imprecation. The sentence of the Session was that "Agnes Reid, being found guilty of cursing and flyting, be rebuked publicly the next day." Another illustration of cursing in the sense of malediction is given in a minute of date 1675. Two women named Heleson Wilson and Bessie Morton were delated for flyting and cursing, and evidence was produced. "Jean Morton, sworne, depont that she saw Heleson Wilson sit down on her knees to curse Bessie Morton, but heard her not do it." The result was that the two women were both found guilty of the minor charge of flyting, and "Heleson Wilson confest *intended* cursing." They were let off, therefore, with a sessional rebuke and a certification that if they were found flyting again they would have to stand a public admonition.*

---

* Similar cases of cursing may be found in other Session Records. For instance, in 1622, a man appeared before the Kirk Session of Dumbarton, and confessed, that in his passion of anger, he had "cursitt the Turks for no deteinning and holding of John Campbell, sailor, when the uthers of his companie wes takene, and that he had wissit that he nor nane of his companie sould evir cum home againe, and that he had wissit all Dumbartane to be in ane fyire." For these evil wishes and cursings he was ordained "to stand ane Sabbothe bairfootit and leggit in the haire goune at the Kirk door, betwixt the second and third bells, and thairafter in the public place of repentance in tym of preiching."

In 1659 a case of blasphemy, which was also very like a case of cursing, came before the Kirk Session of Rothesay. A man was accused of having said, "Let God either mend the weather or destroy it." The man denied he had said so, but admitted he had made the philosophic remark, "that if God would not mend the weather the earth would be destroyed." Proof that condemned the man was however forthcoming, and he was ordered to stand in sackcloth till he shewed signs of repentance.

The following cases of cursing appear in the Galston Records :—In 1657 one man alleged that another " sat doune on his knies and wissed the judgment of God

It may perhaps appear strange that so much importance should have been attached to idle imprecations, as if they had had some mysterious and miraculous potency. But strange as it may appear, the fact is nevertheless certain, that such imprecations were supposed to have power and to prevail. In Luther's Table Talk, which has been already referred to in this Lecture, we have a good illustration of the popular superstition on this point,—" A man," says Luther, " had a habit, whenever he fell, of saying, Devil take me. He was advised to discontinue this evil custom lest some day the prince of darkness should take him at his word. He promised to vent his impatience by some other phrase, but one day having stumbled, the old expression escaped him, and he was killed upon the spot." We can see, therefore, why imprecations were made so much of at one time.

The laws of Moses ordained that whoever cursed his father or his mother should be put to death. And in the year 1661 the malediction of a parent was made a capital offence in Scotland. The act declared that any son or daughter above sixteen years of age, who cursed his father or mother, should be "put to death without mercie." It might have been expected, therefore, that some very special ecclesiastical act regarding the cursing of parents would have been in force in the Church of Scotland long ago. I am not aware that there was any, but my ignorance is not to be counted knowledge. The cursing of parents was, nevertheless, regarded and justly regarded by Kirk Sessions as a very abominable form of sin. In our Session Records there are several cases of people being

---

to come on him ;" and in 1675 a woman confessed that she "malinsount " another woman, and "did it upon her bare knies." Even self-cursing was included under the sin of imprecation. A Galston woman had in 1652 to stand out of her seat in Church and submit to public rebuke for saying in her haste "the Divel tak her if ever she knew of such things."

called to account for cursing their parents. The language libelled in such cases as expressing "horrid imprecations," was just the kind of language that unfortunately is too often heard at the present day both at street corners and in playgrounds, in railway carriages and at Parliamentary elections. But it was not allowed to pass unnoticed by Kirk Sessions. In the year 1749 a shoemaker was delated to the Session of Mauchline for undutiful behaviour to the minister and for cursing his mother. The minutes shew that it was the second of these offences that the Session considered the more serious, and what the Session thought of it may be inferred from the facts that the case was submitted to the Presbytery for advice, and the shoemaker was thereafter ordained to appear before the congregation, in the place of repentance, four several times, namely, on the first Sabbaths of July, August, September, and October. In a learned book, published in 1835, a Scottish antiquarian says, with an air of satisfaction, that "the gradual refinement of social intercourse has fortunately expelled those oaths and execrations, formerly so much incorporated with common converse, or they are heard very seldom from the temperate." I heartily wish that I were able to confirm that statement, but I fear that although the habit of profane swearing may be nearly expelled from some circles of society, it is not dying out in the country. On the contrary, in descending to a lower level of society, it has become more prevalent, and although in our old records we fall in occasionally with both naughty and blasphemous language, "unfit," as a respectable witness under examination by the Mauchline Kirk Session said, "to be rehearsed in Christian ears," the swearing of the present day being further down the social scale is more filthy and more brutal still.*

---

* In the Records of the Presbytery of Ayr, I find that in 1644 a man "laitlie

As might be expected, there are in our Parish Records several instances of people being brought before the Session on charges of heresy and schism. Ecclesiastically these are very grave offences, and for the "atrocity of their scandal" Kirk Sessions are directed not to conclude processes anent them without seeking the advice of the Presbytery. In 1694 a man was delated to the Kirk Session of Mauchline for venting erroneous opinions on one of the fundamental doctrines of the gospel. The man was a person of indifferent character, and at the time he was delated for venting heresy he was under scandal for one of the sins of the flesh. He was so far straightforward that he did not deny having said the words imputed to him and that they bore a heretical construction, but he alleged they were spoken by way of mirthful argument. The Session would not accept that statement as a sufficient apology, and for his mirthful argumentation and his other offence conjoined he was ordered to compear "in publick four several Sabbaths successively."

In 1767 the Session had to deal with a very peculiar case of schism. The person charged with the offence was an elder, and the offence could not be overlooked for this reason among others, that it affected the question of the constitution of the Kirk Session. To retain the elder in the Session would have been absurd as well as wrong, but in order to strike him off the Session, the prescribed form of

---

receaved in the Kirk of Machlin," compeared before the Presbytery for an infraction of the seventh commandment. "And as he wes gravely challenged, did confess the sinne of blasphemie in his drunkenness by taking the body, wounds, blood, and bread of God in his profane mouth, he was remitted to the Session of Machlin to satisfie the discipline of the Kirk." In 1650 another Mauchline man designated a "blasphemer" compeared before the Presbytery in sackcloth, and having humbly acknowledged his offence, was remitted to the Kirk Session of Mauchline.

process had to be gone through. It is pleasant to say that all the proceedings in that unhappy business were conducted in the most friendly spirit. The elder had nothing to object to either the doctrines of the Church or the preaching of Mr. Auld. Nor had he any complaint against the Kirk Session of Mauchline for any thing he had ever seen them do. But he was not satisfied with the Presbytery of Ayr. He said that when sitting in the Presbytery as ruling elder he had seen members of Presbytery refuse to subscribe the Confession of Faith. This statement is so strange that I cannot but think the elder must have been under some misconception. The records of the Presbytery bear uniform testimony to the Presbytery's zeal and faithfulness in requiring subscription to the Confession of Faith from all office-bearers in the Church.* But one or two things happened in the Presbytery that may have been misunderstood and misrepresented. In 1761 the Presbytery's subscription book was lost, and a new one had to be got. In 1766 the new subscription book was lost also, and Mr. Dalrymple of Ayr, in moving that the clerk be examined on oath "as to what he knows about this affair," stated that "the loss of the old subscription book had given occasion to the inventing and spreading of several very injurious reports, and that these are likely to be revived

---

* Not only did the Presbytery demand a subscription of the Confession of Faith, but for a while she insisted on the subscription of what is termed in the records, "the Act assertory of the divine right of Church Government by Presbyteries." This so-called Act bound subscribers to "constancy to the true principles of the covenanted work of Reformation in this land," and adherence to "Presbyterial government in opposition to . . . Prelacy." This was from 1705 to at least 1708 if not later. In 1717 the Presbytery of Auchterarder required their licentiates to subscribe in addition to the Confession of Faith a formula which the Assembly declared to be "unsound and most detestable," namely that it is not orthodox to teach men that they must forsake sin in order to their coming to Christ and instating themselves in covenant with God.

and confirmed upon the supposed loss of the subscription book lately purchased." A student too was that year actually licensed to preach, without having signed the confession, but it was because the subscription book was not forthcoming ; and license was granted on the student's express engagement to sign the formula whenever it should be presented to him. After 1767, another thing happened which, if it had happened before that date (and something like it may have happened), would have completely explained the dissatisfaction of the Mauchline elder with what he saw in the Presbytery. Between 1770 and 1780 Mr. Dalrymple, who in 1766 seemed so concerned about the "injurious reports" that had arisen on the "loss of the subscription book," repeatedly objected to the subscription of the formula, on the ground that that subscription had never been legally enjoined by the Church. His contention, as appears from a minute of Presbytery, dated June, 1771, was that "the questions and formula of subscription contained in the Act of Assembly, 1711, were not regularly transmitted to the different Presbyteries in Scotland, or at least did not receive the consent of a majority of them, without which it can be no standing law of this Church."*

I may mention here that the Presbytery of Ayr, while zealous in the matter of requiring subscriptions to the Confession of Faith from those that held office in the church, was kindly considerate and tender with all that were troubled with any difficulties or doubts in regard to any of the multitudinous articles embraced in the Confession. In 1750 the Presbytery minuted "that students may be allowed modestly to propone the difficulties that may occur to them as to their subscribing some articles in the Confession of Faith, and that the Pres-

---

* For notice of Mr. Dalrymple see Appendix E.

bytery may give their opinion as to the weight and importance of them, in order to their satisfaction and the candidate's." In connection with this matter a curious passage at arms occurred in 1771 between Mr. Auld and the Presbytery, which looks like a sequel to the case of schism in Mauchline four years before, and is not so well cleared up in the Presbytery records as one could wish. Mr. Auld was as rigid as a mast, and he was orthodox to the mast head. He would not stand evasive answers to plain questions, and if he got the least scent of heresy, or of views divergent from what he considered the inflexible standards of immutable truth, he would have a thorough exploration. At the licensing of a student in 1771 there had been some haggling over one or more of the questions that Mr. Dalrymple complained of for being unlawfully put to such as are to be licensed. The matter had been got over, however, and license was granted. But Mr. Auld, minister of Mauchline, dissented from the Presbytery's procedure, "because when the second question appointed to be put to candidates was put to Mr. S. he, in answer, declared that there were some expressions in the Confession of Faith, which he either did not understand or was not satisfied with, and when Mr. Auld insisted that the Moderator should ask Mr. S. what these expressions were, the Presbytery thought fit to refuse to put such a question, and he apprehended if such an answer were sustained by Presbyteries the same answer might be given to the Alcoran." This was the entry made on behalf of Mr. Auld, but the Presbytery, "in justification of themselves and of their licentiate, appointed it to be recorded that the question, as stated by Mr. Auld in his dissent, to be put to Mr. S., was not so proposed by him to the Presbytery, and that he had given an imperfect account of the *res gestae* in this matter."

If Mr. Auld misunderstood what he saw and heard in the Presbytery, and failed to perceive distinctions that made all the difference between regular and irregular procedure, much more may his elder in 1766 have done so. But, in justice to both Mr. Auld and the elder, it must be admitted that neither is the alleged non-subscription of the Confession before 1767, nor the answering of the questions in 1771 fully explained.

To return, however, to the case of the elder. If what he alleged was correct (but that must be held doubtful), the Presbytery had committed an irregularity, and could have been brought to book.* In 1790 the General Assembly found the conduct

---

* In one of Burns' letters, of date 7th February, 1790, the following passage occurs, "You must have heard how the Rev. Mr. Lawson, of Kirkmahoe, seconded by the Rev. Mr. Kilpatrick, of Dunscore, and the rest of that faction, have accused in formal process the unfortunate and Rev. Mr. Heron of Kirkgunzeon, that in ordaining Mr. Neilson to the cure of souls in Kirkbean he, the said Mr. Heron, feloniously and treasonably bound the said Neilson to the Confession of Faith, *so far as it was agreeable to reason and the Word of God.*" In regard to this case, the Clerk of the Presbytery of Dumfries has furnished me with full particulars from the Presbytery records. The ordination at Kirkbean took place on the 17th Sep., 1789, and the minute bears that Mr. Neilson gave satisfactory answers to the questions appointed to be put to such as are to be ordained. The clerk had not a copy of the Confession of Faith with him, but Mr. Neilson signed at next meeting of Presbytery. No notice of any irregularity in the procedure was taken till the 2nd Feb. 1790, when Mr. Lawson informed the Presbytery that Mr. Heron, in putting to Mr. Neilson the question, "do you sincerely own and believe the whole doctrine contained in the Confession of Faith," added the words mentioned above by Burns. Mr. Lawson then made a motion, and required that Mr. Heron should be heard on it, but Mr. Heron declared "he was there as a judge, and would not be interrogated as a party, that he was not ashamed of his conduct at Kirkbean, would not retract a word he had said, and would answer everything in its proper place." At their next meeting in April the Presbytery pronounced their judgment on the matter as follows, " Approve highly of the attention Mr. Lawson has paid to the standards of this Church, but considering the present circumstances of the case they do not judge Mr. Heron censurable, disapprove, however, of every deviation from the questions appointed by the law of this Church to be put to ministers at their ordination, and recommend to all the ministers of the Presbytery to pay due attention to these laws, and for that purpose appoint their clerk in all future cases to furnish the minister who shall be appointed to preside, with the Acts of this Church

of a Presbytery in Forfarshire unjustifiable and deserving of censure in proceeding to settle a minister without requiring him to sign the Confession of Faith and Formula. And had the Mauchline elder complained to the Assembly in 1767 of the conduct of the Presbytery of Ayr in dispensing with subscriptions required by law, he would doubtless, if the facts he stated had been found true, have brought down censure on the Presbytery. But the elder took what he thought a simpler and less troublesome course. Instead of calling down fire from heaven on the offenders, he went to another church, and, in the words of our Session Records, "joined himself to the Seceding congregation." The Session, in dealing with him, proceeded with the greatest deliberation, and gave him ample time to reconsider his resolution, and to change his mind, if he saw fit. It was on the 5th of March, 1767, that proceedings against him were instituted, and on the 3rd December the following deliverance was minuted :—"Compeared John Smith. The Session having read to him the minutes relating to this affair, he was talked with in a friendly manner as to the reason and grounds of his secession from the Church, and his deserting his office of elder in this congregation, are unanimously of opinion that they ought to depose him of his office, but delay their final judgment till their meeting on the first Thursday of January." On the first Thursday of January the affair was delayed till the first Thursday of February, and what was done then we can only conjecture, for there is a blank in the records from 7th January to 3rd March. The Session plainly did not wish to take extreme measures—but extreme measures could not be averted.

The common way of dealing with seceders in Mr. Auld's

---

containing these questions." The irregularity would thus seem to have been not an intended disregard of the law of the Church.

day was to let them alone. If people chose to separate themselves from the services of the Parish Church, they were allowed to do so, and depart in peace. But if they afterwards applied to the Kirk Session for testimonials they had to submit their conduct to investigation and scrutiny.* In the year 1775, for instance, a shoemaker named Fisher applied to the Session for a testimonial of good behaviour, but the answer he got was that the "Session could not grant his desire until he gave them satisfaction as to the sin of schism, viz.: of following the Moravians and Burgers, etc., wherewith they are informed he is chargeable." Besides Mr. Fisher there was another schismatic in the Parish in 1775. This was John Richmond in Bargour. He seems never to have troubled the Session, and the Session seems never to have troubled him. His name was placed on the list of those to whom tokens were to be refused, and the reason of the refusal was stated to be schism, but I have failed to find any other notice of him in the Records. He was just quietly struck off the roll for a reason that the Session, if called upon, would be prepared to vindicate, but he was not subjected to any sort of scandal by a summons to appear before the Session. This is what we may call the beginning of that toleration which Mr. Tod, in his statistical

---

* At an earlier date course was taken with dissenters. The following minute occurs in the records of the Presbytery of Ayr for 1708:—" The Presbytery having gott an account from brethren of disorders committed in their bounds by Mr. Farquhar, did order their Clerk to write to the Clerk of the Commission that the said Mr. Farquhar, upon a Sabbath in one or other of the days of April last, preached within the paroch of Galstone, and upon the Thursday thereafter he preached in the paroch of Dalgain without a call from the minister or eldership of these paroches." This minute may be explained by Act of Assembly 1708, No. VI., for suppressing schism, which states *inter alia* that the Assembly " refers the disorders and schismatical courses of Mr. James Farquhar, minister of Tyrie, &c., entirely to the Commission . . . hereby empowering the Commission to call these persons before them, and to censure them as they shall be found to deserve."

account of the Parish, declared to be so pleasant a feature in the Parochial life fifty years ago.*

There is only one other matter I have now to refer to. In 1680, a man named John Aird appeared before the Session of Mauchline and acknowledged his guilt and scandal "in taking the bond." The minute adds that he was rebuked and absolved. It is hard to say what category this offence should be placed under. Aird himself probably thought his taking the bond was an act of some kind of schism. The Bond was an Erastian document. It was drawn up by the Lords of Council in 1677 with the view of binding people to keep aloof from conventicles and have no intercourse with vagrant preachers or outed ministers. The excitement created by its publication and by the descent of the Highland Host to enforce subscriptions to it was indescribable. Papers were drawn up by Spiritual Independents to shew how illegal and sinful was its tenor, and several persons who had been persuaded to sign it made afterwards a solemn recantation of their deed and professed their sorrow for having ever put

---

* Religious tolerance, however, was but in its infancy last century. In 1769 a Dissenter in Mauchline committed suicide, and the Session Clerk had actually the malignity to exult over the occurrence. In the Register of Deaths he inserted in large text, as if announcing the immediate doom of dissent, " HUGH CAMPBELL, A SECEDER, CUT HIS OWN THROAT, 3RD JANUARY." This extraordinary entry, standing out in great characters in the middle of a page, may be seen by any visitor at the Register House, Edinburgh.

Mr. Dun in one of his volumes of sermons (1790) says :—" We were most publicly told in the General Assembly 1784 that there were about 400,000 dissenters in Scotland. This seems to arise, 1st, From the degeneracy of the human heart ; 2nd, Men licensed to preach the gospel who might be very useful at Johnny Groat's house, but are very unfit for the High Church of Edinburgh, and yet they must be settled where the patron pleases." Dr. M'Kelvie shews clearly enough how dissent grew in Scotland. It was not from the gradual recognition of any religious or ecclesiastical principle, but from dissatisfaction with something or other in the Parish Church—the settlement of a minister—the singing of paraphrases—intimations from the pulpit of civil acts, etc., etc.

their names to so odious a paper. But it was nevertheless a bold proceeding on the part of the Session of Mauchline to administer rebuke to a man for signing a bond required by the State and to record in their minutes that such a rebuke was given. It is not to be wondered at that Mr. Veitch was sometimes called by his betters to account for his conduct.*

I may state, however, that in the time of the civil troubles political misconduct was a frequent subject of ecclesiastical censure. Common history tells how men like Montrose and M'Donald were excommunicated, and how their sentence of excommunication was publicly intimated over all the country, and the records of church courts tell how smaller offenders in the same or a similar line were dealt with. In 1646 the Church courts were particular vigilant in looking after political miscreants. The Laird of Underwood was that year brought to book by the Presbytery of Ayr "for taking of a protection for himself and family from the publict enemie." † To some people this might seem a common act of prudence, but it was not so accounted by the covenanting clergy, and the Laird was "remitted to his minister for tryal of his sense of that sinne," and on giving satisfaction he was to be "received in his own seat." The same year there was a man called

---

* In the account of James Veitch's ministry in Mauchline it is said that in 1681 he was accused of having excommunicated people for signing the bond. The accusation had not been entirely groundless. He had rebuked people for signing the bond, and absolved them when they confessed their penitence. Apropos of Spiritual Independence there is a very curious grievance referred to in the Presbytery Records. In 1715 the Commissioners to the General Assembly from the Presbytery of Ayr were instructed to represent to the Assembly "that addressing of the house of Peers in the common form is straitening to our consciences, and our refusing ought not to be improven against us."

† Montrose's troops were in command of the country after the battle of Kilsyth, in August, 1645. And Baillie says it was "marvellous how few handfuls of the enemy went through Ayrshire, etc., without any opposition, but a general submission of all who did not flee.'

before the Kirk Session at Fenwick "for making merchandise with the enemy," and another for "subscribing a bond with the enemy for protection." And the Mauchline people were as much cowed as their neighbours by the "handfuls" of Montrose's troopers. In September, 1646, the Minister, Mr. Thomas Wyllie, "wes desired by the Presbytery to intimat a day of publict humiliation to be keiped in the Kirk of Machlin for the whole Parochinars, for taking away the sinne of complying with the publict enemie, by taking a general protection from them." The Galston folks, too, were led into good deal of sin by the enemy's temptations. For buying plundered goods from the enemy, several persons in that Parish had to make public confession of a fault, and one man was ordained to "bring the goods to the kirk and let them lye there till they be owned." Another fellow was summoned to the Session for "slaying of a bull in the time of confusion." To that sin he was charged with adding the further sin of slander, in accusing another person of being art and part with him in the butchery. And so, for these two offences conjoined he had very properly to make public appearance in church, and pay the price of the bull.

After the Revolution, some of the sins and defections in the previous times of persecution were brought by the Church Courts to remembrance. In 1693 one Muir of Bruntwood compeared before the Session of Galston, and, having stated how in "the lait tymes" he had been induced to swear and subscribe the Test, "did publicly, before the Session and several others sitting with them in the Session, express the sense he had of that horrid sin, and his willingness to make profession of the same in the most public place of the church if it might be judged more for the glory of God, and if the Church had seen fit to lay down such a method for removing such scandals."

This Test, it may be explained, was first appointed in 1681 to be subscribed by the occupants of certain offices, civil and military, and was again in 1685 appointed to be subscribed by all Protestant heritors and tacksmen over eighteen years of age. Under pretence of securing religion against the machinations of Papists and Fanatics, it opened, as Wodrow says, "a gap for Popery, by renouncing the national covenant, the great bulwark of Scotland against that wicked idolatry, and obliging the swearers to receive a Papist successor." Hence the public horror of the Test, and the public outcry against those that signed it, as well as the public demonstration made over all recantations of subscription. It need scarcely be said therefore that Mr. Muir was leniently dealt with, if not somewhat puffed up, by his Session for his declaration of contrition, and very soon afterwards his name was placed on a list of suitable persons for the Eldership in Galston.

It will now be seen that the old discipline of the Church had a wide range. The number and variety of offences that Kirk Sessions took cognisance of were well nigh infinite. And in next lecture it will be shewn that Kirk censures were both numerous and varied also.

LECTURE VI.

CHURCH DISCIPLINE IN OLDEN TIMES.

Censures—Rebukes—Sometimes in private and sometimes before Congregation—Delinquent sometimes stood in his own seat—Sometimes in the public place of Repentance—Sometimes in his usual clothing and sometimes in sackcloth—Repeated compearances for rebuke, called a course of repentance—Cautioners for compearance and for subsequent conduct—Bands for good behaviour—Disuse of cutty stool—Excommunication—Corporal and pecuniary punishment—Session Bailies—Joggs—Fines—Warnings—Deference paid to Kirk Sessions—Cases of Disrespect and Disobedience—Aid of Magistrate needed—Insolence to the Session—State of Parochial morality at different dates—Street fight in Mauchline between a merchant and a lawyer, with the Bailie looking on—Village Rowdyism—Poosie Nansie and her household—Social progress—Causes to which progress is due—Grounds of hope for the future.

Two lectures have already been devoted to the Kirk Session as the Parochial court of ecclesiastical discipline. The first of these lectures was occupied with an account of the institution and constitution of Kirk Sessions, and of their modes of inquisition. The second lecture was intended to shew the scope and extent of the Kirk's jurisdiction, or in other words the different kinds of offences that Kirk Sessions took cognisance of in olden times. In this lecture we have to consider the several forms of censure and punishment that Kirk Sessions either directly inflicted or caused to be inflicted, and the measure of respect in which the authority of Kirk Sessions was held by the community.

Rebuke was always part of the Session's censure. And rebuke was administered in different ways. Sometimes it was administered in private, that is in presence of the Kirk Session only. But in some cases when it was administered in private it was afterwards publicly announced from the pulpit. At other times when the offence was of a heinous character, or had been aggravated by repetition or other circumstances, the rebuke was delivered in face of the congregation. And old Session Records shew, what is not generally known to have been the fact, that in old times (say from 1600 to 1650 or a little later) public rebukes were administered in three different ways, according to the amount of scandal created by the offence. Sometimes the delinquent stood up in his own seat, made confession of his sin, and was reprimanded. At other times he had to present himself in front of the pulpit for admonition. And when the scandal was great he had to mount an elevated stand, technically designated the public place of repentance, and commonly called the repentance stool. In later times this threefold classification of public rebukes was not observed. Public censures came to be more and more confined to the graver class of offences, and the subjects of such censures had generally, if not always, to stand in the public place.

In one of his letters written on a Sunday morning in July, 1786, Burns states that he was that day going to put on sackcloth and ashes in Mauchline church—not literally, for his offence did not require such an amount of degradation—but metaphorically in the sense of humbling himself in public. But he adds, " I am indulged so far as to appear in my own seat." *

---

* As I was in the act of revising this lecture, I was honoured with a visit from an American, who said he was informed that I possessed the cutty stool on which Burns stood before the congregation of Mauchline, and he was curious to see such an interesting relic of a great man !! I asked if he himself was a poet, but he said No !

A collector of local traditions about Burns (Rev. Dr. Pollock, Kingston, Glasgow), wrote in 1859 that some wiseacres in Mauchline took it into their heads that it would be a grand "spec" to have an assortment of snuff boxes made out of

And Burns correctly describes his permission to stand in his own seat as an indulgence. Had he lived and sinned a century, or even half a century, earlier, it is doubtful if any such concession would have been made to him. It was about 1736 that favours of this kind began to be extended in Mauchline Parish to sinners of Burns's type, and at that time the allowance of the favour, together with a narrative of the circumstances under which it was voted, was specially recorded in the Session minutes. For instance, on the 2nd May, 1736, it was minuted that the minister, Mr. Maitland, informed the Session that a man "had spoke with him and proposed to give six pounds Scots to the poor, and stand in his father's seat twice." The Session, it is then added, did, after reasoning on this tempting proposal, agree that the man "should appear two days in his father's seat," and pay a penalty of ten shillings sterling. This was not precisely what the man offered; but after a little haggling the Session modified their terms, and allowed the man to expiate his offence to the Church by the payment of £6 Scots, and penance in his father's seat *twice*, that is forenoon and afternoon, on one Sabbath. In 1698 a small laird in Mauchline Parish had the hardihood to make trial of the Session's squeezability. He represented his desire to be relieved of a scandal he lay under, but "refused to goe to the pillar, pretending that he had made a promise against it." His alleged conscientious scruples were disregarded, however, by the Session, and the "laws of the Church" were explained to him. Two months later the Session recorded that the laird had repeatedly shifted them with frivolous excuses and con-

---

the old Repentance Stool, "associated as it had been with a solemn event in the history of the Poet." Adam Armour, a brother of Mrs. Burns, accordingly got possession of the stool, but it was found so worm-eaten that it was good for nothing. In point of fact, however, Burns never had to sit on the Mauchline Repentance stool.

tumacies which they would no longer tolerate. It was therefore agreed that he should be formally cited "to compear on the common place of repentance against the next Lord's day." The laird did not make his appearance next Sabbath as required, and the officer complained that in serving the Session's citation he had been "mocked and flouted" by the laird. This was voted contempt of court, and the laird was handed over to the tender mercies of the civil magistrate.*

The practice of Kirk Sessions in the matter of censures was never at any period uniform all over the Church. What is expedient has sometimes to be considered as well as what is lawful. And expediency is a matter on which there will always be differences of opinion. While the Kirk Session of Mauchline in 1698 thought it very expedient that stubborn purse-proud people should be brought to their senses, the Kirk Session of Fenwick about the same date thought it more expedient to give way to the stiff humours of mulish parishioners. In 1692 they minuted a resolution regarding a man accused of using profane language, that "he being of a stiffe proud humour should only be rebuked before the Session." But this ill-judged leniency, as might have been foreseen, emboldened other sinners to assume high and proud airs, and not long afterwards the Session had to minute regarding a different offender that "considering the bad humour of the said Robert," his sentence was deferred.

One of a score of complaints given in to the Presbytery of Ayr against the minister of Maybole in 1718 was his "conniving at scandals in allowing some persons secret unusual corners to

---

* In 1698 a schoolmaster applied to the Presbytery of Ayr for leave to stand in his own seat when undergoing a public admonition, but he was ordered to go to the public place of repentance.

appear in, though people of the very commonest sort, without minding something to the poor in such a case." This complaint implied that the Parishioners of Maybole would have had no objection to dispensations from the repentance stool provided that the persons so indulged had been made to suffer somewhat more in penalty for the good of the poor. And that was the feeling in Mauchline Kirk Session in 1736. But in 1766 a Mauchline man wished to draw the Kirk Session a little farther out. He offered a handsome present to the poor, if the Session would release him from appearing before the Congregation at all. That offer, however, was rejected by Mr. Auld as being overmuch mercantile in its character, and the man was ordered to satisfy the Church in public as other offenders in the like condemnation did.

I have said that it was customary, during at least the first half of the seventeenth century, to allow some offenders, whose scandals were not of the grossest, to do public penance in their own seats. Instances of this are to be found in the Session records both of Fenwick and Galston. In 1650 a Galston dame was delated to her Session for "raileing on ye Ladie Barr, cursing, swearing, and divilish passione." She had the candour to confess all she was charged with, and she was ordained to give "signs of repentance out of her awin seatt the next Lorde's day," with certification that "the first tyme she sould be fund in the lyk sche sould stand *heich*." Other offenders, I said, had to appear *in front of the pulpit* for public rebuke. At one period this was the common place for the repentance stool. Mr. Morer states that in the beginning of last century the usual position of "the stool or bench of penance was under the precentor's desk." But it was not so always. It had once a higher elevation. And during the period that the church "pillar" was the conspicuous object in church, there were some favoured offenders that were allowed to stand "laigh," and be rebuked in front of the pulpit. In 1644 there was a slanderer in Galston ordained "to give signs of his grieff at the pulpit foot the next Sabbath day, because he war ane auld man." In 1676, a man who had been convicted of mending his sack on a Sunday, was appointed by the same Session to be publicly rebuked "in the body of the kirk near the pulpit." And in 1693 we read of a young couple in Galston, who had been married under a cloud, and for that scandal were made to stand several days "in *a* place before the pulpit": not *the public place*, but a place just a little less public.*

The place, however, where delinquents had commonly to stand when undergoing public rebuke, was what was called the repentance stool. The expression stool is apt to convey to the modern reader an erroneous impression, as if it were a tall, three-legged seat like what lawyers' clerks are perched on at the present day. Neither in structure nor situation were repentance stools always of one pattern. In the latter days of the old church of Mauchline the repentance stool, so far as I can learn, was just a common pew, a little exalted above its neighbours, and situated on the left hand of the pulpit under the drop of the west gallery. At an earlier period repentance stools were much more conspicuous objects. They were generally, if not always, "high places," and in old records they are so designated. The sentence pronounced on Paul Methven by the General Assembly in 1566 was that he be "planted in the public spectacle above the people in tyme of sermon," in

---

* As far back as 1583 the General Assembly appointed Mr. David Russell, bailie of St. Andrews, for calling the Presbytery a "rabble," and using other "outrageous words," to appear "before the pulpit, in the paroche Kirk of St. Androis, before noon, after the sermon, and immediately before the prayer," and there make confession that he had "heavily offendit his God and sclanderit the haill Kirk of God within this realme." Book of Univ. Kirk.

the Kirk of Edinburgh on two preaching days. How elevated the public place in Galston church was, may be inferred from several minutes that appear in the Session records of that parish. In 1635 "the Session gave libertie to Matthew Ross and John Walker in Galston to set up ane seat and dask to themselves under the repentance stools at the north-west kirk doore." In 1675, again, there was a delinquent who pled before the same Session " his inabilitie to stand high in the public place, by reason of a distemper in his head, and desired humbly that they would allow him to stand laigh in any place of the church they pleased."* The Session, it is recorded, acceded to the man's request and "appointed a chair to be set at the foot of the stair of the public place the next Lord's day." In Fenwick, also, the old repentance stool must have been a high place, for in 1674 there was an order given by the Session of that Parish that one of two delinquents should stand below and the other in the public place. And from what is stated in the records of the Presbytery of Ayr, it is evident that the repentance stool in Monkton Church, both before and after 1650, was a small gallery " above the kirk doors."

There were some churches in which the public place of repentance was furnished with different rooms or stances to indicate different grades of infamy. In the old Session Records of Perth there is a minute of date 1605 ordaining that " a more public place of repentance be biggit with all diligence, and in it certain degrees, that therein offenders may be distinguished and better discerned both by their place

---

* The term by which the public place of repentance was in very old times commonly designated, was the pillar. In 1591 it was minuted by the Session of the West Kirk, Edinburgh, that "John Howisone and John Gairns had agreit for twa hundreth marks to big ye laft and a pillar for" misdoers. If this pillar was a high and an unfenced stand we can see how some people, like the Galston man in 1675, had not nerve enough to mount it.

and habit." But the threefold classification of public rebukes already described superseded the necessity in Ayrshire of "degrees" in the place of repentance. Some offenders were made to "stand heich," others were allowed to "stand laigh." Some that "stood laigh" had to do so in front of the pulpit, and others were allowed to do so at their usual place of sitting. In all churches, however, the gravity of a man's offence was indicated by the dress in which he appeared for rebuke. As a rule, people came up for admonition in their very best church clothes, but in cases of grievous scandal they were required to appear in sackcloth or linen sheets. An entry in our Session Records shews that in Mauchline there was in 1686 a sum of £2 5s. expended on "harn to be a sackcloth and the making of it."* In 1748 another sackcloth was got and the making of it cost £1 13s. 6d. The discontinuance of sackcloth as a penitential garb is nowhere that I remember referred to in our Session Records, and it is certain that as recently as 1781 an offender appeared in Mauchline Church in that dishonoured and uncomfortable habiliment. In Galston there were at least two robes of shame, and in 1676 two sinners were appointed to appear in Galston Church, "the one with the sackcloth gown and the other with the sheets." But whether there was much difference in the infamy of these respective dresses is not made clear. In 1626 a Galston damsel appeared "in the publict place of repentance with ane uther habite than was enjoined to her be the Session," and therefore for this act of disobedience she was "ordainit to apeir the next day in sackcloth or in ane window claith."†

---

* In the Galston records for 1642 there is an entry " for harden to be ane *sackbratt* 38s., mair for the making thereof 6s."

† In 1573 the General Assembly ordained that great men deserving sackcloth

And whether arrayed in window claith or sackcloth, or attired in their best silks and broad cloth, it was not once only that offenders had to appear in public. They were appointed to undergo what was termed "a course of repentance." The minimum number of compearances required in the case of particular offences was specified in acts of the General Assembly, but when there was no satisfactory sign of humiliation and penitence the compearance was ordered to be continued longer.* And Kirk Sessions were very chary in accepting professions of repentance. In 1708 Mr. Maitland reported to the Session of Mauchline that a certain person under scandal, and with whom he had been appointed to converse, shewed "some seeming sense of sin with some small knowledge."† This was not thought sufficient to warrant absolution, and the delinquent was therefore appointed to

---

should be made to wear the same as well as the poor, and that no superintendent should dispense therewith for a "pecunial composition." Women would sometimes fain have covered their heads with a plaid when they stood in the place of penitence, but remorseless Kirk Sessions ruthlessly ordered plaids to be removed on such great occasions.—*Aberdeen Records.*

* An Act of Assembly, 1648, appointed public compearances to be made in some cases on three, in others on six, in others on twenty-six, in others on thirty-nine, and in cases of incest or murder, on fifty-two Sabbaths, if "the magistrate do not his duty in punishing such crimes capitally." In inflicting censures Presbyteries were occasionally a shade more merciful than Kirk Sessions were inclined to be. In 1697, a man from Cumnock craved leave from the Presbytery of Ayr to appear before the Congregation twice in one day "for his more speedy absolution." The circumstances were peculiar. The Parish was vacant, and there was preaching only at rare intervals. The Presbytery thought therefore that the request might be granted, if the Session found that it was "not offensive to the congregation." The inferior Court asserted its independence, and "found it not expedient to follow the Presbytery's mind, as not being an ordinary practice." That was exceeding the Presbytery's remit, and the Session were told in reply that the Presbytery "disliked their carriage.'

† In 1692 the Galston Session finding a delinquent "grossly ignorant, and so, out of case to give moral evidence of his repentance, delayed his absolution for some time and enjoined him to go to the minister to his own chamber for instruction."

submit to another admonition. The same year a young married couple were ordered to submit to rebuke one day in public and "to ly under the rebuke for some time until their walk appear more suitable after their sin." In 1693 an ill doer in this Parish was continued under scandal for several months, although she had previously stood publicly in the church in sackcloth for nine several Sabbaths! In 1749 a roguish shoemaker in the village had the effrontery or the satirical humour, it is hard to say which, to apply to the Session for a certificate of good behaviour. The shoemaker, however, brought coals of fire on his head by this presumptuous petition, for the minister informed the elders that the petitioner had been guilty of "undutiful carriage towards him (Mr. Auld) in time of catechising and visiting." The Session thereupon authorised the minister to grant the shoemaker such a testimonial as an undutiful member of the congregation deserved. That would just have been a certificate of impudence. But no sooner had this dry courtesy been condescended on than something else came unexpectedly to the Kirk Session's ears. Information was lodged that the son of Crispin had not only been disrespectful to his minister but had been guilty of gross insolence to his own mother; and when this report was investigated it was found that the shoemaker had repeatedly cursed the old lady with horrid imprecations, and had on one occasion aggravated the offence by committing it on a Sabbath day. Instead of a dainty testimonial, therefore, the shoemaker was provided with a seat on the repentance stool for four successive Sabbaths, and got the benefit of an admonition from the pulpit in face of the congregation.

As affording a sample of rigorous discipline, the following minute from the records of the Presbytery of Ayr may be quoted. The date of the minute is 1643, and the sin confessed was a heinous breach of the Seventh Commandment. "Compeared Y Z and confessed . . . . He was removit and enjoined to return clad in sackcloth and mak his confession, quhilk he did in humilitie upon his knies, the Moderator gravelie laying his sinne to his charge by reason of age and gray haires. He was removit ye second tyme, and returning in the same habite of sackcloth he was enjoined to give signs of his unfeigned repentance in the public in his paroch kirk, clad in sackcloth, and to stand at the kirk door in the same habit of sackcloth from the second bell to the third, and theirafter to present (him in) the public place of repentance, and to enter thereinto ye nixt Lord's day, and to continue from Sabbath to Sabbath after the said order enjoined, by the space of sex months according to the order of the Kirk of Scotland." At the end of the six months he appeared before the Presbytery for absolution, but for vitiating an act of the Kirk Session of Craigie he was ordered to stand two days more "in the habite of sackcloth without ane hatt on his head or band about his craig. As also, that after the same manner he appear at the next meeting of Presbyterie in Ayr and present himself in the public place of repentance, and that upon signs of unfeigned penitence he be received by the brether."

A very notable feature in old processes of discipline was the requirement of certain *cautions* from delinquents. These cautions were of two kinds, or more strictly speaking they were given for two purposes. When people were convicted of scandals long ago they were not all at once admitted to repentance, as the phrase was. They had usually to lie under scandal for some time and bemoan their sins in seclusion from Christian society. After being convicted of scandal they were required therefore to find a cautioner that they would, when called upon, appear before the Kirk Session and satisfy the Church. The following summary of a case that came before the Kirk Session of Galston in 1643 will give a fair illustration of the usual form of procedure in matters of discipline during the first forty years of the 17th century. A. B. and C. D. being "summoned, as suspect of" a conjoint offence, compeared and acknowledged their guilt. They also "found E. F. cautioner for them both, that they shall satisfie the Kirk in penaltie and repentance." The Galston records shew that from 1626 to 1638—that is during the first period of Episcopacy in the Church of Scotland —this form of procedure in discipline was universal or nearly so in Galston parish, and presumably therefore in other parishes. In 1633 the Galston Session made their rule absolute anent finding a cautioner for satisfaction of the kirk, and ordained that whoever appeared before them and refused to find caution to such effect "should not be heard till he laid down double penaltie." After 1638 the rule fell gradually into disuse, and seems to have become within a few years from that date altogether obsolete in Galston. But in some other parts of the country it was put in force long after 1638. In the records of the West Kirk, Edinburgh, for 1687—which, it may be mentioned in passing, was during the second period of Episcopacy—there are instances of delinquents finding caution to give "full and complete satisfaction to the discipline of the Church," and of cautioners being ordered when the proper time came "to cause the parties compeir within a month after advertisement, with certification" that if such compearance is not made, the cautioners shall forfeit the penalty specified in their bonds. It sometimes happened that parties delated to the Session declined to find caution for their subsequent compearance, and in such cases they were taken before the civil court and put under an injunction by the magistrate to obey the Session's summons.

In the burgh records of Dumbarton, for example, there is an instance recorded in 1628 of a woman's finding her brother "caution, that sche sall appeir befoir the ministers, elders, and Sessioun of the kirk onytime they pleiss on aucht dayis warning, for the spaice of ane half yeir to cum." *

Besides finding caution for compearance before the Session to satisfy the kirk, delinquents had long ago to find still further caution. After they had undergone rebuke, and other censure, they were not infrequently required to find security for good behaviour in future. Many instances of this requirement are to be found in the old records of Galston. Like the other kind of caution, however, already described, this form of security fell out of use about the middle of the 17th century. There is no instance of it so far as I remember in the extant records of Mauchline Session, which go back to the year 1669. But, both many and varied were the cases in which this caution was anciently given. Security was demanded from brawlers that they would "keip gude neiborheid" with their adversaries. Security was in like manner required from Sabbath breakers, that they would remember the Lord's day to keep it holy. Security had also to be given by conjoint offenders that they would never meet each other in suspect or quiet places. It sometimes happened in Galston, as it has happened elsewhere, that a man's foes were those of his own household, and we read, therefore, of a man in that strictly disciplined parish who, in 1640, was required to find a "cautioner

---

* Possibly some people went of their own accord to the civil magistrate for that purpose, thinking and thinking rightly that the giving and receiving of caution were civil acts with which Kirk Sessions as spiritual courts had nothing to do.

The cautioner was of course always a friend or relative of the delinquent, but in 1634 there was a married woman in Galston who "found *her husband* cautioner for satisfaction of the kirk."

to observe and keip good order with his wyffe, and to leive in love with her as God's word doth allow." There were also in Galston long ago one or two misguided people, who, either from spiritual indifference or from prejudice against their own minister, gave up church going, and so we read that in 1628 there was a woman required by the Session to find caution that she would "keip the kirk ordinarily every Sabbath, and communicate in our kirk every zeir." She had probably been an extreme Presbyterian who could not brook the ritualism of Episcopal services.

Long after the custom of requiring caution for good behaviour had become obsolete, Kirk Sessions, when they thought proper, required delinquents to subscribe "bands" in pledge of their Christian carriage in time coming. These bands, with the subscribers' names underwritten, were engrossed in the Session Records. In 1680, for instance, an insubordinate villager was delated to the Session of Mauchline for beating his wife. blaspheming God's name, and railing against the magistrates of the town. For these insolences and outrages he was sessionally rebuked, and absolved from scandal, " upon the condition of his engaging himself by his band and subscription to carry faire in time coming, under the penalty specified in the said band." The penalty so specified, it may be stated, was "rebuke in public before the congregation as often as the Session shall appoint, and over and above a payment to the Session of £20 Scots money for the use of the poor in the Parish." Even when Sessions were in the way of demanding caution for good conduct they sometimes were content to dispense with the caution and accept parties' own bands. In 1629, two persons, presumably husband and wife, appeared before the Session of Galston and "actit and obleist thame, that in cais it beis tryit in any tyme heirefter that aither of thame beis fundin swearing, or blaspheming of God's name, or making uther misorder in the house, aither of thame with uther, than and that cais aither of thame quha contravenis this act to pay £20 Scots." The shoemaker in Mauchline who insulted the minister and cursed his mother in 1749 had to sign a resolution of amendment before he got the benefit of restoration to Church privileges. There was no stereotyped form in which these bands of good behaviour were draughted, but the shoemaker's declaration will give a fair sample of the general strain in which they were written. "I, A. B., shoemaker in Mauchline, do acknowledge my rude and undutiful behaviour to my minister both in time of catechising and of visiting. I do also, with deep sorrow of heart, confess my horrid sin of cursing my mother. It is my earnest desire to be forgiven by God, whose holy name I have so dreadfully profaned, and by all of this congregation, those especially whom I have more immediately offended. And, at the same time, it is my sincere resolution, through divine grace, which I heartily implore, that I'll do so no more. And as an evidence of my sincerity, I am willing that this, my humble confession, be recorded in the Session Book and be adduced against me as an aggravation of my crime if ever I shall relapse." Signed A. B. More recent registration of such bands may be found in our Session Books. Down to the close of Mr. Auld's ministry at least, if not later, these bands were now and again required in Mauchline.

Besides requiring bands for good behaviour, Sessions sometimes interdicted sinners from "conversing together." In 1705 a minister reported to the Presbytery of Ayr that two of his Parishioners had broken this instruction, whereupon it was minuted that "The Presbytery being informed that they often converse together . . . . . . cause cite them to the next Presbytery that they may be rebuked for contumacy to their Session's appointment discharging them to converse." One of the parties affirmed that he was not contumacious, but that the other came to his house against his mind, and he kept up no correspondence beyond what "he could in no wise shun." Two hundred years ago (1674 for instance) the Kirk Session of Fenwick occasionally inhibited associates in sin from "one another's company except at kirk and mercat." Similar inhibitions were made in Galston, and in 1647 two persons were made to pay heavy penalties and stand two Sabbaths in the public place "for violation of an act of interdiction," and were "again interdicted of one another's companies save only in kirk and mercat."

Whether public appearances in garbs of sackcloth did or did not humble people with godly sorrow two hundred years ago is a question about which there may be two opinions, but it may be confidently asserted that at the present day such compearances would all the more harden the hearts of one class of offenders and utterly break the spirits of another, while at the same time it would demoralise the public mind by turning sin and scandal into a matter of mirth and mockery. It was not, however, till the year 1809 that public compearances for rebuke were abolished in this parish, during the ministry of Mr. Tod, and it may interest some people to be told that this important change in our parochial discipline was brought about by Mr. Thomas Miller, younger, of Glenlee, who was at that time a member of the Mauchline Kirk Session.

But although it was so long before public rebukes were discontinued in Mauchline there was a somewhat memorable protest made against them nearly seventy years before their abolition. This protest was made by a hoary headed sinner, whose name need not be divulged. He seems to have occupied a good social position, and to have had cultured notions on some things. But every now and again he fell under scandal, and times beyond number he was cited to appear before the Kirk Session. For a long while he disregarded or evaded these citations, and the more he worried and outwitted the Session the more he chuckled and grinned. So unwearied and persistent, however, were the Session in renewing citations that he felt at length constrained to come to terms with his tormentors. First of all he tried the effect of a "partial confession," and when this device failed, he insisted that if any further acknowledgments were made by him he should be "treated to a gentlemanly punishment."* And for once, in the course of his foolish life, he spoke wisely, and indicated the true principles on which Church discipline should be established: for if one of the chief ends of discipline is to reclaim people from evil ways, it is not by ridicule or wanton severity, but by love and entreaty, tenderness and earnest remonstrance, and what might be called Christian gentlemanliness, that that end must be sought.

Rebukes were, of course, spiritual sentences, and they were at times accompanied by other spiritual sentences, such as the lesser or the greater excommunication. The greater excommunication was a very serious matter. Down to the revolution it inferred severe civil penalties. By an Act of Parliament passed in 1573 excommunicated persons might be denounced as rebels and have their goods poinded. But they seldom were so denounced and despoiled. Except in the most violent times of civil and ecclesiastical strife, when passions

---

* That some people long ago were not very much abashed by undergoing public repentance may be inferred from the following minute in Mauchline Records of date 5th August, 1705:—"*Quo die* the Sessions met. J. P. and A. A. from the Parish of Ochiltree supplicate the Sessione yt they would receive ym to the stool."

were abnormally excited, it was rarely that the sentence of greater excommunication was passed, either with or without civil penalties. The execution of that sentence, however, was not altogether unheard of even in rural parishes. There is at least one instance of it recorded in the Session Registers of Mauchline. It was on a man who in 1750 had, to use the words of the record, been found guilty of "cursing his mother in very shocking terms, and otherwise using her most barbarously," and had also, in addition to these offences, been guilty of persistent contumacy and contempt of the Church courts. The cursing of parents, as was shewn in a previous lecture, was not only considered a very gross form of sin, but by an Act of Parliament passed in the reign of Charles the Second, it was declared to be a crime worthy of death. Contumacy, again, is an offence which no constituted Church can put up with. If allowed, it would undo all authority and frustrate all discipline. The Presbytery of Ayr, therefore, in the case remitted to them from Mauchline in 1751 did "unanimously agree that the man be summarily excommunicated, and appointed Mr. Auld to intimate the said sentence of the greater excommunication between and next meeting of Presbytery, when he is to report his diligence." In the records of the Presbytery of Ayr there is mention made of another sentence of excommunication that was passed on a Mauchline man. This was in the year 1650, and the offences libelled were incest and disobedience to the minister, or, in other words, incest and contumacy.* As part of the procedure then customary in such cases the Presbytery ordered the "said excommunication to be intimated next Sabbath by all the

---

* Strictly speaking, the Parish of Sorn is entitled to the credit of this incestuous person, as he hailed from that part of Mauchline Parish which is now, and has for 200 years been, called Sorn or Dalgain.

brethren," that is by all the ministers within the bounds, from their respective pulpits. In the Session records of Galston there is an interesting account of a process of excommunication instituted in 1638, the year in which the National Covenant was revived and reframed, against a man named Mitchell "for not subscryving the covenant, not keiping the kirk, refusing the communion, and uther faults." Three separate times prayers were offered for the man, and then he was summoned to appear before the Presbytery. In the end "he referred himself to the will of the Session," and so escaped the extreme sentence of the Church. In his case, therefore, we have not an account of the full process of excommunication in those days nor of the process of removing the excommunication. This latter process, as might be expected, was at one time a very severe piece of discipline. The General Assembly in 1569-70 ordained that excommunicated persons not fugitive from the laws, and suiting to be received by the kirk, should "stand bareheaded at the kirk door every preaching day betwixt the assemblies, secluded from prayers before and after sermons, and then enter the kirk and sit in the public place bareheaded all the time of the sermons, and depart before the latter prayer."*

---

* Previous to 1571 "all adulterers, murtherers, incestuous persons, and uthers committers of hainous crymes," were required to present themselves to the General Assembly "to resave their first injunction," and to return to the following General Assembly "in linen clothes" and receive a second admonition. It was ordained, however, in 1571, that "as divers of the saids offenders are far distant frae the places of Generall Assemblies, and uthers for poverty and deidlie feids may not nor dare not travell through the countrie to present themselves before the saids Assemblies," all such offenders should in future be called by Superintendents and Commissioners of Provinces "to compeir before them in their Synodall conventions, to be halden by them twyse in the yeir, to receave and take their injunctions, conforme to the order usit before the Generall Assemblies in all sorts." In 1588 a further relaxation of discipline was allowed by the Assembly, and adulterers, homicides, &c., were permitted to give satisfaction to the Kirk "before the Presbyteries, in such forme as they were accustomit before the Synodalls."—*Book of Universal Kirk.*

The sentence of lesser excommunication meant suspension from the Lord's table, and it was a matter of not infrequent occurrence. It is not, however, to be confounded with refusal to grant a token of admission to the Lord's table. That refusal was extended to all that were under any scandal and had not made satisfaction to the Kirk Session. But the lesser excommunication was a special sentence appended to a rebuke. It was intended to shew that the offence censured was in the eye of the Kirk Session heinous in character, not to be all at once forgotten, and that the offender was not fit to be a worthy communicant till a different spirit came over him. It was a sentence also that had to be publicly intimated, and one from which relaxation was not to be granted till the Session were satisfied of the knowledge, seriousness, and reformation of the persons desiring release.

Besides spiritual sentences, such as admonitions and excommunications, Kirk Sessions were in the way long ago of inflicting civil punishments on delinquents. Indeed it may be said that so interwoven are things civil and things ecclesiastic, things spiritual and things social, that to be declared under scandal or to be suspended from the privileges of the Lord's table is itself a species of social ostracism. And in one of the old minutes of our Kirk Session, a minute of date 1705, there is to be found a very apposite expression illustrative of this fact. Two persons " appearing penitent according to the view of man," were absolved, says the minute, from their scandal " and received into society again."* But besides the social degradation that accompanied spiritual sentences, there were civil punishments expressly imposed on offenders by Kirk

---

* The expression "received into the society of the Kirk as a lively member thereof" occurs in the old deliverances of the General Assembly regarding absolution from scandal.—*Universal Kirk*, 45.

W

Sessions. This circumstance was made a matter of accusation against the Presbyterians by Maxwell, Bishop of Ross, in a book called *Issachar's Burden*, and the truth of it was vehemently denied by Baillie in his historical vindication of the government of the Church of Scotland. What Baillie says is very notable and well worthy of quotation. "No Church assembly in Scotland," he says, "assumes the least degree of power to inflict the smallest civil punishment upon any person: the General Assembly itselfe hath no power to fine any creature so much as one groat.* It is true the lawes of the land appoint pecuniary mulcts, imprisonment, joggs, pillories, and banishment for some odious crimes, and the power of putting these laws in execution is placed by the Parliament in the hands of the inferior magistrates . . . . ordinarily some of these civill persons are ruling Elders and sit with the Eldership: So when the Eldership have cognosced upon the *scandall* alone of criminal persons and have used their spiritual censures only to bring the party to repentance, some of the ruling Elders, by virtue of their civil office or commission,† will impose a mulct or send to prison or stocks, or banish out of the bounds of some little circuit, according as the Act of Parliament or Council do appoint it. But that the Eldership should impose its

---

* In the Second Book of Discipline agreed upon in the General Assembly, 1578, it is stated that the office of the Christian Magistrate in the Kirk is "to assist and manteine the discipline of the Kirk, and punish them civilly that will not obey the censure of the same, *without confounding alwayis the ane iurisdiction with the uther.*"

† "In Boroughs it was the almost invariable custom to have some of the Elders chosen from among the Magistrates. This circumstance connected with the nature of the offences usually tried and the punishments decreed against them by the legislation, led to that apparent confounding of the two jurisdictions which is apt to strike those who happen to look into the ancient records of Kirk Sessions as an anomaly and a contradiction to the principles of the Presbyterian Church."— *M'Crie's Life of Melville*, Vol. I., p. 335.

ecclesiastick and spiritual power for any such end none of us doe defend."

According to Baillie, it is only the civil magistrate that can legally impose any civil punishment. And we have seen how frequently the Kirk Session of this Parish referred matters to the civil magistrate in the case of people's squatting in the Parish without testimonials, or refusing to comply with the orders of the Church. There was an old Act of Parliament which empowered Sheriffs of counties to appoint Session bailies in Parishes that were unblest with any resident magistrate. These Session bailies were elders that had commission to put certain laws affecting public morals, such as the laws against profaneness, into execution. It thus happened, as Baillie says, that in some cases where Kirk Sessions imposed spiritual censures an elder in the Session simultaneously imposed a civil punishment. In 1648 the General Assembly recommended that use should be made of the Act of Parliament, 1645, "for having magistrates and justices in every congregation," and that "each magistrate in every congregation exact and make compt to the Session" of the sums payable according to Act of Parliament for the several offences liable to fine. And how the Act of Parliament and the Act of Assembly were sometimes executed will be seen from the following extract from the Burgh Records of Glasgow in 1649. At a meeting of Town Council that year it was agreed that appointment be made to certain persons "quha ar upon the Session, that they, in absence of the present magistratis, have commission to exerce the civille power requirit against delinquentis and uthers lyable to censure that come before that judicatorie." In the Session Records of Mauchline there is no reference, so far as I have observed, to any magistrate under the designation of Session bailie, but that there were

Session bailies in many parishes in Ayrshire both in the seventeenth and the eighteenth centuries is beyond doubt. In 1698 an order was minuted by the Presbytery of Ayr that "each minister in the Presbytery is to use his endeavours to have a magistrate in their Paroch elected by the Session, having deputation from the Sheriff according to law." The Synod of Glasgow and Ayr about the same date or shortly afterwards passed an ordinance to the same effect, and in 1700 this Act was read in the Presbytery of Ayr, and each of the members of Presbytery was severally asked whether there were Session bailies in his Parish or not. The minutes of Presbytery state that most part of the ministers reported that they had such magistrates in their Parishes, and those who had them not were enjoined to do what they could to get magistrates in their Sessions appointed.* We have seen how difficult it was long ago to prevail on people to accept the office of Elder, and when we consider both the restraints and the labours imposed on Elders we can understand why there should have been such reluctance. But it might have been thought that every person in every Parish would have been ambitious to be made a bailie. Yet it was not so. In 1700 the minister of Riccarton, at a Presbyterial visitation of his Parish, reported that "any who were pitched upon would not *condescend* to be their Session bailie," and that the Heritors undertook the

---

* In the records of Fenwick Parish there are several notices of the election of "a Civil magistrate for concurring with the Session to the bearing down of scandal." The election was made by the Heritors and Elders, and in one instance at least after the election was made, a petition was presented to the Earl of Eglinton, "Bailzie Principal of Cunningham, for a commission" in favour of the person chosen to exercise the office. A minute in the Records of Sorn Parish (printed in Paterson's History of Ayrshire) states that in 1700 Hugh Mitchell of Delgain was, "according to the 31st Act of the present Session of Parliament," named and chosen magistrate for the Parish to carry said Act into effect—Sir George Campbell of Cessnock, Sheriff Principal, having given him full powers.

duty by course. The reluctance shewn in 1700 by respectable persons in Riccarton to accept the office of Session bailie seems also to have been found in some other Parishes, for in December of the same year the Presbytery thought fit to delay enforcing the Act of Synod about the appointment of magistrates in Sessions, "till a new Act of Parliament made thereanent came forth more full, to make the nomination of the magistrates effectualle." This desired compulsory Act of Parliament never did come forth, and the difficulty of finding Session bailies increased year after year. In 1723 the Presbytery of Ayr were again exercised about this want in their Parochial equipment, and a committee of Presbytery was "appointed to wait on the Earl of Loudoun, principal Sheriff, to try if he would give a deputation to some fitt person in each Session within the bounds who have not magistrates in the Paroch already," but his Lordship told the committee that he had some difficulties in the matter, and would have to give consideration to these.* We shall not be far wrong if we say that this was the date at which the office of Session bailie practically ceased to be recognised in Ayrshire, and we can understand why we never read of a Session bailie in Mauchline. There was no need for one. There was a resident Burgh bailie, and possibly there were among the heritors other local justices. In a minute of Session in 1696 it is stated that the Session "made application to Netherplace, being present, as one of their members, that he as Sheriff Depute and magis-

---

* In 1717 a deputation from the General Assembly attended at Court to represent the grievances of the Church. This deputation "demanded the restoration of those laws for enforcing the judgments of the ecclesiastical courts by the civil power which had been so adroitly cast out of the statute book in the adjustment of the Revolution settlement. But the statesmen repelled the proposal with a brief emphasis."—Burton, VIII. The views of churchmen and statesmen were evidently at that date pretty wide apart. Hence Lord Loudon's difficulties.

trate in the bounds would take notice of the contumacy" of certain persons named as being under discipline.

There can be no doubt that whether Kirk Sessions had constituent bailies or not, they did inflict civil penalties both "pecunial" and corporal. They ordered fines to be paid for particular offences, and they increased fines at their own discretion. In very old times the first thing required of persons charged with scandals was to find a caution that they would "satisfy the Kirk both in penalty and repentance." The Galston Records shew that this was the uniform practice in Galston Parish during the Episcopal times before 1638, and that the practice had not altogether died out till at least 1644, if not later. So much store too was at one time set on the penalty, that delinquents were not allowed to declare their penitence till they had paid their appointed fines. In 1633 some long-tongued people in Galston were found guilty of slander, and had to satisfy the Kirk in both the spiritual and civil forms of satisfaction. The one form of satisfaction, however, had to be given before the other was accepted, and the delinquents were ordered by the Session "before they go to the hie place to lay down ye penaltie, ylk is decernit to be £5, ilk ane of thame." It is very probable that the assumption of civil power by Kirk Sessions was more common in the Episcopal times before the second Reformation of 1638 than in Presbyterial times since, but a claim to the inheritance of Peter's sword as well as Peter's keys was by no means confined to any Episcopal epoch in the history of the Church of Scotland. Long after the overthrow of Episcopacy in 1638 we find Kirk Sessions ordering and ordaining penalties to be paid by transgressors.

The most common form of corporal punishment that Church Courts in this country inflicted was confinement for an hour or two in the jougs.* These jougs were iron collars that were put round the necks of delinquents. They were part of the paraphernalia of every church long ago. Sometimes they were fixed in a pillar at the church gate, sometimes in a tree in the church yard, and sometimes in the wall of the church itself, at the side of the principal door. At Fenwick, the jougs may still be seen dangling on the church wall about five feet from the ground, and in the old Session Records of that interesting Parish there are cases to be found of culprits being appointed to "stand in the joges from eight till ten, and thence go to the place of repentance within ye kirk." It was only in extreme cases, however, that Kirk Sessions had recourse to the jougs. In 1661 the patience of the Kirk Session of Rothesay was sorely tried by an inebriate member of their congregation, who would not by any amount of persuasion or rebuke be induced to live soberly. As a last resource the Session warned her, that "if hereafter she should be found drunk, she would be put in the joggs and have her dittay written on her face." That there were jougs in Mauchline as well as in other uncivilised places two hundred years ago is quite certain, but the only reference to them that I have observed in the Session Records is an entry of payment of £1 16s. in 1681 "for a lock to the bregan and mending it." The word bregan, or, as it is spelt in *Jamieson's Dictionary* braidyeane,† was the common word in Ayrshire for jougs, and the fact that the Mauchline Session were in 1681 keeping the lock of the bregan in order, is proof that the bregan was at that date either in use or kept for use when occasion should require. In the Session Records

---

* In the days of John Welsh (1604) Sabbath-breakers were by the Kirk Session of Ayr " ordained to be put in the thefis hoal."

† In Galston Records spelt " breggaine," " breggan," " bradzane," and " bredyane."

of Galston there are more explicit references than in ours to the bregan or bredyane and the purpose for which it was meant. In 1628 the Session of Galston passed an Act, that "gif the man fornicator be responsible (that is, have money) and the woman not, the man shall satisfie for baith, and gif the woman be responsible and the man not, then and in that caice the woman shall pey and satisfie for baith. And gif naither the man nor the woman be responsible, they shall stand twa several Sabbaths in the bradzane and uther twa days with thair lynning claiths in the public place of repentance." In 1640 a case occurred in which a poor frail girl was found by the Session of Galston to be not responsible, and, "not having silver to pey her penalties, the Sessioune ordainit her to stand in the bredyane conforme to ane former act maid thereanent." In 1651 the horrors of the breggan were threatened by the Session of Galston for what might now-a-days be reckoned a smaller offence. One John Persene appeared before the Session and confessed that he had been absent from church for the space of five weeks. For this neglect of ordinances he was "injoyned to apeir in the public place of repentance and there to be publicly rebuked, with certificatione that if he be found to be two Sabbaths together absent fra the church he shall be put in the breggan." In Sorn parish, too, as well as in Galston, profanation of the Sabbath was occasionally punished by a lock up in the breggan; but in Sorn the punishment was inflicted in the orthodox way by a magistrate. The record bears that in 1698 a Sabbath breaker "was delated by authority of two magistrates, James Farquhar of Gilmillscroft and Adam Aird of Katarin, and was by them put in the jougges from the ringing of the first to the ringing of the third bell, and then" (that is, to use a common but incorrect phrase, when the church went in) "appeared for rebuke before the congregation." *

Another civil penalty imposed by Kirk Sessions on delinquents was fines, although, strictly speaking, it was only the civil magistrate that could legally inflict and exact the payment of these. But if no magistrate was present in a Kirk Session, it saved trouble to all parties when the Kirk Session just stated what the fines were and took them direct from the delinquent's own hands. In most cases the amount of fine exigible for special offences was fixed by Act of Parliament, and appointed to be handed over for pious uses to the Kirk Session of the parish where the offence was committed. It was not unusual, therefore, for Kirk Sessions to minute, "mulcted in terms of Act of Parliament" £4 or £2, as the case might be.

It must be admitted, also, that Kirk Sessions were fond of mulcting and fining, and for a reason that does them no discredit. The fines went for the good of the parish, and especially for behoof of the poor,† and at a time when there

---

* As shewing the kind of extreme cases in which the breggan was had recourse to, it may be stated that in 1626 a person in Galston guilty of "fourefold fornication" was with "her awin consent" ordained, if "deprehendit in harlotrie again to be banished from this congregation, and for the said falt to stand thric dayes in the braggaine, and upon the publique place of repentance als long as ye Sessione shall think expedient, and farder to pay £8 of penaltie."

† Not in all parishes for behoof of the poor.
In the records of the Dumbarton Kirk Session, published along with the Burgh Records in 1860, there is a very interesting table of the "Debursements of the penalties since the 9th Februar, 1620," till the 12th August, 1622. The fines in Dumbarton at that date were not given to the poor, but applied for the pious uses of repairing the kirk, &c. The following items will shew fairly well where the money went :—

	£	s.	d.
For the thiking of the steeple,	9	13	4
For making the common leddir,	0	16	0
For mending the east end of the brigge,	0	12	0
To Johne Thome (the beddell) for his fie of the zeir, 1622,	10	0	0
For ane sand glass,	0	13	0

was no assessment levied for the poor, and church door collection were inadequate to meet the wants of the needy, Kirk Sessions were disposed to take advantage of all lawful means in their power for relief of the indigent. In 1755, in the days of Mr. Auld, who was a good friend to the poor, and always on the look-out for their welfare and interest, the Session of Mauchline minuted that "considering how much vice and immorality of various kinds abound among us, notwithstanding the many good laws we have for checking and discouraging the same, and being sensible that the not putting of the said laws into execution is in a great measure owing to the negligence and remissness of Kirk Sessions in discharging their duty, whereby among other evils it comes to pass that the poor are robbed of their right, and defrauded of that necessary subsistence which they are entitled to by law, in remedy whereof, the Session resolve to be more strict in adhering to these laws for the future, and particularly do hereby enact and ordain, that the full fines appointed by Act of Parliament, Charles II., Par. 1, Sess. 1st, Chap. 38, against offenders specified therein, shall be exacted by the Kirk Treasurer from each of the said specified delinquents before they be absolved." Even in 1809, when Mr. Millar, younger, of Glenlee, proposed the abolition of public rebukes in Mauchline, except in cases of very gross scandal, he appended to his motion, and doubtless from charitable motives, that larger fines should be exacted in the

For ane airne to sett the said glass into,	-	1	0	0
For setting up the place of repentance, -	-	-	5	0	0
For thrie pund of lead to be tickets to the communicants,	0	6	0
To pay the two mortclothis,	-	-	-	-	23	18	4
To pay clerk of the Presbitirie's fees,	-	-	-	1	0	0

A similar table might, with a little trouble, be drawn up by extracts from the Galston session books. The penalty bag was kept distinct in that parish from the kirk box or collecting box, and penalties were applied in Galston in much the same way as in Dumbarton.

way of discipline.* Every one knows that Kirk Sessions now-a-days are very glad to be relieved from dealing with cases of scandal, and very happy to let such cases be disposed of, when it can be done legally, by neighbouring Parishes. But once it was different, and for the very intelligible reason that there was then a question of pounds, shillings, and pence involved in the matter. In 1785 a man applied to the Kirk Session of Mauchline for leave to go to Sorn to make satisfaction for a sin he had committed in that Parish. The Session, however, declared themselves "unanimously of opinion, that the issue of the scandal belonged to Machline," and they refused to grant the favour craved, unless the petitioner paid "his penalty to the poor of this Parish."

As might be imagined, cases sometimes occurred in which the customary and legal fines were greater than delinquents could afford to pay. In such cases Kirk Sessions exercised a wise and generous discretion in modifying the mulct. In 1686, for instance, a man that had been fined in the Kirk Session of Mauchline in £20 was let off for £12. Even Mr. Auld sometimes relaxed his rigorous rule. In 1776, Racer Jess offered half a crown in payment of her penalty, and "the Session considering her poverty and that she had got no assistance in maintaining her bastard child, which the alleged father continues to disown, accepted the same." And for

---

* Among the sins laid by the Cameronians in 1742 to the charge of the Church of Scotland was "a virtual sale of indulgences by receiving money payments as a substitute for ecclesiastical penance." This was not alleged to be a common practice, but was the practice of the kirk treasurer in Edinburght. (Burton's History, viii. 411.) In 1751 a tailor from Riccarton appeared before the Kirk Session of Galston craving absolution for a sin committed before his marriage, and "begging to be absolved from the disgrace of a public appearance, as his wife was dead." The Session allowed absolution after one appearance in public, "for the peculiar circumstances of the case, upon his giving a *present* to the poor," and to that offer the tailor thankfully agreed.

other reasons than the poverty of a delinquent fines were remitted. Good conduct on particular occasions was taken into consideration, so that Kirk Sessions in being a terror to evil doers should also be a praise to them that do well. In 1671, a man named Johnston had his penalties discharged altogether by the Kirk Session of Mauchline, because of "some services done to the Parish at the re-entry of the minister." A promise of service was also in some instances accepted in lieu of money, as in Galston in 1640, when a man gave signs of repentance "and promised staines for bigging of the bridge for his penaltie."

All these instances of leniency may be regarded as very amiable and commendable, but Kirk Sessions at times made compromises that are scarcely defensible on the score of justice. In 1732, a person under fama in Mauchline offered to pay half a guinea to the poor and stand one day in the place of repentance, if by that means her scandal would be removed, and the Kirk Session considering that no guilt had been proven against the woman accepted the offer. Plainly there should have been guilt either proved or confessed before a fine was accepted or a rebuke administered, and I cannot but think, therefore, that the Session was in this instance guilty of taking undue advantage of amiability. In 1735, an important personage from Cumnock, who had occasion to give satisfaction to the Kirk Session of Mauchline, pled that " he was frequently abroad, and craved therefore to be absolved on his appearing one day, forenoon and afternoon, before the congregation, and paying a fine of £16 Scots, otherwise he would pay the ordinary and appear three days." It is, perhaps, owing to the way in which this offer is worded that it has an ugly look of mingled threats and bribery. The Session probably put the offer in another way before their minds, for it is stated that, after reasoning, a vote was taken and the motion to accept was carried. In 1637, the Kirk Session of Galston were petitioned by a delinquent to "licentiat him to stand in the permitted place in his ordinary habit, and enjoin him to pey the greater penaltie." In considering this request the Session minuted a very ingenuous confession that they were sorely in need of "present moneyie," and they passed a resolution therefore to accept the offer, and enjoin the payment of 40s. extra, besides the cost of "ane sheit, quhilk wes gevin to a puir deid bodie."

There was sometimes a disposition shewn by delinquents to regard the payment of a fine as all the satisfaction they had to give for an offence. They thought the fine a complete condonation of the misdeed, and that it inferred removal of scandal. They did not realise the fact that they were members of two separate corporations—the State and the Church—and that they had to answer to the State for crimes, and to the Church for scandals, or in other words that they were subject to both fines and censures. In 1752, a farmer named Goudie was cited to appear before the Session of Mauchline, on a charge of having "clandestinely, and without giving the least warning of his evil design," knocked down a man in the village by a stroke on the head, and of having afterwards denied the fact with imprecations or curses. Mr. Goudie compeared and confessed himself guilty of the act of assault, but professed to have no recollection of having uttered any maledictions. "At the same time he entered his protest against the Session, for meddling in that affair after the Civil Magistrate had fined him for it, and appealed to the Presbytery, craving an extract of the process, which was allowed him." The result of his appeal can easily be conjectured. He got a new wrinkle in Church law which he was not likely to forget. He was rebuked in the Presbytery, and his rebuke was ordered to be intimated to the Congregation of Mauchline the following Sabbath.

There is an old proverb that prevention is better than cure, and Kirk Sessions long ago were alive to that fact. They may at times have been more inquisitorial than was prudent (or would now be prudent), and at other times more rigorous in their censure than was expedient; but it was always their professed and doubtless their sincere desire, to repress and restrain sin, and promote the practice of holiness. They were diligent in warning therefore as well as in rebuking. In 1696, for instance, the Kirk Session of Mauchline, "considering what scandalous practices some people were guilty of, as in particular, frequent absence from church, laying out cloathes to dry on the Lord's day, and suffering their children to play together in flocks on the said day, thought it fit that the people guilty of such practices should be admonished out of the pulpit, and cautioned against them for the time to come." In 1709 again there is a minute in the records that "the minister is to be minded next Sabbath to intimate to all ins in town not to give drink to excess to any upon any day, and especially to souldiers." Of course it may be presumed that in the days of Mr. Auld's wakeful ministry the prevention scheme would be zealously worked. And so it was. In 1782 it is recorded that the Kirk Session, "taking into consideration the cruel and inhuman custom of cockfighting at fasten e'en,* do forbid the same, and order their

---

* Fasten e'en, the night before Lent,—the last night on which good cheer was allowed by the Catholics till the forty days' fast was over,—was in the time of Burns observed by Presbyterians as a night of extra jollity.

On Fasten e'en we had a rockin—
To ca' the crack and weave our stockin ;

officer to take notice to give up the names of such as transgress; and particularly, they order the schoolmaster to take care that none under his charge do provide or bring cocks for that purpose, and that there be no vacancy in the school that day."

In 1788 the prevalence of bastardy in the Parish had become the subject of remark and comment. Burns had risen into fame, and his poems were widely read; and public attention was directed to local scandals, whether real or fictitious. There were not a few people ready to cry out against the hollowness of religious professions. There were enormous gatherings at communions, devotional exercises both in public and in private were frequent and long, and unmistakable zeal on the part of Kirk Sessions was shown to cleanse the cup and platter of the Church. But still there were a great many bad coppers in the country, and there was much vice both openly and secretly practised.*

The Kirk Session were not undisturbed about this. On the contrary, they thought it was a most humiliating and sorrowful fact, and as was shewn in a previous lecture they drew up in regard to it a solemn admonition and a stringent resolution, which they ordered to be publicly read from the pulpit. Two years before this, they had also ordered a similar admonition and resolution, in regard to Sabbath breaking, to be intimated. And this should shew that in dealing with particular persons for breaches of the Sabbath, the Session of Mauchline were not so much moved by "pique and malice" as has by some people

---

> And there was muckle fun and jokin
> Ye need na doubt:
> At length we had a hearty yokin
> At sang about.

* Almost every year there was a sale of the "bad coppers" put into the Church plate for charity.

been supposed and represented. Their procedure may in some instances have been rigid and unwise, but it was at least directed without partiality or respect of persons. Their declaration on Sabbath observance is worthy of quotation, both because it gives a picture of the times in which Burns lived—possibly an *ex parte* and a coloured picture, but still a picture that as students of these times we cannot leave out of account—and because it shows the zeal and vigour with which the Kirk Session endeavoured to put down every form of what they considered unchristian conduct in the parish. The declaration is dated 23rd April, 1786, and its tenor is as follows:—"The Kirk Session of Machline are informed that the Lord's day is grossly profaned in this place by both men and women, particularly the younger sort, meeting together in parties and cabals after sermon, and are seen walking and traversing the fields and highways in an indecent manner on the evening of that holy day. The Session therefore think it their duty to warn the people in this congregation, young and old, against the sin of Sabbath-breaking, and earnestly exhort parents and heads of families to command their children, servants, and all within their gates, to keep holy the day of the Lord as he has commanded, and particularly to refrain from the profanation of this holy day by idly vaguing together and by profane worldly conversation. And the members of the Session and other heads of families are desired to take notice of, and inform against, such profaners of the Sabbath, that they be spoken to privately, or censured, as the Session or Presbytery shall judge proper." It cannot be doubted that the framers of this declaration acted on the high principle propounded by the prophet, "Oh son of man, I have set thee a watchman unto the house of Israel, therefore if thou wilt not speak to warn the wicked from his way, that wicked man shall die in his iniquity, but his blood will I require at thine hand. Nevertheless if thou warn the wicked of his way to turn from it, and he do not turn from his way, he shall die in his iniquity, but thy soul will be delivered."

We have now considered the main questions regarding parochial discipline by Kirk Sessions: the mode of inquisition adopted, the extent of jurisdiction claimed, and the censures inflicted by these local courts. As a sequel to these discussions we have now to enquire what amount of deference was paid to the authority of Kirk Sessions by the general public long ago.

It is customary to represent Kirk Sessions as having in olden times lorded over congregations and parishes with despotic authority. And there is doubtless some truth in the statement. The Kirk Session, as I said before, was in a very wide sense of the term the local authority in the parish. And, as a rule, people were not only subject to the Kirk Session, but they stood in awe of the Kirk Session. It is the case, nevertheless, that the mandates and citations of Kirk Sessions were not in every instance obeyed obsequiously. In 1734 a self-possessed young woman appeared before the Session of Mauchline in response to a summons, and on being asked what she considered an impolite question, drew herself up and "said that time would tell." Instead of taking this malapertness good humouredly the Session pronounced it contempt of court, and minuted that they would apply to "the public magistrate," if the damsel would not shortly give them satisfaction. Three months passed away and there was no sign of either time telling or of the lady showing any disposition to satisfy Sessional curiosity. A second summons was therefore served upon mademoiselle to compear again before the Lords of the Congregation, but this summons she disregarded altogether.

One of the Elders was thereupon deputed "to speak to the Bailie anent her," and at a subsequent meeting of Session the Elder reported that the Bailie's advice was to try her once more with a citation, and if she then failed to compear, he would interfere magisterially and put "his interloquitor in execution against her"! About forty years before that occurrence there was another case of a Parishioner declining to appear before the Session of Mauchline in answer to citation, and in that case the man was simply "remitted (or as it should been said 'committed') to the civil magistrate, because the Session had sufficient evidence of his intention to delude and evade them." The man, however, who was a reckless slippery fellow that reverenced nobody, and had not the least regard for his own word, seems to have eluded and evaded the magistrate also; for the Session some months afterwards declared him contumacious, and instructed Ballochmyle, junior, to report his contumacy to the Sheriff. Kirk Sessions had also at times to call in the aid of the civil magistrate to enforce their orders and sentences. In the year 1691 a number of matrimonial consignations became forfeit in Mauchline. They had never been deposited. There had only been a bond or a caution given for their payment, if payment should become necessary. The Session, therefore, had not the means of executing their sentence of forfeiture by simply retaining the deposits in their possession. They had to ask cautioners and accepters of bills to fulfil their engagements, and they found on the part of these cautioners and bill accepters more reluctance to do this than might have been expected of honourable men. The Session accordingly passed two resolutions. One of these had for its object the prevention of similar defalcations in future, and the tenor of that resolution was, that neither bond nor caution for consignations would henceforth be received, but that all persons who had consignations to make would have to deposit the sums required. The other resolution was to take steps for the recovery of such consignations as had been already forfeited, and the tenor of this resolution was, that all " forefaulters of consignation be summoned before the barronie court, or their cautioners to be legallie persued, for the recovery of the samine to the Session." In 1697 another case occurred in which the Session of this Parish had to invoke the magistrate's assistance in carrying out a sentence of theirs. A young woman was that year complained of by the Session, for not keeping her appointment and promise to appear for rebuke in the public place of repentance, and for "feigning sickness" as an excuse for her non-appearance. For so doing the Session judged her contumacious, and instructed the minister to speak to the magistrate about her. But in this case, and in many similar cases which occurred from time to time, the Kirk Session might have drawn an obvious inference and taken a salutary lesson to heart regarding the rigour of church discipline. To people of the least sensibility a public compearance was a sore humiliation. It was so sore that they feigned sickness to avoid it, and perhaps it was not a feigned but a real sickness that possessed them. They were made to sorrow with a sorrow that worked death,* and in the interests of religion as well as in pity to individual persons, it was highly expedient that such a form of censure as involved shame

---

* How the shame of public humiliation afflicted some people may be seen from the account of Paul Methven's contrition in 1566 for dishonouring his cloth by a sin that involved deposition from the ministry and excommunication. " He prostrate himself before the haill brethren in the General Assembly with *weeping and howling.*" Book of Univ. Kirk. In his survey of Ayrshire Aiton avers that public penance on the repentance stool led to a good deal of child murder.

and ridicule more than womanly feelings could bear, should have been abolished. Another kind of sentence that Kirk Sessions had sometimes to seek magisterial assistance to carry out, was parochial exile. Kirk Sessions, as we have seen, were very careful to exclude from the parish all persons that they thought would not prove respectable parishioners. People from Lesmahagow or Ecclefechan, or in fact from any place whatever, near or remote, were not allowed to squat in the parish at their own sweet wills without producing testimonials of character. The Session had accordingly to give intruders notice to quit. But where were the poor creatures to go? They were bidden move to the other side of the river, and when they did so they were told on the other side to go back by the way they came. They were thus in a strait betwixt two. They sat still, therefore, and by no amount of sessional persuasion or sessional authority would they be induced to rise and walk. The civil magistrate in these cases was appealed to, and the magistrate issued an interlocutor which in substance declared (what was very hard), that people's right of habitation was subject to ecclesiastical permission.

Delinquents had sometimes the hardihood to show positive insolence to the high authority of the Kirk Session.* In 1732

---

* In 1645 there was a woman brought before the Session of Fenwick for "upbraiding of the Session from off the public place of repentance, when she should have made confession of her fault." The following year another offender in the same place was called to book for "unbeseeming speeches on the place of repentance," and in 1649 several people were rebuked for "extenuating their fault on the place of repentance." In Galston, in 1640, one John Wylie, who had confessed that "he gave his wyff a shott with his hand upon ye Sabbath day," came up for penance, but "the said John, upon the high place, argued with the minister, speaking something of the gentlemen and noblemen of the paroch, and of new toyes, quhilk could not be cleirlie understood." The said John was therefore ordained to come back next Sabbath to the same place, and "there to confess and purge himself, that he spak nothing of the noblemen and gentlemen of the paroch in

the officer reported to the Session of Mauchline that on his citing a parishioner to appear before her betters she saucily said to him that "she would not go the length of her foot." And grosser cases of insolence than that sometimes occurred. The sectarian soldiers of Cromwell, we are told, used, when in Scotland, to shew their contempt for Presbyterian discipline by pulling down repentance stools or mounting them for sport when they went to church. And similar feats have been heard of in times much less distant. Many a repentance stool has been maimed and mutilated, dislocated and destroyed, cast down and trampled on, both in mirth and wrath, by people that bore it a grudge for no greater offence than offering them a seat when they were bidden stand before the congregation. In our own Parish Records there is a case of this sort reported. In 1675 deposition was made to the Session by John Campbell that one Sunday about four in the morning he was sent for to the house of Matthew Campbell, a vintner, and on going there he found three men sitting bareheaded. On making inquiry he learned that their bonnets had been poinded for payment of their potations. John, in a fit of generosity which he afterwards had cause to regret, advanced them a mark-piece to clear their account and recover their caps. The three liberated lads in their gratitude to John for his generosity escorted him home with midnight honours: and when his door was opened John politely thanked his friends, and wished them good morning and a pleasant walk to their respective lodgings. The revellers, however, in their maudlin affection were loath to part, and requested admittance into John's house. Such a dear amiable man too was John that he

---

raising of new toyes, and that if he spak onie thing of them he did it out of a rash humour, not knowing what he said, and so craved God and them forgiveness." A similar case of insolence occurred in Galston in 1693.

would fain have let them in, but his better half resented such an untimeous invasion of super exhilarated strangers, and told them it was late and her husband must go to his bed. "For this cause," says the minute of Kirk Session, "one of the three men cast down his benefactor at his own door," and then the whole party, staggering like landsmen aboard a schooner in a hurricane, made their way arm-in-arm for Netherplace. The story reached the ears of the Kirk rulers, and the roysterers being found guilty both of drunkenness and Sabbath breaking, were ordered to be publicly rebuked. The day for rebuke arrived and the three men, come to their sober senses, made their appearance at the place appointed. But sobriety does not bring with it every other form of good behaviour, nor does it by any means always put a man in a proper and civil frame of mind. Instead of shewing signs of penitence and humiliation, these sobered liquorers, say the Records, "did strive all the time to break the stools whereon they stood, and which accordingly they did." A most unchristian miscarriage surely! And that was just what the Session called this act of sacrilegious vandalism. But the Session took care that the three scorners should not be allowed to think they had scored a parochial triumph by their impudence, or that by playing pranks at the place of repentance people might laugh the pains out of penance. For attempting to cast ridicule on public reproof, the three delinquents were subjected to the greater penalty of lesser excommunication, and were left to learn at leisure, by the inconvenience of seclusion from Christian society, the folly as well as sin of poking fun at ecclesiastical authority.*

---

* Curate Calder tells a story which is meant to be marvellous, and may perhaps be only a fabrication, about a presumptuous fellow who went to the repentance stool

Exhibitions of temper too were occasionally witnessed in the Kirk Session. In 1682 a credulous excitable man in this Parish had been taunted in jest by one of the Elders in a way that should have subjected the Elder to censure. Taking in earnest what was said in jest, the man flared up in an instant, reviled the Elder for all that was unmentionable, and swore by his Maker that he would not rest till he made the Elder's blood as cold as clay. For this outburst of foolish passion the man was summoned before the Session, and if he could only have restrained himself so far as to compear peaceably and tell his story correctly he would doubtless have received a fair hearing and a just sentence. But he was beside himself with rage, and he came to the Session like a man possessed with demons. Instead of waiting outside among the tombs, as the custom was, till he was called into the church, he went up to the door and thundered there as if he had come with fire and sword to take over the premises. And when at length he got admittance into the church, he bellowed like a madman, called the Elder who had insulted him a pestilent fellow, and swore in high terms that he would stand to every word he had previously said. The sequel is not worth mentioning, for the

---

and "behaved liker a light fool than a penitent sinner, for he powdered his wig and put on his new clothes, and almost stared the minister out of countenance." A much more astonishing thing than that, however, happened at Cumnock in 1643. A day of solemn humiliation had been appointed by either the Presbytery or the General Assembly, and one of the Elders in Cumnock chose to "misregard" it. For that offence he was ordered to submit to public rebuke, but instead of either submitting humbly to admonition or taking a resolute stand on some intelligible ground of principle against the sentence of the Session, he went to the "publict place of repentance with his head covered and with his sword about him!" His conduct was brought under the notice of the Presbytery at a Presbyterial visitation of the Parish, and for his folly and hardihood he was "suspended from the office of Eldership until the entry of a new minister or a new visitation." Not a very hard sentence for contemptuous conduct by one that was set for an example to the flock.

fact that I am at present concerned in shewing is merely that Kirk Sessions were not regarded with such reverence that they were always secure against acts of insolence. Even Mr. Auld, austere and authoritative, and every inch a minister as he was, did not escape an occasional insult in his Parish consistory. In 1784 the bellman was summoned before the Session for exacting some small charges he was not entitled to make. The bellman, however, thought he was justified in doing what he had done, and that he was very ill-used in being called in question for his conduct. Smarting under the pain of injured innocence, he incautiously let drop an oath in the audience of the Session. For that act of irreverence he was there and then rebuked. But the rebuke inflamed his resentment all the more, and a few weeks later at a meeting of Session he was again complained of for defaming the minister, and calling him a villain, with an adjective before it, the precise meaning of which is best known to theologians.

It is to be observed, however, that instances of contempt and insubordination to the Kirk Session's authority occurred only now and again, and that as a rule the Kirk Session enjoyed both the respect and the confidence of the people. One of the best proofs of this is the fact that fines were promptly paid by delinquents, although the legality of these fines might often have been contested. But delinquents, generally, and almost universally, felt that Kirk Sessions in administering discipline acted justly and with a view to public good, and offenders acquiesced accordingly in the sentences of Kirk Sessions when guilt was not disputed.

Seeing then that Kirk Sessions were in olden times so zealous both in the prevention and the repression of sin, and that they were armed with such large powers both for inquisition and punishment, it may now be asked what was the general state of morality over Scotland a hundred or two hundred years ago, compared with what it is at the present time.

We often hear it said at the present day that the people of Scotland are drinking themselves to death. And there doubtless is a great deal of drunkenness in the country. But it is now looked down upon. On the other hand drunkenness a hundred years ago was regarded as a jovial and gentlemanly thing, and it was not principle but poverty that restrained the masses from going to the same excesses as the gentry. In his traditions of Edinburgh Dr. Chambers says that "in the early part of last century rigour was in the ascendant in Scotland, but the free and easy comprised a considerable minority who kept alive the flame of conviviality with no small degree of success. In the latter half of the century—a dissolute era all over civilised Europe—the minority became the majority, and the characteristic sobriety of the nation's manners was only traceable in certain portions of society. In Edinburgh seventy years ago (which would be about 1780) intemperance was the rule to such a degree that exception could hardly be said to exist."

The newspaper record of divorces at the present day reveals an amount of domestic immorality and misery that would have been thought incredible had it not been brought to light. But old church registers have stories to tell quite as startling. In 1644, when the so-called Second Reformation was in its full glory, no fewer than thirteen couples appeared in sackcloth before the Presbytery of Ayr for *literal* breaches of the seventh commandment, and in 1643 there were at least eleven couples that for the like cause appeared before the same court in the like habit. What is still more astonishing, it was reported to the Presbytery of Ayr in 1690 that "a public brothel house was kept at Dalmellington." It may be presumed, however, that this social nuisance and source of moral corruption was but of brief continuance, for it is added in the records that the Presbytery appointed the minister of the parish "to write to the President for suppressing it."*

The accounts of female termagancy in old records read very much like good jokes now, and we are amused to hear of women brought before magistrates for stoning men to the effusion of their blood and chasing them into their own houses. In point of fact, however, such incidents imply a fearful state of Amazonianism at the time they occurred, and few lovers of antiquity would care for a return of such ancient manners in Scotland.

But, to limit our enquiry, and come nearer home, let us consider what our own Session Records have to say about the state of morality in Mauchline parish at different dates. We may pass over all general statements made by the Kirk Session from time to time, because these only indicate opinions and are apt to be either over or under coloured, according to the spiritual temperament of those that penned them. But "facts are chiels that winna ding." Let us look then at some authentic facts bearing on the state of Parochial morality at different periods, and let us begin with the oldest period of which we have any extant Parochial record—the times of the covenants and the persecutions.

We are in the way of looking back to the Covenant times as to times that were specially distinguished for purity and piety,

---

* By the old laws of Scotland adultery was punishable with death, and in a note to Creech's letters it is said that as recently as 1694 a man was hanged in Edinburgh for adultery, and his paramour was beheaded. In 1763, says Creech, the sin was very rare, and the sinner was boycotted; in 1783 the sin was not uncommon in the Metropolis, and the sinner was received in society.

and were sanctified to an unusual degree by spiritual refreshing. The Drumfork case, however, which has already been alluded to, shews that corruption and profanity, drunkenness and devilry, were not in the days of Charles II. confined to royal courts and London society, but were to be found as well in the country districts of Ayrshire, in the houses of farmers and bonnet lairds. And that the Drumfork squabble was not an exceptional manifestation of the life of that period, is made plain by another case which came before the Session of Mauchline the same year, viz., in 1673. This was a case in which two men named Mershall, presumably brothers, were delated for fighting with and cursing each other. There would have been nothing strange in that, if the men had been a pair of village waifs, flushed by drink. But the men were men of some account. The one was a merchant and the other was a "nottar," who held the public office of Council Clerk; and yet they had so little regard for decency, so little sense of dignity, and so little consideration of public opinion, not to say of brotherly relationship and Christian duty, that after falling out on some matter, they proceeded like a pair of modern roughs to settle their differences with fisticuffs and profanation. And not only so, but the fight was witnessed by a small and select group of spectators without a word of remonstrance. James Peathin and John Jamie both deponed to the Session that they saw the two brother burgesses, neither of them publicans albeit both of them sinners, sparring in a field, and not by way of friendly scientific contest, but in *bona fide* bloody conflict, beating and buffeting each other till failing strength or failing eyesight put an end to the *melee*. But, said Mr. Peathin, with the view of shewing that in this blackguardly business there was nothing unbecoming gentlemen or Christians or even Covenanters, "I don't remember hearing any particular oaths." "I heard the merchant," said Mr. Jamie, "swear by his Maker once—but that was all." The bailie of the burgh, John Richmond, was another spectator of the combat, and he deponed that he heard swearing on both sides, and yet, magistrate though he was, the resident justice in the place, he did not think proper to interfere with the disputants ; he looked on till he saw the end, smoked his pipe (very likely), and tapped out the dottle on his thumb nail without saying a word,—simply took mental note of what passed, and prepared himself to give evidence when called upon. Two elders were, "in virtue of their former oath," examined regarding the public character of the combatants, and these elders deponed that there was no use in trying to whitewash the delinquents, as if their recent outbreak were something exceptional, and not in keeping with the usual tenor of their lives, for despite their social position they were, both by habit and repute, ordinary swearers. This shews what Mauchline was, and what magistracy in Mauchline was, two hundred years ago.

And what was Mauchline one hundred years ago ? It had an unhappy notoriety, we have seen, for one form of scandal.* But what was the general state of moral conduct, moral feeling, and moral thought at that date ? Were the people

---

* This scandal seems to have been prevalent over the whole country at that date, as the following table, drawn up by George Lorimer, Esq., from the records of the West Kirk, Edinburgh, will shew.

Between 1754 and 1764 :			—Cases of Adultery,	0	—Fornication,	16	—Irreg. Mar.,	8
,,	1764 ,,	1774	,,	,,	4	,,	25	,,	41
,,	1774 ,,	1793	,,	,,	19	,,	115	,,	57
,,	1794 ,,	1811	,,	,,	1	,,	58	,,	22

From Creech's letters it appears that the fines paid for bastard children by the members of the city churches in Edinburgh amounted in 1763 to £154, and in 1783 to £600, and the author adds, "they have since increased." In 1763 there were in Edinburgh five or six houses of evil fame, but in 1783 the number had increased twenty fold.

sober, peaceful, and industrious, or the reverse? It is of course only the misdeeds of the people that are shewn in Session Records. The virtues of the people, save in respect of liberality at collections and attendance at communions, are not brought out there. But what appears in the Session Records shews beyond possibility of dispute that although the population of the parish was much less than it is now, and more agricultural, the people were nevertheless rougher, coarser grained, more insubordinate and more uncivilised than they are at the present day. Mr. Auld, in his account of the parish, written about 1790, laments the loss of its Burghal Charter, and hence of its village magistrate; because he says there is a great deal of disorderly and riotous conduct that needs to be repressed. And the Session Records confirm Mr. Auld's statement. For although it is true that one swallow does not make summer, nor the presence of one lawless fellow in a parish prove that the whole parish is turbulent, we may yet draw general inferences from particular cases of misconduct. And the instances of turbulent behaviour that I shall now give, will probably satisfy any one who is willing to be convinced by evidence, that Mauchline a hundred years ago was not a Paradise of either innocence or Christian virtue.

Tradesmen, who in Ayrshire are commonly called merchants, might, as I have said before, be expected from their social position to be favourable specimens of village manners. If merchants are found pestilent fellows, what must we not suppose people inferior in the social scale to be. Well, in 1771, one of the merchants of Mauchline, whose name need not be given, was libelled by the Kirk Session for two very grave offences. He was accused of "uttering and propagating erroneous opinions contrary to the word of God." He was accused also of "transgressing the second table of the moral law by beating, bruising, and defaming his neighbour." His chief heresies were a denial of the doctrine of original sin and a refusal to acknowledge some parts of the Scripture as the word of God.* But although this merchant alleged himself to be untainted by original sin and professed to be wise above what was written, the terms of the libel served upon him, and which were proved against him, will shew that his practical code of morals was neither holy nor harmless, neither super-refined nor super-excellent in wisdom. After reciting the heresies he had vented, the libel proceeds to say :—" You did also in one or other of the months of May, June, or July, 1769, beat and bruise Henry Richmond in Mauchline to the danger of his life, according to proof led against you in the Sheriff Court of Ayr. You did again in one or other of the months of May, June, or July, 1770, attack James Lamie, merchant in Mauchline, at or near Hunter's yeards, and by the assistance of your son William did throw down the said James Lamie, and might have murdered him, had he not been relieved by some people who came thither. After that, you and your foresaid son did at Henry Richmond's midden throw the said James Lamie into the middenstead or hole, and abuse him in the dirt and might have put an end to his life had he not been again relieved. Lastly, when James Lamie told you that your horse was tethered on his possession of Hunter's yeards, as the marches had been pointed out by several witnesses, you said

---

* There is a very remarkable likeness in the terms of this libel against the Mauchline merchant in 1771 to what is said about " Goudie's Bible " in the history of Kilmarnock : " Goudie, terror o' the Whigs, published Essays on various important subjects, moral and divine, being an attempt to distinguish true from false Religion. This book was nicknamed Goudie's Bible, and set forth peculiar views respecting original sin and particular portions of Scripture." Goudie's book, however, was not published till 1780, whereas the Mauchline merchant was libelled for heresy in 1771.

that some of the witnesses were damned already, and that if James Lamie lived he would see them all damned in a year or two, for they were like Ahab's witnesses hired and perjured." Of course we cannot suppose that all the merchants in the village were of a piece with this cross-grained and addle-headed unbeliever, but the fact that any well-to-do man, with a reputation to depend upon, could be found acting as this libelled madcap did, shews that there was very little surrounding culture and very little force of educated public opinion to which people in Mauchline felt themselves amenable.

A few years later, namely, in 1777, the Session were informed that a journeyman blacksmith in the village had been guilty of a series of outrages and acts of devilry which are thus recited: First, about the time of the June fair in 1776 he threatened to murder his wife, and was only prevented from doing so by the kirk officer's coming to her rescue: secondly, at Martinmas thereafter, he threatened to murder the kirk officer for interfering between him and his wife in their domestic quarrels: thirdly, about Ware last, he fought his cock with the minister's cock on a Sabbath day and during the time of divine service: and fourthly, at the Yule fair last, he took a hammer from the smithy, in order, as he said, to knock down all that came in his way, and he also ran through the streets with an open knife, swearing that he would rip up every man, woman, and child he met. This blacksmith may be considered as a sample of the village rowdy, and although rowdyism is personal and eccentric, not uniform and typical, his conduct will at least go a long way in proving that rowdyism in 1777 was more lawless and savage than it is now-a-days in small rural towns.

There is only one other illustration that I shall give of the worst forms of village life in Mauchline about a hundred years ago, and it may have interest as bearing upon one, at least, if not on two, of the poems of Burns. Among the masterpieces of the poet, the cantata entitled the Jolly Beggars is universally admitted to have a conspicuous place. The subject of the poem is in one sense repulsive. The characters depicted are the lowest of the low and the vilest of the vile, but they are delineated with inimitable power. Such as they were, the beggars and their chums are set before us; and such a scene of rollicking mirth, boisterous revelry, and audacious profanity, lit up here and there with outbursts of the rarest eloquence and highest patriotism, as well as broadest humour and liveliest wit, has seldom been turned into shape by poet's pen. One of the most outstanding figures in the poem is a tozie drab of consummate impudence and shameless morals. That person, whoever she was, we must suppose was not a fictitious but a real character, whose lewd conduct the poet witnessed, and whose wanton words the poet heard. It may be impossible to identify her with any person of whom we have any record, but the person referred to in the minute of Session I am about to quote, might, so far as character went, have been the drab that sat for the portrait of the unblushing virago, who was not ashamed to tell that she had no remembrance of an innocent maidenhood. And in speaking for the moment somewhat harshly of this abandoned woman, or rather poor wretched creature, we may well ask what it is but Divine grace, in the shape of a more favoured outward lot and more civilising surroundings, that has made any of ourselves to differ from her. She was, as she tells us, a child of misfortune, and she might have said, as a poet of no mean order, who was also one of society's illegitimates, and who fell into evil habits of life, sadly said of himself—

> "No mother's care
> Sheltered my infant innocence with prayer,

No father's guiding hand my youth maintained,
Called forth my virtues, and from vice restrained."

But to return to the cantata and the drab. The date of the minute will shew that the person mentioned therein might have been, and *probably was*, in Poosie Nansie's house the night in which Burns and his friend were admitted to see and join in the beggars' carousals. The poem was written in 1785, that is in the autumn of 1785, "when lyart leaves bestrewed the yird," and "infant frosts began to bite." The date of the minute is the 6th March, 1786, and the woman mentioned in the minute is said to have been *for more than six months previous entertained by George Gibson* and by another person called Black, who seems to have kept a house similar to Gibson's. But if there be any doubt about this woman's having been the tozie drab of the cantata, there can be no doubt of her having been the " jurr " referred to in Adam Armour's prayer. The scandalous conduct of this "jurr," as we know, led to a public demonstration of feeling in the village, in which demonstration Adam Armour took a prominent part, and for so doing was brought into trouble. Burns was ever ready to give a jocular turn to any mishap that befell his friends, and he accordingly wrote, under the title of "Adam Armour's Prayer," a satirical poem, in which he invoked the pains of everlasting torment on Adam's persecutors—"black Geordie," who was George Gibson, and his spouse, "auld drunken Nanse," who was Agnes Ronald.* The minute is interesting, therefore, as bearing on

---

* In the admirable edition of Burns's poems published by Mr. Paterson, the Adam Armour of the prayer is said to have been in no way related to Jean Armour's family. The representatives of Jean's family tell me that they never heard of any Adam Armour in Mauchline in the days of Burns, except Jean's brother. In the Baptismal and Burial Registers of Mauchline Parish there is no trace of the birth of any Adam Armour in the parish between 1730 and 1786, except Jean's brother, who

points of literary history, besides giving a picture of Mauchline town and Mauchline life a hundred years ago. Its date is 6th March, 1786, and its tenor is as follows :—" The members of the Kirk Session having seen a petition signed by the inhabitants of Machlin, to be presented to the Honble. Justices for preserving the peace of this place, do unanimously concur in the same, and beg leave to add the following particulars—That there is a vagrant woman called Agnes Wilson, of bad fame in the parish and places whence she came, who for more than six months past has been haunted and entertained by Elizabeth Black and George Gibson—That the bad reputation of this woman, as being lewd and immoral in her practices, has been the occasion of a late disturbance in this place, which the Session greatly disapprove of and resolve to inquire into—That it is the opinion of the Session that if this woman be allowed to continue here it will tend much to corrupt the morals of the youth and to disturb the peace of the whole inhabitants—That in these circumstances the Session think it their duty, in regard there is no magistrate in the place, to apply to the Honble. Justices to get the said woman removed—Lastly, that George Gibson and Elizabeth Black, who haunt and entertain in their houses such vagrant persons of suspicious and bad characters, may be laid under proper restrictions and obliged to secure and maintain the peace and safety of the

---

was born in February, 1771; and there is no trace of the death of any Adam Armour in the parish between 1786 and 1820. Adam Armour, Jean's brother, was just such a fellow as would be sure to be in a village row. He was fond of fun and mischief to the end of his days, and many queer stories are told of him. He was rather under middle size, but his being only fifteen years old in 1786 explains how he is called in the poem "little," and "scarce as lang's a guid kail whittle." In the edition of Burns's poems published in 1842 by Virtue, London, the editor, Allan Cunningham, states that he got the verses from Adam Armour, Jean's brother, and that Adam told him the circumstances in which the prayer originated.

neighbourhood under such legal penalties as to the honourable court shall appear relevant."

Looking then to the facts which these extracts reveal, we cannot doubt that two hundred years ago, and even one hundred years ago, there were in Mauchline parish elements of disorder and turbulence that are happily unknown at the present day. Whether there were more vice and secret sin is another matter, which no man that can't see through a millstone need attempt to discover. But it is clear that long ago the people of this parish were ruder, rougher, and coarser than they are now, and it is to be hoped that a hundred years hence the parish minister will be able to tell a parish audience that the progress noted from 1684 to 1784 and from 1784 to 1884 has been continued in an increasing ratio to 1984. The poet laureate has said in words which have long since become hackneyed by frequent use,

"That through the ages one increasing purpose runs,
And the thoughts of men are widened by the process of the suns."

I would add, that the hearts and the habits of men, and the conditions and forms of human life are, like ripening fruit, all meliorating, too, with the same solar procession.

But to what has progress in civilization and good order been due in time past, and what is it that inspires us with hope for the continuance of that progress in time coming? All social progress is effected by social forces, and these forces are of two kinds—educative and repressive. The Church and Kirk Sessions in olden times made use of both forces to the best of their judgment and the best of their means. The Church furnished pastors and doctors, ministers and readers, to instruct the people in the knowledge of religious truth. Aided by the Kirk Sessions of particular parishes the Church also set up schools for the instruction of youthhead, long before the State acknowledged responsibility for the education of the young. And the Church and Kirk Sessions were no less zealous in attempting to keep down disorders, and restrain vice and immoralities. It was for these ends that a rigid discipline was instituted and executed. The lawless and the ungodly were rebuked and censured, ostracised from society and suspended from the enjoyment of valued privileges, fined and jogged, made to go mourning in sackcloth, and subscribe bands of good behaviour.

It is to the use of similar forces that we still look for all social improvement. The educative forces are much stronger to-day than they were either one hundred or two hundred years ago Not only is school attendance made compulsory on all children, but there is a public opinion of such strength created by the diffusion of periodical literature that few men now-a-days dare to outrage society by the freaks and pranks, high jinks and low orgies, that were once commonly practised with impunity and without shame. And it is to the growth and culture of this public opinion that we must mainly look for the extirpation of some vices that still infest the land, such as profane swearing and the nasty calumnies of low correspondents in low newspapers. And not only are the educative forces stronger to-day than they once were, but the repressive forces are stronger also. The modes of repression are changed, and changed for the better. It is true that Church discipline is relaxed. But civil government is much firmer, and a system of rural police has been established, which for vigilance, inquisition, and probation of crime, far surpasses the Kirk Session in its palmiest days. When Mr. Auld wrote his account of the parish, nearly a hundred years ago, he expressed his sorrow that the old charter of the burgh had been destroyed, and consequently that the people of the town had lost their ancient right of choosing magistrates. "This," he says, "is much to be regretted, as that privilege, if properly exercised, might contribute much to the public good by checking riots and disorders which are at present too frequent." But in truth what was wanted in Mauchline a hundred years ago was not so much a resident magistrate as a resident policeman. In 1673 Mauchline had the full benefit of a burghal charter, and she enjoyed the services of a magistrate freely chosen by her own burgesses. But the magistrate was a man of like passions as the people. He stood and looked at the town clerk pounding a merchant, and never tried to save the weaker brother. A policeman would have done better. He would have said to the pugilists, "*Arcades ambo*, you are both my prisoners, and no matter which, if either, of you is in the right, you must settle your disputes according to the laws of a civilised country." And so, when we compare past times with present times, we must keep in mind that there is one potent cause of order in modern society that was unknown in rural districts till the second quarter of the present century. No one will say or suppose that it is in the power of a policeman to make men good and virtuous, but every one must know and see that a policeman can do, and actually does, a great deal by his presence and his note-book, his authority and his hand-cuffs, to make a community orderly and quiet. All honour, then, to the **policeman** for his work's sake. Repressive legislation, too, has within the last few years done much, and in years to come may do still more, to promote peace and sobriety. Publicans are now compelled to close their premises before men have had time to be well drunken, and that is no small gain to the cause of order; and legislators will doubtless be guided by sound considerations in determining how much farther, repression should be carried for the public weal. We must neither be bugbeared nor bamboozled with words and their associations. Repression is a word that sounds harsh, and freedom is a word that takes the heart and the imagination by storm. But it must be remembered that unrepressed rowdyism means rampant terrorism, and unrestricted freedom is unmitigated tyranny—power to the strong to do as they please with the weak. Side by side, therefore, we should hope to see educative and repressive forces at work, public opinion growing daily more enlightened and more potent, and restraints imposed wherever they are clearly and loudly called for—and then we may feel confident for the future—confident that society will, generation after generation, become more pure and peaceful, more virtuous and more happy.

APPENDIX.

APPENDIX.

A.

THE EXERCISE, THE PRESBYTERY, AND THE CLASSICAL ASSEMBLY.

These phrases are sometimes used interchangeably as if they were of the same import. It is at least certain, however, that they were sometimes used in official records with a distinction of meaning.

The *Exercise* was the phrase that, during the first twenty years after the Reformation, was applied to the convention of ministers within walking distance of a common centre.

The *Presbytery* was a term that came into use about 1580, when the Second Book of Discipline was approved by the General Assembly.

The expression *Classical Assembly* is what the Westminster Divines, in their form of Church government, approved by the Church of Scotland in 1645, applied to the intermediate Court of the Church, or what we now call the Presbytery. "It is lawful and agreeable to the Word of God," they said, "that the Church be governed by several sorts of Assemblies, which are Congregational, *Classical*, and Synodical."

Wherein, then, it may be asked, did the Exercise and the Classical Assembly differ from the Presbytery, if either differed from the Presbytery at all?

In 1579, an overture was made in the General Assembly that "*Presbyteries be erected in places where publick exercise is used* unto the tyme the policy of the Kirk be established by law." This looks as if the framers of the overture supposed that the Presbytery was something different from the Exercise. The declaration of the Assembly, however, was that the Exercise may be judged a Presbytery.

Bishop Sage finds fault with this judgment of the Assembly. He says that Presbyteries were never heard of in Scotland till this overture was brought forward in 1579, and that what was formerly called the Exercise was something quite different from a Presbytery. "It was," he says, "nothing like a Court," it had no jurisdiction, and it exercised no discipline.*

---

* At page 185 reference is made to the fact that the fundamental Court of the Church described in the Second Book of Discipline was, in respect of its size and

The Exercise was a meeting of ministers and readers for the purpose of mutual instruction in Scripture and religion. There were two speakers previously appointed to expound and argue—the first "to exercise or prophesy" and the second "to add"—and in 1576 there were severe punishments ordained by the Assembly to be inflicted on all such as failed to fulfil these appointments. "If either of the two faile, for the first fault, they shall confess their offence upon their knees in presence of the brethren of the Exercise; for the second, they shall make the like submission before the Synodal Assembly; for the third, they shall be summoned before the General Assembly and receive discipline for their offence; and for the fourth they shall be deprived of their offices and functions in the ministry."

After Presbyteries were erected, the Exercise continued to be regarded as something distinct from the Presbytery. In the General Assembly of 1582 there were several "articles" recorded as answers to certain doubts concerning Presbyteries, and from these we learn that ruling elders had seats in the Presbytery, but there is nothing said about their duty to attend the Exercise. Ministers, on the other hand, are declared to be subject to penalties if they do not resort to the Exercise *and* Presbytery. It was also thought meet that the day appointed for the Exercise be "in like manner the day of ecclesiastical processes," but if the brethren think it necessary they may appoint days and places for processes "by" or besides the day of the Exercise.

In 1610, the King and the Bishops, with the view of making the abolition of Presbyterial jurisdiction in the Church more easy, endeavoured to bring about the disuse of the word Presbytery, and for that unpleasant word the substitution of the phrase, "Brethren of the Exercise."

When Presbyterial government was restored in the Church in 1638 and 1639, Exercises and Presbyteries were held together on the same day and in the same place, just as general meetings and special meetings of railway companies are said to be held at present.

In the oldest extant records of the Presbytery of Ayr—those from 1642 to 1650—we find that when there was to be an Exercise as well

---

membership, more like a modern Kirk Session than a modern Presbytery, but that in respect of its functions it was the reverse. It may be stated here that the scheme of small Presbyteries—comprising "ane or twa," "thrie or four" kirks—was never carried out. The very year in which the Second Book of Discipline was registered (1581) the King submitted to the General Assembly a "forme how elderships may be constitute of a certain number of parochines lyand together," and in this form all the parishes in Scotland were grouped under fifty Presbyteries, "twenty to every Presbytery, *or thereabouts*." This form, with modifications, became the basis on which Presbyteries were erected, and hence, when Presbyteries were so large, it was meet that some jurisdiction should be conceded to Kirk Sessions, as was craved by the Church in 1586 (Book of Univ. Kirk, and Calderwood, Vol. IV., p. 568), and allowed in the Act of Parliament 1592. The existence of Kirk Sessions as constituent Courts seems to be further recognised in a resolution of Assembly, 1587, which declares that "particular Sessions of Kirks and Congregations are, and should be, subject to their Presbyteries." Book of Kirk, 319.

as a Presbytery held, it was commonly minuted, "The Exercise was established in the person of A. B., the first speaker, and of C. D., the second," or "C. D. to add."

While the Exercise was said to be established in the persons of only two speakers, there was an Act of Assembly, passed in 1598, that from its intrinsic reasonableness might be said to be of perpetual standing, which ordained "that every member of the Presbytery study the text whereupon the exercise is to be made." Another clause in the same Act ordained that "ane common head of religion be intreatit every moneth in ilk Presbyterie, both by way of discourse and disputation," or by way of exercise and addition.

In 1705 an attempt was made to have a complete book of discipline compiled anew, as a directory for the several Church Courts. Such a book was compiled and published, but it never obtained either ecclesiastical or civil sanction. It nevertheless throws light on old usages, and what it says about Presbyterial exercises may be quoted. It declares that part of the work of a Presbytery is to begin every meeting with a sermon by one or two of the brethren on a text appointed at the former meeting of Presbytery, and this piece of business is called a Presbyterial exercise. One half of the time allowed in this work is to be taken up with explication, and this is called exercise; the other half of the time is to be occupied in raising doctrines on the text, and this is called "addition." "After the exercise is over, and the Presbytery met in their own meeting-place, and the meeting constituted, the censure of the exercise they have heard useth always to be the first work of the Presbytery. Besides the above exercise they used in Presbyteries frequently to have common heads in Latin with disputes, but if it be *coram populo* it should be in the vulgar language."

The Exercise at one time was a laborious business. The Presbytery of Edinburgh in 1597 ordained that "the first speikar sall occupy na langer tyme nor an hour, the second half an hour preciselie . . . and that the prayer before and efter the exercise be short." And the censure of the exercise was no sham. Speakers were plainly told to have a feeling of what they delivered, to "eschew affectat language, and to utter their words with gretar force." Occasionally, however, complimentary language was used, and speakers were informed that they had done "mervellous." M'Crie's *Life of Melville*, i. 477.

From what is said not only in the Westminster Form of Church Government, but in Baillie's Dissuasive, we might think that a Presbytery and a Classical Assembly are one and the same thing, "A Presbytery, as it is called in Scotland," says Baillie, "or a Classis, as in Holland, or a Collogue, as in France, is an ordinary meeting of the pastors of the churches nearly neighbouring, and of the ruling elders deputed therefrom, for the exercise chiefly of discipline, so far as concerns those neighbouring churches in common." Dissuasive, p. 198.

The word Classis, however, was used in a different sense from this in the Presbytery of Ayr. The Classis was not the whole Presbytery, but a part of the Presbytery. In a minute of date 1697 we read that "the several classes that meet sometimes for prayer are appointed to meet—those of Carrick at Dailie, and those of Kyle at Symington, St. Quivox and Auchinleck." Another minute, of date 1737, states expressly that in the Presbytery there were four classes, those of Cumnock, Galston, Ayr and Maybole. It will be seen, too, that the classes in the Presbytery of Ayr met for prayer, and we may say religious conference, rather than for discipline, as alleged by Baillie.

The Rev. Dr. Chrystal informs me that when he came to Auchinleck, in 1833, the Carrick Class was still in the way of holding meetings. At these meetings an essay or paper was read by one of the members, and criticised by the others, as is done at present at the half-yearly conferences of the Presbytery of Ayr. It is said that it was at these meetings of the Carrick Class that Dr. MacKnight laid the foundation of his well-known work on the New Testament.

In the Mauchline Session Records there is at least one reference to the local Classical meeting. In 1765 Mr. Auld reported "from the Presbytery that P. Q. (a man who denied the truth of a charge made against him) appeared there, and was ordered to appear at a Classical meeting at Cumnock on the 20th November." His appearance before the Classical meeting at Cumnock, however, was not for censure, but for trial, as is shewn by a subsequent minute of Session, which states that the *Presbytery*, after hearing all the evidence on the case, assoilzied the man from scandal.

The several classes in the Presbytery seem to have formed the first set of Committees of Presbytery for the examination of schools. In 1738 the Presbytery of Ayr appointed " the brethren of the class of Ayr, and with them Messrs. Fisher, Cooper and Younger, to visit the Grammar School of Ayr the Tuesday before next Presbytery. And the Classes of Cumnock, Maybole and Galston are each appointed to visit the Grammar Schools that are in each of their bounds at their first Classical meeting, and an account of their diligence to be carried on in the minutes."

B.

FAST-DAYS AND DAYS OF ATONEMENT.

How Fast-days were meant to be observed in the Church of Scotland may be gathered from the following sentences in the Westminster Assembly's Directory for Public Worship :—

" A religious fast requires total abstinence, not only from all food, but also from all worldly labour, discourses, and thoughts, and from all bodily delights (although at other times lawful), rich apparel, ornaments, and such like, during the fast, and much more from whatever is in the nature or use scandalous and offensive, as gaudish attire, lascivious habits and gestures, and other vanities of either sex."

"Before the public meeting, each family and person apart are privately to use all religious care to prepare their hearts to such a solemn work, and to be early at the congregation."

"Before the close of the public duties, the minister is, in his own name and the people's names, to engage his and their hearts to be the Lord's, with professed purpose and resolution to reform whatever is amiss in them, and more particularly such sins as they have been more remarkably guilty of."

How scandalously at variance with these directions Fast-day services have in recent years become in large cities, and even in rural parishes traversed by railways, the following paragraph, which appeared in the newspapers about two years ago, will show :—

GLASGOW — THE FAST-DAY AND ITS EFFECTS. — Following the Glasgow Fast, yesterday was exceptionally busy at the City Police Court, there being no less than 319 cases, as compared with 248 on the same day last year. There were 90 cases of drunkenness, being an increase of 36.

On the other hand, that it may be seen how Fasts were appointed and held by good and godly people long ago, I subjoin here from Brodie's Diary an account of what is termed a day of humiliation and *atonement*. The occasion of the solemnity was a raid committed in the North by Glencairn's soldiery in 1654 :—

"1654, January 20th.—Glencairn burnt the corns and houses of Leathin. O Lord, sanctify and help us to understand and be humbled under this hand of thine. 24th. This day I went to Leathin and determined to give a stack of oats and straw to his poor people because of his freedom and their safety, both in duty of love and obedience and in sign of thankfulness, for his safety was from Thee. We appointed a day of search, and a day of humiliation and *atonement*" (the word is italicised in the printed copy of the Diary) "and of supplication, on the 30th and 31st of January. . . January 31st, 1654, was the solemn humiliation at Leathin for the causes and reasons contained in the paper which is in my Latron.

"After Leathin and Francis did, with some measure of tenderness, confess and bewail their particular guilt of covetousness, passion, pride, unrighteous dealing, worldly mindedness, youthful lusts of uncleanness, and promise-breaking to God of many duties which they had bound themselves unto, we were all affected with the work of God on their spirits, and besought the Lord on their behalf that He would not let the wound close till it were thoroughly healed. After some measure of assistance and countenance on the day, Mr. Joseph preached on John xxii. 20, 21, etc., Mr. John on Joel ii. We closed the exercise with a solemn engagement of ourselves to God, and did come under a new, firm, inviolable covenant with God, that we should be His and He should be ours. We gave up and surrendered our soul, body, estates, lands, rents, houses, families, wives, children, servants, wit, parts, endowments, friends, wealth, and all that we had or ever should have or attain unto in this world, to be the Lord's for ever, that He might call for, make use, and dispose of it and mark it as his own. We besought the Lord to accept the free-will offering of our lips and of our hearts, and not to permit us to depart from Him.

"Mr. John acknowledged his predominant sins of worldliness, passion, pride, and unfaithfulness in his calling, and entered his soul bound to endeavour to mortify these sins, and every sin, and to labour for more fidelity in his ministerial calling than ever, but, renouncing himself, desired to believe in the grace of God through Christ for this effect.

"Mr. Joseph acknowledged and bewailed the same sins, unconscionableness in his calling, and doing duty for some outward respect of credit or honesty, and not from pure love to God in Christ, and now desired to give up himself to the Lord.

"Old Leathin renewed his acknowledgments, and prayed the Lord for a willing, honest heart, to make good what was in his heart.

"Young Leathin professed his willingness to consecrate him and his to God, and that as long as he had a house or family it should be the Lord's. He alone should be worshipped in it; he should have no God but him.

"Old Francis renewed his confession, with tears, confessing the Lord to be just in casting him out of his family and making it desolate, for he had polluted his body with unclean lusts, &c., &c., and therefore the Lord was just in burning up his house and substance.

"Young Francis desired to consent and to subscribe his name to the Lord for ever, and sought their prayers that were present that he might never fall back.

"Joseph, David and Mr. James each confessed his shortcomings, and prayed for strength.

"Janet expressed meikle distrust of herself, but desired to come under a new bond for the Lord.

"The Lady Leathin dared promise little of herself, but professed that of all there she was most bound, both to take with guilt and the cause of his anger above any others, although they had taken it on themselves: and now that none had so great cause to engage their hearts to the Lord as she had, therefore in the faith of the Lord Jesus and his might, she did and would give up herself to the Lord, and all hers.

"John Brodie, Woodhead, acknowledged much guilt, and great need of this day's work. He was lying under some bonds to God already, and this should add to the former bonds.

"John of Main engaged for an humble and unfeigned endeavour, as to honour God in his own spirit so to be an instrument to Godward for his wife, children and family, that they also and he might be the Lord's.

"Mr. Robert Donaldson desired of God to discover if there were any iniquity in his way or in his heart, for which he was spared while others were smitten.

"Katherine, his wife, burst forth in the complaint of her woful, sad, deserted case, but if he would accept, there was not anything in all the earth which should so content and satisfy her as that the Lord would condescend to that bargain to become her God, and to take her and accept of her as his for ever. It was replied the bargain was sure enough, if she were willing for her part.

"Jean Symington, albeit a stranger among us, yet desired to be upholden by his grace.

"John Brodie, my boy, professed an unfeigned desire to know the Lord more, and to cleave to him more, and to be for him and to his glory all his days.

"John Tweedie absent at the time.

"All of us for ourselves, and for our little ones, and for our wives that have them, and families and interests, do stand before the Lord this day, making supplication and confession on their and our behalfs, and do take burden on us, according to our several stations and callings as aforesaid, that the Lord shall be our God, and we shall be his people, on the bare condition of his new covenant, that he will give us another heart and write his law within us.

"On the 1st of February this was written, and letters of exhortation to every one of them for putting them in remembrance.

"My soul this morning desired for its own part to rejoice before the Lord in trembling, and to consent unto this new oblation and covenant, and besought his majesty for a blessing on it, and on all their souls who had consented to or were concerned in it."

C.

THE OLD OATH OF PURGATION.

THE oath of purgation, as given in the form of process approved by Act of the General Assembly in 1707, is of a very solemn tenor, and it might well be directed that in taking that oath "all tenderness and caution is to be used." But there were more ancient oaths of purgation in use in the Church of Scotland before the present form of process was enacted. In a fly leaf of a volume of the records of the Presbytery of Ayr, commencing at the date 3rd August, 1687, there is a copy of the Presbytery's "oath of purgation," written out in full, and the terms of this old oath of the Covenant times are as follow :—

"I   do, therefore, in the presence of the great and dreadfull Majestie of the etternall, ever living and ever blessed

God, the searcher of hearts and reins, in his holy sanctuary, humbly upon my knees, with my hands lifted up to heaven, protest and swear by the holy and dreadfull name of the Lord, the only true God, and as I shall be answerable to his Majestie in that great and terrible day, when he shall judge the world in righteousness by Jesus Christ, whom he hath appointed the judge of quick and dead, that I never committed the abominable sin of   with   , &c. And this oath I take in presence of the all-seeing and sin-revenging God, as said is, with a clean and innocent conscience, in righteousness, truth, and judgment, without all equivocation or mental reservation, that is to say, without all deceitfull meaning, dissembling in or concealling of any part of the truth of this matter, and I take God to record on my soul, of my truth and sincerity herein, whom I know to be a swift witness against him that sweareth falsely by his name, and who hath threatened that his curse shall enter into their house and consume it, with the stones and timber thereof, and who hath brought on very terrible, tremendous, and dreadfull judgments in this life upon such, and who may bring forth his everlasting curse upon me if I have so done, wishing the Lord may no otherwise help me in my greater need, nor prosper me in any thing I have to doe, but exemplarly punish me in this lyfe and with the everlasting fire of his wrath in the lyfe to come, if I be not every way free in this matter. So be it."

The following is the oath of purgation in use in the West Kirk of Edinburgh in 1680:— I —— do swear by the great Eternal God, as I shall be judged at the last and most terrible day, that I never —— : wishing that all the plagues threatened and pronounced against the breakers of the law may be inflicted on me, both in this life and the life to come, if this be not the truth as I have sworn."

D.

PRESBYTERIAL VISITATIONS OF PARISHES.

WITH the view of shewing how these visitations were conducted, I subjoin the following accounts of visitations of the parish of Mauchline in 1642 and 1723. They are extracted from the records of the Presbytery of Ayr, and they afford specimens of Presbyterial action, both when there was nothing amiss and when there was much amiss in a parish.

Presbiterium Machlinense, 16th Maii, 1642—The qlk day after preaching as wes appointed, and after incalling of the name of God. Mr. George Young, minister, being removed, Mr. James Bonner, moderator, enquyred the Session then present if they had anything to object against the doctrine, discipline, life, or conversation of their minister. The Session all in one voyse approved the said Mr. George in all things.

"Thairefter, the said Mr. George being called in and the Session's approbation declared unto him, the said Mr. George was demanded if he had any objection against the members of the Session, and he affirmed he had nothing to say of them bot good.

"And, further, the said Mr. George declared, as he was requyred, that he preached twyse on the Sabbath, and every Twysday once, sumtyme by preaching and sumtyme by catechising, and declared the frequent meeting of the people to that effect.

"And, further, he declared that publict prayers wer used and reading of the Scriptures morning and evening, and that familie exercise wes also observed.

"The Session books were presented, visited, and approven. Being demanded concerning his glebe, manse, and maintenance, the said Mr. George produced ane decreet of the Lords, dated ye twentie-eighth of January, 1635, wherein it wes found that the said Mr. George had allowed unto him fourtie bolls victualls, belonging of old to the minister of Machlin, and of moneye thrie hundreth pundis and ane hundreth merks, sixty of the same with this provision, except the heritors suld cause carie to his house yearlie ane laid of coales and peitts for every merkland in the parochin, the said coales and peitts being provydid and trysted before, upon the said Mr. George his proper expenses. Moreover, the said Mr. George declared that Mr. John Gemmell, thair reader and scholmayster, had demitted his places, and that the Session had agreed with Mr. John Grey, son lawfull to umqle Mr. James Grey, minister at Newmylnes, for supplying of that charge, whereunto the Presbyterie condiscended also.

"Machline, 12th September, 1723.—This day, according to advertisement givin, Mr. John Dickson, probationer, preached from Gal. v. 18, also Mr. John Fergushill delivered his popular sermon from John xiv. 21, likewise Mr. Maitland preached from Rom. viii. 14; all which discourses were approven. And Mr. Maitland being asked if he made intimation of this meeting to all concerned, he told he did. He was asked if he had anything to object against his eldership or people, and said he had nothing. And, he being removed, the eldership were called in, upon which there appeared six, and they were asked the usual questions as to their minister visiting the paroch. They told he had not visited the whole of it since the celebration of the Lord's Supper about three years ago, except once, after which time he visited some parts of it and not others, but that he has not catechised it since the said time, and that they have weekly sermons very unfrequently. The minister being recalled, he and they were asked the usual questions, and particularly as to their session book, which was required to be produced now; to which it was answered that their register is yet in Mr. Blackwood, their late clerk, his hand, as was represented last visitation, and that he has not given it up, and that severall of their minutes were carried off by another clerk since his time, and others of them are in Mr. Gilchrist, their last clerk, his hands, which they will gett up. As to their register which Mr. Blackwood has, the clerk is to write to him to give up the book to Mr. Maitland, and Mr. Orr is to be present when he gives it, to hear about an aledged claim Mr. Blackwood pretends to be resting him, and the Session of Mauchline is to order the filling up of their register from what minutes they have and can recover (which they are to be at pains to gett), and where there is want of minutes, that they record the reason of that want in the book. As to the sum that is restand to the Session by Ballachmile,* they tell they proceeded against him as to personall diligence, but had done nothing so as to affect his reall estate with others of his creditors; and so it appears that there is no expectation of recovering it, which negligence the Presbytery disprove, and do intimate to them their former resolution thereanent for the said negligence, viz., that they might be pursued for the said sum. As to the fifty merks mentioned in the last visitation due by John Colvill, they inform it is since uplifted by them, and is applied for the use of the poor of the paroch. As to the uttensills for the Sacrament, it is so as it was last visitation. They being removed, the heritors and heads of families were called in, and there compeared a great number of both these, and being asked the usual questions as to their minister and the elders, they answered that their minister was often absent from his charge, and they often wanted publick ordinances, and that he does not enter so soon to publick worship on the Lord's day as were desirable, much of the Sabbath being thereby idly and sinfully misspent, and generally they complained that he had not visited and catechised the paroch save once these three years. There was no complaint against the elders. The fabrick of the kirk is in good condition. The Presbytery called in Mr. Maitland, but delayed to enquire into the said complaints, there being some persons of note waited on who wanted to have their affairs discussed.

"The Presbytery entered on the consideration of what was aledged against Mr. Maitland by his Session and people, and the same being read to him, he answered that he had been often under much indisposition of body and that he had fallen under sundrie difficulties in his affairs that obliged him to be often abroad contrair to his inclination, which had hindered him to gett the particulars of visiting and catechising his people and to dispense public ordinances more than he intended, which he had formerly acquainted the Presbytery of when called on to an account by them. And as to that of his being long in entering to publick ordinances on the Sabbath, he acknowledged it

---

* He seems to have fallen into pecuniary difficulties, for we find "John Reid, of Ballochmyle, advocate, prisoner in the Tolbooth of Ayr, 30th April, 1720." Paterson's History of Ayrshire, 553.

was a fault, but that it was often owing to his indisposition of body, and that he would endeavour to help it in time coming.

"And he being removed, the Presbytery found from some members present that the said difficulties that occasioned his avocation were true and that he was put (to) a necessity of it. But that he should be exhorted to amend these things, viz., to visit families and catechise his people in order to the celebration of the Sacrament, which has been much omitted, and that he enter earlier to public ordinances on the Sabbath, and that he observe to have week dayes' sermons according to former manner, and that the session register be filled up in order to be revised. And, being called in, he was accordingly exhorted to these things, and the Presbytery is to enquire afterwards how these things are observed."

E.

DR. DALRYMPLE OF AYR.

Mr. Dalrymple was a native of Ayr, and, to use his own words, "notwithstanding had the honour of an unanimous call to minister to so large a congregation" as that of his native place. Writing in 1787, he said, "for nighest to forty years past a good and gracious God has judged proper to enable me for the discharge of common parochial duties, with apparent general acceptance, which I speak to the praise of his unmerited love."

That he was a man of more than common excellence of personal character may be inferred from the words of Burns,

> "D'rymple mild, D'rymple mild,
> Though your heart's like a child's,
> And your life like the new driven snaw."

But he was more than an amiable man. He was a man of weight and authority in the Church, and was appointed Moderator of the General Assembly in 1781.

His orthodoxy, however, was suspected, especially on the question of our Saviour's nature. He has left behind him several publications. One of these is entitled, "A History of Christ for the Use of the Unlearned." It is not of much literary or theological merit, and is simply a paraphrase of the Gospels in the style of Doddridge's "Family Expositor." It was published in 1787, and the object of its publication was thus stated in his dedication of it to his parishioners, "At a time of life when an approach of dissolution may be soon expected, it is natural for the warmth which I owe to an obliging people to look beyond them to their posterity, and if possible to serve both parents and offspring in absence."

The following paraphrase of a few verses in the 14th chapter of St. John's Gospel will indicate pretty clearly Dr. Dalrymple's views on the point on which he was popularly considered unsound, "Whither I go ye may surely know, and the way of coming thither ye may likewise know. Thomas, yet weak in belief, and desirous that he should be still more explicit, saith unto him, Lord, we know not so surely yet whither thou goest, and how can we, then, without some clearer instructions, know the way that leads thither? Jesus, in great affection, saith unto him, I am the way by my example, the truth by repeated promise, and the life by an endless reward, no man cometh to the Father for the enjoyment of this perfect, eternal existence but by means of me. If, therefore, ye had known me aright, and the nature of my kingdom, ye should have known the chief glorious manifestation of my Father also, and from henceforth ye know him more fully than ever, and have, as it were, seen him in his divine attributes of wisdom, goodness, holiness and power. . . He that hath seen me perform such miracles in confirmation of a heavenly doctrine hath in effect seen the Father."

The colleague of Dr. Dalrymple in Ayr in 1787 was Dr. M'Gill, whose book on "the sufferings and death of Christ, considered by way of practical essay," made, on its appearance from the press, such a commotion in the West country that Burns took up his pen and immortalised the ecclesiastical uproar in satirical verse, which he entitled the Kirk's Alarm. The most curious passage in Dr. Dalrymple's History of Christ is a sentence in the dedication, in which, all unconscious and unsuspicious of the storm that was gathering, he refers to the essay of his worthy colleague, Dr. William M'Gill. "There is little doubt," he says, "from its piously condescending manner, the simple elegance of its composition, exactness of method, and whole tendency to excite and cherish the best affections, it will prove universally acceptable. He will pardon me, after perusing the whole in manuscript, to have cast in this mite of tribute without his knowledge; less could not be said, and more might have been liable to misconstruction, besides doing hurt where modesty wishes to be spared. . . . . My trust and hope in the divine mercy is that you may yet long continue to enjoy and value his sacred ministrations, and to set a special mark of regard, as you now do, upon the unremitting accuracy with which the truths of Scripture are explained and applied by lectures."

Dr. Dalrymple had taken a very inaccurate guage of public sentiment when he wrote these kindly and complimentary words, for such a storm as M'Gill's essay raised, shortly after it was published, was never heard of in connection with any literary subject in Ayrshire.

Mr. Dun, of Auchinleck, in the preface to one of his sermons—"A Discourse on the Divinity of our Lord and Saviour Jesus Christ, in the Latin language, which a late publication has called for"—says, "I am sorry that a co-presbyter of mine has published an attack on the dignity of our Lord, under the dark title of a Practical Essay on the death of Jesus Christ, . . . and has not given the fair hint where to find what has been formerly answered to Ebion, Cerinthus, Socinus, and his other friends, whom he copies after."

Notwithstanding Mr. Dun's denunciation, however, the essay of Dr. M'Gill (published in 1786, and dedicated to Dr. Dalrymple) is a very able production, written in an admirable spirit, and evincing an earnest desire to solve the great mystery of redemption and vindicate the ways of God to man through Christ. It is not destructive, but constructive, in its aim. It may be described as a reply to the statement of Archbishop Tillotson that "the death of the Son of God is such a stumbling-block as is very hard for human reason to get over." The following passages will indicate Dr. M'Gill's views :—" Next to the mercy of God, which is never to be forgotten, the benefits of our redemption by Christ flow chiefly from the righteousness and holiness of his life—and particularly from the eminent patience, piety, submission, and benevolence displayed at the close of it—which avail with God in favour of sinners, in the same manner as do the piety and virtue of good men in general, only the effects of such singular excellencies are proportionally greater and more extensive," p. 275. "The worthiness of Christ was most eminently displayed in his endeavouring to save men at the price of his blood. This is of great estimation in the sight of God, who is pleased for the sake of it to show favour to the unworthy, provided they turn from their evil ways and join themselves to the son of his love," p. 279. "What the blood of Christ did," says Dr. M'Gill, "was to ratify and make valid the covenant of grace," p. 360-361.

Although Dr. Dalrymple in 1787 spoke of himself as having reached "a time of life when an approach of dissolution might be soon expected," he lived for twenty-seven years after that date, and died at the age of ninety in 1814. In 1794 he published a treatise on the Mosaic Account of Creation. This was followed in 1796 by his Legacy of Dying Thoughts, and in 1803 he closed his literary career by the publication of a Handbook of Scripture Jewish History. (Scott's Fasti).

F.

CELL, MONASTERY, OR PRIORY—WHICH?—AT MAUCHLINE.

As the Lectures published in this volume were written in the first instance for the entertainment of a parish auditory, I thought proper in Lecture I. to go a little beyond my proper subject, and say something about the church of Mauchline before the Reformation. Not doubting the correctness of what is a common statement, that there was in Catholic times a Priory at Mauchline, I endeavoured to describe what on that supposition would be the form of the buildings around the church, and the life within its walls. It was not till the whole lecture was printed that I was favoured by an eminent authority on Monastic Institutions with a note, in which the writer expresses his belief that there never was at Mauchline any Monastic establishment, in the popular sense of the terms, as a "place where monks lived." Considering the source from which it comes this opinion is, to say the least of it, entitled to very great deference. I shall accordingly insert it here, but before doing so I shall indicate the grounds on which the views expressed in the lecture may be said to rest.

In Chalmers' Caledonia, a book of high authority, it is stated that "The monks of Melros planted at Mauchline a colony of their own order, and this establishment continued a cell of the Monastery till the Reformation."

In Spottiswoode's "account of all the religious houses that were in Scotland at the time of the Reformation"—which is reckoned the chief authority on the subject of which it treats—it is stated under the head of Cistercians, that the Cistercians had thirteen monasteries in Scotland. These thirteen monasteries are then separately named and described, and the one numbered thirteenth is Mauchline.

For an account of Ayrshire ruins and Ayrshire antiquities one naturally turns to the History of Ayrshire, and in Paterson's History of Ayrshire the following sentences will be found in the chapter on Mauchline, "The parish church, or Priory of Mauchline, was no doubt erected by the monks of Melrose, as supposed by Chalmers, after 1165; and the village or Kirktoun of Mauchline gradually sprung up in the vicinity. The church, forming part of the original priory, it is supposed, and with which the tower at Mauchline is believed to have been connected, was situated in the middle of the town, having the churchyard around it."

Just as one goes to Paterson's History for an account of Ayrshire antiquities, so for an account of the early churches in Scotland one goes to the pages of Dr. Walcot, and we there find Mauchline placed in the list of "Priories" attached to the Abbey of Melrose. What Dr. Walcot says of Mauchline is, "a cell of Melrose . . . no trace of it left." It is proper to say, however, that Dr. Walcot refers to Chalmers and Paterson as his authorities for these statements.

Before going to press I put myself in communication with a Reverend Doctor who has written and published a great deal on the subject of monasteries, and I asked his opinion on one or two points about the monastic buildings at Mauchline. He kindly forwarded to me the notes he had gathered about Mauchline, and authorised me to use them as I thought proper. The following sentences are his:—

"The Tower of Mauchline, or Mauchline Castle, may be said to be the only remains of this ancient priory, which is still in good preservation. The old parish kirk taken down many years ago formed part of the original priory, and was connected with the tower.

"Dugdale puts Mauchline in the list of monasteries which were founded by David I., and Spottiswoode says the same. But in the Chartulary of Melrose referred to (that is, the one 'which was not long since in the hands of the Earl of Haddington'), which is very imperfect, there is no such statement, neither does it appear that the Stuarts founded Mauchline and gave it to Melrose.

"It is therefore probable that the convent for Cistercian monks there, was established by the monks of Melrose themselves."

It will thus be seen that it was not without a good shew of authority that I said there was an old monastery at Mauchline under the government of a prior. And for any positive proof that I have to the contrary the statement may yet be found to be correct. But the eminent authority I have referred to writes as follows :—

"I think I cannot be in error in saying that the castle at Mauchline never was a monastic establishment, in the sense of a place where monks lived. The estate belonged to the Abbey of Melrose, but the castle was merely the factor's house and estate office. No doubt the factor was a layman, or at least a clerk not in holy orders. If the Abbey enjoyed a secular jurisdiction, I suppose the hall (the large room on the first floor with the groined ceiling) would have been the place for the legal proceedings, as well as for other estate business, and was no doubt, like the halls in other castles, business-room, sitting-room, dining-room, and partly servants' sleeping place. I don't suppose a monk ever came near the place, unless it were the Procurator (the member of the community charged with its worldly affairs) in discharge of his official duties, or the Abbot making a visitation of the property, or on some other exceptional occasion."

In a postscript it is added that the castle "is a particularly precious monument of Scotch mediæval *domestic* building."

What then are we to say about the establishment which the monks of Melrose had at Mauchline? Was it a religious house or not—and if it was—was it a cell, a monastery, a priory, or what?

The Chartulary of Melrose will naturally occur to people as a source from which light might be got on the subject. There may be a great deal left unsaid about Mauchline in the Chartulary of Melrose. But whatever is said may be relied on. I have not had it in my power to examine the Chartulary (printed copy) as carefully and fully as would justify me in speaking confidently of all the references to Mauchline it contains, but I have looked at it and noted a few particulars.

The index of the Chartulary is made out in such a way as to necessitate the recurrence of the word Mauchline over and over. The term "monasterium," however, is never in the index associated with Mauchline. We find in the index the expressions "Monasterium de Fale," Monastery of Fail; "Abbacia de Dryburgh," Abbey of Dryburgh; "Decanatus de Are," the Deanery of Ayr. But in the index the only terms associated with the word Mauchline are "terrae," lands, and "ecclesia," Church.

In the Chartulary, the place and date are given at which different documents were signed. One deed, for instance, is dated "Apud Monasterium de Passelay," at the Monastery of Paisley. There is another dated at Mauchline, but the words in the deed are not "Apud Monasterium de Mauchline." They are simply "Apud Mauchlyn," at Mauchline, the 11th July, 1342.

Many persons as well as places are named in the Chartulary. There is one Bernard Bell, designated "Monachus Monasterii de Melros ac pensionarius de Mauchlyne," Monk of the Monastery of Melrose and Pensioner of Mauchline. What the word pensioner in this instance may have meant—whether the holding of a religious office at Mauchline or simply the enjoyment of the rents from the lands of Mauchline —I will not presume to say. But besides "Magister Bernardus Bell, pensionarius de Mauchlyne," there is one Richard Biger mentioned in the Chartulary as having been "Monachus de Mauhelin" in the reign of Alexander the Second. The clause in which his name occurs is "Per manum Ricardi de Biger tunc Monachi de Mauhelin." To those uninitiated in the mysteries of monastic nomenclature, this expression, Monk of Mauchline, must seem to imply that there was at least one monk, if not more than one, who lived at Mauchline in the time of Alexander the Second. And, if monks, there would be monastic life at Mauchline, such as is described in Lecture I. Now, however, that doubt has been cast on the common statements about the monastic establishment at Mauchline, further exploration of the subject is necessary, and it is not unlikely that in some of the ancient papers and documents that in recent years have been published, valuable scraps of information will be found.

In a note on page 27 there is a remark made, not seriously, but in the spirit of the last clause of Prov. xxvi. 19, about a St. Maughold or Macallius. It may be stated here that the name of the Mauchline Parish saint occurs in the Melrose Chartulary. The name was St. Michael, as appears from the following clause in a deed drawn up in the reign of William the Lion—"Territorium de Mauchelin et ecclesiam Sancti Michaelis in eo sitam," the district of Mauchline and the Church of St. Michael therein situated. One of the wells in Mauchline, that near the U.P. Church, bears the name of St. Michael's, and is so designated in a precept of *Clare Constat* from Hugh, Earl of Loudoun, in 1712. This document is in the hands of the Trustees of the U.P. Church.

G.

LECTURING ON SCRIPTURE LESSONS.

In addition to what is said in the note at page 63 about the Presbyterian custom of lecturing and the Episcopalian disuse of lecturing, the following extracts from Woodrow's History may be quoted. Vol. I., p. 318, folio edition, 1721 :—" The Prelates complained to the Council that the Indulged ministers lectured and expounded a portion of Scripture to the people before the forenoon's sermon ; which, as it had been most iniquitously laid aside by the Prelatick preachers since the Restoration, so they alleged it was a hurtful innovation ; and what the Indulged had no warrant from Authority for. . . . They (the Indulged ministers) knew that the laying aside Lecturing was one of the Badges of Conformity since the year 1662." On the 13th Jan., 1670, the following act was passed by the Privy Council :—"'The Council understanding that several of the ministers allowed by their special warrant to preach, do use, before they begin their sermon, to lecture upon some part of the Scripture : and considering that this form was never used in this Church before the late troubles and is not warranted by authority, do discharge the same, etc., etc. . . How far the matter of fact is true, which the Bishops make the Council to say in their act, that lecturing was not used before 1638, in this Church, I (says Woodrow) do not know."

INDEX.

Action sermon, 160
Adultery, 329
Alone, living, 260-1
Altars, 7, 8
Ambling with elements, 167
Armour, Adam, his prayer, 337
Assisting ministers at communions, 168, 171
Atonement, days of, 348
Attendance at church, 116, 332

Bakers, scarcity of, 149
Bailie of Mauchline breaking Sabbath, 256-58
Bailie of Mauchline at a street fight, 332
Bailie-session, 307-9
Bands for good behaviour, 299-300
Bell, church, 26-8
„ saint's, 27
„ sermon, 23
„ third, 57
Bleeding above eyes, 269
Bond of 1677, 282
Bradzane or Bregan, 311-12
Bread at communions, distributed, 150
„ „ form of, 148-50
„ „ leavened or unleavened, 148-9
Bread at communions, preparation of, 148
Bread at communions, taken home, 150-51
Brownists, 74-5
Brothel at Dalmellington, 330
Brulie minutes, 2
Burns, 45

Calderwood on Kirk Sessions, 183-4
Candles in church, 113-115
Castle of Mauchline, 358
Catechising on Sundays, 91-2
„ week days, 93-4
Caution for compearance, 296, 298
„ good behaviour, 298-9
Censors, 211

Censure of the exercise, 347
Chancel of church, 7
Choir of church, 7
Churches, interior of, in 17th cent., 16
„ small, long ago, 177
Church service in 1611, 56-7
„ „ 1715, 64
Churchyard dyke, 52
„ „ houses on, 50-1
„ „ of Mauchline, 45-9
Churchyards, 43, 47, 48
„ filthy state of, 50
Circular satisfaction, 238
Civilisers, 209
Classical Assemblies, 347
Clergy, number of, in ancient churches, 7
Clocks on churches, 29, 31
„ „ how kept, 30
Cokalanes forbidden, 202
Cock-fighting, 318
Collogues, 347
Communion crowds, 169, 172-4, 177
„ in the evening, 159
„ „ morning, 158-9
„ frequency of, 152-7
„ scandals, 174-6
„ service, order of, 160
„ successive Sabbaths, 157-8
„ taken fasting, 158
Confession of Faith, not subscribing, 276-8
Confession of Faith, objections to, 194
„ „ subscribed by Elders, 193, 194
Confession of Faith, subscribed by ministers, &c., 277-280
Consignations, 205-6
Corbies on lum-head, 264
Covenanters not Democrats, 185-6
Covenants subscribed before communion, 164
Cups for communion, 140-2
Cursing, 268-272
„ parents, 273

Dalrymple, Dr., 355

364 Index.

Dates of communion changed, 179-80
Debarring from communion, 153, 162-3
Deference to Kirk Sessions, 321, 328
Deil's address to Burns, 175
Delations, 200-4
Desks in churches, 15, 16
Discipline at different dates, 195-201, 208
Dismantling idolatrous houses, 10
Disorders in church, 109, 110
Distribution of elements, 166-7
Districts for elders, 206-8
Doxologies, 70-3
Drink for workmen, 36, 138
Drumfork, Reids of, 262-3
Drunkenness, 240-5

Early age for communicating, 120
Elder, ruling, 189
  ,,   ,,   misuse of phrase, 190-1
  ,,   ,,   how designated by Westminster Divines, 60
Elder, ruling, presbyter or lay ruler, 189
Elders originally appointed for one year, 191
Elders ordained now for life, 191-2
  ,, ordination of, 192-3
  ,, to keep Presbytery by turns, 191
  ,, censure of, 221-5
  ,, hours, 242
  ,, one of Mauchline, accused of homicide, 222-3
Eldership sometimes meant Presbytery, 189-90, 346
Elements for communion, how provided, 143-4, 150
Episcopal and Presbyterian discipline contrasted, 196
Erastian theory of admission to communion, 163
Erastian theory repudiated by Westminster divines, 164
Evidence on oath in Sessions, 215-16
Excommunication and civil penalties, 198, 302-4
Excommunication, lesser, 305
Exculpation, oath of, 217-20
Exercise, the, 345
Eyelists, removal of, 122

Fairs, formal opening of, 14
  ,, in churches, 13, 14
  ,, disorders at, 209
Family exercise enjoined, 203-4
Farm houses in Ayrshire (1811), 39
Fasts, causes of specified, 130-1, 284
  ,, how to be kept, 348-9

Fasts, breaches of, 132
  ,, sacramental, 126-34
  ,,   ,, who should preach on, 131
  ,, monthly, 130, 152
Fasten e'en, 318
Fasting when communion taken, 158
Fellowship societies, 204
Fencing tables, 161-2
Fines, 306-7, 313
  ,, application of, 313-4
  ,, abated, 315-6
  ,, accepted in lieu of penance, 316-7
  ,, did not remove scandals, 317
Fog used in slating, 35
Formula subscribed by elders, 193
  ,,   ,, ministers, 277, 280
  ,, haggling about, 278-9

Galleries in church, origin of, 23
  ,, by whom first built, 24-5
  ,, of rude structure long ago, 24
Gentlemanly punishment, 302
Gibbites, 75, 76
Glass windows, 32
  ,, price of, 33
  ,, (sand) for measuring length of sermon, 105-6
Goudie's Bible, 334
Grass in churchyard rouped by minister, 49

Hats on in church, 57, 111, 112
  ,, at communion, 137
Hawthorne, Mrs., 4
Healths, drinking of, 244
"Heich," standing, 290, 292-3
Heinous crimes, satisfaction for, 304
Heresy, 275
Holy Fair, 178
Holy Willie, 225-229
Hours of service on Sabbath, 115
Hours, untimeous, 209
Hydroparastatae, 147
Hymns, 77-8

Imprecations, 268-269, 273
Inquisition, sessional, 199-202
Insolence to Kirk Session, 324-5
  ,, on repentance stool, 324
Interdict of company and conversation, 300-1

Joggs, 311
Jolly Beggars, 336

Index.

Kneeling in prayer at communion, 161
,, on receiving the elements, 165-6

Ladies provided with desks in church, 15
"Laigh" stand, 291, 293
Lairs in churchyards, 43
Lecturing, 62-3, 360
Leniency ill-judged, 289
Length of communion service, 179
Liturgy in Church of Scotland, 83
Loft, common, 24
Lofts, by whom built, 25
Lunar chronometers on churches, 29

MacGill, Dr., 356
M'Call, Marion, the Mauchline witch, 261
Magistrate invoked, 321-4
Maitland, Rev Mr., 97, 108
Merkland, Jean, 269-70
Manses at Reformation, 36-7
Manse at Mauchline in 1646, 37
Manses, size of, in seventeenth and eighteenth centuries, 38-9
Manses, interior of, last century, 40
,, rickety state of, in Ayrshire, last century, 41
,, inspection and delivery of, 42
Mauchline 100 years ago, 332-9
,, 200 years ago, 331-2
,, castle or tower of, 358-9
,, old church of, antiquity, 5-6
,, ,, ancient beauty 6
,, ,, appearance in 1811, 5
,, ,, interior of in 1827, 10-11
,, new church, in 1837, 4-5
,, Presbyterial visitation of, 352
,, an old parish, 3
Men and women on opposite sides of church, 7
Mixed cups at communions, 147
Michael, St., the parish saint of Mauchline, 360
Michael's, St., well in Mauchline, 360
Moderators, lay, of Kirk Sessions, 187-8
Monk, General, on Church government, 195
Monk of Mauchline, 360
Monasticism, 9
Monastery of Mauchline, 8-9, 357
Monday's service at Communions, 135

Monday's dinner, 135-6
Morer, Mr., author of a book on Scotland, 1715, 27
Morrison, Mary, 46
Murder in Mauchline, 249-50
Music in Church of Scotland, 65

Names of persons refused tokens announced, 124-5
Noise about the sin, 259
Number of elders, 207-8

Officers (town) to stand in church beside their bailie, 12
Ordinary, the, 96, 99
Organs in Church, 65-6

Paraphrases, 74, 80
,, long in being introduced in some churches, 82
Parish, whole, put under oath of purgation, 218
Pardovan's book, 21
Parson different from Stipendiary Minister, 143
Pavement of churches in olden times, 7
Pecunial compositions, 294
Pensioner of Mauchline, 360
Perambulations, 209
Peter, the parish saint of Galston, 27
Pews, origin of, 18-9
,, sometimes erected by Kirk Sessions and let, 20
Pins, wooden, used in slating, 36
Plaids over heads in church, 113
Poetical squibs forbidden by Kirk Sessions, 202
Police rates saved by church, 199
,, rural, desired by church, 211
Policemen, value of, 341
Poosie Nansie, 243
Postures in worship, 73
Prayers, the bidding, 86
,, extempore, 85
,, daily, 88, 90
Preaching, quantity of 87
,, style of, 95
,, on some subjects forbidden, 95
Precentor, 65
Prelacy, meaning of, 189
Preparation sermon, 125-6
Presbyterianism, meaning of, 189
Presbyterian discipline at different dates, 195-8, 200, 208
Presbyterian and Episcopalian discipline contrasted, 196

Presbyteries and Elderships synonymous words, 189, 346
Privy censures, 229-30
Profanity, 274-5
Progress, social, how effected, 339
Protection from the enemy a sin (1646), 283-4
Protesters, 129
Psalm-singing, little in church, 67
Psalms, present metrical version of, 78
,,   in rhyme and metre objected to, 74-6
Psalms given out line by line, 68-70
Public censures too sore, 323
,,   ,,   discontinued in Mauchline (1809), 301
Purgation, oath of, 217-220, 351
Pythonising, 103

Quarters or districts for elders, 206-8

Rae, Peter, of Kirkconnell, 96
Railing on elders and minister, 237-8
Ray, the traveller, 32
Readers, 55
Reader's service, 56-60
,,   office abolished in 1580 and in 1645, 58, 60
Reader's salary, 59
Reader usually schoolmaster, 59
,,   in Mauchline, 65
Readers employed after office abolished, 59, 62, 64
Reader's service joined with preacher's, 61
Reading of Scripture in church, 62, 63
,,   ,,   bare, denounced by Brownists, 63
Rebukes, private or public, 286-7
,,   public, different degrees of publicity, 287-8
Reconciliation before Communion, 122-3
Repair of church fabrics, 34-5
Repentance, course of, 294
Repentance stool, different forms of, 291-3
Repentance stool, dispensations from, 289-90
Repentance stool in Mauchline wrongly associated with Burns, 287-8
Residence in a parish forbidden without testimonials, 214
Resolutioners, 129
Roll, "examine," 124

Sabbath, observance of, 209-211, 252, 257, 318-320

Sackcloth, 293
Sacramental Fasts, 126
Saint's name to churches and fairs, 27
Satisfaction, civil and spiritual, 310
Saturday's sermon before Communion, 124-5
Saving knowledge, sum of, 93
Scandal, people kept under for years, 217-8
Scandal, the "issue" of, 315
Schism, 275
Scriptural songs, 79
Seats in churches for ladies, 15
,,   for ministers' families, 15
,,   squabbles about, 17
,,   erection by warrant of Kirk Session, 20
,,   out of poor's money for benefit of poor, 20, 25, 26
,,   how allocated, 20-1
,,   grievance about, 21-2
Seceder, suicide of, 282
Seceders, course taken with, 280-1
Sermon bell, 23
Sermons, few, in Catholic times, 23
,,   form of, 97
,,   model, 99
,,   length of, 103-6
,,   Scotch, 102
,,   without texts, 100-1
Session records of Mauchline, 2
,,   a good court of justice, 29
Sessions, Kirk, when instituted as courts, 182-3
Sessions, Kirk, constitution of, 187
,,   ,,   functions of, 195, 203
Shots, window, 32
Society, received into, 305
Solo singing in church, 77
Spottiswoode of Fowler, 186
Standing in church, 12, 23
Stiles on churchyard dykes, 52
Stools in church, 12, 22
,,   ,,   letting of, 12, 13
Storm boards, 33, 39
Sunday life in 1722, 92
Sundays, silent, 107-9

Table addresses, 169-70
Tables, communicating at, 136-7
,,   dressing of, 138
,,   erection of communion, 138
,,   number of, at communions, 179
Tent, the, 177
Test, subscribing in 1685, sin of, 284-5
Testimonials, 212-3

Thanksgiving service at communions, 135
Thatch on churches and manses, 39
Theft, 247-8
Tickets for communion (See Tokens)
Times, number of, public compearances made, 294-5-6
Tokens, mode of distributing, 134-5
,, making of, 139
,, strict rules about, 238, 240
Tombstones, 43
Trees in churchyards, 53
Trial of congregations before communions, 119-122

Visitations of parishes, 231-233, 352

Warning by tuck of drum, 34
Warnings from pulpit, 318-320
Weekday sermons, 83-90
Windows in old times, 32, 39, 40
,, particularly glazed up, 40
Wine, kind used at communions, 143-6
,, quantity used at communions, 145-6
,, mixed with water at communions, 147
,, "composure like unto," allowed at communions, 147
,, allegorical meaning of red and white, 146 7
Wire trell ses for windows, 32-3, 40
Witchcraft and quack doctoring, 269-70
Wodrow's great work, 22
Women, boldness of, 246

www.ingramcontent.com/pod-product-compliance
Lightning Source LLC
Chambersburg PA
CBHW030405230426
43664CB00007BB/754